# JOHN

# *John*

## Believing on the Son

# W. Robert Willoughby

*CHRISTIAN PUBLICATIONS*
*CAMP HILL, PENNSYLVANIA*

Christian Publications, Inc.
3825 Hartzdale Drive, Camp Hill, PA 17011
www.cpi-horizon.com

*Faithful, biblical publishing since 1883*

© 1999 by Christian Publications

ISBN: 0-87509-840-1

99 00 01 02 03     5 4 3 2 1

# Contents

## Part XI: The Passion of the Son
### John 17:1-19:42

## Part XII: The Triumph of the Son
### John 20-21

# Introduction

From the obscurity of a carpenter's shop in contemptible Nazareth there emerged a Man who would shake the foundations of His nation. On the far bank of the Jordan River He received His public introduction by a popular preacher of righteousness and judgment. He attracted the cautious curiosity of the common crowd and gained the ardent allegiance of a few faithful followers. But most of Jerusalem's religious establishment remained acrimonious and antagonistic.

Who was this extraordinary Man? What was His origin? What were His claims? What was the meaning of His message? How should people respond to His claims? How *did* they respond? What was His destiny?

To answer such crucial questions, John[1] wrote his Gospel. He wrote it toward the close of the first century, quite possibly in the city of Ephesus.[2] It was the final of the four canonical Gospels.

## John's Readers

Who did the author hope would read his Gospel? Certainly he would have expected the Christian community of his day to study it with eagerness. He selectively offered faith-strengthening accounts of Jesus' miraculous deeds. He mated these with chosen discourses and dialogues calculated to provide encouragement and instruction to believers.

Half a century had elapsed since John the Baptist's meteoric ministry. But he still had his fiercely devout disciples. John speaks of John the Baptist in glowing terms. Certainly he must have hoped the Baptist's remaining disciples would transfer their loyalty to the Christ, just as their leader had done.

And there were the local synagogue congregations in Ephesus and throughout the Roman Empire. John would have hoped that many of his fellow Jews would come to faith in Jesus, the Messiah of Israel, the Revealer of God the Father.

It is also likely that John hoped he could interest devout, thoughtful, non-Christian Gentiles (including Gnostics[3]). He knew that many of them yearned to discover the nature, meaning and source of eternal life. If he could write in terms intelligibly related to their previous religious interests and experience, perhaps he could attract them. Perhaps they might come to believe on the One of whom he wrote.

In brief, John wrote both to edify the church and to evangelize the world. "These [miraculous signs] are written," he says, "that you may believe that Jesus is the Christ, the Son of God, and that by believing you may have life in his name" (John 20:31).

## John's Sources

From what source or sources did the author of the fourth Gospel obtain his information?

First, the writer clearly acknowledges the inspiration of the Holy Spirit in bringing to the remembrance of the apostles the words of Jesus. He acknowledges the Spirit's role in enabling him to interpret those words.[4] Second, this ministry of the Holy Spirit would not preclude John's making use of other sources. For example, he could have been familiar with, and made use of, the earlier Gospels. More probably he, like the other Gospel writers, called on the oral tradition of the life of Christ circulating within the Christian community.[5]

## John's Style

Whatever John's sources,[6] the most casual reader can readily perceive a difference between the so-called Synoptics and John's Gospel. It is a difference both in content and style. For example, whereas "the other Gospels begin with Bethlehem, John begins with the bosom of the Father."[7] The "Christmas stories" of Matthew and Luke are absent in John. In their place are breathtaking utterances about Jesus. In their simplicity and profundity they go beyond anything else in all of Scripture. The "Upper Room" discourses on the ministry of the Holy Spirit are found only in John. So is the "high-priestly prayer."[8] Unique with John is his way of connecting miracles of Jesus with the discourses whose truths they symbolize.

The church historian, Eusebius, tells us what Clement of Alexandria, one of the great teachers of the early church, said about this Gospel: "John, perceiving that the bodily facts had been made plain in the gospel, being urged by his friends and inspired by the Spirit, composed a spiritual gospel."[9] Clement did not intend to insinuate that the other Gospels were not "spiritual." But in John, as another writer puts it, "the words and deeds of Jesus appear to have undergone, by the Holy Spirit, a 'transposition into a higher key' than that with which we are familiar in the synoptic Gospels."[10]

## John's Gospel and the Deeper Life

You are about to read a Deeper Life Pulpit Commentary on the Gospel of John. Perhaps you, like me, hold dear the "Fourfold Gospel"—Christ our Savior, Sanctifier, Healer and Coming King. In John's "spiritual Gospel" is a plenitude of inspiration and teaching to help you know this Christ in a deeper way. You discover Jesus to be the great "I AM" of the Old Testament. You meet Him as the Light of the World, the Bread of Life, the Water of Life. He is the Provider of the New Wine of the Spirit; the Good Shepherd; the Way, the Truth and the Life. He is the Lamb of God who takes away the sin of the world. He is the Resurrection and the Life. He is the Healer of spirit, soul and body. You will want to appropriate this all-sufficient Savior in all His wonderful fullness.

If your heart is hungry for holiness, you will find in this Gospel the encouragement you seek. Do you wish power for service? Meditate on what our Lord teaches concerning the person and work of the Holy Spirit, the gift of the exalted Lord Jesus Christ.

You will find your faith in Christ deepened and strengthened as, throughout his Gospel, John exhorts you to *believe on the Son of God.*

## *Endnotes*

1.  There has been much debate in scholarly circles concerning the actual authorship of the Gospel of John. Not a few believe the author was someone close to the apostle—who put John's thoughts into words. I prefer the classic conclusion of B.F. Westcott, *Commentary on the Gospel According to St. John* (London: John Murray, Albemarle Street, 1967), v-xxi. Westcott notes that (a) the author was a Jew and (b) a Jew of Palestine; he was (c) an eyewitness and (d) an apostle. Therefore he was (e) the Apostle John.

2.  No one can say for certain where John wrote his Gospel. Irenaeus states Ephesus. Others suggest Antioch in Syria, Alexandria or somewhere else in Egypt.

3.  The term *gnostic* means "one who knows." Gnosticism was a syncretistic mix of religion and philosophy, at the root of which was a dualistic view of reality. Gnostics believed that all that is material is evil and only what is spirit is good. Carried to its extremity, this doctrine effectively divides God from the evil world, which He could not have created. Similarly, the Gnostics considered the Incarnation impossible, for God could not have adopted a material (read that sinful) body. Gnostics changed the meaning of redemption from "deliverance from sin" to "deliverance from the material world." Paradoxically, however, many Gnostics were drawn to the fourth Gospel. It is likely that a part of John's purpose was to help Gnostics see in the Christian gospel what they really were seeking. He hoped as well to combat the errors of those leading the Church astray.

4.  See John 14:26, where Jesus promises that the Father will send the Counselor, the Holy Spirit, who will teach the apostles all things and remind them of everything He had said to them.

5.  For what he considers evidences of John's dependence on Mark, see C.K. Barrett, *The Gospel According to St. John* (London: S.P.C.K., 1955), 34ff. However, Leon Morris in *The Gospel According to John* (Grand Rapids, MI: Eerdmans, 1971), 51-52, does not find Barrett's arguments very convincing. He prefers to say that John, like the other evangelists, was familiar with the oral tradition surrounding the life and words of Christ.

6.  C.H. Dodd, in *The Interpretation of the Fourth Gospel* (Cambridge: At the University Press, 1970), 133, sees John as being conversant in a number of areas: the general background of early Christianity, of course, and perhaps with the Pauline writings; with Rabbinic Judaism (the writings of the Jewish rabbis in their commentaries on the Scriptures); with Hellenistic Judaism (as represented in the writings of Philo); and with "higher pagan thought" (represented in the so-called Hermetic literature). It is this familiarity with contemporary literature, says Dodd, that would attract thoughtful Gentile readers to John's Gospel. Dodd, however, is careful to observe that John's Gospel rises far above the secular literature of his day, pointing his readers to Jesus Christ, crucified and risen, as the only hope of eternal life.

    Leon Morris, *The Gospel According to John* (Grand Rapids, MI: Eerdmans, 1971), 39, quotes H.G.G. Herklets, *A Fresh Approach to the New Testament* (London: n.p., 1950), 121, as rightly saying, "This Gospel makes good use of terms intelligible in the Hellenistic world, but it is to impress ideas which are not Hellenistic."

7.  Alexander Maclaren, *The Gospel According to St. John,* vol. I (London: Hodder and Stoughton, 1907), 1.

8.  Chapters 14-17.

9.  Quoted in F.F. Bruce, *The Gospel of John* (Grand Rapids, MI: Eerdmans, 1983), 15.

10. Ibid., 16. Bruce suggests this transposition into a higher key is the effect of the Spirit's enabling John to interpret the story of Jesus to a different public from that to which the earlier Gospels were designed. This interpretation resulted in an expanded version of what Jesus

said in order to bring out the sense more fully. Says Bruce, "To reproduce the words of Jesus which were spirit and life to their first believing hearers in such a way that they continue to communicate their saving message and [are] spirit and life to men and women today . . . is the work of the Spirit of God."

*Part I*


# The Identity of the Son


John 1:1-51

# 1

# The Eternal Word

## John 1:1-9

*In the beginning was the Word, and the Word was with God, and the Word was God. 2 He was with God in the beginning.*

*3 Through him all things were made; without him nothing was made that has been made. 4 In him was life, and that life was the light of men. 5 The light shines in the darkness, but the darkness has not understood it.*

*6 There came a man who was sent from God; his name was John. 7 He came as a witness to testify concerning that light, so that through him all men might believe. 8 He himself was not the light; he came only as a witness to the light. 9 The true light that gives light to every man was coming into the world.*

We come with awe before this profound yet exquisitely unadorned exaltation of our Lord Jesus Christ. Like an overture that delicately intimates all the coming movements of a symphony, our text introduces the grand themes that will follow. Some have suggested that these opening verses might well have been based on a hymn in current use.[1] Whether or not that is so, the poetic-like phrases, lofty in their Christology, elevate us to heights of adoration and praise.

## *The* Logos

The text describes our blessed Lord as "the Word"—the *Logos*. What does this term signify? John's Jewish readers would immediately be reminded of the oft-repeated Old Testament phrase, "the *word* of the Lord." It was used to describe God's powerful *actions* in creation[2] or revelation[3] or deliverance.[4] When God "speaks," something is created, something is revealed or someone is delivered—something happens! In terms that could well be descriptive of the person and ministry of Jesus, God says through the prophet Isaiah, ". . . so is my word that goes out from my mouth: It will not return to me empty, but will accomplish what I desire and achieve the purpose for which I sent it" (Isaiah 55:11).

While this is clearly the background for his use of the term,[5] John would know that *logos* was used by Greek philosophers. They used it to describe the impersonal principle of reason or order in the universe. To them it stood for the principle that imposed form on the material world, that constituted the rational soul in man. Thus, as F.F. Bruce observes, *logos* was a "bridge-word" whereby people raised in Greek thought might find their way into Johannine Christian faith.[6] The Apostle John, ever the evangelist, thus calls both Jewish and Gentile readers to faith. Faith not in some impersonal principle, but faith in a real Person—the Word made flesh, Jesus Christ, the Son of God.

Our text presents seven fundamental truths concerning the *Logos*. John uses these truths to prepare us for the themes he will unfold throughout his entire Gospel. In this chapter we will consider only the first four of these poignant statements concerning our Lord. We must ponder each of them carefully.

## *The Divine Word*

Note first that John presents Jesus as the *Divine Word* (1:1-2). In the first three words of our text, John carries us back in thought to the opening words of the Old Testament.[7] Genesis 1:1 speaks of the beginning of the creation of the heavens and the earth. John, therefore, is saying that at the very moment when God spoke the universe into existence, the *Logos* was already there. "In the beginning *was* the Word."

The tense of the Greek verb[8] suggests what other Scriptures clearly affirm.[9] The Word Himself did not have a genesis as did created things but was in truth *uncreated.* In his superb Colossian Christology, Paul speaks of our Lord Jesus as the "firstborn over all creation" (Colossians 1:15). He is by no means telling us that Jesus Christ was the first created being. Rather, he is saying that Christ is Lord of all creation, the divinely appointed "heir of all things" (Hebrews 1:2). And so, like Paul, John is declaring the *eternality* of the Word.

But not only was the *Logos* eternal, He was *distinctive.* Says John, ". . . and the word was *with* God" (John 1:1, emphasis added). Here and in 1:2[10] the author clearly differentiates between the Word (God the Son) and God the Father. He will proceed immediately to proclaim that "the Word was God." Nevertheless, he first insists that these two are not identical, although they existed in perpetual association. What was that eternal relationship between the *Logos* and God the Father? The answer is suggested in the preposition "with" (the Greek word *pros*), defined by the lexicon as "face to face" or "toward."[11] We dare not read too much into one Greek preposition. But it does seem to intimate, as Westcott remarks, not just simple coexistence but active connection and perfect communion with the Father.[12] We are right in affirming that the Word proceeded eternally from the Father in a living, dynamic identity of thought, purpose, action and, as we shall see next, essence. John is declaring the *distinctiveness* of the Word.

But though the *Logos* possessed His own "personhood," John wants us to be absolutely clear about the *Logos' divinity.* John says, ". . . and the Word was God."[13] Here is unequivocal evidence of the deity of Jesus Christ! In His very nature, the Word was God, distinct from God the Father as to personhood, yet one with the Father in essence. Or as the ancient creed[14] says, ". . . being of one substance with the Father. . . ." Throughout His earthly ministry our Lord continually professed His oneness with the Father. John, in the first verse of our text, prepares us to receive Jesus' testimony about Himself by proclaiming the Divine Word.

## The Creating Word

Second, our Lord is presented as the *Creating Word* (1:3). "Through him all things were made; without him nothing was made that has been made." Here, ever so concisely, our text reveals the *agent* through whom God created the heavens and the earth. The "mouth of the Lord"[15] (the *Logos)* spoke, and His word of command brought the universe into being!

Both Paul and the writer to the Hebrews concur fully with John. "For by [the Son] all things were created: things in heaven and on earth, visible and invisible . . . ; all things were created by him and for him" (Colossians 1:16). And again, ". . . there is but one Lord, Jesus Christ, through whom all things came and through whom we live" (1 Corinthians 8:6). Or this: ". . . but in these last days [God] has spoken to us by his Son, whom he appointed heir of all things, and through whom he made the universe" (Hebrews 1:2).[16] The Scriptures unequivocally declare that God created the heavens and the earth. To the unbiased mind, all nature witnesses to an all-powerful, all-wise, Creator God.[17] Our Lord, the *Logos*, is that Creator God.

## The Enlivening and Illuminating Word

Third, our text proclaims this divine Word as the *Enlivening, Illuminating Word.* "In him was life, and that life was the light of men. The light shines in the darkness, but the darkness has not understood it" (1:4-5).

The *Logos* is the source of natural life. We read that "[the LORD God] breathed into [Adam's] nostrils the breath of life, and the man became a living being" (Genesis 2:7). In His grace, God both gives and sustains natural life.

But our text also implies that the *Logos* is the fount of spiritual and eternal life for believers. The psalmist, addressing the Lord, says, "For with you is the fountain of life" (Psalm 36:9). And John makes this particularly clear in his first letter, "God has given us eternal life, and this life is in his Son. He who has the Son has life; he who does not have the Son of God does not have life" (1 John 5:11-12). Note how in his introduction John is preparing his readers to hear Jesus declare, "I am the way and the truth and *the life"* (John 14:6, emphasis added).

Not only is the *Logos* "life," but the *Logos* is "light." Bruce observes, "This is true both of the natural illumination of reason which is given to the human mind and of the spiritual illumination which accompanies the new birth: neither can be received apart from the light that resides in the Word."[18] In John's Gospel we will hear our Lord Jesus declare, "I am the light of the world. Whoever follows me will never walk in darkness, but will have the light of life" (8:12).

John goes on to assert (1:5) that the light dispels darkness. It is as true in the spiritual world as in the natural. Amid the spiritual darkness of Satan's dominion, the light of Christ shines brightly. John says that "the darkness did not overcome it" (1:5).[19] Could John be referring to that historic moment when the Light would be quenched in death and burial, only to rise again? Satan's kingdom, with all of its ugly, hateful force, could not overpower our Lord. Instead, Satan was vanquished. Truly the *Logos* is enlivening, illuminating and overcoming!

## *The Heralded Word*

Fourth, this One of whom John writes is the *Heralded Word* (1:6-9). Here, the apostle introduces us to the person Isaiah spoke of: "A voice of one calling: 'In the desert prepare the way for the LORD; make straight in the wilderness a highway for our God' " (Isaiah 40:3). John the Baptist fits the description. He was born, as we know, to Zechariah and Elizabeth, both of whom were "well along in years" (Luke 1:7). The angel Gabriel predicted he would "make ready a people prepared for the Lord" (Luke 1:17). John the Baptist comes on the scene as the man "sent from God," that is, a prophet of God. He was sent to bear witness to the coming Christ, in order that all might be brought to faith in Him. Perhaps for the benefit of the Baptist's lingering disciples, the writer makes it clear that John is *not* to be the object of anyone's faith. Rather, he was a witness[20] to "the true light" that "was coming into the world."[21] Here, as before, John is preparing us for the Baptist's story that begins at 1:19, in which he himself affirms that he is not the Christ.

## *Conclusion*

We must leave till the next chapter our study of the three remaining truths in John's portrayal of the *Logos*. In the present text, we have beheld Him who is the Divine Word. We believe this Jesus is none other than God the Son, and we reverently worship Him. Man is content to speak of Him as one of the world's great prophets—perhaps the greatest. People may go as far as to say God spoke through Him as through no other. They will concede that He gave to the world the loftiest ethic ever devised. But John would have us believe that He is the very *Logos* of God—Deity Himself.

Unbelieving mankind sees our universe as the product of blind chance. But John would have us see our world as the marvelous result of a powerfully creative Word. "By faith," says the writer to the Hebrews, "we understand that the universe was formed at God's command, so that what is seen was not made out of what is visible" (Hebrews 11:3).

Self-sufficient humanity supposes it is autonomous and sovereign. John would have us bow in utter humility before the enlivening, illuminating Word—the embodiment of life and truth.

Mankind, enamored by the relativistic philosophy of our age, sees the Christian faith as just one of many "religions." John presents the *Logos* as the only valid object of worship, the only Way to eternal life.

There is but one reasonable response. That is to kneel before this eternal Word in reverent worship. It is to follow Him in loving, Spirit-enabled trust and obedience.

With the ancient hymnist[22] let us unite heart and voice as we sing:

> Of the Father's love begotten,
>     Ere the worlds began to be,
> He is Alpha and Omega,
>     He the source, the ending He,
> Of the things that are and have been,
>     And that future years shall see,
>         Evermore and evermore.
>
> This is He whom seers in old time
>     Chanted of with one accord,

Whom the voices of the prophets
Promised in their faithful word;
Now He shines, the long-expected;
Let creation praise its Lord,
Evermore and evermore.

### Endnotes

1. Among those who make this suggestion is George R. Beasley-Murray, "John," *Word Biblical Themes* (Dallas, TX: Word Publishing, 1989), 19. Other passages thought to have been hymns of praise to Christ are Philippians 2:6-11, Colossians 1:15-20 and First Timothy 3:16.
2. For example, "By the word of the LORD were the heavens made. . ." (Psalm 33:6).
3. For example, "Then the word of the LORD came to Isaiah: 'Go and tell Hezekiah, "This is what the LORD . . . says . . ." ' " (Isaiah 38:4-5).
4. For example, "He sent forth his word and healed them; he rescued them from the grave" (Psalm 107:20).
5. See George Barker Stevens, *The Theology of the New Testament* (Edinburgh: T. & T. Clarke, 1899 [reprinted 1956]), 577ff.
6. F.F. Bruce, *The Gospel of John* (Grand Rapids, MI: Eerdmans, 1983), 28. See also my footnote 6 to the Introduction.
7. The Hebrew title for the first book of the Bible consists of its first words, "In the Beginning."
8. The tense of the Greek verb is imperfect, denoting continuous action in the past.
9. See, for example, Colossians 1:16f; Hebrews 1:2; Revelation 3:14.
10. John 1:2 is saying essentially the same thing as 1:1: The Word was in the beginning and was with God. The Greek *houtos,* meaning "this one," which begins 1:2, only adds emphasis to what has already been said in 1:1.
11. William F. Arndt and F. Wilbur Gingrich, *A Greek-English Lexicon of the New Testament* (Chicago: The University of Chicago Press, 1957), 716, item III.
12. B.F. Westcott, *The Gospel According to St. John* (London: John Murray, Albemarle Street, 1967), 3.
13. To translate this clause, as do cults such as Jehovah's Witnesses, ". . . and the word was a god," shows total ignorance of Greek syntax and grammar. The noun "God" *(theos),* used here without a definite article, indicates "essential nature." Our English indefinite article "a" cannot be inserted. Furthermore, the Greek sentence places the word *theos* first, emphasizing the Deity of the Word.
14. The Nicene Creed expressed the chief articles of the Christian faith as they were summarized by the first Nicene Council. The Council was called in A.D. 325 to refute the views of Arius, a priest of Alexandria, who believed that Christ was not of the *same* essence as God, but of *similar* substance. The Council declared that God and Christ as God are of one substance.
15. This descriptive phrase is found, for example, in Isaiah: "For the mouth of the LORD has spoken" (40:5). That settles the matter!
16. See also Proverbs 8:22-31, where Wisdom personified parallels the *Logos* as active in creation.

17. See Romans 1:18-23. Surely only a willful suppression of the truth could induce anyone, claiming to be wise, to foolishly and thanklessly assert the accidental or eternal existence of such a vast and intricate universe.

18. Bruce, *The Gospel of John,* 33.

19. The verb in 1:5, translated in the NIV "has not understood," is the Greek verb *katalambano,* which can also be translated—and more appropriately here—"did not overcome." The tense used is the Greek aorist, which indicates some particular point in the past—possibly the cross and the resurrection.

20. The word "witness" is very prominent in John's Gospel. We are told of the witness of the Father (5:32, 37); the Son (8:14, 18); the Spirit (15:26); Christ's works (5:36 and 10:25); Scripture (5:39) and the disciples (15:27; 17:23; 21:24).

21. The Greek text of 1:9 presents the translator with some slight difficulty. Should it be translated, "This was the true light that gives light to every man who comes into the world"? Or, as does the NIV, "The true light that gives light to every man was coming into the world"? Leon Morris, *The Gospel According to John* (Grand Rapids, MI: Eerdmans, 1971), 92f, prefers the latter translation, as does Bruce, *The Gospel of John,* 35. The implication is that even before coming into the world as a man, the *Logos* brought to every person in the world a spiritual illumination. On the other hand, R.G.V. Tasker, *The Gospel According to St. John* (London: The Tyndale Press, 1960), 46, prefers the former translation, ". . . to every man who comes into the world," being a rabbinic expression for everyone who is born. Perhaps John has purposely left some ambiguity, since both interpretations make good sense.

22. Aurelius C. Prudentius, "Of the Father's Love Begotten," *Hymns of the Christian Life* (Camp Hill, PA: Christian Publications, Inc., 1978), # 53, stanzas 1 and 2.

# 2

# *The Revealing Word*

John 1:10-18

*10 He was in the world, and though the world was made through him, the world did not recognize him. 11 He came to that which was his own, but his own did not receive him. 12 Yet to all who received him, to those who believed in his name, he gave the right to become children of God— 13 children born not of natural descent, nor of human decision or a husband's will, but born of God.*

*14 The Word became flesh and made his dwelling among us. We have seen his glory, the glory of the One and Only, who came from the Father, full of grace and truth.*

*15 John testifies concerning him. He cries out, saying, "This was he of whom I said, 'He who comes after me has surpassed me because he was before me.' " 16 From the fullness of his grace we have all received one blessing after another. 17 For the law was given through Moses; grace and truth came through Jesus Christ. 18 No one has ever seen God, but God the One and Only, who is at the Father's side, has made him known.*

In the previous chapter, we examined four truths concerning the *Logos*. We worshiped Him as the Divine One, the Life and Light of mankind, shining triumphantly in the darkness of sin and ignorance. We rejoiced in Him as God's Creative Word. We were introduced to the prophet sent by heaven to bear witness to the Light, so that people might believe. Let us now continue to hear this overture to the symphony that is John's unique Gospel.

## The Offered Word

Fifth, we are brought face-to-face with the *Offered Word* (1:10-13). Note first His presence in the world (1:10). He had dwelt in glorious and intimate fellowship with the Father from before there was a world. He had commanded the world into existence. He came into the world He had created, made Himself known and offered Himself, the Savior, to a world[1] alienated from God through sin.

But see also His rejection by the world (1:10-11). We might have expected that He would be recognized immediately and loved as a friend.[2] Instead, for the most part, He was met with either indifference or outright hostility. This is especially amazing when we consider that His coming to Israel was in reality a homecoming.[3] His own people should have recognized Him and made Him welcome. Instead they rejected Him.

Such a refusal of the Savior was utterly inexcusable. His holiness and exalted character should have been clues to His identity. Likewise His astounding miracles and the supernatural wisdom of His teaching. Israel's scribes should have seen the correspondence of His birthplace, His life, His deeds and His death with the predictions of Scripture. But, alas! As John reports, ". . . his own did not receive him" (1:11).

Notice, in contrast, His reception by believers (1:12-13). Though most in Israel missed their opportunity, there were some who recognized Jesus for who He was. Some gladly received Him as their Lord and Savior. See how John, in graphic detail, describes, first from the human perspective and then the divine, these who became Christ's disciples.

From the human perspective, they were (1) those "who received him" (1:12). When He knocked on the door of their hearts, asking entry, these gladly made Him welcome. They were (2) those "who believed on his name" (1:12). For us today, names are simply a way to distinguish one person from another. But in the world of Jesus' day, the name stood for the individual's whole personality. Thus to "believe on his name" means to trust in Him as He really is—God incarnate, Lord and Savior of the world. Those who believe on His name have entered into a relationship of trustful obedience[4] to Jesus. They recognize Him for who the Gospel claims Him to be: their Lord and Savior.

From the divine side, believers are (1) those to whom the divine Word "gave the right to become children of God" (1:12). What momentous Gospel truths are contained in these few words! They speak of the *gift* of grace, "freely bestowed on all who believe." It is "by grace [we] have been saved, through faith—and this not from [our]selves, it is the gift of God—not by works, so that no one can boast" (Ephesians 2:8-9). It is "not because of righteous things we had done, but because of his mercy" that he saved us (Titus 3:5).

The words of our text speak of the change of *status* into which grace brings us.[5] We were "objects of God's wrath" (see Ephesians 2:3) under the dominion of the kingdom of darkness. But God has brought us "into the kingdom of the Son he loves" (Colossians 1:13).

They speak also of the new *disposition* that we possess as children of God.[6] We have been made "participa[nts] in the divine nature" (2 Peter 1:4). Through the indwelling of the Holy Spirit, we begin to manifest the fruit of the Spirit (Galatians 5:22-23), that is, the likeness of Christ. We begin to be "imitators of God . . . as dearly loved children" (Ephesians 5:1).

Moreover, from the divine perspective, believers are (2) "children born not of natural descent,[7] nor of human decision[8] or a husband's will" (John 1:13). John is anxious to make clear that we are not children of God by virtue of our natural ancestry. The Jews of Jesus' day were proud to be descendants of Abraham. They considered their racial connection to Abraham, certified by circumcision, sufficient grounds for their acceptance by God. Not so, says John. As Paul puts it, "If you belong to Christ, then you are Abraham's seed, and heirs according to the promise" (Galatians 3:29).

Again, from the divine side, believers are described positively as (3) those "born of God" (John 1:13).[9] As we will be told in John 3, they have been "born again" or "born from above" by the action of the Holy Spirit. Becoming a child of God involves a supernatural act. New *spiritual* life (God's seed—see 1 John 3:9) is implanted in the believer. The person becomes "a new creation" (2 Corinthians 5:17) in Christ. He or she, as we already noted, begins to exhibit godly traits, concurrently repudiating the practice of sin (see 1 John 3:9).

What a marvelous, marvelous thing it is to be a child of God through faith in the living Word of God!

## *The Incarnate Word*

Sixth, from seeing Him as the offered Word, we behold Him as the *Incarnate Word* (John 1:14). How poignant is John's three-point Christmas story! (1) "The Word became flesh . . ." Not "The Word took on the seeming appearance of a man."[10] Not "The Spirit of the Heavenly Christ came temporarily upon the man Jesus."[11] But simply, "The Word became flesh"[12] God became Man in the person of Jesus. Jesus was conceived in the womb of the virgin Mary by the Holy Spirit. He was born in a cattle cave in the Judean town of Bethlehem. God incarnate! Tremendous mystery! Glorious historical, saving reality!

John's marvelous Christmas story continues: (2) ". . . and made his dwelling among us." The translators of our version have sought to bring out the meaning of the Greek word *skenoo* (literally "tabernacled"). The word implies a temporary rather than a permanent residence. The desert tabernacle may well have been in John's mind. More likely he was thinking of the Shekinah,[13] the glorious presence of God that resided in both the Mosaic tabernacle and Solomon's temple.[14] John is saying, in effect, that in the incarnate Word the true Shekinah glory is radiantly manifest.

And, in fact, he goes on (3) to say, "We have *seen* his glory." How was Christ's glory seen by John and his fellow apostles? Surely the whole earthly career of Jesus revealed that glory. His words, His deeds, His miracles (see especially John 2:11), His transfiguration (Matthew 17:2) revealed that glory. But it was on the cross that His glory was preeminently manifested. Our Lord "humbled himself and became obedient to death" (Philippians 2:8). On the cross He made atonement for sin. In His resurrection He defeated death and ascended in glory to the Father's right hand.

This glory is brought out yet more completely in the ensuing phrase. John describes Jesus as being "full of grace and truth." The words could very well be connected grammatically with the word "glory."[15] That is to say "grace and truth" are manifestations of Christ's glory. John may have in mind that remarkable Old Testament interchange between Moses and God. The great leader of Israel requests of God, "Now show me your glory" (Exodus 33:18). And God replies, "I will cause all my goodness to pass in front of you, and I will proclaim my name, the LORD, in your presence" (33:19). God's glory is to be seen in His "goodness."

Then a little later, as God passed in front of Moses, He elaborates on His goodness, proclaiming, "The LORD, the LORD, the compassionate and gracious God, slow to anger, *abounding in love and faithfulness . . .*" (34:6, emphasis added). Thus God's glory is to be seen in His abounding love and faithfulness. John's phrase, "full of grace and truth (faithfulness)," clearly parallels the words of God to Moses.

Clearly the glory revealed to Moses at Sinai is the same revealed in the grace and faithfulness of God's "One and Only." It was a goodness that led Him to become flesh and lay down His life for sinners on a shameful cross.

## The All-Surpassing Word

Finally, John would have us see our Lord as the *All-Surpassing Word* (John 1:15-18). He surpasses Israel's two greatest prophets: His contemporary, John the Baptist, and the ancient law-giver, Moses.

John the Baptist, whose testimony concerning Christ will be amplified in 1:19-34, is not reluctant to declare Jesus' superiority. Although the Baptist's ministry predated Jesus', he knew that the Lord preexisted him. Jesus Christ far surpassed him.

As revered as Moses was in the Jewish mind, Jesus has "greater honor than Moses" (Hebrews 3:3). As hallowed as was the law Moses mediated, it was only a temporary measure. Neither the apostles nor Jesus would have demeaned the Law of God.[16] Jesus said He came not to destroy the law but to fulfill it (Matthew 5:17). Paul declared it to be "our schoolmaster to bring us unto Christ" (Galatians 3:24, KJV). He called it "holy, righteous and good" (Romans 7:12), a vehicle used by the Spirit to convict of sin (see 7:7ff).

But the law provided no permanent means of freeing sinners from the guilt and power of their sin. It could only condemn the sinner. God intended its ritual and symbolism to point man to Christ. He alone, through His grace and truth, has a remedy for sin. From Mount Sinai, enshrouded by dark clouds, thunder and lightning, he was "given" the Law. But from Mount Calvary and the darkness that covered the world "came" grace and truth. "What the law was powerless to do in that it was weakened by the sinful nature, God did by sending his own Son in the likeness of sinful man to be a sin offering. And so he condemned sin in sinful man, in order that the righteous requirements of the law might be fully met in us, who do not live according to the sinful nature but according to the Spirit" (Romans 8:3-4).

What a Savior! What grace! What truth!

John 1:18 in a sense sums up the entire prologue, if not John's entire Gospel. The Son of God, the Word made flesh, who came from God, has given us the perfect—and final—revelation of God's nature. In this statement, John prepares us to hear the words of Jesus: "Anyone who has seen me has seen the Father."

## Conclusion

We have finished the overture that introduces the symphony to come. Let us prayerfully consider how we might apply this text to our lives. Should my reader be one who has been rejecting the Lord Jesus as He offers Himself in the Gospel, let me solemnly remind you that in your spiritual blindness, like the unbelievers of our text (1:10-11), you are repelling and wounding Him who is your only hope of eternal life.

In Wales, there is a romantic village named Beddgelert—"the grave of Gelert." Gelert was a dog, the hound of Llewellyn the Great. Returning one day to his castle, Llewellyn discovered the bloodied corpse of his child and the hound Gelert beside it. In a blind rage Llewellyn plunged his sword into the poor animal. Too late he saw nearby the lifeless form of a huge wolf and realized his awful mistake. It was the wolf, not Gelert, that had attacked and killed his child. Faithful Gelert had in turn killed the wolf. In his rage, Llewellyn had slain a faithful friend.

In a far more terrible sense, that is what all who reject Jesus Christ do. In their spiritual blindness they repudiate their truest Friend and Savior.

To you, reader, who have believed in the name of our Lord Jesus (1:12-13), I have a few words. Remember that God's grace alone has rescued you from the kingdom of darkness. You, like all others, were once blinded and bound by sin. In His mercy, God has transferred you into the glorious kingdom of light, life and truth. He has granted you new status: child of God. As such you have been given God's divine nature within. You are called, then, as one of God's dear children, to reflect in your disposition and behavior the likeness of your heavenly Father. This is only possible as you yield yourself, body, mind and spirit, to the moment-by-moment control of the Holy Spirit. The Holy Spirit is the Spirit of Christ. Allow Him to be "at home" in you, producing His lovely Christlike fruit in your life.

Meditate long on the glory, full of grace and truth, which with John we have seen in Christ. You will sense it in His perfect life, His atoning death, His glorious resurrection and His ascension to the Father.

> God and Father, we adore Thee
>    For the Son, Thine image bright,
> In whom all Thy holy nature
>    Dawned on our once hopeless night.
>
> Far from Thee our footsteps wandered,
>    On dark paths of sin and shame;
> But our midnight turned to morning,
>    When the Lord of Glory came.
>
> Word Incarnate, God revealing,
>    Longed-for while dim ages ran,
> Love Divine, we bow before Thee,
>    Son of God and Son of Man.
>
> Let our life be new created,
>    Ever-living Lord, in Thee,
> Till we wake with Thy pure likeness,
>    When Thy face in heaven we see;
>
> Where the saints of all the ages,
>    Where our fathers glorified,

Clouds and darkness far beneath them,
   In unending day abide.


God and Father, now we bless Thee,
   For the Son, Thine image bright,
In whom all Thy holy nature
   Dawns on our adoring sight.[17]


### Endnotes

1. John uses the word "world" three times in this verse, twice with reference to the material world, including mankind, and once with reference to fallen mankind, alienated from God through sin.
2. This is the meaning in 1:10 of the verb *ginosko,* "to know."
3. The expression in 1:11 is "he came *eis ta idia."* We find the same expression in John 19:27, where the writer reports that John received Mary *eis ta idia,* "into his home."
4. In both Old and New Testaments, the meaning of the word "believe on" is to trust and obey.
5. The word translated "right" is the Greek *exousia.* It means not "power" but rather "authority" or "status."
6. The New Testament in Romans 8:14, for example, refers to believers as "sons of God." This alludes to the rights that Christ confers on us as His adopted offspring. Here in John 1:12, believers are called "children of God" (Greek *tekna*), which speaks of the fact that believers are partakers of a new divine nature.
7. Literally, "not of bloods." There was an idea in the ancient world that birth took place as the result of the action of blood, perhaps here the blood of both parents.
8. Literally, "of the will of the flesh," that is, of man's natural sexual appetite.
9. The word translated "born" here is the Greek *gennao,* "to beget." The emphasis is on the father's part in the birth process.
10. As the so-called Docetists or the Gnostics would have it, denying the reality of Christ's human body.
11. As the so-called Arians would have it, denying the deity of the man Jesus.
12. In contrast to the heresies of Docetism and Arianism, the orthodox doctrine, promulgated at Chalcedon, A.D. 451, holds that in the one person, Jesus Christ, there are two natures, a human and a divine. Each has completeness and integrity, and these two natures are organically, indissolubly united, without forming a third nature. As it is often put, orthodoxy forbids us either to divide the person or to confound the natures.
13. The Greek verb *skenoo,* "tabernacled," is commonly associated with the Hebrew verb *shakan,* "to settle down, abide, dwell." See William Gesenius, *A Hebrew and English Lexicon of the Old Testament* (Oxford: The Clarendon Press, 1955), 1014. The word *shekinah,* "dwelling" (Gesenius, 1015)—God's dwelling among His people—came to be linked with the glory resulting from the immediate presence of the Lord in the tabernacle. So we speak of the "Shekinah glory."
14. See, for example, Exodus 40:34; 1 Kings 8:10f.

15. For example, F.F. Bruce, *The Gospel of John* (Grand Rapids, MI: Eerdmans, 1983), 411, takes it that way and goes on to relate the phrase "full of grace and truth" to God's word to Moses in Exodus 34:5f, where He describes Himself as "abounding in love and faithfulness."
16. Here the "Law" refers both to the decalogue, and to the Torah, the first five books of Moses. But perhaps it also refers to the whole pre-Christian Judaism as it was based on Scripture.
17. "God and Father, We Adore Thee," *The Church Hymnody* (London: Oxford University Press, 1927), # 59. Stanza 1 is attributed to John Nelson Darby and stanzas 2-6 to Hugh Falconer.

# The Consecrated Lord

John 1:19-34

*19 Now this was John's testimony when the Jews of Jerusalem sent priests and Levites to ask him who he was. 20 He did not fail to confess, but confessed freely, "I am not the Christ."*

*21 They asked him, "Then who are you? Are you Elijah?"*

*He said, "I am not."*

*"Are you the Prophet?"*

*He answered, "No."*

*22 Finally they said, "Who are you? Give us an answer to take back to those who sent us. What do you say about yourself?"*

*23 John replied in the words of Isaiah the prophet, "I am the voice of one calling in the desert, 'Make straight the way for the Lord.' "*

*24 Now some Pharisees who had been sent 25 questioned him, "Why then do you baptize if you are not the Christ, nor Elijah, nor the Prophet?"*

*26 "I baptize with water," John replied, "but among you stands one you do not know. 27 He is the one who comes after me, the thongs of whose sandals I am not worthy to untie."*

*28 This all happened at Bethany on the other side of the Jordan, where John was baptizing.*

*29 The next day John saw Jesus coming toward him and said, "Look, the Lamb of God, who takes away the sin of the world! 30 This is the one I meant when I said, 'A man who comes after me has surpassed me because he was before me.' 31 I myself did not know him, but the reason I came baptizing with water was that he might be revealed to Israel."*

> *32 Then John gave this testimony: "I saw the Spirit come down from heaven as a dove and remain on him. 33 I would not have known him, except that the one who sent me to baptize with water told me, 'The man on whom you see the Spirit come down and remain is he who will baptize with the Holy Spirit.' 34 I have seen and I testify that this is the Son of God."*

The day on which the events of our text took place was a day of extraordinary significance for its two main characters. For the one it marked the end of a powerful revival ministry. For the Other it marked the beginning of a singular pastoral ministry.

For the one, the purpose of his heavenly calling was now complete. For the Other, the purpose of His calling would now begin to unfold. The mission of the one was to proclaim the identity and mission of the Other and then fade away. The mission of the Other was to popularly proclaim the kingdom of God, to die in shame, to rise again in power and glory.

It is no easy circumstance for a renowned preacher to find himself superseded by a younger man whose popularity transcends his own. It is still more difficult for that same prominent preacher to encourage his followers to transfer their allegiance. John the Baptist did exactly that, not hesitantly, but with determination. He did it the very day he saw Jesus passing by. It was a rare but becoming example of genuine humility! No wonder the Lord declared, "I tell you the truth: Among those born of women there has not risen anyone greater than John the Baptist" (Matthew 11:11).

This was a day, I say, of vital importance to our Lord. It marked His ordination to a ministry of teaching, healing and deliverance. Our text parallels the accounts in the other Gospels of His water baptism and His consecration to service. But we will view the events here through the eyes of the Baptist. We will see Jesus first as the announced Messiah, then as the atoning Redeemer and finally as the anointed Baptizer.

### The Announced Messiah (1:19-28)

The Spirit of God was moving in convicting power on the far bank of the Jordan. The rough-hewn, leather-belted eater of locusts and wild honey was calling people from all walks of life to repent and be baptized. He spared no one. Self-righteous Pharisee to disreputable soldier—all were warned to flee from God's wrath and produce the fruits of genuine repentance (Matthew 3:1ff).

In the air was a widespread spirit of expectation. Rome's army occupying in the land of Israel had created an intense longing for the promised Messiah. Jews expected this Messiah to overthrow the conquerors and deliver their nation from bondage. This sense of expectancy had reached into the very top echelons of Jerusalem's religious establishment.

John the Baptist's phenomenal following along the Jordan had not escaped the notice of these leaders. Might he possibly be the deliverer they were anticipating? Could he be the Messiah? They had best find out!

And so they sent a delegation of priests and Levites to ascertain the truth about this ever-so-outspoken preacher of righteousness (1:19). Their question evoked (1) *John's Confession:* "I am not the Christ." Had he been less forthright (see 1:20), there would have been not a few willing to bestow the title on him. Note how the Jerusalem delegation continued to press him.

"Then who are you?" they wanted to know. "Are you Elijah?" (1:21). There was much about his message and appearance[1] that reminded them of that Old Testament prophet. And had not Malachi predicted, "See, I will send you the prophet Elijah before that great and dreadful day of the LORD comes" (Malachi 4:5)? But John, humble man that he was, could not see himself as fulfilling such a prediction (John 1:21). It was Jesus who later identified John with Elijah (see Matthew 11:14).

Another possibility came to mind. "Are you the Prophet?" Moses had foretold, "The LORD your God will raise up for you a prophet like me from among your brothers. You must listen to him. . . . I will put my words in his mouth, and he will tell them everything I command him" (Deuteronomy 18:15-18). But to their question John replied with a firm "No." Even John's emphatic denials were a truly positive confession to Jesus' Messiahship.

The Jerusalem deputation was getting nowhere. They needed to take some answer back to the religious leaders who had sent them. So they asked John point blank. "Who are you? . . . What do you say about yourself?" (John 1:22).

This concluding question produced a statement of (2) *John's Commission* (1:23-26). In genuine humility of spirit, John answered their question by echoing the prophet Isaiah's words. "I am the voice of one calling in the desert, 'Make straight the way for the Lord' " (see Isaiah 40:3). John's job description was to prepare the way for Christ's coming. His was the arduous task of elevating the valleys of discouragement and despair. He was to bring down the mountains of self-righteousness and self-security. He had been called to level the rough ground of dishonesty, to shave off the rugged places of unapproachable pride. He was at work so the glory of the Lord could be revealed.[2]

Before John the Baptist's birth, the angel Gabriel had described John's ministry to Zechariah his father. "He will . . . turn the hearts of the fathers to their children and the disobedient to the wisdom of the righteous—to make ready a people prepared for the Lord" (Luke 1:17).

John's ministry was to take the penitent into the baptismal waters. By that act of symbolic cleansing they declared their intent to follow John in the way of righteousness. All of this was in the commission of the rugged revivalist John.

Some members of the delegation had a further question. It would appear that in the eyes of the Pharisees baptism was an eschatological rite. It should be administered by one of the expected end-time figures. So they demand to know why John, if he was not the Christ nor Elijah nor the Prophet, would dare to baptize. John does not answer their question directly. Instead, he turns their attention to Jesus, and we hear (3) *John's Concession* (1:26-27): "I baptize with water, . . . but among you stands one you do not know. He is the one who comes after me, the thongs of whose sandals I am not worthy to untie."

It is as though John is saying, "Yes, my baptism in water is important, but it is not an end in itself. Its purpose is to point people to Jesus, the Christ, whom I am announcing to you. Jesus, whom you do not yet know, is already among you." John makes clear how great this One is by conceding that he is totally unworthy to perform for Him even the most menial task.[3]

Second, John would have us see Jesus as . . .

## The Atoning Redeemer (1:29-31)

The time came for the Baptist and the Christ to meet. John had already identified Him as the one who, though coming after him, surpassed him (1:15, 30). Now, the day following his interchange with the Jerusalem committee, he sees Jesus "coming toward him" (1:29). As a herald shouts out the identity of arriving royalty, John excitedly announces to the assembled multitude, "Look, the Lamb of God, who takes away the sin of the world!"

It will profit us to look carefully at this amazing appellation, "Lamb of God," given to Jesus. It is a title greatly loved by the Apostle John. In his later Spirit-given symbolic visions, John sees "a Lamb, looking as if it had been slain, standing in the center of the throne" (Revelation 5:6). He hears the persecuted saints comforted by an angel who assures him that "the Lamb at the center of the throne will be their shepherd" (7:17). He is told that ten kings and the beast "will make war against the Lamb, but the Lamb will overcome them because he is Lord of lords and King of kings" (17:14).

The picture of Christ as the Lamb is clearly Old Testamental. For example, on their way to the sacrifice on Moriah, Abraham's son Isaac says to his father, "The fire and wood are here, . . . but where is the lamb for the burnt offering?" To which Abraham in faith replies, "God himself will provide the lamb for the burnt offering, my son" (Genesis 22:7-8). Stopped by the angel as he was in the act of slaying the boy, Abraham looked up. There in a thicket "he saw a ram caught by its horns" (22:13) which he sacrificed as a burnt offering instead of his son.

On the eve of the Israelites' exodus from Egypt, "each man [was] to take a lamb for his family," slaughter it at twilight and sprinkle its blood "on the sides and tops of the doorframes of the houses" where they would be eating the lambs. The Lord assured them, "When I see the blood, I will pass over you. No destructive plague will touch you when I strike Egypt" (Exodus 12:3-13).

Or again, in Isaiah's vivid portrayal of the Suffering Servant (Christ Jesus), he declares that "he was led like a lamb to the slaughter, and as a sheep before her shearers is silent, so he did not open his mouth" (Isaiah 53:7). Any of these Old Testament Scriptures, and more, could well account for John's description of Jesus as "the Lamb of God."

And what does the Lamb accomplish? He "takes away the sin of the world." Under the Old Covenant, an Israelite who sinned was to place his hand upon the head of an unblemished, sacrificial lamb. It symbolized the transference of the person's sin to an innocent substitute which was slain in his stead (see Leviticus 1:4). So at the cross the sins of the world were laid on

Jesus. He died in our stead—a death that made full atonement for sin. Isaac Watts had it right when he wrote:

> Not all the blood of beasts
>   On Jewish altars slain
> Could give the guilty conscience peace,
>   Or wash away the stain.

> But Christ, the heavenly Lamb,
>   Takes all our sins away;
> A sacrifice of nobler name
>   And richer blood than they.

> My faith would lay her hand
>   On that dear head of Thine,
> While like a penitent I stand,
>   And there confess my sin.

> Believing, we rejoice
>   To see the curse removed;
> We bless the Lamb with cheerful voice,
>   And sing His bleeding love.[4]

Thus our Atoning Redeemer bears away the sin of the world. But that is not all he does! John also would have us see Jesus as . . .

## The Anointed Baptizer (1:32-34)

First, let it be understood that Jesus Himself was anointed for His ministry by the Holy Spirit. The Spirit came upon Him at the Jordan (1:32).[5] All that He did—healing, exorcising demons, teaching, working miracles and offering Himself to die on the cross—He did as a Spirit-filled person. He exercised those gifts of the Spirit that were necessary for the proper fulfillment of His God-ordained work. Peter reported to the household of Cornelius: "God anointed Jesus of Nazareth with the Holy Spirit and power, and . . . he went around doing good and healing all who were under the power of the devil, because God was with him" (Acts 10:38).

Luke records Jesus' understanding of the descent of the Holy Spirit upon Him. In the Nazareth synagogue Jesus read from the prophet Isaiah:

> The Spirit of the Lord is on me,
>> because he has anointed me
>> to preach good news to the poor.
> He has sent me to proclaim freedom for the prisoners
>> and recovery of sight for the blind,
> to release the oppressed,
>> to proclaim the year of the Lord's favor.
>>> (Luke 4:18-19)

Returning the scroll to the attendant, Jesus announced to the congregation, "Today this scripture is fulfilled in your hearing" (4:21).

Second, the Lord intended that His disciples would perpetuate His ministry through the same anointing of the Holy Spirit. Note what John the Baptist says God told him: "The man on whom you see the Spirit come down and remain is he who will baptize with the Holy Spirit" (John 1:33). Shortly after His resurrection, Jesus gave this instruction to His disciples: "I am going to send you what my Father has promised; but stay in the city until you have been clothed with power from on high" (Luke 24:49).

This promised enduement was fulfilled initially on the Day of Pentecost. The Holy Spirit came upon the 120 assembled disciples, purifying their hearts and empowering them for their own ministries. The crowd that quickly gathered was both amazed and perplexed. Peter told them it was the ascended Jesus who "has poured out what you now see and hear" (Acts 2:33).

But Acts makes it clear that this same "pentecostal" anointing of the Holy Spirit is available to all believers. In fact, as not a few have discovered, it is quite impossible to effectively fulfill one's Christian service without such a personal baptism of the Holy Spirit. D.L. Moody, for example, attempted the work of evangelism without much success. Then, at the urging of some concerned Christian women, he sought and received the infilling of the Holy

Spirit. Would that all the Lord's people availed themselves of the Exalted Christ's provision for them!

## Conclusion

How critical it is that believers in the Lord Jesus receive Him in all the aspects of His gracious salvation! Through His atoning death and glorious resurrection He has made available a full pardon for sin. And through His exaltation at the Father's right hand He has made available the free gift of the Holy Spirit. This gift enables both holiness of life and ability in service. Like the gift of salvation, it is received by appropriating faith.

Years ago, Dr. A.B. Simpson, founder of The Christian and Missionary Alliance, penned these still-appropriate lines:

> Oh, what a solemn spectacle it is to see the Son of God spending thirty years on earth without one single act of public ministry until He received the baptism of power from on high. Then He concentrated a whole lifetime of service into forty-two short months of intense activity and almighty power!
>
> But He has left to us the same power which He possessed. He has bequeathed to the Church the very Holy Spirit that lived and worked in Him. Let us accept this mighty gift. Let us believe in Him and His all-sufficiency. Let us receive Him and give Him room. Let us go forth to reproduce the life and ministry of Jesus. And let us perpetuate the divine miracles of our holy Christianity through the power of the blessed Comforter.
>
> This is the mighty gift of our ascended Lord. This is the supreme need of the Church today. This is the special promise of the latter days. God help us to claim it fully. In the power of the Spirit, let us go forth to meet our coming Lord.[6]

In our day, too, the world needs to see the Lord Jesus in and through His followers. Let us heed Simpson's vital words. Two stanzas from a once-familiar Simpson song close this chapter:

> Jesus is our Sanctifier,
>     Cleansing us from self and sin,

And with all His Spirit's fullness,
    Filling all our hearts within.

Jesus only is our power,
    He the gift of Pentecost;
Jesus, breathe Thy power upon us,
    Fill us with the Holy Ghost.[7]

To which every heart hungry for the deeper life must respond, "Amen!"

### Endnotes

1.  Second Kings 1:8 describes Elijah as a man, like John, "with a garment of hair and with a leather belt around his waist."
2.  By way of explaining the necessary preparation of the way of the Lord, see Isaiah 40:3-5, which follows the verses John quotes.
3.  Leon Morris, *The Gospel According to John* (Grand Rapids, MI: Eerdmans, 1971), 141, observes, "Loosing the sandal was the task of a slave. A disciple could not be expected to perform it. To get the full impact of this we must bear in mind that disciples did do many services for their teachers. . . . But they had to draw the line somewhere, and menial tasks like loosing the sandal thong came under this heading. . . . John selects this task . . . and declares himself unworthy to perform it."
4.  Isaac Watts, "Not All the Blood of Beasts," *Hymns of the Christian Life* (Camp Hill, PA: Christian Publications, Inc., 1978), # 86.
5.  The other Gospels inform us that this happened in connection with Jesus' own baptism in water by John the Baptist.
    I recognize that others take the position that Jesus did His miracles in the power of His deity. But the biblical evidence supports my view: He did them through the empowering of the Holy Spirit, who descended on Him at His baptism. Apart from Jesus' forgiveness of sins (which He did as God, of course), His disciples did the same miracles Jesus did. And surely there is contemporary evidence that Spirit-anointed individuals continue to work miracles by the same power that rested on Jesus.
    Surely, too, Peter's words to Cornelius and his household (Acts 10:38), which I quote in the text, lend credence to my viewpoint.
    A.B. Simpson states: "The Holy Spirit [came upon] the Christ, and in the strength of this indwelling Spirit, henceforth He wrought His works, spoke His words and accomplished His ministry on earth." He adds, "Oh, if the Son of God did not presume to begin His public work until He had received this power from on high, what presumption it is that we should attempt in our own strength to fulfill the ministry committed to us and be witness unto Him!" [A.B. Simpson, *The Holy Spirit: Power from on High,* ed. Keith M. Bailey (Camp Hill, PA: Christian Publications, Inc., 1994), 309-310].
6.  Quoted from Simpson, *The Holy Spirit: Power from on High,* 314.
7.  A.B. Simpson, "Jesus Only," *Hymns of the Christian Life,* # 398, stanzas 3 and 5.

# 4

# The Compelling Rabbi

John 1:35-51

35 The next day John was there again with two of his disciples. 36 When he saw Jesus passing by, he said, "Look, the Lamb of God!"

37 When the two disciples heard him say this, they followed Jesus. 38 Turning around, Jesus saw them following and asked, "What do you want?"

They said, "Rabbi" (which means Teacher), "where are you staying?"

39 "Come," he replied, "and you will see."

So they went and saw where he was staying, and spent that day with him. It was about the tenth hour.

40 Andrew, Simon Peter's brother, was one of the two who heard what John had said and who had followed Jesus. 41 The first thing Andrew did was to find his brother Simon and tell him, "We have found the Messiah" (that is, the Christ). 42 And he brought him to Jesus.

Jesus looked at him and said, "You are Simon son of John. You will be called Cephas" (which, when translated, is Peter).

43 The next day Jesus decided to leave for Galilee. Finding Philip, he said to him, "Follow me."

44 Philip, like Andrew and Peter, was from the town of Bethsaida. 45 Philip found Nathanael and told him, "We have found the one Moses wrote about in the Law, and about whom the prophets also wrote—Jesus of Nazareth, the son of Joseph."

46 "Nazareth! Can anything good come from there?" Nathanael asked.

> *"Come and see," said Philip.*
>
> *47 When Jesus saw Nathanael approaching, he said of him, "Here is a true Israelite, in whom there is nothing false."*
>
> *48 "How do you know me?" Nathanael asked.*
>
> *Jesus answered, "I saw you while you were still under the fig tree before Philip called you."*
>
> *49 Then Nathanael declared, "Rabbi, you are the Son of God; you are the King of Israel."*
>
> *50 Jesus said, "You believe because I told you I saw you under the fig tree. You shall see greater things than that." 51 He then added, "I tell you the truth, you shall see heaven open, and the angels of God ascending and descending on the Son of Man."*

O nce again, John the Baptist, this time in the company of two of his disciples, seeks to transfer their allegiance to Jesus. Perhaps they were not present the previous day to hear John call Jesus "the Lamb of God." Regardless, John repeats his declaration (1:36). John has been faithful to point these followers to Christ. In this way John frees them to pursue Jesus. At the same time he creates in them a curiosity—more than that, an eagerness—to know more about this One to whom their teacher faithfully pointed. There is a compelling magnetism about Jesus; their minds are open to know the truth; their hearts are seeking. They are now hungry to know Him.

## *A Hunger Created (1:35-38)*

Our text does not describe Jesus' calling of these men to the apostleship which they would later obtain.[1] Before that can happen, they must desire to really get to know Him. They must be willing to be all that is in His plan for them. This the Spirit of God places within the hearts of these two disciples of John. As Jesus passes by they begin to follow Him, and He responds by asking them, "What do you want?" (1:38). He is searching out their motives.

Surely He knows what is in their hearts, but it is important that they themselves express this in His presence. Were they only looking for an exhilarating discussion about some particular theological controversy? Did they want to impress Him with their already-acquired insights? Did they, perhaps, wish to acquire a place of prominence among whatever community He might establish? Were they looking to better their lot in life? Had such unworthy motives been in their minds, it is doubtful that Jesus would have invited further conversation.

To His question, they reply, "Rabbi[2] . . . where are you staying?" (1:38). They are saying to Him, in effect, "Our motives are pure. We recognize that You are a teacher sent by God. We want more than a passing acquaintance with You. We have questions we want to ask You that cannot be answered hurriedly. We want to know who You are. We desire to know why John wants us to follow You instead of him. What exactly is involved in being Your disciples?" Then, as now, Jesus is always willing to converse with sincere seekers after truth. And so He invites them: "Come . . . and you will see" (1:39). It was by then four o'clock in the afternoon.[3] Likely they stayed the night with Jesus. What a life-changing evening that turned out to be!

## A Longing Satisfied (1:39-42)

One can only imagine what truths Jesus conveyed to Andrew and his partner[4] during those quiet hours together. Doubtless He would have quoted the Scriptures, showing them those things about Himself that they were ready and able to hear.[5] What a feast Jesus provides for those who truly desire to know Him! They would have discovered that He "satisfies the thirsty and fills the hungry with good things" (Psalm 107:9). They would have sensed in their hearts that this man was the answer to their every quest. Whatever else was said, they came away convinced that they had been with none other than Israel's Messiah (John 1:41).[6]

So great was the joy of his new discovery that Andrew immediately thought of his brother, Simon. Simon should know the Christ, too! Eagerly "he brought him to Jesus" (1:42).[7] The text says Jesus "looked at him."[8] Seeing the potential in Peter, He gave him a new name that indicated what Simon would become by the power of God.[9] No one of us can foresee, when we bring a person to Jesus, what Jesus will make of that person!

## A Skepticism Dispelled (1:43-51)

Philip, like Andrew and Peter a native of Bethsaida,[10] heard the call of Jesus and joined the other two. He also sought to bring another to the Master. He assured his friend Nathanael that this One they had discovered indeed fulfilled the Old Testament Messianic prophecies (1:45). But when Nathanael heard that Jesus was from Nazareth, he was skeptical (1:46). Doubtless he and Philip had discussed many Old Testament prophecies concerning the Messiah. He knew of none predicting that the Christ would come from such a no-good village as Nazareth.[11] Quite possibly some of his skepticism was due to the usual rivalry existing between small country villages. Nathanael's hometown was Cana (see John 21:2), a not-too-distant neighbor of Nazareth!

Philip wisely made no attempt, through argument, to change Nathanael's mind. He knew it would be sufficient for his friend to meet Jesus face-to-face. And so the skeptic and the Savior came together. Jesus at once disarmed Nathanael by accurately describing the character of the man he had never previously known.

"Here is a true Israelite," Jesus said, "in whom there is nothing false"(1:47).[12]

Nathanael, guilelessly showing no false modesty, immediately questioned the source of Jesus' knowledge of Him. He was utterly astounded when Jesus declared, "I saw you while you were still under the fig tree[13] before Philip called you" (1:48). Prompted by this manifestation of Jesus' insight into his innermost thoughts, Nathanael took an utter leap of faith.

"Rabbi," he declared, "you are the Son of God; you are the King of Israel" (1:49). The skeptic is not won over by human argument, but by a manifestation of the supernatural power of God.

Jesus' reply to Nathanael's confession was to assure him that he would see greater manifestations of God's power (1:50). And then, speaking to more than Nathanael,[14] Jesus tells them, in effect, that they will come to see that He is the true "Jacob's ladder" (Genesis 28:10ff). He is the saving link between heaven and earth.

## Conclusion

Prayerfully consider five lessons we may learn from our text. First, concerning John's two disciples, it was their hunger for the truth that turned them toward Jesus. Here we discover a first principle of the deeper life. It begins with an intense desire to have all that God has for us in Jesus.

"Blessed are those who hunger and thirst for righteousness," said Jesus, "for they will be filled" (Matthew 5:6). It is not that God is disinclined to fill our lives with Himself; it is just that He loves to be pursued. He will not thrust Himself upon someone disinterested or unwilling. And yet, the truth is, He creates in us the hunger that He alone can satisfy. We must learn not to quench the hunger for God that He places in our hearts.

Second, as the disciples found their spiritual longings fully met in Jesus, so can we. The deeper life is a continual discovery of how fully Jesus satisfies the deep yearnings of our hearts. Do we long to be holy? The indwelling Christ offers Himself to us as our holiness! Do we long to know our Father, God? Christ is the Revealer of the Father! Do we long for power that enables a fruitful ministry? Christ, by His Holy Spirit, is that power! As we study John's Gospel, we will discover the gracious provision that God has made available for us in Christ. It is a provision that we may readily appropriate through faith.

Third, just as Andrew shared his discovery of Jesus with Peter, so we will want to share Christ with others. The joy and reality we find in Christ is to be passed on! The deeper-life Christian experiences "streams of living water [flowing] from within" (John 7:38). Such a person can witness to the sufficiency of Christ for human need.

Fourth, think of Peter, the impetuous Galilean fisherman, who would learn the untrustworthiness of his self-assured heart. One moment, he would stand by his Lord no matter what others did. The next, he was denying any knowledge of Jesus. Peter teaches us not to put confidence in ourselves but in Christ who lives within. We can be glad that Jesus saw Peter not only as he *was,* but as he *would be*—by God's grace. Though all we have to offer Him is failure, Jesus can turn our failures into blessings.

Finally, think of Nathanael, the cautious skeptic. He is converted to Christ as he sees before his very eyes the supernatural power of God. How our world needs to see the manifestation of God's mighty power joined to the Church's verbal witness! There is an increasing hunger out there for the supernatural. We can see it in the New Agers' interest in occult phenomena. The occult is demonically inspired. In the Old Testament, the presence of the ark of God caused a Philistine idol to topple (1 Samuel 5:1ff). So the display of supernatural power that originates in the action of the God and Father of Jesus must demolish Satan's deceiving wonders.

How compelling is this One whom the disciples of our text address as "Rabbi!" May the Spirit of God graciously compel you, my reader, to follow Him who is "the Son of God, the King of Israel."

### Endnotes

1. The call to apostleship is recorded in the other Gospels: Matthew 4:18-20; Mark 1:16-18; Luke 5:10-11.
2. "Rabbi" means "my great one." It is the title the Jews gave to their teachers.
3. "The tenth hour." The Jews measured their days from sunset to sunset and divided both night and day into twelve hours.
4. It has been thought from early times that this was the beloved disciple, John, the author of this Gospel. See Leon Morris, *The Gospel According to John* (Grand Rapids, MI: Eerdmans, 1971), 155.
5. As he did for the two with whom He walked on the road to Emmaus (Luke 24:13ff).
6. The Hebrew *Messiah* and the corresponding Greek *Christ* both mean "Anointed One." In the Old Testament three classes were anointed for their task: the king (1 Samuel 16:6), the priest (Leviticus 4:3) and the prophet (Psalm 105:15). Jesus fills all three of these offices.
7. Each time Andrew appears in this Gospel he is bringing someone to Jesus! (See 6:8 and 12:21-22.)
8. The Greek word is *emblepein,* meaning "to gaze intently." The thought here is that Jesus saw right into Peter's heart.
9. Both Cephas (Aramaic) and Peter (Greek) mean "rock."
10. A fishing village just a little northeast of the Sea of Galilee.
11. It is difficult to pinpoint the reference in Matthew 2:23, "So was fulfilled what was said through the prophets: 'He will be called a Nazarene.' " What Old Testament references is Matthew referring to? Perhaps, as some have suggested, the reference is to Isaiah 11:1, which mentions a shoot or branch (Hebrew *natzer)* which shall spring out of Jesse's stump or root.
12. The Greek is *dolos,* meaning "guile" or "deceit." The equivalent Hebrew term, *mirmah,* is used in Genesis 27:35 of Jacob before his change of heart. Thus the basis of Temple's translation, "an Israelite in whom there is no Jacob" (see Morris, 166).
13. The expression "under the fig tree" is subject to varying interpretation. William Barclay, *The Gospel of John,* vol. 1 (Philadelphia: The Westminster Press, 1975), 93, for example, comments that "to the Jews the fig tree always stood for peace. Their idea of peace was when a man could be undisturbed under his own vine and his own fig tree (cf. 1 Kings 4:25; Micah 4:4)." Barclay observes that likely Nathanael had been praying and meditating on the promises of God under the tree's shady branches. Now he sensed that Jesus had seen into the very depths of his heart. Morris, 167, considers the fig tree a symbol of home, where Nathanael had had outstanding experiences of communion with God.
14. The "you" of 1:51 is plural.

## Part I

## *Questions for Reflection or Discussion*

1. How does John 1 demonstrate the deity of Jesus Christ?
2. What two vital ministries of Jesus are set forth in John 1:19-34?
3. Evaluate this statement: "All that Jesus said and did was done in the power of the Holy Spirit."
4. What other New Testament book proclaims the superiority of Jesus to Moses? In what ways is Jesus superior?
5. What first principle of the deeper life is illustrated in the lives of John's two disciples (1:35-39)?
6. In what ways can it be said that Jesus meets the deepest longings of our hearts?
7. Do you think our world still needs to see manifestations of God's supernatural power as Nathanael did? If so, why?

*Part II*

# The Authentication of the Son

John 2:1-22

# The Water Transformed

John 2:1-11

*On the third day a wedding took place at Cana in Galilee. Jesus' mother was there, 2 and Jesus and his disciples had also been invited to the wedding. 3 When the wine was gone, Jesus' mother said to him, "They have no more wine."*

*4 "Dear woman, why do you involve me?" Jesus replied. "My time has not yet come."*

*5 His mother said to the servants, "Do whatever he tells you."*

*6 Nearby stood six stone water jars, the kind used by the Jews for ceremonial washing, each holding from twenty to thirty gallons.*

*7 Jesus said to the servants, "Fill the jars with water"; so they filled them to the brim.*

*8 Then he told them, "Now draw some out and take it to the master of the banquet."*

*They did so, 9 and the master of the banquet tasted the water that had been turned into wine. He did not realize where it had come from, though the servants who had drawn the water knew. Then he called the bridegroom aside 10 and said, "Everyone brings out the choice wine first and then the cheaper wine after the guests have had too much to drink; but you have saved the best till now."*

*11 This, the first of his miraculous signs, Jesus performed at Cana in Galilee. He thus revealed his glory, and his disciples put their faith in him.*

## *The Wedding (2:1-2)*

I have repeated the words ever so often:

> Jesus, His mother and His disciples gladly responded to the wedding invitation to witness and participate in the happiness of the occasion. It was there that He began His ministry of power, adding to the pleasure of those assembled. Thus we come to witness the vows and pledges _____ and _____ are to make to each other and to participate in the happiness of the occasion, sending them forth in their new estate of wedlock with our prayers and Christian greetings.

So reads the introduction to "An Alternate Wedding Ceremony" in my well-worn copy of the original *Pastor's Handbook.*[1] Often in the prayer of invocation I invite the Lord Jesus to be present at this wedding just as He was at the wedding in the Galilean town of Cana. I ask Him to sanctify again the holy estate of matrimony and bring joy and delight to the whole event.

And when He receives this wedding invitation, He always returns His RSVP insert, saying, "Jesus of Nazareth will be pleased to attend!"

Those who imagine that Jesus' presence at a wedding reception would quench the congenial mirth do not know Him well. He who could weep with the sorrowful and rejoice with the joyful would feel right at home. He would join in the lighthearted laughter prompted by the humorous reminiscences of the couple's mischievous "friends." Jesus delights to share all of life's joys with His loving children.

Certainly the bride and groom of our text did not hesitate to invite both Jesus and His disciples to participate in the gala banquet. It just so happened that His mother was there as well, evidently having something to do with the wedding arrangements. Could the happy bride—or groom—have been her relative?[2]

We know some details about a first-century Jewish wedding. It was preceded by a betrothal, a much more serious matter than an engagement is today. It meant the solemn pledging of the couple to each other. It was so binding that to break it would necessitate divorce proceedings. At the conclusion of the betrothal, the marriage took place. If the bride was a virgin, the wedding took place on a Wednesday. If a widow, on Thursday.

Accompanied by his friends, the bridegroom would make his way to the bride's home. This was often at night so there could be a spectacular torch-light procession. The bride and groom then returned in procession to the house of the groom. There the wedding banquet would take place. It might last as long as a week. The wedding ceremony itself took place late in the evening after the feast.

After the ceremony, the guests conducted the couple by torchlight, a canopy over their heads, to their new home. For a week the newlyweds kept open house. One can happily visualize our Lord's glad-hearted participation in these festive events.

## *The Wine (2:3-10)*

All was going well at the wedding feast. As in every Jewish wedding, wine flowed freely. What would a wedding reception be, said the rabbis, without this social necessity—this symbol of joy? There would be no carousing or drunkenness, for these were frowned upon, and the wine was well diluted.[3] The "master of the banquet"[4] would have every reason to feel good about the way things were progressing.

But then, for some reason or other, what should never have happened, happened. Whether uninvited guests had "crashed" the party, or the planners simply had miscalculated, the wine ran out. For the host it was a most humiliating turn of events, terribly damaging to his reputation.[5] What should he do?

The mother of Jesus was on the scene. She knew what to do. Jesus was there, and He would have the answer to their dilemma. If she asked Him, her Son would take care of everything! She knew who He was. She knew His birth had been miraculous. She knew there was something quite different about His life. She knew He was the Messiah. Mary knew that all she had to do was draw Jesus' attention to the need. He would listen to His mother!

And so her brief statement: "They have no more wine" (2:3). What a model prayer of petition! To come to the Savior in simple trust, expressing one's need of the moment. He will do what needs to be done! I am reminded

of "Daddy" Whiteside of Pittsburgh. It is alleged that in a time of dire financial pressure, he literally spelled out his petition: "God, we need money—
m-o-n-e-y!"

But Jesus' reply to Mary, though courteous,[6] seems to indicate their
changing mother-son relationship was changing. With His entry into public
ministry, He was not so much the son of Mary as the Son of Man.

"Why do you involve me?" He asks.[7] "My time has not yet come." Yet in
spite of what appears to be a mild rebuke to Mary, she was not put off by His
reply. She still believed that Jesus would not allow this modest Galilean
family to be shamed in the presence of their friends.

"Do whatever he tells you," Mary instructs the servants. It is instruction
still appropriate for us who follow Jesus today.

What ensues is drama at its best! A natural process that would have taken
weeks is compressed into a few miraculous moments. Before the eyes of the
servants, ordinary water is transformed into wine of exquisite bouquet. The
master of the banquet, tasting it, utters his amazed commendation (1:10).
The emergency is over! The host is saved! The party can proceed!

## The Meaning (2:11)

The text concludes with John's words of explanation: "This, the first of
his miraculous signs, Jesus performed in Cana of Galilee. He thus revealed
his glory, and his disciples put their faith in him."

Notice first *the true nature* of this event. It was "a miraculous sign."[8] The
spectacular character of the phenomenon which the disciples had just witnessed was a marvel which had no natural explanation. It was nothing less
than a special demonstration of the power of God. It was an authenticating
sign that Jesus' claim to be the Son of God was true. Therefore His disciples
must heed all He taught. They must believe in Him.

But the actions of Jesus and the turning of the water into wine were a
"sign" in another important way. C.H. Dodd observes, "John writes in a
world in which phenomena—things and events—are a living and moving
image of the eternal, and not a veil of illusion to hide it. . . ."[9] Therefore,
while the story in our text is factually true, it also is a sign of an underlying
reality; it signifies a deeper truth.

What is the underlying spiritual truth that John would have us glean? Surely it is that the old symbolic Jewish order of sacrifice, ceremony, temple and tradition is being replaced. It is being replaced by the reality of new life that Christ provides through the Spirit. See how the wedding at Cana beautifully illustrates this.

Take, for instance, those six stone water jars—"the kind used by the Jews for ceremonial washing" (2:6). They served the practical purpose of providing water to wash the dusty feet of sandaled travelers. They also would have fulfilled the ritualistic hand-washing obligation before eating.[10] They represented, in a sense, the entire Mosaic system. Their filling "to the brim" (2:7) was a sign that this entire Old Testament pattern had run its course. The change from water to wine portrayed the change from life under law to life in union with the Holy Spirit.

Notice also *the grand effects* of the event. (1) "[Jesus] thus revealed his glory." In our study of the prologue to John's Gospel, we learned that the glory of Christ was revealed in all His earthly life. This was especially so in His acts of mercy and compassion—His goodness. Surely this miraculous provision of an overabundance of wine for a needy family was a lovely act of glorious compassion. But there was another important effect: (2) "And his disciples put their faith in him." The purpose of the sign was thus fulfilled.

## Conclusion

What helpful truths may we apply to life from our text? I suggest two. One is from the straightforward detail of the story. The other is from its underlying reality. In supplying the very real need of an ordinary Galilean family, we see our Lord's concern for our temporal, physical necessities. "Give us today our daily bread," He taught us to pray (Matthew 6:11). "Do not worry about your life, what you will eat or drink; or about your body, what you will wear" (6:25). "Your heavenly Father knows that you need [these things]" (6:32). And His apostle Paul adds, "My God will meet all your needs according to his glorious riches in Christ Jesus" (Philippians 4:19).

I well recall an incident that occurred in our home when I was just a small boy. It happened in the 1930s, when my father was a not-very-well-paid pastor. On one particular day, he and Mother were suffering the enervating effects of the flu, and she remarked, "Wouldn't it be nice if we had some chicken soup." Father agreed, but they had neither money to buy a chicken nor energy to get to the store. I remember my father saying, almost nonchalantly, "Lord, You know we could all do with chicken soup."

Hardly were the words out of his mouth when there was a knock at the door. One of our church members entered, carrying a large basket. First she sent my father back to bed. Then she prepared the most wonderful chicken soup we had ever tasted. Before that day was over, *five* chickens and one duck had come uninvited to our home—far more than we possibly needed. All of them came through the kindness of loving church members prompted by our heavenly Father. It was a case of water turned to broth! How lovingly our Lord cares for His children's needs!

Second, from the underlying reality of John's story, we may learn how abundant is our Lord's provision for our spiritual need. He turns the "water" of fruitless, joyless living under law into the "wine" of abundant, joyful life lived in the Spirit. He transforms our impotent, guilt-ridden *past* into a fruitful, powerful, Spirit-controlled *present*.

Certainly the law served an important purpose in the plan of God. Paul teaches us that one of its functions was to define the nature of sin and convict us of our guilt. "For I would not have known what coveting really was if the law had not said, 'Do not covet' " (Romans 7:7). Furthermore, the law, through its commandments, its ceremonies, its sacrifices and its curse, served to prepare its followers for the coming of the One who would redeem us from its curse (Galatians 3:13).

But the law was powerless to enable the kind of behavior and attitude it required. And the more we tried in our own strength to meet its demands, the more we despaired of ever succeeding. We found ourselves identifying with the testimony of despairing Paul: "For I have the desire to do what is good, but I cannot carry it out. For what I do is not the good I want to do; no, the evil I do not want to do—this I keep on doing. . . . What a wretched man I am!" (Romans 7:18-19, 24).

It was then that we made the wonderful discovery of the Spirit-filled life! We learned that we had "died to the law through the body of Christ, that [we] might belong to another, to him who was raised from the dead, in order that we might bear fruit to God" (7:4). We ceased from our vain attempts to overcome sin and our self-efforts to be holy. We counted ourselves "dead to sin but alive to God in Christ Jesus" (6:11). We offered ourselves in full surrender to God, receiving by faith the gracious gift of His Holy Spirit. His indwelling and anointing brought His beautiful fruit into our lives. We began to see the fruit of "love, joy, peace, patience, kindness, goodness, faithfulness, gentleness and self-control" (Galatians 5:22-23). It was indeed a whole new kind of life—Christ living in us.

When on the day of Pentecost the 120 disciples were filled with the Holy Spirit, they broke out into joyous praise. It is fascinating that the amazed onlookers interpreted their joy as the effect of "too much wine" (Acts 2:13)! It is equally as interesting to hear the instruction of Paul to the Ephesians: "Do not get drunk on wine, which leads to debauchery. Instead, be filled [literally, keep on being filled] with the Spirit" (Ephesians 5:18). The new wine of the Spirit!

### Endnotes

1. *The Pastor's Handbook* (Camp Hill, PA: Christian Publications, Inc., 1958), 18-19.
2. William Barclay, *The Gospel of John,* vol. I (Philadelphia: The Westminster Press, 1975), 96, writes, "One of the Coptic gospels tells us that Mary was a sister of the bridegroom's mother. There is an early set of prefaces to the books of the New Testament, called the Monarchian Prefaces, which tell us that the bridegroom was no other than John himself, and that his mother was Salome, the sister of Mary." Whether or not these details are accurate, we cannot say. But the accounts are very early.
3. The usual dilution was one part wine to three parts water.
4. We would likely refer to him as the head waiter.
5. J. Duncan M. Derrett, cited by Leon Morris, *The Gospel According to John* (Grand Rapids, MI: Eerdmans, 1971), 177, points out that in the ancient Near East there was a strong element of reciprocity in weddings. For example, in certain circumstances it was possible to take legal action against a man who failed to provide the appropriate wedding gift. Derrett thinks that when the supply of wine failed, the bridegroom and his family could well have become the targets of a lawsuit.
6. Jesus does not address Mary as "Mother" but "Woman" (Greek *gunai),* which in Greek is not as cold as in English. It could be translated, as does our version, "Dear woman" or "Dear lady."
7. The original words are *ti emoi kai soi*—literally, "What to me and to you?" Besides our version, other translations have it: "Let me handle this my own way" (William Barclay, *The Gospel of John,* vol. I [Philadelphia: The Westminster Press, 1975], 95); "Why dost thou trouble me with that?" (F.F. Bruce, *The Gospel of John* [Grand Rapids, MI: Eerdmans, 1983], 69); "What have you to do with me?" (RSV); "What have I to do with thee?" (KJV).

8. Our translators have interpreted John's one word *semeion,* "sign," by inserting the word "miraculous" to emphasize that what happened here could not be explained on the basis of a natural phenomenon. It was indeed a "miraculous sign."

9. C.H. Dodd, *The Interpretation of the Fourth Gospel* (Cambridge: At the University Press, 1970), 142.

10. See, for example, Matthew 15:1-2, where the Pharisees reproved Jesus for not insisting that His disciples hold to the tradition of the elders by washing their hands before they ate.

# 6

# The Temple Cleansed

John 2:12-22

*12 After this he went down to Capernaum with his mother and brothers and his disciples. There they stayed for a few days.*

*13 When it was almost time for the Jewish Passover, Jesus went up to Jerusalem. 14 In the temple courts he found men selling cattle, sheep and doves, and others sitting at tables exchanging money. 15 So he made a whip out of cords, and drove all from the temple area, both sheep and cattle; he scattered the coins of the money changers and overturned their tables. 16 To those who sold doves he said, "Get these out of here! How dare you turn my Father's house into a market!"*

*17 His disciples remembered that it is written: "Zeal for your house will consume me."*

*18 Then the Jews demanded of him, "What miraculous sign can you show us to prove your authority to do all this?"*

*19 Jesus answered them, "Destroy this temple, and I will raise it again in three days."*

*20 The Jews replied, "It has taken forty-six years to build this temple, and you are going to raise it in three days?" 21 But the temple he had spoken of was his body. 22 After he was raised from the dead, his disciples recalled what he had said. Then they believed the Scripture and the words that Jesus had spoken.*

The Subject of our present text is no sentimentally soft, "gentle Jesus, meek and mild." Nor is He a Man in an uncontrollable rage. We are looking at genuinely righteous anger, directed against blatant social injustice perpetrated in the name of religion. Here is a manifestation of the pure wrath of God against sin. Here is passionate emotion channeled into effective action. This well may be an example of what the prophet meant when he said to faithless Judah, "Then suddenly the Lord you are seeking will come to his temple. . . . But who can endure the day of his coming? Who can stand when he appears? For he will be like a refiner's fire or a launderer's soap" (Malachi 3:1-2).

We remember another occasion. Jesus faced bigoted, tradition-bound Pharisaical hypocrisy, and Mark says, "He looked around at them in anger" (Mark 3:5). It is true the Scriptures exhort us to "rid yourselves of . . . anger" (Colossians 3:8). We should not give place to anger that is selfish, mean, spiteful, vengeful. But there are some evils, some injustices, some forms of craftiness that demand a Christian response. If we are to be fully Christlike, there is place for godly anger that stirs planned, positive, productive endeavors.

### An Earthly Temple Purged (2:12-17)

Jesus and His disciples[1] had come from the new family home in Capernaum (2:12)[2] to Jerusalem to celebrate Passover. Jesus did not like what He found in the temple courts.[3] We note first *the cause of His anger* (2:13-14). To this greatest of all Jewish feasts came not only Palestinian Jews, but Jews from all over the world. Every Jew over nineteen years of age was required to pay the temple tax, equivalent to almost two days' wages. The money made possible the daily rituals of worship and sacrifice. This tax had to be paid in Galilean shekels or in shekels of the sanctuary—"clean" Jewish coins suitable for temple use. Thus, pilgrims arriving from other countries needed the services of "money changers." And like Shakespeare's Shylock, these greedy money changers charged exorbitant rates. Sometimes the loss amounted to as much as fifty percent—and this for pilgrims who could ill afford it.

It enraged Jesus. So did the flagrant extortion practiced by the vendors of cattle, sheep and doves. The law required that any animal offered in sacrifice to God must be perfect—unblemished. Temple inspectors, appointed to examine the offered animals, charged fees for their service. And they usually determined that any animal or bird procured on the outside (at a fraction of the inside cost) was unfit. It was extortion in the name of religion!

But something else contributed to the Lord's wrath. The temple area consisted of a series of courts leading into the temple proper: first the Court of the Gentiles, then the Court of the Women, then the Court of the Israelites. Finally came the Court of the Priests. The merchandisers used the Court of the Gentiles. It was the only place in the temple area where Gentiles might go if they wished to pray or meditate. Instead of worshiping in peace and quiet, they found themselves "in the midst of a noisy bazaar."[4] The place that should have been "a house of prayer for all nations" (Mark 11:17, quoting Isaiah 56:7) had become a market.[5] This total desecration of His Father's house—the injustice, the greed, the irreverence of it all—cried out for redress.

Notice, second, *the expression of His anger* (John 2:15-16). How electrifying to behold the blazing eyes of the Master wielding His improvised whip! With matchless moral authority He drove out the lowing, bleating livestock. He overturned the tables of the money changers, scattering their filthy lucre across the pavement. He ordered out the dove merchants and their stock! The Refiner's fire had indeed come to His temple.

Third, see *the response to His anger* (2:17-18). One can only imagine how quickly word of Jesus' impassioned, daring deed spread throughout Jerusalem, and the varied responses. John records the reaction of two groups—Jesus' disciples (2:17) and official Judaism (2:18). When the disciples discussed the event among themselves, as they must have done, they remembered how Jesus had called the temple "*my* Father's house" (2:16, emphasis added).[6] There came to their minds the unquestionably Messianic prophecy of Psalm 69:9—"Zeal for your house consumes me." Who but Messiah could be so zealous for the reputation of the Father?[7] Who but Messiah could so defy the temple authorities? Who but Messiah could hold to such special intimacy with the Father? The disciples' certainty about Jesus increased, and John expects his account of the event will increase his readers' certainty.

Unlike the disciples' response, the reaction of Jerusalem's "establishment" was to confront Jesus. They perceived Him to be a pseudo-messiah, and they challenged Him to prove Himself. Like the disciples, they knew only Messiah had authority to take such action. But they were not at all prepared to believe that Jesus was He. Arrogantly, they demanded a sign to demonstrate His authority.[8]

### *A Spiritual Temple Created (2:18-22)*

Jesus, who more often than not refused to submit to requests for signs,[9] in this case was willing to comply. But the sign that He offered thoroughly mystified the leaders. "Destroy this temple," Jesus declared, "and I will raise it again in three[10] days" (2:19). The Jews, thinking He referred to the literal temple He had just cleansed, mocked such an impossible feat (2:20). Work on this temple, built by Herod to please His Jewish subjects, had been proceeding for forty-six years (2:20).[11] Did Jesus suppose He could erect it in a mere three days?

The Jews could hardly be expected to understand the sign He was giving them. The disciples themselves did not understand it until after its fulfillment at Jesus' resurrection (2:22). It was only then that John could explain that "the temple he had spoken of was his body" (2:21). The statement indicates Jesus' consciousness that His body was the very special temple of God. For the disciples, the conclusion was inescapable. They believed both what the Scriptures foretold[12] and the words of Jesus Himself (2:22).

### *Conclusion*

Clearly, John has juxtaposed two "sign" stories in this part of his Gospel. One is the changing of water into wine; the other, the cleansing of the temple. We can say, first, that both of these events clearly authenticated Jesus' Messianic claim. Both resulted, as intended, in a deepening of faith in the hearts of His disciples. But we are reminded that there is also an inner, spiritual reality illustrated in both. In our previous chapter we saw how the changing of water into wine portrayed the end of the old legal Levitical order. Its ceremonies and sacrifices were no longer appropriate. In their place was a new spiritual reality—life lived in the "new wine" of the Holy Spirit. So also the cleansing of the temple portrayed the end of a worship order necessitating a tangible building. It marked the beginning of a spiritual worship, in a spiritual temple, which is Christ's body, the Church.

Consider the very fundamental truth of the Church as the temple of the Holy Spirit. Thinking biblically, the Church is not an edifice of wood or stone or brick. It is a living fellowship of redeemed, Spirit-indwelt people. And this living "body" of Christ is no less than His dwelling place, the very temple of God.

We need to remind ourselves of what Paul said to the Corinthians: "Don't you know that you yourselves[13] are God's temple and that God's Spirit lives in you? If anyone destroys God's temple, God will destroy him; for God's temple is sacred, and you are that temple" (1 Corinthians 3:16-17). Or again, "What agreement is there between the temple of God and idols? For we are the temple of the living God. As God has said: 'I will live with them and walk among them, and I will be their God, and they will be my people' " (2 Corinthians 6:16). And to the Ephesians he writes: "In [Christ] the whole building is joined together and rises to become a holy temple in the Lord. And in him you too are being built together to become a dwelling in which God lives by his Spirit" (Ephesians 2:21-22). The Apostle Peter echoes the same truth: "As you come to him, the living Stone—rejected by men but chosen by God and precious to him—you also, like living stones, are being built into a spiritual house to be a holy priesthood, offering spiritual sacrifices acceptable to God through Jesus Christ" (1 Peter 2:4-5).

The garments of Aaron and his sons, in the ancient precursor of the temple, were said to be "for glory and for beauty" (Exodus 28:2, 40, KJV). If the Church is the temple of God, how important it is that she manifest the beauty and glory of our God! Her love and unity, her Spirit-gifted ministry, her Christ-centered fellowship should evidence God's beauty and glory. Nothing that could mar this temple's sacred loveliness must remain unjudged.

In reality, only God Himself can accomplish such a cleansing. Believers concerned for the health of Christ's Church must pray earnestly that God will bring her healing and well-being.

Two millennia ago, Jesus came to Jerusalem's temple. He cast out what was ugly—those things that found their source in the spirit of the world. He disallowed the works of the flesh and the designs of the devil. May we, His Church, submit ourselves to the same intense judgment. May the Church of Jesus Christ be a "radiant church, without stain or wrinkle or any other blemish" (Ephesians 5:27).

Let Charles Spurgeon's prayer for revival flow from your redeemed heart:

> O God, send us the Holy Ghost! Give us both the breath of spiritual life and the fire of unconquerable zeal. O Thou who art our God, answer us by fire, we pray Thee! Answer us both by wind and fire, and then we shall see Thee to be God indeed. The kingdom comes not, and the work is flagging. Oh, that Thou wouldst send the wind and the fire! Thou wilt do this when we are all of one accord, all believing, all expecting, all prepared by prayer.
>
> Lord, bring us to this waiting state! God, send us a season of glorious disorder. Oh, for a sweep of the wind that will set the seas in motion and make our ironclad brethren, now lying so quietly at anchor, to roll from stem to stern!
>
> Oh, for the fire to fall again—fire which shall affect the most stolid! Oh, that such fire might first sit upon the disciples, and then fall on all around! O God, Thou art ready to work with us today even as Thou didst then. Stay not, we beseech Thee, but work at once.
>
> Break down every barrier that hinders the incoming of Thy might! Give us now both hearts of flame and tongues of fire to preach Thy reconciling word, for Jesus' sake! Amen!

### Endnotes

1. And possibly His mother, Mary, and His brothers. See John 2:12.
2. Capernaum, "the village of Nahum," stood—and stands—on the northwest shore of the Sea of Galilee, about sixteen miles from Cana. It appears that the holy family had moved from Nazareth to Capernaum, which became Jesus' headquarters for His Galilean ministry. See F.F Bruce, *The Gospel of John* (Grand Rapids, MI: Eerdmans, 1983), 73.
3. The wording and timing of this account in the Synoptic Gospels gives rise to the debate as to whether there were two occasions when Jesus cleansed the temple. There is no reason to think that there could not have been two cleansings, one at the beginning and one at the

end of Jesus' ministry. Remembering, however, the "spiritual" nature of John's Gospel, the important thing for him would not be the chronology of the incident but its "sign" content.

4. Leon Morris, *The Gospel According to John* (Grand Rapids, MI: Eerdmans, 1971), 95, footnote 68.

5. Mark (11:17) records Jesus accusing the money changers of highway robbery.

6. It is significant that Jesus does not speak of the temple as "our Father's house" or "your Father's house," but as "*my* Father's house," indicating that He saw Himself as the unique Son of God, Israel's promised Messiah.

7. C.H. Dodd, *The Interpretation of the Fourth Gospel* (Cambridge: At the University Press, 1970), 300f, interprets this quotation from Psalm 69 as saying that just as the righteous sufferer of the Psalm paid the price for his loyalty to the temple, so the action of Jesus in cleansing the temple will bring Him grief.

8. Israel as a nation expected that with the dawn of the Messianic age God would perform many mighty miracles. It was thought, for instance, that Messiah would repeat Moses' miracle of causing bread to come down from heaven. See John 6:30ff.

9. See, for example, Mark 8:11f; John 6:30.

10. That is, within the space of three days.

11. The temple was not actually completed until A.D. 64.

12. John may mean that the truth of the resurrection is part of the general tenor of Old Testament teaching, or he may be referring to particular passages, such as Psalm 16:10, Isaiah 53:12 or, less likely, Hosea 6:2.

13. Other passages make clear that the individual believer is also the temple of the Spirit, but in this case, it seems that Paul is speaking about the corporate body, the Church.

## Part II

## *Questions for Reflection or Discussion*

1. What was the purpose of Jesus' miraculous signs?

2. How do the New Testament epistles compare life under the law and life in the Spirit? How does the turning of water into wine illustrate the difference?

3. What was it that angered Jesus when He cleansed the temple?

4. What does the New Testament teach us concerning the Church as the Temple of God?

5. Under what conditions might anger be justified?

*Part III*

# The Universality of the Son

John 2:23-4:42

# 7

# In Jerusalem:
# A Pharisee's Quest

## John 2:23-3:21

*23 Now while he was in Jerusalem at the Passover Feast, many people saw the miraculous signs he was doing and believed in his name. 24 But Jesus would not entrust himself to them, for he knew all men. 25 He did not need man's testimony about man, for he knew what was in a man.*

*1 Now there was a man of the Pharisees named Nicodemus, a member of the Jewish ruling council. 2 He came to Jesus at night and said, "Rabbi, we know you are a teacher who has come from God. For no one could perform the miraculous signs you are doing if God were not with him."*

*3 In reply Jesus declared, "I tell you the truth, no one can see the kingdom of God unless he is born again."*

*4 "How can a man be born when he is old?" Nicodemus asked. "Surely he cannot enter a second time into his mother's womb to be born!"*

*5 Jesus answered, "I tell you the truth, no one can enter the kingdom of God unless he is born of water and the Spirit. 6 Flesh gives birth to flesh, but the Spirit gives birth to spirit. 7 You should not be surprised at my saying, 'You must be born again.' 8 The wind blows wherever it pleases. You hear its sound, but you cannot tell where it comes from or where it is going. So it is with everyone born of the Spirit."*

*9 "How can this be?" Nicodemus asked.*

*10 "You are Israel's teacher," said Jesus, "and do you not understand*

*these things? 11 I tell you the truth, we speak of what we know, and we tes-*
*tify to what we have seen, but still you people do not accept our testimony.*
*12 I have spoken to you of earthly things and you do not believe; how then*
*will you believe if I speak of heavenly things? 13 No one has ever gone into*
*heaven except the one who came from heaven—the Son of Man. 14 Just as*
*Moses lifted up the snake in the desert, so the Son of Man must be lifted up,*
*15 that everyone who believes in him may have eternal life.*

*16 "For God so loved the world that he gave his one and only Son, that*
*whoever believes in him shall not perish but have eternal life. 17 For God*
*did not send his Son into the world to condemn the world, but to save the*
*world through him. 18 Whoever believes in him is not condemned, but*
*whoever does not believe stands condemned already because he has not*
*believed in the name of God's one and only Son. 19 This is the verdict:*
*Light has come into the world, but men loved darkness instead of light be-*
*cause their deeds were evil. 20 Everyone who does evil hates the light, and*
*will not come into the light for fear that his deeds will be exposed. 21 But*
*whoever lives by the truth comes into the light, so that it may be seen*
*plainly that what he has done has been done through God."*

It was quiet in Jerusalem now. Night had fallen, and the streets that had
been jammed with jostling Passover crowds were deserted. The Rabbi
would be alone, and the Pharisee and He could converse without the unre-
lenting intrusions of the common throng. Nicodemus yearned to hear from
God. He had felt the barrenness of lifeless Judaism long enough. Now, just
maybe, there was Someone who could show him a better way.

And so it was that this representative of Jerusalem's Jewry came to Jesus.
He came with a heart and a quest that was different from others who had so
quickly "believed" on the Miracle Worker from Galilee.[1]

I once heard A.W. Tozer, addressing a congregation, quip, "I don't know
*you,* but I know *people!*" Our text (2:23-25) says that Jesus knew people.
His dramatic miracles during Passover had attracted many who espoused an
altogether too superficial faith in Him. Some sought the spectacular for its
own sake. Others, concerned about their own physical needs, would follow
Him as long as He was a popular healer. None had understood the deeper
significance of the "signs." When confronted with the terms of a genuine
commitment to the Son of Man, they would draw back and no longer follow
Him.[2]

As then, so now our Lord Jesus sees into the hidden depths of every human heart. Wherever He beholds sincere faith, He commits Himself to that person without reserve. But it must be a faith that receives Him as Lord and Savior, for thus it is that He offers Himself in the gospel. It must be a faith prepared to "take up [its] cross and follow [Him]" (Matthew 16:24). To that kind of faith He will entrust His Spirit, reveal His will, divulge His purposes and share His secrets.

Unlike the "fair-weather" belief of the Passover crowds, Nicodemus desired to go deeper in his search for truth.[3] He approached Jesus respectfully and courteously, addressing Him as "Rabbi," a "teacher who has come from God" (John 3:2).[4] Nicodemus had grasped the significance of the "signs" Jesus had performed. Unlike many of his Sanhedrin colleagues, he was willing to concede that this man was indeed genuine. In fact, he may even have come to ask some very specific questions. "Are You the Messiah?" or, "Is the earthly kingdom of God near, as Your miracles seem to indicate?" Whatever, his positive approach opened the way for the first of Jesus' life-giving discourses recorded by John. It is a message to Jerusalem about new birth.

## New Birth—Its Necessity (3:3)

Nicodemus had been schooled in rabbinic tradition. He was a Pharisee and a member of the Jewish ruling council.[5] But if he was expecting Jesus to feel honored by his presence, our Lord's abrupt reply must have startled him. Jesus went right to the heart of the elderly Pharisee's real need: "I tell you the truth, no one can enter the kingdom of God unless he is born of water and the Spirit" (3:5).[6] Nicodemus needed to know that the kingdom of God[7] is first and foremost a present and inward kingdom. He would not find this personal presence of God in his old life of legalistic, self-righteous Pharisaism. Nothing short of a radical rebirth from above could bring the gracious spiritual reign of God into his present life. And only that could qualify him afterward to enjoy the blessing of eternal life[8] in the age to come. In short, Nicodemus needed to be begotten by God.[9]

## *New Birth—Its Meaning (3:4-8)*

Nicodemus responded to Jesus' startling statement with a question. On the surface his question seemed to indicate he completely misunderstood our Lord's words (3:4). But was he really so foolish as to think that Jesus could be talking about a physical rebirth? Hardly! Leon Morris explains Nicodemus' question this way:

> A man, Nicodemus might have said, is the sum of all his yester-days. He is the man he is today because of all the things that have happened to him through the years. He is a bundle of doubts, un-certainties, wishes, hopes fears and habits good and bad built up through the years. It would be wonderful to break the entail of the past and make a completely fresh beginning. But how can this possibly be done? Can physical birth be repeated? Since this lesser miracle is quite impossible how can we envisage a much greater miracle, the remaking of man's essential being? Regener-ation is sheer impossibility![10]

But this new birth from above, of which Jesus was speaking, *is* possible. Nicodemus needed only to know the conditions for receiving it. He must be born "of water and the Spirit" (3:5).[11] What did Jesus mean? How would Nicodemus understand these words? When Nicodemus heard Jesus speak of being born of "water," he quite likely thought of John the Baptist. Nicodemus and his Sanhedrin colleagues had proudly rejected the wilder-ness prophet. John the Baptist had claimed to be sent from God (see John 1:33). To the contrite sinner, John's baptism had signified the washing away of sins through repentance and the forgiveness offered by God.[12] Jesus was insisting, therefore, that if Nicodemus was to enter the kingdom of God, he must die to his self-righteousness. He must come to God as a guilty sinner, receiving His mercy and pardon. The Holy Spirit responds to the repentant heart by silently yet surely communicating a whole new kind of life. This eternal life qualifies a person to enter God's kingdom.

All of this was a complete enigma to Nicodemus (3:7). How was one to explain this mysterious regenerating power of the Spirit? The noisy and pompous appearance of the kingdom of God in the Pharisaic program he un-derstood. But this inner, life-giving work of the Spirit was something else.

Possibly, as Nicodemus was pondering Jesus' words, a gust of wind blew across the rooftop where the two men conversed. Our Lord, ever the Master at using the natural to illustrate the spiritual, seized the moment (3:8).[13]

"Nicodemus, can you explain that gust of wind?" Jesus asked in essence. "By what rule does it operate?"

Nicodemus did not know! The *effects* of wind are obvious, both to eye and ear, but whence it comes and where it goes, no one can tell. So with the Spirit. There is something utterly inexplicable about the Spirit's invisible work of regeneration. And there is something quite baffling about those born of the Spirit. Daniel Whittle put it this way in his gospel song:

> I know not how the Spirit moves,
>> Convincing men of sin,
> Revealing Jesus through the Word,
>> Creating faith in Him.[14]

We may not be able to explain the "how" of the Spirit's work. But just as the effects of wind are visible, so the reality of the Spirit's work is evident in the believer's words and deeds.

## New Birth—Its Means (3:9-15)

Nicodemus listened to the penetrating words of the teacher "come from God" (3:2). What must have been going on within this Pharisee so steeped in Judaism? "How can this be?" he asked (3:9). Was it the question of a proud man, unwilling to accept what reason could not explain? Many today let intellectual pride stand in the way of believing in Jesus. Or was Nicodemus acknowledging himself to be a total stranger to the knowledge and experience of the Holy Spirit? Such honesty is indeed commendable. Or was he genuinely inquiring how new birth can come to be? Jesus' reply seems to indicate that this was the case.

Whatever the motive behind Nicodemus'question, our Lord first gently chided him for his lack of understanding (3:10). He was a student of the Old Testament Scriptures. He should have seen Jesus' teaching implicit in passages such as, for example, Jeremiah 31:33: " 'This is the covenant I will make with the house of Israel after that time,' declares the LORD. 'I will put my law in their minds and write it on their hearts. I will be their God, and

they will be my people.' " God says through Ezekiel, "I will give you a new
heart and put a new spirit in you; I will remove from you your heart of stone
and give you a heart of flesh. And I will put my Spirit in you and move you
to follow my decrees and be careful to keep my laws" (36:26-27).

These and other Old Testament passages[15] should have helped
Nicodemus understand Jesus' instruction concerning new birth.

But then, out of the very depths of His being,[16] the Master Teacher began
to share the gospel with Nicodemus. He explained how he and his Jerusalem
colleagues[17] could enter the kingdom of God. First, they must acknowledge
that Jesus and His disciples spoke from experience in describing the ministry of the Spirit (John 3:11). Theirs was no hearsay message. It was based on
personal testimony. They knew what they were talking about!

Furthermore, Nicodemus and his Sanhedrin colleagues must believe Jesus' witness concerning His origin. He was the Son of Man come down from
heaven (3:13) and therefore qualified to speak concerning "heavenly
things" (3:12).[18] In other words, Nicodemus and his friends must be prepared to confess the deity of Jesus of Nazareth.

Again, they must understand that eternal life[19] (entrance into God's kingdom) was not at all through their own righteousness. It was by believing in
Him who had to be "lifted up" on a cross if mankind were to be saved
(3:14-15).[20]

Did his nighttime tryst with Jesus have a lasting effect on Nicodemus?
Seemingly so. Did he come to believe on the Son? We do not really know.
Two later actions make us hopeful. One was his protest to his colleagues on
the Jewish Council. They wanted to condemn Jesus without hearing His
own explanation of His actions (7:50-51). The other was his part in the em-
balming and burial of the body of Jesus (19:38ff).

## New Birth—Its Result

Likely, with verse 15, the words of Jesus to Nicodemus end. Beginning
with verse 16, the Apostle John appears to be sharing with readers his own
profound meditations on Jesus words.[21] Here (3:16) is probably the
best-known, most memorized and most loved verse in the entire Bible. It
tells us of that immense, divine, self-sacrificing love *(agape)* that motivated

God to give up His only Son. Through faith in Jesus, who died in humanity's stead, no one need perish. All of us, through spiritual rebirth, can possess life eternal.

The measure of love is always its willingness to give, its capacity for sacrifice. If we would measure God's love, we must do so by Calvary. There God sacrificed the One who was closest to His heart. But more than that, in the giving of His Son, the Father gave Himself. The Scriptures declare, "God was in Christ reconciling the world to Himself in Christ" (see 2 Corinthians 5:19). The Lord Jesus is not merely a representative through whom God dispatches the message that He loves us. He is God Himself actually come to earth, loving us. He does not merely expound the love of God: He *is* the love of God incarnate. The songwriter penned these oft-sung lines that so movingly portray God's love:

> Could we with ink the ocean fill,
>   And were the skies of parchment made,
> Were every stalk on earth a quill,
>   And every man a scribe by trade,
> To write the love of God above
>   Would drain the ocean dry.
> Nor could the scroll contain the whole,
> Though stretched from sky to sky.[22]

## Conclusion

In the closing words of our text, we face the eternal consequences of our relationship to Jesus Christ, God's Son. For all who believe in Him: eternal life. For all who do not believe in Him: continuing condemnation (3:17-18). And what is the reason for this condemnation? John's answer is clear. Jesus has brought Light into the world—a Light that exposes the evil in the human heart. Unbelievers, wishing to persist in evil, refuse to come to the Light, and their evil deeds condemn them (3:19-20).

How we respond to the Light determines our eternal destiny! That is the awesome truth. If we refuse the Light and persist in the works of darkness, we stand condemned. But if we come in faith to Jesus, confessing the sin that the Light of His presence reveals, we receive eternal life. Our changed lives demonstrate that now God is at work in us (3:21).

You may be, like Nicodemus, a man of superior religious principles. You may hold the man Jesus in high regard, acknowledging Him to be a great prophet—even the greatest. But the word of our text comes to you with unmistakable clarity: "Unless a man is born again, he cannot see the kingdom of God."

Will you respond to God's love by coming to Him just as you are? Will you repent of your attempts to live life without Him, turning from all you know to be sin? Will you, in simple, childlike faith, receive Jesus Christ as your Lord and Savior? In response to your repentance and faith, He will give you His Holy Spirit to live in you, and you will know what it means to be *born again.*

### Endnotes

1. That Nicodemus came to Jesus "at night" may suggest he feared fellow members of the Sanhedrin would see him with Jesus. Some scholars suggest that the phrase "at night" is not to be taken literally at all. Rather, it is symbolic of the darkness describing his old life as Nicodemus emerges into the Light of Christ (see Leon Morris, *The Gospel According to John* [Grand Rapids, MI: Eerdmans, 1971], 211). I prefer to give Nicodemus the benefit of the doubt. I suggest he came at night simply because he wanted uninterrupted conversation with Jesus.
2. See, for example, John 6:53ff, especially 6:66.
3. Chapter 3 begins with the postpositive conjunction *de,* commonly used as an adversative particle, translated "but" or "however" or "on the other hand." If that is the force of the word here, John seems to contrast the people whom Jesus could not trust with one man, Nicodemus, whom He could.
4. In the original Greek, Nicodemus's words translated "from God" appear in an emphatic position in the sentence.
5. In 3:10 Jesus calls Nicodemus, literally, "*the* teacher of Israel." Thus Jesus implies a place of great importance in the Jewish religious hierarchy.
6. However, Jesus softens the pointed words that are obviously directed to Nicodemus personally by using the more general expression "no one" and "he."
7. The "kingdom of God" is interpreted to mean not only the realm in which God reigns, but primarily the reign itself. For a thorough treatment of the meaning of the kingdom of God, see George Eldon Ladd, *The Gospel of the Kingdom* (Grand Rapids, MI: Eerdmans, 1959), 13ff.
8. In John's Gospel, "entering the kingdom of God" is equivalent to receiving eternal life. Compare Mark 9:43, 45, 47.
9. The Greek word translated "born" in our version is *gennao,* which more often than not describes a father's part in the birth of a child.

10. Morris, *The Gospel According to John,* 215. F.F. Bruce, *The Gospel of John* (Grand Rapids, MI: Eerdmans, 1983), 83, wonders if Nicodemus' question is figurative for "You can't teach an old dog new tricks."

11. Various interpretations of the words "born of water and the Spirit" have been proposed: Some, for example, B.F. Westcott, *Commentary of the Gospel According to St. John* (London: John Murray, Albemarle Street, 1967), 50, tell us that Nicodemus would have understood Jesus to be referring to the ministry of the Baptist and the consequent work of the Spirit in regeneration. He suggests that in the Christian society, baptism in water and baptism in the Spirit are joined together. See also F. Godet, *Commentary on the Gospel of St. John,* vol. II (Edinburgh: T. & T. Clarke, 1881), 49.

   John Calvin, *Commentary on the Gospel According to John,* vol. I, (Edinburgh: The Calvin Translation Society, 1847), 111, thinks that "water" and "the Spirit" mean the same thing, as in the expression, "the Holy Ghost and fire." He states, "By *water,* therefore, is meant nothing more than the inward purification and invigoration which is produced by *the Holy Spirit.*"

   R.G.V. Tasker, *The Gospel According to St. John* (London: The Tyndale Press, 1960), 71, writes, "But in the light of the reference to the practice by Jesus of water baptism in 3:22, it is difficult to avoid construing the words of *water* and *the Spirit* conjunctively, and regarding them as a description of Christian baptism, in which cleansing and endowment are both essential elements."

   Morris, *The Gospel According to John,* 216, cites the use of "water" in rabbinic sources as being connected to procreation and takes "born of water and the Spirit" as meaning "a spiritual seed."

12. Compare Peter's call at the close of his sermon on the day of Pentecost: "Repent and be baptized, every one of you, in the name of Jesus Christ for the forgiveness of your sins" (Acts 2:38).

13. The word translated "wind" and "spirit" is the same Greek word, *pneuma.* So the illustration Jesus gives from the wind is highly appropriate to His statement concerning the Spirit.

14. Daniel W. Whittle, "I Know Whom I Have Believed," *Hymns of the Christian Life* (Camp Hill, PA: Christian Publications, Inc., 1978), # 319, stanza 3.

15. Bruce, *The Gospel of John,* 86, cites three such Old Testament parables of new birth truth: Genesis 6:13-9:19 (Noah starting life anew in a new world); Exodus 14:15-15:21 (Israel crossing the Red Sea, a people set apart for God); 2 Kings 5:14 (Naaman the Syrian's "baptism" in the Jordan).

16. The implication of the Greek is "Verily, verily," or "Truly, truly."

17. The change from the singular number to the plural, translated in the NIV by "we" and "you people" (3:11), would seem to imply that Jesus is including His disciples, some of whom may have been present on this occasion (see Westcott, *Commentary on the Gospel According to St. John,* 52), as those who "speak what we know"; and Nicodemus's colleagues as those who "do not accept our testimony."

18. The "earthly things" of 3:12 are likely the content of chapter 3 up to this point, i.e., truth that can be illustrated by earthly analogies. The "heavenly things" are likely what Jesus goes on to say about the love of God. God gave His Son to the death of the cross so that believers might have eternal life. That has no counterpart in the natural (earthly) world.

19. This is the first instance in John's Gospel of the phrase "eternal life." While it contains within it the thought of life that has no end, it refers primarily to a quality of life of which believers already have a foretaste through their union with Christ. It is resurrection life, the full enjoyment of which lies still in the future. Compare Colossians 3:1f.

20. The reference to Moses' lifting up the snake in the desert is found in Numbers 21:5-9. The "lifting up" of the Son of Man probably refers both to His being lifted up on the cross and His exaltation to glory. Both were necessary for humanity's salvation.
21. Scholars differ as to exactly where the words of Jesus end and the meditations of John begin. Our version, through its continuation of quotation marks till the end of 3:21 implies that Jesus' words end there. The RSV closes the quote at the end of 3:15.
22. F.M. Lehman, "The Love of God," *Hymns for the Family of God* (Nashville, TN: Paragon Associates, Inc., 1976), # 18.

# 8

# In Judea:
# A Forerunner's Joy

John 3:22-36

*22 After this, Jesus and his disciples went out into the Judean country-side, where he spent some time with them, and baptized. 23 Now John also was baptizing at Aenon near Salim, because there was plenty of water, and people were constantly coming to be baptized. 24 (This was before John was put in prison.) 25 An argument developed between some of John's disciples and a certain Jew over the matter of ceremonial washing. 26 They came to John and said to him, "Rabbi, that man who was with you on the other side of the Jordan—the one you testified about—well, he is baptizing, and everyone is going to him."*

*27 To this John replied, "A man can receive only what is given him from heaven. 28 You yourselves can testify that I said, 'I am not the Christ but am sent ahead of him.' 29 The bride belongs to the bridegroom. The friend who attends the bridegroom waits and listens for him, and is full of joy when he hears the bridegroom's voice. That joy is mine, and it is now complete. 30 He must become greater; I must become less.*

*31 "The one who comes from above is above all; the one who is from the earth belongs to the earth, and speaks as one from the earth. The one who comes from heaven is above all. 32 He testifies to what he has seen and heard, but no one accepts his testimony. 33 The man who has accepted it has certified that God is truthful. 34 For the one whom God has sent speaks the words of God, for God gives the Spirit without limit. 35 The Father loves the Son and has placed everything in his hands. 36 Whoever believes in the Son has eternal life, but whoever rejects the Son will not see life, for God's wrath remains on him."*

Jerusalem, Judea, Samaria, the ends of the earth—thus the proclamation of the universal gospel would later proceed.[1] The steps of the Son of Man took a similar course as He moved from Jerusalem into the Judean countryside and later into Samaria (4:4). It was during this initial Judean ministry, our text informs us, that John's disciples found themselves battling . . .

## A Spirit of Rivalry (3:22-27)

John's followers found it hard to be silent as their own rabbi's[2] disciples diminished while Jesus' increased. The flash point came when Jesus and His disciples arrived along the Jordan and began to baptize.[3] John's followers regarded this as unfair competition. By now, John had moved his base of operation to Aenon, on the Judea-Samaria side of the river, where water was plentiful (3:22-23).[4] To have these two public figures operating in proximity engendered a theological controversy over "ceremonial washing" (3:25).[5] On one side were John's disciples; on the other an unidentified, argumentative "Jew."

The discussion may very well have been broadened to include the relative value of John's baptism and Christ's. Perhaps feeling bettered in the argument, John's disciples came to him looking for support. There is more than a hint of anger in their complaint.

"Rabbi, that man who was with you on the other side of the Jordan—the one you testified about[6]—well, he is baptizing, and everyone is going to Him" (3:26).[7] But John refuses to be a party to their jealous attitude. In him there is no place for a competitive spirit. Rather, this forerunner of Jesus is filled with . . .

## A Spirit of Joy (3:27-30)

Far from being jealous, John the Baptist is overjoyed to see the success of Jesus' ministry. Jesus' success clearly indicates that his own ministry has accomplished its intended purpose. In his thinking, there is no room whatsoever for the spirit of rivalry he sees in his followers. He cites two reasons. First, it is a general principle of spiritual ministry that any person can do only what God ordains and enables that person to do (3:27). It is heaven, not earth, that decides a person's kingdom work. Therefore, each—John and Jesus included—must be content with what God sovereignly assigns to him or her. No one is to covet the place of another.

Second, as to their particular ministries, John's was the God-appointed work of preparing the way for Messiah. He had no desire to do anything else. Had he not made this fact crystal clear the day the Jewish representatives questioned him? They had asked, "Who are you?" and he had replied, "I am not the Christ" (John 1:19ff). His disciples knew this perfectly well (3:28). They should have realized that John's work was accomplished. It was to Jesus that Messiahship belonged. For his appointment and enablement He was as dependent upon God as was John for his. Each man recognized and appreciated the ordination of the other.

To see people going over to Jesus filled John's heart with pure joy. He saw his relationship to Jesus as being something like that of a "best man" in a Jewish wedding—"the friend who attends the bridegroom" (3:29). Writes Barclay,

> The friend of the bridegroom . . . had a unique place at a Jewish wedding. He acted as the liaison between the bride and the bridegroom; he arranged the wedding; he took out the invitations; he presided at the wedding feast. He brought the bride and the bridegroom together. And he had one special duty. It was his duty to guard the bridal chamber and to let no false lover in. He would open the door only when in the dark he heard the bridegroom's voice and recognized it. When he heard the bridegroom's voice he let him in and went away rejoicing, for his task was completed and the lovers were together.[8]

John sees Jesus as the bridegroom and himself as the friend of the bridegroom.[9] And he sees that now that the bridegroom and the bride are together, his work is finished. To see Jesus and His people united together in love brings great rejoicing to his heart. He must now fade into obscurity; Jesus must attain the place of greatest prominence (3:30).

Except for the Baptist's plaintive question as Herod's prisoner, this may be his last recorded statement.[10] If so, it is a fitting final word for the man of whom Jesus spoke so highly. "I tell you the truth," Jesus said. "Among those born of women there has not risen anyone greater than John the Baptist" (Matthew 11:11).

If indeed the remaining words of our text (3:31-36) are the author's, they shift our focus from John's joy to Jesus. On Him—on the One who comes from above—rests . . .

## *The Spirit without Limit (3:31-36)*

In a lofty Christological conclusion, our text declares seven grand realities concerning the Lord Jesus. They are reflective of Jesus' words to Nicodemus.

### His origin

Unlike John the Baptist, whose origin was "from the earth," Jesus is "from above"—the one who "comes from heaven" (3:31).[11] We were told at the beginning of John's Gospel that Jesus was the eternal Word who dwelt with the Father (1:1). He created all things (1:3). He "came" (1:11) to earth as a man and "made his dwelling among us" (1:14). He described Himself to Nicodemus as "the one who came from heaven—the Son of Man" (3:13). We will hear Him pray when He is about to go to the cross, "And now, Father, glorify me in your presence with the glory I had with you before the world began" (17:5).

### His exaltation

Twice in our text He is said to be "above all" (3:31). That is to say, He is sovereign over all created things. We see Him portrayed in Scripture as Creator and Sustainer of the universe.[12] We behold Him as the one who, as a reward for His incarnation, suffering and death, was exalted to the highest possible place and given a name that is above every name (Philippians 2:9; Ephesians 1:20ff.). We acknowledge Him to be "head over everything for the church" (Ephesians 1:22). And we bow before Him who is "KING OF KINGS AND LORD OF LORDS" (Revelation 19:16).

### His words and works

John informs us that Jesus "testifies to what he has seen and heard" (3:32) and that He "speaks the words of God" (3:34). To Nicodemus He declared, "we testify to what we have seen" (3:11) and asserts He will "speak of heavenly things" (3:12). He will later avow that He "can do nothing by himself; he can do only what he sees his Father doing" (5:19). "The words I say to you are not just my own. Rather it is the Father, living in me, who is doing his work" (14:10). In the words and works of our Lord Jesus we have received a true revelation of the mind and will of the Father. To "see" Jesus is to "see" the Father (see 14:9).

### His rejection

Sadly, even though Christ spoke the words and did the works of God, His testimony was not generally believed (3:32). "He came," the prologue told us, "to that which was his own, but his own did not receive him" (1:11). John will later explain the reason for this rejection. It was due to the stubborn, willful unbelief of Jesus' hearers, and it issued in God's blinding of their understanding (12:37ff). What sadness this brought to the heart of our Lord! He cried out, "O Jerusalem, Jerusalem . . . how often I have longed to gather your children together, as a hen gathers her chicks under her wings, but you were not willing" (Matthew 23:37).

### His reception

Not all rejected the testimony of Christ. John the Baptist believed it,[13] as did some secret believers (John 12:42f), and not a few who became disciples. "To all who received him, to those who believed in his name, he gave the right to become children of God" (1:12). The profound fact is that in accepting the words of Christ, God's accredited messenger, we are accepting the teaching of God. We are solemnly witnessing that God is truthful (3:33). It follows conversely that to reject the words of Jesus is to make God out to be a liar (see 1 John 5:10).

### His anointing

Only of Jesus Christ can it be said that "God gives the Spirit without limit" (John 3:34). The Holy Spirit came upon the Old Testament prophets in mighty power. He enabled them to say, "Thus says the Lord." He came upon John the Baptist, the last of those Old Testament prophets, enabling him to recognize the Messiah at the Jordan. It was this same John who said, "I saw the Spirit come down from heaven as a dove and remain on him" (1:32). The identical Spirit came upon the disciples at Pentecost, enabling them to bear witness to Christ and perform mighty signs. But upon no one, either before or after Jesus' ministry on earth, did the Spirit come in such un-measured power. It was this unlimited anointing of the Spirit that enabled Him to speak perfectly the words of God. The Spirit enabled Him to do the works that He saw the Father doing.

### His authority

Because of the Father's love for the Son, He has given to Him complete authority to act in His Name. Our text states: "The Father loves the Son and has placed everything in his hands" (3:35). To His disciples Jesus declared, "All authority in heaven and on earth has been given to me" (Matthew 28:18).

This God-given authority permits Jesus to "give eternal life to all those [the Father has] given him" (John 17:2). He also has "authority to judge be-cause he is the Son of Man" (5:27). Thus our text concludes, as did our pre-vious one (3:18), by reemphasizing a destiny-determining truth: "Whoever believes in the Son has eternal life, but whoever rejects the Son will not see life, for God's wrath remains on him" (3:36).[14]

## Conclusion

The attitudinal difference between the Baptist and his disciples is a lesson for all who serve in Christ's kingdom. We need to see ministry from God's point of view. John's disciples saw themselves as competitors of Jesus' dis-ciples. They supposed they were vying for the larger following. This percep-tion evoked anger and jealousy. John the Baptist saw both his ministry and that of Jesus as God's particular calling and gifting. Each had his own heaven-designed work. If more went over to Christ than came to him, this was the will of God. So be it!

How tragic to see some Christian leaders competing with each other for popularity and position! "What is your church's membership?" or, "How large is your Sunday morning congregation?" How frequently those questions are asked between ministers! "How much does your church give to missions?" Pastors of small congregations are jealous of pastors of large congregations. Evangelists become so desperate for results that they water down the gospel, cheapening eternal life. How unlike John's godly perspective!

William Barclay tells a story that illustrates John's attitude:

> There was a certain American minister—a Dr. Spence. Once he was popular and his church was full. But as the years passed his people drifted away. To the church across the road came a new young minister who was attracting the crowds. One evening in Dr. Spence's church there was a very small gathering. The doctor looked at the little flock. "Where have all the people gone?" he asked. There was an embarrassed silence. Then one of his office-bearers said: "I think they have gone to the church across the street to hear the new minister." Dr. Spence was silent for a moment. Then he smiled.
>
> "Well, then," he said, "I think we ought to follow them." And he descended from his pulpit and led his people across the road.

Barclay concludes the story, "What jealousies, what heartburnings, what resentfulness we might escape if only we would remember that someone else's success is given to him by God. If only we were prepared to accept God's verdict and God's choice!"[15]

How pathetic also to see workers in Christ's kingdom jealous of the gifts of others! Paul deals with this unspiritual attitude in First Corinthians. He reminds the Corinthians that it is the Spirit who endows each member of the body with a gift that will build up the whole. No Spirit-given ministry is unnecessary, and no one person possesses all the gifts. It takes all the members of the body working together to fulfill the work of Christ.[16]

John's desire was this: "He must become greater; I must become less" (3:30). Read the prayer of the hymnwriter:

> Not I but Christ be honored, loved, exalted;
>     Not I but Christ be seen, be known, be heard;
> Not I but Christ in every look and action;
>     Not I but Christ in every thought and word.

> Oh, to be saved from myself, dear Lord!
>     Oh, to be lost in Thee!
> Oh, that it might be no more I,
>     But Christ that lives in me![17]

### Endnotes

1. It was the pattern announced by Jesus to His disciples just prior to His ascension (Acts 1:8). The Acts testifies to how closely the pattern was followed, nudged along at times by persecution.
2. They addressed John as "rabbi" (3:26)—a term that seems hardly to fit such a revivalist prophet.
3. Later (4:2) we are informed that Jesus' disciples actually did the baptizing.
4. *Aenon* likely means "a spring of water."
5. Verse 25 is connected to 3:23 by the word *therefore* (Greek *oun),* making the double baptizing of Jesus and John the cause of the controversy described in 3:25.
6. See again John 1:29-34.
7. B.F. Westcott, *Commentary on the Gospel According to St. John* (London: John Murray, Albermarle Street, 1967), 58, explains the connection, as he sees it, between the argument of 3:25 and the outburst of 3:26 as follows: "We cannot but believe that Christ, when He administered a baptism through His disciples, explained to those who offered themselves the new birth which John's baptism and this preparatory baptism [Jesus' baptism] typified. At the same time He may have indicated, as to Nicodemus, the future establishment of Christian baptism, the sacrament of the new birth. In this way nothing would be more natural than that some Jew, a direct disciple, should be led to disparage the work of John, contrasting it with that of which Christ spoke; and that John's disciples, jealous for their master's honor, should come to him complaining of the position which Christ had taken." This may or may not be a plausible connection.
8. William Barclay, *The Gospel of John*, vol. I (Philadelphia: The Westminster Press, 1975), 143-144.
9. The picture of Israel as the bride of God, sometimes faithful, sometimes unfaithful, is a familiar one in the Old Testament. See such passages as Isaiah 62:4ff; Jeremiah 2:2; 3:20; Ezekiel 16:8; 23:4; Hosea 2:19-20. In the New Testament the Church is portrayed as the bride of Christ (2 Corinthians 11:2; Ephesians 5:25-29, 32).
10. It is difficult to know where the words of John the Baptist stop and the words of John the apostle begin. The NIV has the Baptist speaking from 3:27-36. Others, like Westcott,

*Commentary on the Gospel According to St. John,* 60, suggest that 3:31-36 is the apostle's clarification of the previous words of the Baptist. In the final analysis it makes no great difference!

11. For passages in which Jesus is described as the one who "comes," see Matthew 11:3; 21:9; 23:39; Mark 11:9; Luke 7:19f; 13:35; 19:38; John 1:15, 27; 11:27; 12:13.

12. See Colossians 1:15ff for Paul's powerful presentation of the exalted position of Christ.

13. "The man" of 3:33 may be a direct reference to John the Baptist.

14. Compare First John 5:10. The "wrath of God" is the sure and certain connection that exists between sin and judgment. See Romans 1:18; 2:5; 9:22; Ephesians 5:6; Colossians 3:6; 1 Thessalonians 5:9; Revelation 14:10.

15. Barclay, *The Gospel of John,* 142-143.

16. For an exposition of Paul's teaching concerning ministry, see chapters 4, 15 and 16 of my book, *First Corinthians: Fostering Spirituality* (Camp Hill, PA: Christian Publications, Inc., 1996).

17. Mrs. A.A. Whiddington, "Not I, But Christ," *Hymns of the Christian Life* (Camp Hill, PA: Christian Publications, Inc., 1978), # 264, stanza 1 and chorus.

# 9

# In Samaria:
# A Woman's Discovery

John 4:1-42

*The Pharisees heard that Jesus was gaining and baptizing more disciples than John, 2 although in fact it was not Jesus who baptized, but his disciples. 3 When the Lord learned of this, he left Judea and went back once more to Galilee.*

*4 Now he had to go through Samaria. 5 So he came to a town in Samaria called Sychar, near the plot of ground Jacob had given to his son Joseph. 6 Jacob's well was there, and Jesus, tired as he was from the journey, sat down by the well. It was about the sixth hour.*

*7 When a Samaritan woman came to draw water, Jesus said to her, "Will you give me a drink?" 8 (His disciples had gone into the town to buy food.)*

*9 The Samaritan woman said to him, "You are a Jew and I am a Samaritan woman. How can you ask me for a drink?" (For Jews do not associate with Samaritans.)*

*10 Jesus answered her, "If you knew the gift of God and who it is that asks you for a drink, you would have asked him and he would have given you living water."*

*11 "Sir," the woman said, "you have nothing to draw with and the well is deep. Where can you get this living water? 12 Are you greater than our father Jacob, who gave us the well and drank from it himself, as did also his sons and his flocks and herds?"*

13 Jesus answered, "Everyone who drinks this water will be thirsty again, 14 but whoever drinks the water I give him will never thirst. Indeed, the water I give him will become in him a spring of water welling up to eternal life."

15 The woman said to him, "Sir, give me this water so that I won't get thirsty and have to keep coming here to draw water."

16 He told her, "Go, call your husband and come back."

17 "I have no husband," she replied.

Jesus said to her, "You are right when you say you have no husband. 18 The fact is, you have had five husbands, and the man you now have is not your husband. What you have just said is quite true."

19 "Sir," the woman said, "I can see that you are a prophet. 20 Our fathers worshiped on this mountain, but you Jews claim that the place where we must worship is in Jerusalem."

21 Jesus declared, "Believe me, woman, a time is coming when you will worship the Father neither on this mountain nor in Jerusalem. 22 You Samaritans worship what you do not know; we worship what we do know, for salvation is from the Jews. 23 Yet a time is coming and has now come when the true worshipers will worship the Father in spirit and truth, for they are the kind of worshipers the Father seeks. 24 God is spirit, and his worshipers must worship in spirit and in truth."

25 The woman said, "I know that Messiah" (called Christ) "is coming. When he comes, he will explain everything to us."

26 Then Jesus declared, "I who speak to you am he."

27 Just then his disciples returned and were surprised to find him talking with a woman. But no one asked, "What do you want?" or "Why are you talking with her?"

28 Then, leaving her water jar, the woman went back to the town and said to the people, 29 "Come, see a man who told me everything I ever did. Could this be the Christ?" 30 They came out of the town and made their way toward him.

31 Meanwhile his disciples urged him, "Rabbi, eat something."

32 But he said to them, "I have food to eat that you know nothing about."

33 Then his disciples said to each other, "Could someone have brought him food?"

34 "My food," said Jesus, "is to do the will of him who sent me and to finish his work. 35 Do you not say, 'Four months more and then the harvest'? I tell you, open your eyes and look at the fields! They are ripe for harvest. 36 Even now the reaper draws his wages, even now he harvests

*the crop for eternal life, so that the sower and the reaper may be glad to-
gether. 37 Thus the saying 'One sows and another reaps' is true. 38 I sent
you to reap what you have not worked for. Others have done the hard
work, and you have reaped the benefits of their labor."*

*39 Many of the Samaritans from that town believed in him because of
the woman's testimony, "He told me everything I ever did." 40 So when
the Samaritans came to him, they urged him to stay with them, and he
stayed two days. 41 And because of his words many more became believers.*

*42 They said to the woman, "We no longer believe just because of what
you said; now we have heard for ourselves, and we know that this man really is the Savior of the world."*

Our Lord Jesus was very conscious that the Father's *timing* was important in His life and ministry. At the wedding in Cana of Galilee, for example, He told his mother, "My time has not yet come" (2:4). He knew all
His Father had sent Him to do. He knew there was a future hour when it
would be time for His crucifixion.

But that God-ordained hour of His death was still three years away. When
Jesus learned of the Pharisees' distress because His baptized disciples ex-
ceeded John's (4:1-2), He prudently decided to leave Judea. He was well
aware of Jerusalem's reputation for killing prophets they did not want to
hear (Matthew 23:37). Lest the jealous Jewish leaders take steps to arrest
and kill Him prematurely, He would get out of harm's way (4:3).[1]

The shortest route to Galilee was through Samaria—a three-day trek. Because of the hostility between Jews and Samaritans, many Jews circum-
vented Samaria and walked twice as far to do so. But racist fire did not burn
in Jesus' breast. He would go *through* Samaria (4:4). And it was this walk
north that occasioned . . .

## The "Chance" Encounter at the Well (4:4-9)

It is not necessary to believe that by spiritual discernment Jesus knew He
would meet the Samaritan woman of our text. But it is important to believe
that divine providence brings about events and circumstances that we sometimes attribute to mere "chance."

Recently a newspaper story told how a husband and wife, separated in Europe by World War II, were reunited. A diplomat, whose plans for the day suddenly changed, "happened" to take a particular subway he had not used before. He "chanced" to sit beside the husband and in conversation heard the man's account. When the man told him his wife's name, the diplomat recalled that he had once met a woman by that name at a gathering some time previously. He managed to contact the woman and eventually was able to reunite the grateful couple. The newspaper reporter concluded that more than "chance" was involved in those events. "God was riding that subway train," he decided.

And so it was in the providence of His Father God that a travel-weary Jesus came face-to-face with a needy woman. It was at Jacob's well near the small village of Sychar in Samaria (4:4-6).[2]

How different is this account and the Nicodemus story of chapter 3! Nicodemus was a well-educated, important Jewish official, concerned about the kingdom of God. The Samaritan woman was a peasant whose main interest was getting the water she needed. Jesus ministered to the Pharisee through a graphic Old Testament story from the Torah. He ministered to the woman through a parable of eternal life, suggested by Jacob's well. Jesus presented Himself to Nicodemus as God's one and only Son; to the woman, as the true Messiah. Both needed the new life that Jesus offered. Together the two stories illustrate the universality of the gospel. Rich or poor, high or low, Jew or Gentile, moral or immoral, religious or irreligious—it does not matter. All are invited to come to Jesus and freely partake of the salvation He offers.

See now how the story develops. It was the noon hour. The disciples had gone into the village to purchase food. Jesus, alone, tired and thirsty from the long journey, sat down by Jacob's well. A Samaritan came by herself—and at an unusual hour—to draw water from the well.[3] Jesus' disciples were not there to get water for their Master (4:8), so Jesus unabashedly asked the woman for a drink (4:7).

The woman was utterly astonished! She recognized His accent and could not imagine any male Jew having anything to do with her. "How can you ask me for a drink?" she asked (4:9).

So that his readers will understand the irony of the situation, John explains that "Jews do not associate with Samaritans" (4:9).[4] Their mutual hostility was rooted far back in history. The Samaritans were half-Jews. When in 722 B.C. the Northern Kingdom fell to the Assyrians, Sargon II deported most of the Israelites to Assyria (2 Kings 17:23). In their place he brought in other conquered people—"from Babylon, Cuthah, Avva. Hamath and Sepharvaim" (17:24). So the Samaritans owed their ethnic origin to the intermarriage of the Jewish remnant and these imported settlers. Consequently idolatry corrupted their worship (see 17:26ff). The returning Jewish exiles under Ezra and Nehemiah rejected offers of cooperation from the Samaritans. In Jesus' day this racial and religious animosity still ran deep.

Furthermore, the woman was amazed that Jesus, a male, would so much as speak to her. Jewish men were advised not even to talk to their own wives in public.[5] Certainly no woman was considered fit to engage in theological discussion. At least one rabbi publicly thanked God that he had not been born a woman! But this Man who asked her for a drink was neither racist nor sexist. Utterly remarkable! And then our Lord presented to her . . .

## The Free Offer of Living Water (4:10-15)

Jesus responded to her how-can-you question by informing her that He possessed "living water" (4:10).[6] And He added that He was prepared to give it to her. Like Nicodemus before, she misunderstood Jesus' words, supposing He was speaking about natural well water. Jacob's well was more than a hundred feet deep. It was fed by an underground spring that rarely failed.[7] The woman could see that Jesus had no means of reaching the water, and He would certainly not use a Samaritan's bucket! She wondered from what source He would procure fresh, pure water. Surely this poor, weary traveler was not more powerful than the patriarch Jacob, who had dug the well in the first place, was He? (4:12).[8]

But then Jesus increased the woman's desire for the water He had to offer. He assured her that, unlike the water from Jacob's well, His was a permanent cure for thirst. It would be like a spring bubbling within her being, issuing finally in *eternal life* (4:13-14). He was speaking, of course, about the Holy Spirit, whom He would impart to His people. The Holy Spirit, dwelling within them, would be a perpetual wellspring of refreshment and life.[9] The Spirit would be a foretaste of eternal glory.[10]

Still the woman misunderstood. Hoping to preclude her daily return to the well, she asked for the water Jesus offered (4:15). In doing so, and without realizing it, she opened the door for Jesus to reveal to her His Messiahship. He proceeded to do so by declaring to her . . .

### The Nature of True Worship (4:16-26)

Jesus asked the woman to get her husband and bring him back with her (4:16). Did Jesus, at this point, know by the Spirit the woman's checkered past? And if so, why would He make this request of her? Some scholars suggest it was to arouse her slumbering conscience. Jesus wanted to awaken conviction of sin within her as her past life loomed before her mind's eye.[11] Others are of the opinion that Jesus was insisting that she "live in the truth."[12] Another suggests that Jesus simply did not wish to influence her, a dependent person, without the participation of her husband. Jesus wanted the *family* to be the nucleus of the kingdom of God in Samaria.[13]

Whatever the reason, Jesus' request did in fact bring out the truth of her past. In a potentially misleading reply, she volunteered, "I have no husband" (4:17). It was the truth—but not the whole truth. By a word of knowledge[14] Jesus compelled her to admit to her five marriages and her present common-law arrangement (4:17-18).[15] Thus it became clear to the woman that she was dealing not with an ordinary Jew. Rather, He was a bona fide prophet of God (4:19).

Right then, she might have confessed her sin. Instead, she saw in this Prophet of God an opportunity to clarify a theological question. Finally she could know the proper place to worship God. Was it in the temple on Mount Gerizim, where the Samaritans worshiped? Or was it in the temple at Jerusalem where the Jews worshiped (4:20)? The Samaritans, adjusting history to suit themselves, taught that on Mount Gerizim Abraham had tried to sacrifice his son. On Mount Gerizim Melchizedek had appeared to Abraham. On Mount Gerizim Moses had first built an altar and sacrificed to God when the people entered the promised land.[16] The Samaritan woman had been schooled to regard Mount Gerizim as the most sacred spot in the world. She had also been schooled to despise Jerusalem. Now, through this prophet, she hoped to discover the truth.[17]

Her question became the springboard for our Lord's definitive teaching concerning true worship (4:21-24). Until this time, Jewish worship had, indeed, been superior. The Samaritans' veneration of God on Mount Gerizim was directed to One whose true character the Samaritans did not know. They were unacquainted with the God revealed through Israel's prophets and Scriptures (4:22). Jewish worship may have been of the letter and not the Spirit. But they were familiar with the nature, will and unfolding purposes of the God they worshiped in Jerusalem (4:22).

"A time is coming," said Jesus, "when you will worship the Father neither on this mountain [Gerizim] nor in Jerusalem" (4:21). The question concerning the correct location for a temple would soon be passé. Soon the true worship of God would not be confined to man-made temples in particular places.[18] Instead, worship would take place within the human spirit. Through the indwelling Holy Spirit we may have immediate communication with the Father. At the same time we may have a true concept of the Object of our worship, thanks to Jesus Christ. God has revealed Himself in Jesus Christ. It will be "in spirit and truth," which is the kind of worship the Father desires (4:23).

Thus Jesus invited the woman to leave behind her doubts and questions. He invited her to become a true spiritual worshiper of the living God. What the prophet was saying to her rang true, but the Samaritan felt she must wait for the coming Messiah to clear up all these religious problems (4:25).[19] Jesus had good news for her.

"You need wait no longer," Jesus said in effect (see 4:26). "I *am* the Messiah!"

## The Believing Response of the People (4:27-42)

Just about then, the disciples, who had been in Sychar on their quest for food, returned. They were surprised to see their Master talking with a woman. But they had learned by this time that Jesus did not fit into the traditional mold. He must have had some good reason for this conversation, so they said nothing about it (4:27). The woman, forgetting why she had come to the well in the first place, rushed back to her village. Turning evangelist, she invited all her fellow Samaritans to "come, see a man who told me everything I ever did. Could this be the Christ?" (4:29). Her hyperbole can be forgiven her. And even the lingering suggestion of doubt.[20] All of this was so new, so unanticipated.

Some of her friends were indeed prepared to believe that Messiah was out there by the well. They began making their way toward Jesus (4:30).

The disciples, meanwhile, were concerned that the Lord had eaten nothing and pressed Him to take some food. He refused, explaining that He had "food" they could not comprehend (4:32). Nicodemus had interpreted the "second birth" literally. The Samaritan woman had interpreted the "living water" literally. Now Jesus' disciples interpreted "food" literally and wondered who might have fed Him while they were away (4:33). But Jesus knew that "man does not live on bread alone" (Deuteronomy 8:3). The spiritual food that sustained Him was to do the Father's will. It was to finish the work He had been sent to do (4:34). His mission was to turn the old water of Judaism into the new wine of the Spirit. He was sent to raise a new spiritual temple, to give new birth to a Pharisee, to offer living water to a Samaritan woman. He had been commissioned to complete the work of our salvation. Even as He was speaking, He saw the harvest—men and women from Sychar who eagerly approached Him.

"Your proverb, 'Four months more and then the harvest,' is not appropriate," He said in effect to His disciples. "Open your eyes and look at the fields! They are ripe for harvest" (4:35). Jesus had sown the seed in the heart of a Samaritan woman. Already He and His disciples were about to reap the harvest. These Samaritans would be the firstfruits of Gentile believers. Others had helped in the sowing. There was John the Baptist and the long line of God's messengers. All had made the harvest possible (4:37-38).

By this time, the villagers from Sychar had arrived at the well. They saw and heard for themselves this Man about whom the woman had told them. Their faith, and the faith of many more who believed on Jesus during His two-day stay, was based on firsthand experience.

"We no longer believe," they told the woman, "just because of what you said; now we have heard for ourselves, and we know that this man really is the Savior of the world" (4:42).

## Conclusion

What an abundance of "food and drink" is in this text for the souls of deeper-life seekers! To receive the Spirit from the exalted Savior is to discover within us a refreshing, ever-present, life-giving well of living water. It is a foretaste of glory! And we say with the ancient hymnwriter, "We drink of Thee, the Fountainhead, and thirst our souls from Thee to fill."[21] The more we drink at the Fountainhead, the more we long to drink of this precious Spirit of Jesus. We can identify with the testimony of another songwriter:

> I tried the broken cisterns, Lord;
> But, ah, the waters failed.
> E'en as I stooped to drink they'd fled
> And mocked me as I wailed.
>
> Now none but Christ can satisfy,
> None other name for me;
> There's love and life and lasting joy,
> Lord Jesus, found in Thee.[22]

And this spring of living water "welling up to eternal life," this indwelling Spirit of God, prompts genuine spiritual worship. Our great Triune God is worthy of adoration. True worship is only possible when we sense the awesome presence of God or recall such a sense. It is this awareness of God's nearness that the Spirit brings to our hearts. Worship, the declaring of God's worth, must undergird all of our life and ministry. Let us cultivate the art of worship! Let us be worshipers!

Let us bow before the Lord our Maker and our God.

### Endnotes

1. F.F. Bruce, *The Gospel of John* (Grand Rapids, MI: Eerdmans, 1983), 101, interestingly suggests this reason for Jesus' leaving Judea: Jesus expected the Pharisees would try to exploit the possible feelings of resentment within John's disciples over His greater success. And Jesus regarded John so highly that He would not tolerate the possibility of a cleavage between them.

2. For the Old Testament background of 4:5, see Genesis 33:19; 48:22; and Joshua 24:32.

3. B.F. Westcott, *Commentary on the Gospel According to St. John* (London: John Murray, Albemarle Street, 1967), 68, reports that an ancient legend gives her name as Photina.

4. A more literal translation would be, "Jews do not use dishes that Samaritans have used." The reason, of course, was their fear of ritual defilement.

5. Bruce, *The Gospel of John,* 112, cites this remark by one rabbi: "He who prolongs conversation with a woman brings evil upon himself, ceases from the words of the law, and at the last inherits Gehenna."

6. Westcott, *Commentary on the Gospel According to St. John,* 69, interprets "the gift of God" here as a general reference to all the blessings given through Jesus the Son.

7. See Bruce, *The Gospel of John*, 101.

8. The Greek negative *me* at the beginning of 4:11 indicates the woman expected a "No" answer to her question.

9. Compare John 7:37-39.

10. Paul calls the Holy Spirit "a deposit guaranteeing our inheritance until the redemption of those who are God's possession" (Ephesians 1:14). To the Romans he writes, "If the Spirit of him who raised Jesus from the dead is living in you, he who raised Christ from the dead will also give life to your mortal bodies through his Spirit, who lives in you" (8:11). Paul is saying in different words what Jesus said to the woman at the well. The Holy Spirit's presence in us guarantees eternal life.

11. See R.G.V. Tasker, *The Gospel According to St. John* (London: The Tyndale Press, 1960), 76.

12. See Bruce, *The Gospel of John,* 106.

13. F. Godet, *Commentary on the Gospel of St. John*, vol. II (Edinburgh: T. & T. Clarke, 1881), 110. Godet believes that only after she confessed that she had no husband did Jesus have a revelation of her past failed marriages.

14. See First Corinthians 12, where one of the manifestations of the Spirit is "the word of knowledge." It must be remembered that Jesus performed all His ministry as a Man anointed by the Holy Spirit.

15. Apparently each of her previous marriages had ended in legal divorce. Now she was living common-law—a situation not expressly forbidden by Mosaic regulations. See Westcott, *Commentary of the Gospel According to St. John,* 71. However, as Godet, *Commentary on the Gospel of St. John,* 111, points out, the Greek construction *nun hon echeis estin sou aner* ("now the one you have is not *your* husband") could imply that she was living common-law with another woman's husband and thus was guilty of adultery.

16. But see Deuteronomy 27:4-5 for the truth.

17. I prefer this interpretation of her 4:20 comment rather than to suppose it a diversionary tactic to avoid further exposure of her personal life. Nor do I see her as a person who cannot engage in religious conversation without raising points of disagreement.

18. Jesus is foretelling what both Hebrews 9 and First Corinthians 3 state as fact. The temple of God is now the people of the Church, wherever they are assembled.

19. The Samaritans conceived of Messiah not as a conqueror but as a perfect law-giver; as a prophet, not a king.

20. Again, the construction and vocabulary of the Greek indicates she may have expected the townspeople to say "No."

21. Ray Palmer, trans., "Jesus, Thou Joy of Loving Hearts," *Hymns of the Christian Life* (Camp Hill, PA: Christian Publications, Inc., 1978), # 35, stanza 3.

22. Anon. in *Hymns of the Christian Life*, 1962 edition, # 458.

## Part III

## *Questions for Reflection or Discussion*

1. What does it mean to be "born of water and the Spirit"?
2. What New Testament Scriptures back up the appropriateness of John's attitude described in 3:27-30? If God's people imitated John, what difference might this make in contemporary church life?
3. What is the New Testament doctrine of the providence of God? How is this doctrine illustrated in the story of the woman at the well?
4. Contrast the Old Testament practice of worship with the New.

*Part IV*

# The Life in the Son

John 4:43-5:47

# 10

# *Eternal Life Portrayed*

John 4:43-5:15

*43 After the two days he left for Galilee. 44 (Now Jesus himself had pointed out that a prophet has no honor in his own country.) 45 When he arrived in Galilee, the Galileans welcomed him. They had seen all that he had done in Jerusalem at the Passover Feast, for they also had been there.*

*46 Once more he visited Cana in Galilee, where he had turned the water into wine. And there was a certain royal official whose son lay sick at Capernaum. 47 When this man heard that Jesus had arrived in Galilee from Judea, he went to him and begged him to come and heal his son, who was close to death.*

*48 "Unless you people see miraculous signs and wonders," Jesus told him, "you will never believe."*

*49 The royal official said, "Sir, come down before my child dies."*

*50 Jesus replied, "You may go. Your son will live."*

*The man took Jesus at his word and departed. 51 While he was still on the way, his servants met him with the news that his boy was living. 52 When he inquired as to the time when his son got better, they said to him, "The fever left him yesterday at the seventh hour."*

*53 Then the father realized that this was the exact time at which Jesus had said to him, "Your son will live." So he and all his household believed.*

*54 This was the second miraculous sign that Jesus performed, having come from Judea to Galilee.*

*5:1 Some time later, Jesus went up to Jerusalem for a feast of the Jews. 2*

*Now there is in Jerusalem near the Sheep Gate a pool, which in Aramaic is called Bethesda and which is surrounded by five covered colonnades. 3 Here a great number of disabled people used to lie—the blind, the lame, the paralyzed. 5 One who was there had been an invalid for thirty-eight years. 6 When Jesus saw him lying there and learned that he had been in this condition for a long time, he asked him, "Do you want to get well?"*

*7 "Sir," the invalid replied, "I have no one to help me into the pool when the water is stirred. While I am trying to get in, someone else goes down ahead of me."*

*8 Then Jesus said to him, "Get up! Pick up your mat and walk." 9 At once the man was cured; he picked up his mat and walked.*

*The day on which this took place was a Sabbath, 10 and so the Jews said to the man who had been healed, "It is the Sabbath; the law forbids you to carry your mat."*

*11 But he replied, "The man who made me well said to me, 'Pick up you mat and walk.' "*

*12 So they asked him, "Who is this fellow who told you to pick it up and walk?"*

*13 The man who was healed had no idea who it was, for Jesus had slipped away into the crowd that was there.*

*14 Later Jesus found him at the temple and said to him, "See, you are well again. Stop sinning or something worse may happen to you." 15 The man went away and told the Jews that it was Jesus who had made him well.*

The two days spent in Sychar must have brought great joy to the heart of the Savior. Many Samaritans had become believers on the basis of His words alone (4:41). And now, encouraged and rested, He was ready to continue His journey. In Judea, He had found Himself to be a "prophet without honor." As He progressed into Galilee, He was welcomed with open arms.[1] Many of the Galileans had been in Jerusalem for the Passover Feast. Likely they had heard about Jesus' astonishing cleansing of the Temple—or even witnessed it! Possibly they had seen some of the miraculous deeds He had performed. Now they were eager to see what "wonders" He would do in Galilee.

Not surprisingly, Jesus chose to return to Cana, the site of His previous need-supplying miracle. Turning water into wine had symbolized the giving way of Judaism's barren legalism to the new life in the Holy Spirit. Out of the staid stone water jars had flowed wine much better than the guests had tasted earlier. In Cana, where He had first "revealed his glory" (2:11), He would perform another miraculous sign. This one would be a miracle of healing—the son of a royal official was near death. Along with the healing of the invalid at Bethesda pool (5:1-15), it speaks of eternal life, lovingly and freely given. Jesus makes this life eternal available to all who believe on His name.

## *Life for a Dying Son (4:46-54)*

In Capernaum, a town some twenty miles from Cana, the son of an official in Herod's court[2] lay dying. The officer loved his son and was desperate to find healing for him. News of what Jesus had done in Cana had reached the man. Discovering that Jesus was now back, he determined to go personally to Him and intercede for his son.

We can imagine this official's turmoil as he left his dying son to beg the merciful intervention of a village Carpenter (4:47). But desperation and deep love for his son pushed him on. Only to have Jesus meet his entreaty with what must have sounded like a rude brush-off: "Unless you people see miraculous signs and wonders, . . . you will never believe" (4:48).

This was hardly the time for a disapproving lecture. What was in Jesus' mind to prompt such a response? Although His words appear directed to the distressed father, they probably were aimed much more broadly. Jesus may have been speaking to the entire unbelieving populace of Galilee. Or to Herod's inquisitive entourage whom the officer in effect represented.[3] Jesus' words were not so much a reply to the father's plea as they were His sad-hearted reflection occasioned by it.[4] He was saying, in effect, "You people want to make Me nothing more than a Wonder-worker.[5] Unless I play the part, you will not believe what I have to say."

No matter how he may have understood Jesus' words, the royal official refused to be deterred.

"Sir," he insisted, "come down before my child[6] dies" (4:49). Jesus' response was a stiff test of the man's faith. "You may go," He said. "Your son will live" (4:50). Likely the officer assumed Jesus' power to heal was linked inseparably to His physical presence. Now, with no visible sign and only Jesus' word, he was expected to return home to Capernaum. *And he went!*

Obediently trusting Jesus' life-giving word, all feverish sense of hurry gone from his soul,[7] he started home. Even before he arrived, his servants met him with the good word: his son was well! Then he learned that the time of the boy's recovery coincided with Jesus' word of promise! He and his entire family surrendered themselves in faith to Jesus (4:51-53). They received the eternal life[8] of which the son's restoration to physical life was a striking symbol.

### *Healing for a Crippled Man (5:1-15)*

John the apostle wants further to prepare His readers for the discourse on eternal life that will follow (5:16-30). So he adds another vivid "sign" narrative. This time he shows how the word of Christ brought hope and vitality to a helpless cripple. The scene shifts from Cana back to Jerusalem. Jesus was attending an unidentified "feast of the Jews" (5:1).[9] The setting is a pool, Bethesda ("house of mercy"), located near the Sheep Gate on the east side of the city. The pool was not far from the Temple.[10] The five covered colonnades at the pool were a favorite gathering place for invalids. They believed that an angel periodically disturbed the water in the pool. When that happened, whoever first stepped into the water would be healed.[11]

What a pathetic sight met our Lord's ever-compassionate eyes as He neared the pool! Before Him were "the blind, the lame, the paralyzed" (5:3). What a picture of sin-sickened humanity! One man in particular caught Jesus' attention. Jesus learned[12] that he had been in this pitifully hopeless condition for thirty-eight years! Jesus knew that an Eastern beggar often lost a modestly good living by being cured of his disease. So He asked the man if he truly desired to see his circumstances changed (5:6). Jesus knew, too, that if the power of God was to be manifested, the bedridden man must intensely *want* to be healed.[13]

Lack of desire was not the man's problem. But he had no caring friends to hurry him into the water (5:7).[14] Knowing neither Jesus' identity nor His power, he naturally would seek the only means of healing he knew. Jesus, both compassionate and able, must have detected a rising tide of faith within the man's spirit.

"Get up!" Jesus ordered. "Pick up your mat and walk" (5:8). What excitement! What joy! The man who for thirty-eight years had been dependent felt sudden strength in his paralyzed limbs. He was walking![15] Perhaps, like Peter's beggar, this one went into the temple "walking and jumping and praising God" (see Acts 3:1ff).

Sadly, not everyone present shared the man's ecstasy. There were in Jesus' day, even as now, certain small-minded, self- righteous souls more concerned about legal minutiae than changed lives. Never mind that a hopeless, pitiable, lonely cripple had been given a brand-new lease on life. He was carrying his pallet on the Sabbath! Did he not know that such action contravened the law (5:10)?[16]

A dark cloud suddenly loomed in the man's blue sky. According to Jewish regulations, he could be stoned to death for carrying his mat on the Sabbath. He absolved himself with an age-old excuse: *He told me to do it!* The Man whose name he did not know had told him to pick up his mat and walk (5:11, 13). The Jews pressed the issue, demanding to know who had encouraged this defiance of their law. Not being willing to concede a miracle, they did not ask, "Who healed you?" Rather, "Who told you to pick it up and walk" (see 5:12)?

In the Temple, where likely the man was offering thanks to God for his healing, he and Jesus came face to face again (5:14). Jesus assured him of the permanence of his cure[17] provided he stopped the sin originally responsible for his condition. We need not, like John Calvin, conclude from Jesus' words that all sickness is caused by the ailing person's sin.[18]

On a different occasion, Jesus' disciples asked Him, "Who sinned, this man or his parents, that he was born blind?" Jesus replied, "Neither" (9:2-3). But in the case of the man at the Bethesda pool, some evil in his past had triggered his sorry condition. We are left to imagine what it might have been.

## Conclusion

In our next chapter we will look at the interaction between Jesus and the Jews because of this Sabbath healing. The motif of opposition to our Lord will come once again to the fore.[19]

For now, let us draw together two lessons that our text would teach us.
First, we learn of our Savior's tender compassion in the face of physical suf-
fering. It is true that Jesus' miracles were for the purpose of authenticating
His Person. That includes the miracles of healing. His miracles proved that
He was indeed sent from God, that He was who He professed to be. There-
fore we should attend carefully to His words.

But Jesus' miracles point us as well to deeper spiritual truths. His ministry
of healing flowed out of a divinely compassionate heart. It was a heart that
grieved over the brokenness of people. It longed for their wholeness. Jesus
knew that disease and deformity were the dastardly work of the prince of
darkness. Satan's intent has always been the vicious destruction of God's
beautiful handiwork. Jesus knew the atonement He accomplished on Calvary would secure the total defeat of the kingdom of darkness. He knew it
would make possible not only the forgiveness of sins but the healing of disease and the mending of deformity. And so He would look upon the sick and
afflicted as victims of satanic tyranny. With divine authority mixed with
tender pity, He commanded demons to flee and fevers to vanish. He told sei-
zures to cease and diseases to depart. His healing hands brought sight to the
blind and hearing to the deaf.

As Albert B. Simpson wrote in his great testimonial song, Jesus was—
and is—Christ our Healer:

> Jesus only is our Healer,
> All our sicknesses He bear,
> And His risen life and fullness
> All His members still may share.[20]

And this:

> There is a great Physician still
> Whose hand has all its ancient skill;
> At His command our pains will flee—
> "I am the Lord that healeth thee."[21]

"A great Physician still." Still today He attends to the desperate pleas of
distraught fathers and mothers whose children lie at the point of death. Still
today He looks with tender sympathy upon the blind, the lame, the para-

lyzed. He sees them lying helpless in the "five covered colonnades" of this world. He asks, "Do you want to get well?" And still today He responds with healing power to those who reach out to Him in faith.

Barbara (not her real name) proved this to be true. She had been bedridden for months. Two major surgeries had left her weak and helpless. The medicines prescribed by her well-meaning doctors produced further complications. Her condition worsened. Then, when all medical hope was gone, in desperation she cried out to the Lord.

That very day God answered her prayer. God showed Barbara His way to wholeness. Within a few days she was walking and on her way to a health and strength she had never before known. God had indeed healed her!

But there is a greater miracle than the healing of physical bodies. God's power that brought new *physical life* to a dying boy in Capernaum and a paralyzed man in Jerusalem is a "sign." It points us to God's gracious intervention in granting *eternal life* to all who believe on the Lord Jesus. It is fitting for the possessors of this abundant life to remember, as the Apostle Paul often did, the death from which we were delivered. The Scriptures remind us that at one time

> [we] were *dead* in [our] transgressions and sins, in which [we] used to live when [we] followed the ways of this world and of the ruler of the kingdom of the air. . . . But because of his great love for us, God, who is rich in mercy, made us *alive* with Christ even when we were dead in transgressions. (Ephesians 2:1-4, emphases added)

Before God intervened in our lives, we were like corpses, unaware of the physical world that surrounded us. We were dead to God, having no awareness of the invisible spiritual world that encompassed us. We were utterly unable to bring life to ourselves. But the Spirit of God breathed into our dead spirits the breath of divine life, and we became alive to Him. Again, the Scriptures tell us:

> At one time we too were foolish, disobedient, deceived and enslaved by all kinds of passions and pleasures. We lived in malice and envy, being hated and hating one another. But when the kindness and love of God our Savior appeared, he saved us . . . so that,

having been justified by his grace, we might become heirs having
the hope of *eternal* life. (Titus 3:3-7, emphasis added)

Before Jesus reached out to us with healing power, our minds were
twisted and distorted by sin. Our spiritual eyes were blind to eternal truth.
Our spiritual ears were deaf to the voice of God. Nothing or no one on earth
could heal us. We were hopelessly enchained in a dark prison of our own
making. No earthly power could set us free. But now, by God's grace, we
can joyfully sing:

> Saved! saved! saved! my sins are all forgiven;
> Christ is mine! I'm on my way to heaven;
> Once a guilty sinner, lost, undone,
> Now a child of God, saved through His Son.

> Saved! saved! saved! by grace and grace alone;
> Oh, what wondrous love to me was shown,
> In my stead Christ Jesus bled and died,
> Bore my sins, for me was crucified.

> Saved! saved! saved! O joy beyond compare!
> Christ my life and I His constant care;
> Yielding all and trusting Him alone,
> Living now each moment as His own.[22]

May we never be guilty of minimizing either the enormity of our desperate condition or the immensity of God's great salvation.

### Endnotes

1. Various attempts have been made to make sense of Jesus' use of the proverb (4:44). If, as
   some like F. Godet, *Commentary on the Gospel of St. John,* vol. II (Edinburgh: T. & T.
   Clarke, 1881), 134, believe, Nazareth in Galilee was His "own country," then the welcome
   He received there would seem to deny the truth of the proverb. However, as F.F. Bruce,
   *The Gospel of John* (Grand Rapids, MI: Eerdmans, 1983), 116, R.G.V. Tasker, *The Gos-
   pel According to St. John* (London: The Tyndale Press, 1960), 80, and B.F. Westcott,
   *Commentary on the Gospel According to St. John* (London: John Murray, Albermarle
   Street, 1967), 77, each point out, Jerusalem in Judea was the "hometown" of every true Is-
   raelite wherever he might be living, and it was in Jerusalem that Jesus was without honor.

2. This "royal official" *(basilikos)* was likely attached to the entourage of Herod Antipas, tetrarch of Galilee from 4 B.C. to A.D. 39 (compare Mark 6:14-15). It is doubtful that he could have been Cuza (Luke 8:3), as some suggest.

3. See Luke 23:8 for Herod's interest in Jesus.

4. Godet, *Commentary on the Gospel of St. John,* vol. II, 136. John Calvin, *Commentary on the Gospel According to John,* vol. I (Edinburgh: The Calvin Translation Society, 1847), 180, has this comment on 4:48: "The wicked contempt for the word of God, which at that time prevailed, constrained [Jesus] to make this complaint." He goes on to say that the Jews depended so much on miracles that they left no room for the word.

5. The term *wonders (terata)* is used only here in John's Gospel. Leon Morris, *The Gospel According to John* (Grand Rapids, MI: Eerdmans, 1971), 290, describes a "wonder" as a portent defying rational explanation.

6. The father calls his son by the very affectionate word *paidion.* In 4:50, Jesus calls the boy *huios,* a term, according to Godet, *Commentary on the Gospel of St. John,* vol II, 137, of dignity, expressing the worth of the child, as representing the family. In 4:51, the servants refer to the child as the official's *pais,* a term expressive of family life.

7. The phrase "yesterday at the seventh hour" (1:00 p.m.) in 4:52 seems to indicate that the official did not rush home. Perhaps one reason was the peace in his heart which his faith inspired, or the desire to stay a little longer with Jesus. Since, however, for the Jews the day closed at sunset, "yesterday" does not oblige us to suppose that a whole night had elapsed since the miracle.

8. The reader is encouraged to review previous passages concerning eternal life: John 1:4; 3:15-16, 36; and 4:14.

9. The identification of this feast is in doubt. If, as some scholars believe, the content of chapter 6 originally preceded chapter 5, then the feast of 5:1 is Passover (see 6:4). Godet, *Commentary on the Gospel of St. John,* vol. II, 148, is quite sure that the reference is to the feast of Purim, which celebrates the deliverance of the Jews by Queen Esther.

10. The gate referred to in Nehemiah's account of the rebuilding of Jerusalem's wall (3:1; 12:39) would have taken its name from the adjoining sheep market where sacrificial animals were sold for use in temple worship.

11. As noted in the NIV, there is considerable manuscript evidence that the words "and they waited for the moving of the waters" and verse 4 (KJV) in its entirety were not in the original Gospel. The likelihood is that these verses were inserted later by someone wanting to give a supernatural explanation to a natural phenomenon referred to in 5:7 as the "stirring" of the water, perhaps a subterranean stream that every now and then bubbled up and disturbed the water. See Tasker, *The Gospel According to St. John,* 90, and others. Westcott, *Commentary on the Gospel According to St. John,* 82, thinks that the healing properties of the pool may have been due to its mineral content. He cites the historian Eusebius, who comments on the "marvelously red" color of the water, an indication of its iron content.

12. Our version translates the Greek *ginosko* as "learned," implying, I think correctly, that Jesus got His information about the man from bystanders. However, *ginosko* also means "to know," and it is quite possible, as Godet, *Commentary on the Gospel of St. John,* vol. II, 154, points out, that this is one of those "instantaneous perceptions by which the truth became known to Jesus according as the task of the moment demanded." In other words, we may have here another example of the "gift of knowledge" that was manifested in Jesus' ministry to the Samaritan woman at the well.

13. Calvin, *Commentary on the Gospel According to John,* vol. I, 189, proposes a novel but unlikely reason for Jesus' question. He asks, "Do you want to get well?" to get the atten-

tion of the witnesses present who, if they had been thinking of something else, might have missed the miracle.

14. The most common meaning of the Greek *ballo,* translated "help" (5:7), is "to throw," perhaps underlining the necessity of great haste.

15. The tense of the verb *walked* (5:9) is the Greek imperfect. It means, literally, "He was walking." There is a hint of joyous amazement as the man suddenly realizes that he is doing something he had given up all hope of ever doing.

16. The Jews were very aware of God's word to Jeremiah (17:19-27) and of the actions of Nehemiah (13:15-19), who forbade the carrying of a load on the Sabbath. However, even the most casual reading of those passages indicates that what was forbidden was *working* on the Sabbath, not carrying one's mat home at Jesus' command. According to William Barclay, *The Gospel of John,* vol. I (Philadelphia: The Westminster Press, 1975), 181, the rabbis argued that a man was sinning if he carried a needle in his robe, artificial teeth or a wooden leg on the Sabbath. Their man-made law said, "If anyone carries anything from a public place to a private home on the Sabbath intentionally, he is punishable by death by stoning." It was just such gross misinterpretations of the law that angered the Lord.

17. The verb is in the perfect tense, *gegonas,* indicating an action that had continuing results. The statement could be translated, "See, you are, and will continue to be, well."

18. Calvin, *Commentary on the Gospel According to John,* vol. I, 193, incorrectly (I think) avows, "All the evils which we endure ought to be imputed to our sins; for the afflictions of men are not accidental, but are so many stripes for our chastisement."

19. Compare John 2:18-20, where John first introduces this motif.

20. A.B. Simpson, "Jesus Only," *Hymns of the Christian Life* (Camp Hill, PA: Christian Publications, Inc., 1978), # 398, stanza 4.

21. A.B. Simpson, "The Branch of Healing," ibid., # 275, stanza 4.

22. Oswald J. Smith, "Saved, Saved, Saved," ibid., # 494.

# 11

# Eternal Life Extended

John 5:16-30

*16 So, because Jesus was doing these things on the Sabbath, the Jews persecuted him. 17 Jesus said to them, "My Father is always at his work to this very day, and I, too, am working." 18 For this reason the Jews tried all the harder to kill him; not only was he breaking the Sabbath, but he was even calling God his own Father, making himself equal with God.*

*19 Jesus gave them this answer: "I tell you the truth, the Son can do nothing by himself; he can do only what he sees his Father doing, because whatever the Father does the Son also does. 20 For the Father loves the Son and shows him all he does. Yes, to your amazement he will show him even greater things than these. 21 For just as the Father raises the dead and gives them life, even so the Son gives life to whom he is pleased to give it. 22 Moreover, the Father judges no one, but has entrusted all judgment to the Son, 23 that all may honor the Son just as they honor the Father. He who does not honor the Son does not honor the Father, who sent him.*

*24 "I tell you the truth, whoever hears my word and believes him who sent me has eternal life and will not be condemned; he has crossed over from death to life. 25 I tell you the truth, a time is coming and has now come when the dead will hear the voice of the Son of God and those who hear will live. 26 For as the Father has life in himself, so he has granted the Son to have life in himself. 27 And he has given him authority to judge because he is the Son of Man.*

*28 "Do not be amazed at this, for a time is coming when all who are in their graves will hear his voice 29 and come out—those who have done*

*good will rise to live, and those who have done evil will rise to be con-*
*demned. 30 By myself I can do nothing; I judge only as I hear, and my*
*judgment is just, for I seek not to please myself but him who sent me."*

In the previous chapter we examined two healing narratives. The first concerned the son of a royal official. Near death at his home in Capernaum,
the boy received new physical life through the intervention of Jesus Christ.
In the other, a man of Jerusalem, paralyzed for thirty-eight years, suddenly
could walk. Both aptly illustrate Jesus' offer of eternal life set forth in the
discourse which is our present text.

What an amazing, powerful discourse it is! In it our Lord makes some astounding claims. Wrote Bishop J.C. Ryle, "Nowhere else in the Gospels do
we find our Lord making such a formal, systematic, orderly, regular statement of His own unity with the Father, His divine commission and authority, and the proofs of His Messiahship, as we find in this discourse."[1] Our
Lord is giving His hearers an *invitation,* a call to *decision.* He is offering
eternal life to all who will believe His claims and submit to His Lordship.
Notice first that this offer of eternal life is extended by . . .

## *The Divine Son (5:16-18)*

The developing pattern of Sabbath healings had aroused Jewish indignation. In response to their unwarranted persecution, Jesus makes this reply:
"My Father is always at his work to this very day, and I, too, am working"
(5:17). At least three things about this statement angered the Jews:

- It implied that the Sabbath-day healings were in reality the work of
  God and therefore not an unlawful breaking of the Sabbath-rest, as
  the Jews were asserting.[2]

- It implied collateral action with God in a field where God's action
  was considered exclusive.[3]

- His use of the words "my Father" implied a relationship of equality
  with God, which in their eyes was blasphemy.[4]

Altogether, the Jews rightly perceived that Jesus was asserting His Divine Sonship. But notice, second, the offer of eternal life is extended by . . .

## *The Obedient Son (5:19)*

"I tell you the truth," said Jesus, "the Son can do nothing by himself; he can do only what he sees his Father doing, because whatever the Father does the Son also does." Doubtless Jesus was remembering boyhood days in the carpenter shop at Nazareth learning His father's craft. As an apprentice, He would never act on His own initiative. Rather, He would watch His father at work and imitate each operation.

Now He lived in the invisible workshop of heaven, obediently doing what He saw His heavenly Father doing. He was not God's rival. On the contrary, He could do nothing but give unqualified obedience to His Father's wishes. He acted in complete unity with Him. Not one moment and not one action was anything but a perfect expression of the life and action of His Father. When He cleansed the temple, when He turned water into wine, He was doing what He "saw" His Father doing. When He healed the son of the royal official, when He caused the paralyzed man to walk, He was following His Father's actions. When He conversed with Nicodemus or the Samaritan woman at the well, He was obeying His Father. Later, when He agonized in Gethsemane, His only concern was that His Father's will should be done. He could pray, "I have brought you glory on earth by completing the work you gave me to do" (John 17:4). He was ever *the Obedient Son.*

Third, the offer of eternal life was extended from . . .

## *The Beloved Son (5:20-23)*

The Son's obedience to the Father was made possible by the Father's intense desire to reveal His will to Jesus. This desire sprang from the tender affection which God the Father had for His Son. God spoke at the transfiguration: "This is my Son, *whom I love*; with him I am well pleased" (Matthew 17:5, emphasis added). He said through Isaiah, "Here is my servant whom I have chosen, *the one I love,* in whom I delight," (see Isaiah 42:1). Remember the parable of the vineyard tenants? "What shall I do?" asked the vineyard Owner. "I will send my son, *whom I love*; perhaps they will respect him" (Luke 20:13, emphasis added). And in our text, Jesus declared, "The Father *loves the Son* and shows him all he does" (5:20, emphasis added).[5] All Jesus' activity on earth was in response to a loving heavenly Father "showing" Him what to do.

But then Jesus went on to say, in effect, "You haven't seen anything yet! If you have been amazed at what you have seen Me do thus far, wait! You will marvel even more when you see the greater works My Father will show Me" (5:20). Godet comments, "The Jews opened their eyes wide at the healing of [a paralyzed] man. What will it be when, at the voice of this same Jesus, mankind will recover life spiritually, and even one day physically! A poor healing amazes them; what will a Pentecost do, and a resurrection from the dead!"[6]

And these are precisely the more amazing works that Jesus went on to define. The miracle of physical healing pales when compared to resurrection from the dead, sovereignly accomplished by the Father (5:21).[7] Whether physical life to one in the grave (11:43-44) or spiritual life to one dead in transgressions (Ephesians 2:4-5), these are miracles!

And the Father has entrusted this power to His Son Jesus (John 5:21). It was He who made the offer of abundant life to Nicodemus. It was He who gave new life to the woman at the well and to the other Samaritans who believed on Him. It is the exalted Jesus who "clothes" all whom the Father gives Him with His regenerating, fruit-bestowing, gift-giving Spirit. And it is Jesus whose voice will call forth the dead from their graves when He returns in glory (5:28-29).

There is another "more amazing" work that the Father has bestowed upon His beloved Son Jesus. That is the work of judgment (5:22)—a work that was already going on in Jesus' earthly life. To the man born blind, whose eyes He opened, Jesus declared, "For judgment I have come into this world, so that the blind will see and those who see will become blind" (9:39).

True, in another context Jesus declares, "As for the person who hears my words but does not keep them, I do not judge him" (12:47). He adds, "I did not come to judge the world, but to save it." The fact is, unbelievers who deliberately reject Christ's offer of pardon bring God's judgment upon themselves. Jesus does not need to judge them.

But the judgment Jesus exercised in His earthly life was only a prelude to His judgment at the last day. Paul advised the Athenians that God "has set a day when he will judge the world with justice by the man he has appointed" (Acts 17:31). Those who find themselves wanting on that day are to be pitied above all others (Revelation 20:15).

Power to give life! Authority to judge! These are the two "greater works" that the Father has entrusted ("shown") to His dearly loved Son. And for what purpose? "That all may honor the Son just as they honor the Father" (John 5:23). In a gem-like passage in his letter to the Philippians, Paul describes this Lord Jesus Christ:

> [Jesus], being in very nature God,
>> did not consider equality with God something to be grasped,
> but made himself nothing,
>> taking the very nature of a servant,
>> being made in human likeness.
> And being found in appearance as a man,
>> he humbled himself
>> and became obedient to death—even death on a cross!
> Therefore God exalted him to the highest place
>> and gave him the name that is above every name,
> that at the name of Jesus every knee should bow,
>> in heaven and on earth and under the earth,
> and every tongue confess that Jesus Christ is Lord,
>> to the glory of God the Father. (Philippians 2:6-11)

> Far above all, far above all;
> God hath exalted Him far above all.
> Low at His footstool, adoring we'll fall;
> God hath exalted Him far above all.[8]

So inseparably united are the Father and the Son whom He loves that to honor One is to honor the Other. In the realm of international diplomacy, to slight an ambassador is to insult the sovereign who posted him. So, in the heavenly kingdom, to dishonor Christ is to dishonor the Father who sent Him (John 5:23).

Finally, notice the offer of eternal life is extended by . . .

## The Empowered Son (5:24-30)

Jesus sums up the declaration of His claims by asserting: "As the Father has life in himself, so he *has granted* the Son to have life in himself. And he *has given him authority* to judge because he is the Son of Man" (John 5:26-27, emphasis added).[9] The risen Jesus declared to His followers: "All authority in heaven and on earth has been given to me" (Matthew 28:18). This is the Father's empowering of the Son. And it is because our Lord has been thus empowered that He can invite all the world to hear His words and believe God (see John 5:24). The one who believes God will assuredly believe His Son.

It is because of this empowering that He can unequivocally assert the *consequences* of believing. Negatively, that person escapes condemnation (eternal death). Positively, the person receives and possesses eternal life (again, see 5:24).

Furthermore, because Jesus is thus empowered by the Father, He can even now *command* life for the spiritually dead (5:25). And because He is thus empowered, He will one day *command* the graves to open. Out of those graves the dead, "great and small" (Revelation 20:12), will rise to appear before Him. They will receive God's just verdict—life for "those who have done good"; condemnation for "those who have done evil" (John 5:28-29).

## Conclusion

What a text! What a Christ! What an offer! Eternal life extended from the hand of the divine, obedient, beloved and empowered Son of God. William Barclay describes the significance of Jesus' words this way:

> For Jesus to speak like this was an act of the most extraordinary courage. He must have known well that to make claims like this would sound the sheerest blasphemy to the orthodox Jewish leaders and was to court death. The man who listened to words like this had only two alternatives—he must either accept Jesus as the Son of God or hate him as a blasphemer.[10]

Yes! Our text confronts us with the necessity of making a destiny-determining decision. We have the awesome freedom to choose. We may believe on the Lord Jesus and have eternal life. Or we may reject His claims and His gracious offer. We have the freedom to choose, but not the freedom to determine the results of our choice. How we choose determines our eternal future. If you, my reader, have not believed on the Lord Jesus, I beg of you to do so now, without further delay.

Again, our text precludes the popular attempt to believe on the true God apart from believing on His Son. There is a "gentle intolerance" about the gospel! We cannot have God without having Jesus. Such truth offends modern mankind, who prefers to believe there are as many ways to God as there are religions in the world. But to espouse that notion is to pronounce the Jesus of the Bible a deluded deceiver. If these words of Jesus recorded in our text are not the truth, it follows that Jesus is not worthy of our allegiance. Thank God, they *are* true!

As believers, we may learn from the relationship between Jesus' work and the work of the Father. Jesus was led by what He saw the Father doing. So we are to have a similar relationship with Jesus. The more we devote ourselves to faithfully doing the will of Christ, the fuller the understanding He gives us. And the better we understand it, the more we desire to enter into it at every point of life.

Jesus' statement in 5:20 about the "greater things" reminds us of a later similar statement He made. He was talking to His disciples shortly before His crucifixion. "I tell you the truth," He said, "anyone who has faith in me will do what I have been doing. He will do even *greater things* than these, because I am going to the Father" (14:12, emphasis added). Jesus was speaking here about the descent of the Holy Spirit, the Pentecostal gift from His Father and Him to believers. It is through God's Spirit that we do even greater works than Jesus did—greater in number and in scope. Fifty days after His resurrection, Jesus' made good His promise to send the Holy Spirit. In an upper room in Jerusalem, the 120 disciples found themselves empowered and their hearts purified by faith. That same promise is open to every New Testament believer of every era. The Spirit has been given; He is ours to receive!

> May the mind of Christ, my Savior,
> 	Live in me from day to day,

By His love and power controlling
    All I do and say.

May the Word of God dwell richly
    In my heart from hour to hour,
So that all may see I triumph
    Only thru His power.

May the love of Jesus fill me,
    As the waters fill the sea;
Him exalting, self abasing—
    This is victory.[11]

### Endnotes

1. Quoted by Leon Morris, *The Gospel According to John* (Grand Rapids, MI: Eerdmans, 1971), 311.
2. The question whether or not God actually rested on the seventh day, debated in the Jewish schools, is superfluous to our discussion here. It was generally concluded that God rested from His work of creation but not from His work on the wicked and on the righteous and His work of sustaining the universe.
3. A strict Jewish monotheist, says C.H. Dodd, *The Interpretation of the Fourth Gospel* (Cambridge: At the University Press, 1970), 327, would take Jesus' words as asserting His competence in and by Himself to perform divine actions. Like Lucifer (Isaiah 13:13), He was setting Himself up as a rival to the one true God.
4. Jews never addressed God as "*my* Father" but rather "*our* Father." They might, if in private prayer, say "Father in Heaven." "My Father" was unheard of and outrageous.
5. Two verbs in Greek, *agapao* and *phileo,* can be translated "to love." While careful study will show that these two can be used interchangeably, *phileo* may seem to be the more affectionate of the two words. F. Godet, *Commentary on the Gospel of St. John*, vol. II (Edinburgh: T. & T. Clarke, 1881), 165, believes that *phileo* expresses the feeling of tenderness which the Father has for His Son. It accords perfectly with the intimacy of the relationship.

   B.F. Westcott, *Commentary on the Gospel According to St. John* (London: John Murray, Albemarle Street, 1967), 85, concurs.
6. Godet, *Commentary on the Gospel of St. John,* vol. II, 167.
7. Morris, *The Gospel According to John,* 314, quotes a rabbinical saying: "Three keys are in the hand of God and they are not given into the hand of any agent: namely, that of the rain (Deuteronomy 28:12), that of the womb (Genesis 30:22), and that of raising the dead (Ezekiel 37:13)."
8. I personally heard Alan Redpath recite this verse in a sermon. I have not been able to document its origin. He said he preferred it to "Oh, that will be glory for me."

9. The reference to the Son of Man takes us back to Daniel 7:13ff. In a night vision Daniel sees "one like a son of man" being given "authority, glory and sovereign power" and "an everlasting dominion that will not pass away."

10. William Barclay, *The Gospel of John*, vol. I (Philadelphia: The Westminster Press, 1975), 187.

11. Kate B. Wilkinson, "May the Mind of Christ, My Saviour," *Hymns of the Christian Life* (Camp Hill, PA: Christian Publications, Inc., 1978), # 257, stanzas 1, 2 and 4.

# 12

# Eternal Life Rejected

John 5:31-47

*31 "If I testify about myself, my testimony is not valid. 32 There is an-other who testifies in my favor, and I know that his testimony about me is valid.*

*33 "You have sent to John and he has testified to the truth. 34 Not that I accept human testimony; but I mention it that you may be saved. 35 John was a lamp that burned and gave light, and you chose for a time to enjoy his light.*

*36 "I have testimony weightier than that of John. For the very work that the Father has given me to finish, and which I am doing, testifies that the Father has sent me. 37 And the Father who sent me has himself testified concerning me. You have never heard his voice nor seen his form, 38 nor does his word dwell in you, for you do not believe the one he sent. 39 You diligently study the Scriptures because you think that by them you possess eternal life. These are the Scriptures that testify about me, 40 yet you re-fuse to come to me to have life.*

*41 "I do not accept praise from men, 42 but I know you. I know that you do not have the love of God in your hearts. 43 I have come in my Father's name, and you do not accept me; but if someone else comes in his own name, you will accept him. 44 How can you believe if you accept praise from one another, yet make no effort to obtain the praise that comes from the only God?*

*45 "But do not think I will accuse you before the Father. Your accuser is Moses, on whom your hopes are set. 46 If you believed Moses, you would*

*believe me, for he wrote about me. 47 But since you do not believe what he*
*wrote, how are you going to believe what I say?"*

How heartbreaking was the response of the Jews to the invitation in Jesus' heartfelt words! Jesus had assured them, "Whoever hears my word and believes him who sent me has eternal life and will not be condemned; he has crossed over from death to life" (5:24). Faced with the overwhelming evidence in Jesus' words and works, anyone of rational mind should have believed in Him. Instead, our Lord was compelled to utter what are perhaps His most woeful words ever: ". . . yet you refuse to come to me to have life" (5:40). He was describing people in whose hearts was what the Scottish preacher, Alexander Whyte, called "a stone of obstinacy." These were people who *would* not see. They were rejecting, resolutely, a fivefold objective witness to Jesus. None but arrogant lovers of the praise of men (5:44) would dare question Jesus' verity.

In a scathing rebuke, our Lord unmasked their jealously evil hearts. He confronted them with the testimony concerning Himself that they so proudly had rejected. Conceding that a single witness could not be received as truth,[1] He charged them with rejecting a massive bank of evidence. First was . . .

## *The Testimony of John (5:33-35)*[2]

The Baptist, speaking prophetically, had witnessed to Jesus' Messiahship. When "the Jews of Jerusalem sent priests and Levites to ask him who he was" (1:19), he had answered clearly. He Himself was neither the Messiah nor the Prophet. He had been sent to prepare the way for Messiah. He had identified Jesus as the atoning sin-bearer and the anointed Spirit-baptizer, the very Son of God (1:23-34). About all this, Jesus reminds His antagonists (5:33). Not that His claims were dependent on human witness (5:34). Even though the forerunner was off the scene,[3] his testimony, which they could understand and appreciate, remained in their minds.[4] If they would but believe it, as others had done, they would be saved (5:34).

They ought to have taken heed to John's message. True, he was not *"the* light" (1:8), but he was a burning lamp that brightened the path until daybreak. His earnest calls to repent, his solemn warnings and his unwavering witness to Christ showed men the way to God. Then, when the "true light" (1:9) appeared, his work of preparation was complete (5:35). Alas! These Jews did not take John's revival message seriously. That is reflected in Jesus' description of their response to it: "you chose for a time to enjoy[5] his light" (5:35). They rejoiced in the prospect that God would intervene on Israel's behalf. They exulted in God's gift of a prophet to their generation. But they misunderstood His mission, disregarded His warnings and spurned His witness.

Not only did the Jews reject the testimony of John the Baptist, second, they rejected . . .

## *The Testimony of Jesus' Works (5:36)*

In our Lord's view, His miracles carried even more weight than John's spoken testimony (5:36). Jesus said, in effect, *"You Jews* received your witness concerning me from John the Baptist, a witness that was assuredly the truth. But the testimony which *I* accept and rely upon, *in contrast to yours,* is not a human, but a Divine testimony."[6] This divine testimony was undoubtedly comprised of everything[7] that Jesus was commissioned and enabled by the Father to do. Especially it encompassed those miracles of healing which took place before the very eyes of these Jewish unbelievers. They had seen many of His miraculous signs (2:23). Some of them had witnessed the healing of the paralyzed man at the pool of Bethesda. And they would yet see more of these works until He had finished everything assigned to Him by His Father (5:36). But the unbelieving Jews, prejudiced by malice, willfully refused to recognize these works as attestations of Jesus' Messiahship.[8]

Not only did the Jews reject the testimony of John the Baptist and the testimony of Jesus' works. They rejected, third, . . .

## *The Testimony of the Father (5:37-38)*

Already, Jesus had claimed that His Father ("another") was bearing true witness to His divine Sonship (5:32). Now He re-echoed this truth in the words, "And the Father who sent me has himself testified concerning me" (5:37). One may well ask, "How has the Father given this testimony?" Three possibilities come to mind. (1) There was that awesome moment during Jesus' baptism when the Voice from heaven spoke. "This is my Son, whom I love; with him I am well pleased" (Matthew 3:17).[9] (2) There was also the Father's testimony in Old Testament prophecy.[10] (3) And there is the unseen witness by the Spirit of God in each person's heart. John says in his first letter, "Anyone who believes in the Son of God has this testimony in his heart" (1 John 5:10).[11]

But the Jews rejected God's testimony to Jesus. He described their unbelief in a threefold assertion (5:37-38) graphically explained by Morris:

> (i) They have never heard God's voice. Moses heard that voice (Exodus 33:11), but they are no true followers of Moses, otherwise they would have heard God's voice in Jesus (3:34; 17:8). (ii) They have never seen God's form. Israel [Jacob] saw that form (Genesis 32:30f), but they are no true Israelites. Were they, they would have seen God in Jesus (14:9). (iii) They have not God's word abiding in them. The Psalmist laid up God's word in his heart (Psalm 119:11), but they do not share his religious experience. Had they done so they would have received that word from Jesus (17:14).[12]

The truth is that there can be no life-giving assimilation of the Word of God apart from faith in Jesus. As Barrett rightly states: "The observer cannot sit in judgment upon [the Word] and then decide whether or not he will believe in Jesus. He must believe in Jesus first and then he will receive the direct testimony from God."[13]

This important truth was illustrated to me in an evening's intense discussion with a former theology student. He had withdrawn from his pastoral training because of "all the contradictions in Scripture, its irreconcilable inconsistencies, its historical inaccuracies." He insisted he would have to find clear answers to these problems before he could ever believe on the Lord Jesus. When I presented to him what to me were logical answers to his problems, he was unable to receive them as such. Unwilling to commit himself to One who would be his Master, he rejected, as did the Jews, the testimony of the Father.

Fourth, the Jews rejected . . .

## The Testimony of Scripture (5:39-44)

A.W. Tozer saw a vast difference between being "Bible-taught" and "Spirit-taught."[14] He did not mean that one can be guided by the Spirit without the Scriptures. Rather, a person can be intellectually familiar with the Scriptures without their truth impacting his or her life. Such was the case with the Jews who opposed Jesus. They were indeed Bible-taught. They believed that the very act of carefully studying the letter of the Law gained for them eternal life (5:39).[15] But they were not Spirit-taught. With all their diligent investigation, they failed to recognize Christ in the Bible. Consequently they refused to come to Him who alone is the only source of eternal life (5:40). How utterly heartbreaking! One can hear our Lord's painful lament over the unbelieving nation: "O Jerusalem, Jerusalem, you who kill the prophets and stone those sent to you, how often I have longed to gather your children together, as a hen gathers her chicks under her wings, but you were not willing. Look, your house is left to you desolate" (Matthew 23:37-38).

Our Lord now gets to the very core of the Jews' problem. How alluring to the unregenerate heart is the praise of men! Jesus loved His Father intensely. He desired only God's approval. What others said or thought about Him did not matter (John 5:41). The Jewish leaders, in whose hearts was no real love for God (5:42), "loved praise from men more than praise from God" (12:43). They prayed to be seen praying. They loved the front seats in the synagogues. They loved the deferential greetings of men on the street. And the praise of men shaped their attitudes and behavior toward Jesus. Not love for God, but credibility with peers determined their behavior. They were quite prepared to listen to any self-accredited prophet. If he confirmed their own opinions, he would receive their applause. But for fear of what others would think, they refused to listen to Jesus. Jesus had come "in [His] Father's name" (that is, with His Father's authority). He expressed everything the Father stood for (5:43). But for these His antagonists, with their man-centered focus, how could there be any saving faith in Jesus (5:44)?

Finally, fifth, these unbelieving Jews rejected . . .

## *The Testimony of Moses (5:45-47)*

Concluding one of his sermons, Alexander Whyte dramatized the fate of the rich ruler who refused Jesus' offer of eternal life. As he portrayed the moral man's descent into hell, Whyte leaned over the pulpit. Imitating the terrifying laughter of demons, he cried out, "He kept the Law!"

In the final verses of our text, Jesus addresses men who hung their hope of eternal life on law-keeping. But they had not allowed the holy law of Moses to do its intended work—to convict them of sin. Through the law they should have sensed their deep need of a Savior. Its symbolism of priests and sacrifices and ordinances was to point guilty sinners to Messiah. It was He on whom their hopes should have been set. He would make the real atonement for sins. He was the one great High Priest who could plead their cause before the Father. But their self-righteous hearts missed the whole meaning of the law. And so Jesus transformed Moses, their hoped-for advocate, into a prosecuting attorney. Moses would be their accuser before God the Judge. It would not be Jesus, the Savior, who would accuse them at heaven's bar. It would be Moses, whose message their darkened minds failed to grasp (5:45-47).

We can almost hear Moses's opening statement as he rises to present heaven's case against the Jews:

"Your Honor: Under Your Spirit's inspiration I wrote what these defendants call the *Torah.* I set down the promises You made to our Fathers—Abraham, Isaac and Jacob. I chronicled our miraculous deliverance from slavery in Egypt. I recorded the commandments You gave us—Your law. And the beautiful design of Your earthly dwelling place, the tabernacle. I wrote out the sacrificial rituals of Your altar and the ordinances of the priesthood. I foretold Your promised Prophet. In all these things, I was writing of Him in whom they would find all of these things fulfilled. If the defendants had understood the symbols, they would have known the law was pointing guilty sinners to Jesus. They would have believed this One of whom I wrote. But they missed the whole meaning of the law. I accuse them of rejecting not only me and my message, but their Messiah."

We wait to hear the rebuttal of a defense attorney, but no one stands to plead their cause. *They have no defense.* And as they descend into the abode of the doomed, the laughing, mocking demons cry out, "They kept the Law!"

## Conclusion

Faced with incontrovertible testimony to the truth of His claims, Jesus' persecutors rejected outright the evidence. The testimony of the Baptist, Jesus' miracles, the Father's voice, the Scriptures, the Mosaic law—all failed to draw the Jews to Jesus. What unspeakable hardness of heart! What satanically wrought blindness! What awful depravity of the human will!

Of Jesus it could never be said that some flaw of character caused people to reject His message. There was no want of clarity in His presentation of truth. He lacked no Spirit-bestowed anointing. There was no deficiency in His message. His hearers had only themselves to blame. The Sower was wise and faithful. The Seed was living and powerful. The fault was with the soil.[16]

Let faithful, prayerful, godly, Spirit-filled pastors and evangelists remember this. Let them take heart from Jesus' experience. When the message they so clearly preach fails to produce faith, they may not be at fault.

Consider how often a negative response to the Word of God is because people desire others' approval rather than God's. Who knows what untold spiritual blessings are forfeited through the fear of what people will think or say!

I think of a man who, Sunday after Sunday, literally shook when invited to receive the Lord Jesus into his life. Had he responded, he would have lost family, business, friends—all on earth that was dear to him. He would not pay the price.

That same fear has prevented believers from entering into the fullness of Christ. "Will my peers reject me if I am filled with the Spirit?" they wonder. "Will I be considered a fanatic if I earnestly seek and find all that God has for me in Christ?" "Will they think I am trying to be more spiritual than they?" These and other questions serve to frighten hungry people from the deeper life.

I cannot experience the "full blessing of Pentecost"[17] until all that matters is what God thinks about me. If Christ is to become my all, every idol that would usurp God's place must be torn down, no matter how legitimate or harmless it may appear in the eyes of even fellow Christians. A woman once approached a missionary speaker whose life evidenced a deep knowledge of God. "I'd give all I have to know God the way you know Him," she said. The missionary replied, "That's exactly what it cost me!"

Gerhard Tersteegen's prayer might well be yours—and mine—as we seek to experience the deeper Christian life:

> Is there a thing beneath the sun
> That strives with Thee my heart to share?
> Ah! tear it thence, and reign alone,
> The Lord of every motion there;
> Then shall my heart from earth be free,
> When it has found repose in Thee.[18]

### Endnotes

1. Jesus would have had Deuteronomy 19:15 in mind. The NIV has Jesus saying that His testimony alone would not be "valid." The Greek word *alethes* would better be translated "dependable." The validity of the testimony was not in question, but that it was a single witness.
2. Actually the first objective testimony to which He refers in 5:32 as that of "another" was the testimony of the Father, to which witness He returned in 5:37.
3. Note the verb "was" in 5:35. It may allude to John's imprisonment. It could allude to his death at Herod's hand (see Mark 6:16ff).
4. The verb "has testified" is in the Greek perfect tense, which indicates a completed past action with lasting results going on into the present.
5. Literally, "to rejoice." The word indicates overflowing, enthusiastic happiness. See Leon Morris, *The Gospel According to John* (Grand Rapids, MI: Eerdmans, 1971), 327. Marcus Dods, *"The Gospel of St. John," The Expositor's Greek New Testament,* vol. I (Grand Rapids, MI: Eerdmans, n.d.), 744, writes, "The expression seems intended to suggest the thoughtless and brief play of insects in the sunshine or around a lamp." He gets this metaphor from another writer, Hausrath, who describes the Jews as "gnats playing in the sunshine." Dods continues: "[They are] like children following in a bridal procession, dancing in the torchlight; the type of sentimental religionists reveling in their own emotions."
6. The italicized words fairly represent the import of the original Greek text.
7. Such as His authoritative teachings, His exorcisms, His judgments, His healing miracles, His raising of the dead and all His other supernatural acts.
8. In fact, the Jews attributed Jesus' exorcisms to ability given Him by the devil (Matthew 12:24). They accused Him of being demonized (John 8:48).
9. F. Godet, *Commmentary on the Gospel of St. John*, vol. II (Edinburgh: T. & T. Clarke, 1881), 191, citing other earlier interpreters, thinks that this is the only appropriate explanation of Jesus' statement.

10. John Calvin, *Commentary on the Gospel According to John*, vol. I (Edinburgh: The Calvin Translation Society, 1847), 216, for example, writes, "I explain, therefore, that God testified concerning his Son whenever in past times he held out to the ancient people the hope of salvation, or promised that the kingdom of Israel would be fully restored. In this manner the Jews must have formed an idea of Christ from the Prophets before he was manifested in the flesh." Similarly Morris, *The Gospel According to John,* 329, writes, "The entire revelation of the Father from the very beginning has prepared the way for the coming of the Son."

11. William Barclay, *The Gospel of John*, vol. 1 (Philadelphia: The Westminster Press, 1975), 197.

12. Morris, *The Gospel According to John,* 329.

13. Quoted by Morris, *The Gospel According to John,* 330.

14. Tozer writes on pages 76-77 of *The Pursuit of Man* (Camp Hill, PA: Christian Publications, Inc., 1978): "The doctrine of the inability of the human mind and the need for divine illumination is so fully developed in the New Testament that it is nothing short of astonishing that we should have gone so far astray from the whole thing. Fundamentalism has stood aloof from the liberal in self-conscious superiority and has on its own part fallen into error, the error of textualism, which is simply orthodoxy without the Holy Ghost. Everywhere among conservatives we find persons who are Bible-taught but not Spirit-taught. They conceive truth to be something which they can grasp with the mind. If a man holds to the fundamentals of the Christian faith he is thought to possess divine truth. But it does not follow. There is no truth apart from the Spirit. The most brilliant intellect may be imbecilic when confronted with the mysteries of God. For a man to understand revealed truth requires an act of God equal to the original act which inspired the text."

15. As is indicated, for example, in the saying of Hillel, "The more study of the Law, the more life. . . . If he has gained for himself words of the Law he has gained for himself life in the world to come." Quoted by Morris, *The Gospel According to John*, 330.

   The KJV translates 5:39 in the imperative mood: "Search the Scriptures." The NIV, considering the context, uses the indicative mood: "You diligently search the Scriptures . . . ."

16. This is the message of the parable of the sower in Luke 8. The variety of soils is symbolic of the spiritual receptivity of the hearers of the word. Jesus' admonition is, "Take heed how you hear" (KJV).

17. Andrew Murray's description of the infilling of the Spirit.

18. "Thou Hidden Love," *The Church Hymnal* (London: Oxford University Press, n.d.), # 459. Translated from the German by John Wesley.

# Part IV

## *Questions for Reflection or Discussion*

1. How do the two stories of John 4:43-5:15 illustrate the gift of eternal life which Jesus offers?

2. What may believers learn about their relationship to Jesus from His relationship with the Father?

3. What three things about Jesus' statement in John 5:17 angered the Jews?

4. According to John 5:31-47, what testimonies concerning Jesus did the Jews reject?

5. What are some of the truths that Moses wrote about Christ?

6. How could accepting praise from men hinder our deeper life walk with God?

*Part V*


# The Provision of the Son

John 6:1-71

# Bread for the Outer Man

John 6:1-15

*Some time after this, Jesus crossed to the far shore of the Sea of Galilee (that is, the Sea of Tiberias), 2 and a great crowd of people followed him because they saw the miraculous signs he had performed on the sick. 3 Then Jesus went up on a mountainside and sat down with his disciples. 4 The Jewish Passover Feast was near.*

*5 When Jesus looked up and saw a great crowd coming toward him, he said to Philip, "Where shall we buy bread for these people to eat?" 6 He asked this only to test him, for he already had in mind what he was going to do.*

*7 Philip answered him, "Eight months' wages would not buy enough bread for each one to have a bite!"*

*8 Another of his disciples, Andrew, Simon Peter's brother, spoke up, 9 "Here is a boy with five small barley loaves and two small fish, but how far will they go among so many?"*

*10 Jesus said, "Have the people sit down." There was plenty of grass in that place, and the men sat down, about five thousand of them. 11 Jesus then took the loaves, gave thanks, and distributed to those who were seated as much as they wanted. He did the same with the fish.*

*12 When they had all had enough to eat, he said to his disciples, "Gather the pieces that are left over. Let nothing be wasted." 13 So they gathered them and filled twelve baskets with the pieces of the five barley loaves left over by those who had eaten.*

*14 After the people saw the miraculous sign that Jesus did, they began to*

*say, "Surely this is the Prophet who is to come into the world." 15 Jesus,
knowing that they intended to come and make him king by force, withdrew
again to a mountain by himself.*

It was time for a season of solitude![1] For one thing, the disciples had been on the road in an evangelistic mission. Jesus had commissioned—and enabled—them to preach repentance, exorcize demons and heal the sick (Mark 6:7-13). A relaxed debriefing, which the incessant crowds prevented, was essential (6:30-31).

Furthermore, news had reached Jesus of John the Baptist's execution. The courageous reformer had dared to rebuke Herod the tetrarch for his immoral relationship with his sister-in-law, Herodius. It had aroused the anger of that evil woman, who succeeded in having the Baptist beheaded (see Matthew 14:3-12). Jesus and His disciples needed a quiet time to reflect on John and his faithful ministry. They needed to sort out the implications of his untimely death.

Not only that, but word was out that this same Herod was anxious to meet with Jesus (Luke 9:7-9). He hoped to discover exactly who this Man really was. For safety's sake, it was prudent for Jesus to avoid such an encounter with "that fox" (13:32). He was not to be trusted. Thus Jesus and His disciples, bent on restful solitude, privately set out across Galilee for the northeastern shore. Their objective was a quiet hillside not far from the village of Bethsaida (John 6:1-4). John observes that it was near Passover time.[2]

### The Hungry Crowd Gathered (6:1-4)

Not for long was the little band to find the seclusion they sought. Ever since His return to Galilee from the stressful events in Jerusalem (chapter 5), Jesus had been continually hounded by crowds. They wanted to witness the healing miracles He was performing.[3] Not surprisingly, therefore, His departure for the other shore could not be kept secret. The eager crowd took off on foot (Mark 6:33). Hurrying around the north shore of Galilee, they found Jesus on the hillside with His disciples (John 6:5).

Would He send them away? *His* designs for solitude were clearly being thwarted. Yet His compassionate heart would not let Him ignore the needs of these "sheep without a shepherd" (Mark 6:34). Forsaking His own plans and acquiescing to the plans of His Father, He took up again His healing and teaching ministry (Matthew 14:14; Mark 6:34). As the day wore on, He was mindful of the people's need for physical nourishment. Thus Jesus proceeded with His already determined plan of action (John 6:6). Part of it was to test a disciple's creativity and level of faith in a well-nigh impossible situation.[4]

## *The Realistic Disciple Tested (6:5-9)*

Philip was from Bethsaida (1:44). Therefore it was natural for Jesus to consult him concerning the availability of food in the area (6:5). But even with an adequate source, Philip the realist could not imagine how the thirteen of them could possibly afford it. By later count there were 5,000 men, plus women and children! Food for that many would require more than 200 denarii. It was an amount far beyond their meager resources.[5] It did not occur to him to say, "Master, You could do here the same sort of miracle we saw You do at Cana!"

Meanwhile, Andrew had been scouting the crowd. He found a boy[6] with "five small barley loaves and two small fish" (6:9).[7] Even for the youth it was an inadequate picnic lunch. But as we might expect of Andrew, he brought the boy to Jesus. Like Philip, Andrew could see only the impossibility of the situation (6:9). Neither did it occur to him to suggest, "Master, there must be something *You* can do about our need." Obviously, the disciples were failing the test. How much they had yet to learn about the power of God! How much they needed to learn of faith in His bounteous goodness!

## *The Benevolent Miracle Wrought (6:10-13)*

It was time for Jesus to put His miracle plan into operation! He would show Philip and Andrew and His other disciples that with God nothing is impossible. He would give the people another sign that He was the Son of God. With calm authority, He instructed His disciples to have the people (literally, the "men"[8]) recline[9] on the green grass (6:10 and Mark 6:39). We can imagine with Alexander Maclaren that "some of them seated themselves with a scoff; and some with a quiet smile of incredulity; and some half sheepishly and reluctantly; and some in mute expectancy; and some in foolish wonder."[10] In what must have been a poignant moment, Jesus took the barley loaves from the hands of the boy. Lifting His face toward heaven (Mark 6:41), He returned thanks to God (John 6:11).

"Blessed art Thou, O Lord our God, who causest to come forth bread from the earth" was the mealtime prayer spoken by every Jewish father. It may have been Jesus' prayer that day.

Then the miracle happened! It was not that Jesus encouraged the selfish to share their food with those who had none. That would never have produced the results described in 6:12-13! Nor was it a sacramental meal in which each person received but a tiny fragment. Hungry people are not satisfied with crumbs. What happened that day for all to see was nothing less than a miraculous sign. With the solemnity befitting a Passover meal, Jesus broke the bread, evenly distributing the pieces to His disciples. The disciples, in turn, passed their portions to the first person in the "groups of about fifty each" (Luke 9:14). As the food was passed, person to person, section upon section, each took as much as he or she wanted.[11] And the *food left over* filled twelve baskets![12]

## *The Political Response Resisted (6:14-15)*

The response of the people to such a miraculous sign created one of the most dangerous moments in Jesus' ministry. They were convinced He was the Prophet promised by Moses (see Deuteronomy 18:18), indeed, their Messiah. The fiercely nationalistic throng was prepared right then to revolt against Rome under Christ's leadership (John 6:15). Once before, following His baptism, Jesus had resisted Satan's temptation to receive an earthly kingdom (see Luke 4:5-8). Now, again, this insistent crowd posed the same temptation. Had He caved in, He would have forfeited forever His spiritual kingdom. Our hope of salvation through His death and resurrection would have been eternally dashed.

What the crowd was pressing upon Him was not the will of His Father. Jesus knew that. The cross had to precede the crown! Jesus therefore took two strategic steps to resist the coercion of the multitude. He immediately sent His disciples to the west side of the lake,[13] thus preventing them from being unduly influenced by the powerful sentiments of the zealots. They had not yet come to understand the true nature of His mission. They might very easily have sided with the crowd's political ambitions. Besides sending away His disciples, He dismissed the crowd and "withdrew[14] again to a mountain by himself" (John 6:15). There in prayer, away from the shouting crowd, He was strengthened in His Father's will (Matthew 14:23).

## *Conclusion*

There is much that we may take to heart from our text. We see, first, Jesus' compassionate concern that the people be fed. Mark expresses Jesus' word to His disciples as a command: "You give them something to eat" (Mark 6:37). Still today our Lord's compassion reaches out to the starving multitudes of earth. We hold that our primary work as believers is to proclaim the gospel to those who have never heard it. Yet we cannot minister to mankind's spiritual needs if we ignore their physical needs. Such an attitude demonstrates an inadequate, unbiblical view of people's unified nature. Nor dare we feed the hungry just as an entree for the gospel. Whether or not a hungry person is receptive to spiritual bread, we have an obligation to provide that person with physical bread. Thus our support of agencies which care for the physical person is both appropriate and imperative. We must attach no strings to our ministry to the hungry.

Second, our text encourages us to believe that nothing is impossible with God. The disciples were faced with the hopeless task of feeding the multitude with five loaves and two fish! Their own resources were totally inadequate. Yet it was in that very circumstance that the Lord displayed His adequacy. In one of his deeper-life sermons, Allan Redpath tells how the proud owner of a brand new Rolls Royce wrote to the company to ascertain the horsepower of the car's engine. It happened to be information that the manufacturer did not make public. When he received no reply, he wrote again. And again. Finally, in exasperation, he fired off a telegram to Rolls Royce, demanding, "What is the horsepower of my engine?" The company sent back a one-word reply: "Adequate."

So with the resources our God has made available to His children. They are totally adequate to meet every need. Is it wisdom we lack? We may ask of God "who gives generously to all without finding fault" (James 1:5). Are we unable to carry out a God-appointed task or to live up to His calling? We may know God's "incomparably great power" that "raised [Jesus] from the dead" and seated Him at God's right hand (Ephesians 1:19-20). The resources are ours in Christ. Too often we fail to appropriate them.

So often we are like the farmer who lived and died in abject poverty. Only after his death was a vast supply of oil discovered under his land. He had been a potential millionaire all his life! How many of the Lord's people are living like spiritual paupers! They have never discovered that all they need for life and godliness is in Christ Jesus. It is to be received through faith.

Third, like the boy in our text, we need to put at Jesus' disposal whatever we are and however much we have. Someone has remarked that God looks less at our *ability* than at our *availability*. He is not looking for great talent as much as for total yieldedness. He is looking for clean, surrendered people whom He can fill with His Spirit.

Somewhere in her writings, Amy Carmichael observes that we need not ask God to "use us." If we are clean and filled with His Spirit, He *will* use us. Mary E. Maxwell understood this well when she wrote "Channels Only":

> How I praise Thee, precious Saviour,
>     That Thy love laid hold of me;
> Thou hast saved and cleansed and filled me
>     That I might Thy channel be.
>
> Emptied that Thou shouldest fill me,
>     A clean vessel in Thy hand;
> With no power but as Thou givest
>     Graciously with each command.
>
> Witnessing Thy power to save me,
>     Setting free from self and sin,
> Thou who boughtest to possess me,
>     In Thy fullness, Lord, come in.
>
> Jesus, fill now with Thy Spirit
>     Hearts that full surrender know;

That the streams of living water
From our inner man may flow.[15]

### Endnotes

1. Some of the details that follow, which John omits from his account, are provided by the Synoptic Gospels. See especially Matthew 14:13-21; Mark 6:30-44; Luke 9:16.

2. There may be more to this than just a chronological reference. F. Godet, *Commentary on the Gospel of St. John,* vol. II (Edinburgh: T. & T. Clarke, 1881), 203, has this insightful comment on John's reference to the Passover: "Proscribed to a certain extent, [Jesus] is Himself prevented from celebrating the Passover at Jerusalem; and seeing the multitude flocking after Him in the desert, perishing for the bread of life, His heart is touched with pity, and He immediately recognizes in this unexpected circumstance the Father's signal. Transporting Himself in thought to Jerusalem, He says to Himself, for His disciples, for the multitude: We, too, will keep a Passover!"

3. It is significant that the verbs in 6:2 translated "followed," "saw" and "performed" are all in the Greek imperfect tense, which signifies continuous action in the past. The NIV seems to miss this nuance.

4. John has *Jesus* taking the initiative concerning the feeding of the crowd. In the Synoptics the disciples broach the subject. See Matthew 14:15; Mark 6:35-37; Luke 9:12-13. For John the important detail is Jesus' question, "Where shall we buy bread for these people to eat?"

5. The NIV helps us to know the practical value of this amount—"eight months' wages." William Barclay, *The Gospel of John,* vol. I (Philadelphia: The Westminster Press, 1975), 202, has it, "more than six months' wages." One denarius was the standard day's wage for a working man.

6. The Greek word is *paidarion,* "little boy, child." The word can also be translated "a youth" (William F. Arndt and F. Wilbur Gingrich, *A Greek-English Lexicon of the New Testament* [Chicago: The University of Chicago Press, 1957], 608).

7. According to Barclay, *The Gospel of John,* vol. I, 202, barley bread was the cheapest of all bread—the contemptible bread of the very poor. The "fish" may have been a kind of salted fish eaten as a relish along with the barley bread.

8. The Greek uses the generic *anthropous.* John then goes on to tell us that the number of males *(andres)* that sat down was 5,000. Only the men were counted. Eastern women and children always kept a respectable distance from husbands and guests.

9. The verb is *anapipto,* "to lie down," "to recline." The green grass provided a comfortable picnic atmosphere. Mark observes that "they sat down in groups of hundreds and fifties" (6:40). It was at Jesus' order (see Luke 9:14), doubtless to expedite the distribution of food and, as it turned out, to count the males present.

10. Alexander Maclaren, *The Gospel According to St. John,* vol. I (London: Hodder and Stoughton, 1907), 257.

11. One is reminded of the similar miracle during the ministry of Elisha (2 Kings 4:42-44). Twenty loaves of barley bread were multiplied to feed 100 men, with bread to spare, as the Lord had promised.

12. Barclay, *The Gospel of John,* 203, informs us that at Jewish feasts the regular practice was to leave something (called the Peah) for the servants.

13. The wording of Matthew 14:22 and Mark 6:45 makes this clear.

14. George R. Beasley-Murray, *Word Biblical Themes* (Dallas, TX: Word Publishing, 1989), 58, observes that important early manuscripts of John's Gospel do not support the reading *anechoresen*, "withdrew." They use a much stronger verb, *pheugei*, "to flee." He thinks that the reading "He withdrew" is a later watering down of the text by copyists, who could not believe that Jesus would actually flee. That Jesus "fled" from the scene lends credence to the idea that acquiescing to the Galilean crowd was indeed tempting.
15. Mary E. Maxwell, "Channels Only," *Hymns of the Christian Life* (Camp Hill, PA: Christian Publications, Inc., 1978), # 375.

# 14

# Bread for the Inner Man

John 6:16-71

*16 When evening came, his disciples went down to the lake, 17 where they got into a boat and set off across the lake for Capernaum. By now it was dark, and Jesus had not yet joined them. 18 A strong wind was blowing and the waters grew rough. 19 When they had rowed three or three and a half miles, they saw Jesus approaching the boat, walking on the water; and they were terrified. 20 But he said to them, "It is I; don't be afraid." 21 Then they were willing to take him into the boat, and immediately the boat reached the shore where they were heading.*

*22 The next day the crowd that had stayed on the opposite shore of the lake realized that only one boat had been there, and that Jesus had not entered it with his disciples, but that they had gone away alone. 23 Then some boats from Tiberias landed near the place where the people had eaten the bread after the Lord had given thanks. 24 Once the crowd realized that neither Jesus nor his disciples were there, they got into the boats and went to Capernaum in search of Jesus.*

*25 When they found him on the other side of the lake, they asked him, "Rabbi, when did you get here?"*

*26 Jesus answered, "I tell you the truth, you are looking for me, not because you saw miraculous signs but because you ate the loaves and had your fill. 27 Do not work for food that spoils, but for food that endures to eternal life, which the Son of Man will give you. On him God the Father has placed his seal of approval."*

28 Then they asked him, "What must we do to do the works God requires?"

29 Jesus answered, "The work of God is this: to believe in the one he has
sent."

30 So they asked him, "What miraculous sign then will you give that we
may see it and believe you? What will you do? 31 Our forefathers ate the
manna in the desert; as it is written: 'He gave them bread from heaven to
eat.' "

32 Jesus said to them, "I tell you the truth, it is not Moses who has given
you the bread from heaven, but it is my Father who gives you the true
bread from heaven. 33 For the bread of God is he who comes down from
heaven and gives life to the world."

34 "Sir," they said, "from now on give us this bread."

35 Then Jesus declared, "I am the bread of life. He who comes to me will
never go hungry, and he who believes in me will never be thirsty. 36 But as
I told you, you have seen me and still you do not believe. 37 All that the Father gives me will come to me, and whoever comes to me I will never drive
away. 38 For I have come down from heaven not to do my will but to do the
will of him who sent me. 39 And this is the will of him who sent me, that I
shall lose none of all that he has given me, but raise them up at the last day.
40 For my Father's will is that everyone who looks to the Son and believes
in him shall have eternal life, and I will raise him up at the last day."

41 At this the Jews began to grumble about him because he said, "I am
the bread that came down from heaven." 42 They said, "Is this not Jesus,
the son of Joseph, whose father and mother we know? How can he now
say, 'I came down from heaven'?"

43 "Stop grumbling among yourselves," Jesus answered. 44 "No one
can come to me unless the Father who sent me draws him, and I will raise
him up at the last day. 45 It is written in the Prophets: 'They will all be
taught by God.' Everyone who listens to the Father and learns from him
comes to me. 46 No one has seen the Father except the one who is from
God; only he has seen the Father. 47 I tell you the truth, he who believes
has everlasting life. 48 I am the bread of life. 49 Your forefathers ate the
manna in the desert, yet they died. 50 But here is the bread that comes
down from heaven, which a man may eat and not die. 51 I am the living
bread that came down from heaven. If anyone eats of this bread, he will
live forever. This bread is my flesh, which I will give for the life of the
world."

52 Then the Jews began to argue sharply among themselves, "How can
this man give us his flesh to eat?"

53 Jesus said to them, "I tell you the truth, unless you eat the flesh of the
Son of Man and drink his blood, you have no life in you. 54 Whoever eats

*my flesh and drinks my blood has eternal life, and I will raise him up at the last day. 55 For my flesh is real food and my blood is real drink. 56 Whoever eats my flesh and drinks my blood remains in me, and I in him. 57 Just as the living Father sent me and I live because of the Father, so the one who feeds on me will live because of me. 58 This is the bread that came down from heaven. Your forefathers ate manna and died, but he who feeds on this bread will live forever." 59 He said this while teaching in the synagogue in Capernaum.*

*60 On hearing it, many of his disciples said, "This is a hard teaching. Who can accept it?"*

*61 Aware that his disciples were grumbling about this, Jesus said to them, "Does this offend you? 62 What if you see the Son of Man ascend to where he was before! 63 The Spirit gives life; the flesh counts for nothing. The words I have spoken to you are spirit and they are life. 64 Yet there are some of you who do not believe." For Jesus had known from the beginning which of them did not believe and who would betray him. 65 He went on to say, "This is why I told you that no one can come to me unless the Father has enabled him."*

*66 From this time many of his disciples turned back and no longer followed him.*

*67 "You do not want to leave too, do you?" Jesus asked the Twelve.*

*68 Simon Peter answered him, "Lord, to whom shall we go? You have the words of eternal life. 69 We believe and know that you are the Holy One of God."*

*70 Then Jesus replied, "Have I not chosen you, the Twelve? Yet one of you is a devil!" 71 (He meant Judas, the son of Simon Iscariot, who, though one of the Twelve, was later to betray him.)*

On the grassy slope near Bethsaida above Galilee's eastern shore, Jesus had fed a famished crowd. Someone even took a head count: 5,000 men plus women and children. That miraculous provision of physical nourishment for the multitude symbolized the spiritual truths set forth by Jesus in our present text.

Jesus' twelve disciples had set out by boat to return to Capernaum. Jesus remained behind to pray (Matthew 14:23). Sometime after dark, still on the lake, the disciples encountered strong winds and rough waters. They were terrified when they saw a human apparition walk toward them on the water. When Jesus identified Himself, their fear melted, and they took Him aboard. "Immediately," John informs us, "the boat reached the shore where they were heading" (John 6:16-21). The episode reminds us that Jesus then—and yet—cares for His followers in the turbulence of life. He will see us safely to the shore!

The multitude who had been supernaturally fed also made their way to Capernaum looking for Jesus. They concluded He had somehow joined His disciples there. Finding Him, they demanded to know how long He had been there (6:25). Jesus ignored their question and confronted them with their real motive in seeking Him (6:26). They had seen the food miracle only as a hopeful sign of more, failing to perceive its symbolic significance. Against that background, Jesus entered the Capernaum synagogue (see 6:59) and commenced His discourse on the bread of life. In effect, He explained the symbolism of the food miracle.

The discourse sets forth seven vital truths concerning Jesus, the Bread of Life. First, He is the . . .

## *Heaven-Sent Bread (6:32-33, 38, 41-42, 50)*

Six times Jesus informed His audience that the unspoiling bread (6:27) needed for their spiritual welfare had its source in heaven, not on earth. The material manna associated with Moses has been superceded by the real bread from heaven. God had sent the physical manna to Israel. Now God was giving to the world the spiritual reality, of which the manna was only a picture (6:32). The manna was, in fact, a valuable type of the Bread of Life. It came down from God to undeserving sinners, whom it preserved and nourished. But only in a comparatively crude sense could it be called "bread from heaven." It was perishable, and those who ate it remained mortal and subject to recurring hunger.

The true Bread from Heaven is nothing else than Jesus Himself. He was sent by the Father (6:33) as His authorized agent for its bestowal (6:27).[1] Previously John said that the Word with God in the beginning (1:1) "became flesh and made his dwelling among us" (1:14). His mission in coming from heaven to earth was to do His Father's will, not His own (6:38). He foreknew what this involved. In Gethsemane, Jesus literally sweat blood. "My Father," He prayed, "if it is possible, may this cup be taken from me. Yet not as I will, but as you will" (Matthew 26:39).

The people in the Capernaum synagogue were incensed by Jesus' claim to have come from heaven (John 6:41). Like their forefathers in the wilderness (Exodus 16:2, 8f), they "grumbled." To all appearances, Jesus was the natural-born son of Joseph, a Galilean carpenter, and his wife, Mary. They knew both parents (John 6:42). How could He truthfully say, "I came down from heaven"? But appearances are often deceiving. In fact, Joseph was not Jesus' father. Had the Jews known the truth about Jesus' parentage, they would have had to admit that He spoke the truth. He was indeed the heaven-sent Bread of God.

Second, our text affirms that Jesus is . . .

## *The Life-Giving Bread (6:27, 33, 39-40, 44, 51)*

Like their materialistic counterparts today, the people of Jesus' day were interested only in the satisfaction of their physical appetites. They saw in Jesus a possible permanent source of bread (6:26). Our Lord charges them to adjust their priorities by making their higher goal food for the inner person (6:27). This abiding spiritual food, unlike "food that spoils," would provide eternal life to the believer (6:27). We are reminded of the Samaritan woman, whose quest was a perpetually available source of natural water. Jesus had in mind for her the "spring of water welling up to eternal life" (4:14-15).

The eternal life which Jesus extends is not merely a future life without end. That is the believer's sure and certain hope. But our Lord offers Himself as "he who comes down from heaven and *gives* [present tense] life to the world" (6:33, emphasis added). The Father wills for believers to have eternal life now (6:40).[2] It is to be a here-and-now possession! It is an entirely new *quality* of life. It is the life-giving presence of Jesus' Spirit within us. Jesus will speak again about this life and His purpose on earth: "I have come that they may have life, and have it to the full" (10:10). It is the life we pray for when we sing,

> Live Thou Thy life in me;
> All fullness dwells in Thee;
> Not I, but Christ in me,
>     Christ all in all.[3]

It is the very life of God in us!

But having that life in us now insures that we shall, in fact, live forever. Paul says those who have believed are "marked . . . with a seal, the promised Holy Spirit" (Ephesians 1:13). He calls the Spirit "a deposit guaranteeing our inheritance until the redemption of those who are God's possession" (1:14). In other words, we are sealed until we receive our new glorified bodies. Paul says elsewhere, "If the Spirit of him who raised Jesus from the dead is living in you, he who raised Christ from the dead will also give life to your mortal bodies through his Spirit, who lives in you" (Romans 8:11). Paul further promises that, at the coming of the Lord, "the dead in Christ will rise first" (1 Thessalonians 4:16).

Three times in our text, Jesus in slightly different language makes the same promise. He said, "I will raise them [or "him"] up at the last day" (John 6:39-40, 44).[4] Once He says, "he who believes has *everlasting life*" (6:47, emphasis added). And once He says, "If anyone eats of this bread, he will *live forever*" (6:51, emphasis added). Eternal Life! Precious present possession! Hope of future glory!

Third, our text tells us that the bread which Jesus offers is . . .

### Satisfying Bread (6:35)

"I am[5] the bread of life," Jesus declared. "He who comes to me will never go hungry, and he who believes in me will never be thirsty" (6:35). Jesus clearly implied satisfaction. As we continue to "come" to Him and "believe" (that is, "abide") in Him, He continually satisfies our spiritual hunger and thirst.[6] The medieval hymn writer had it right:

> We taste Thee, O Thou living Bread,
>     And long to feast upon Thee still;
> We drink of Thee, the Fountainhead,
>     And thirst our souls from Thee to fill.[7]

Paradoxically, the more we feast upon this Bread of Heaven, the more we hunger for Him. The more we drink of the living water, the more we thirst for Him. The Welsh poet, William Williams, expressed it this way: "Bread of Heaven, feed me till I want no more."[8] He might have said, "Feed me forever!"

No one and nothing satisfies but Jesus! How often have we heard the testimonies of once-popular, successful, prestigious people. At the pinnacle of
their careers they found only inner emptiness, loneliness, guilt—until they
met Jesus. He filled their emptiness, vanquished their loneliness, removed
their guilt. What this world's pleasures, pomp, prosperity and position could
not offer, the Bread of Life could!

Fourth, Jesus in His discourse offers . . .

## Faith-Procured Bread (6:29, 35, 37, 45, 47)

This life-giving, satisfying, bread of life from heaven is obtained through
*faith* in Christ. The Jews asked Jesus, "What must we do to do the works
God requires?" (6:28). They looked for salvation as the result of their own
efforts, that is, by "works of the law." Jesus replied that there is only *one*
work[9] that God requires—"to believe in the one he has sent" (6:29). Elsewhere in our text, this "work" of faith is described as coming to Jesus (6:35,
37, 44); believing in Him (6:35, 47); and looking to Him (6:40). Each of
these phrases is full of meaning. *Coming* to Jesus speaks of discovery. A
person has found Jesus to be the source of spiritual bread. *Believing*[10] under-
scores the necessity of faith. A person enters into this relationship by faith.
He or she walks the Jesus way by faith. *Looking* points up "the discerning vision which recognizes the eternal reality behind or within the phenomenal
facts of the life and death of Jesus Christ."[11]

It is vital that we understand the true nature of "saving faith." Often in
these days, faith in Christ is construed as the single act of "accepting" Him
as Savior. This is not the biblical concept of faith. "Believing on Jesus"—faith in Him—is an ongoing, lifetime trust in Him. It is a permanent
commitment to Him as Lord. Both in the Old Testament and the New, the
meaning of "believe" may be summed up in the phrase "trust and obey."[12]

This faith in Christ is itself a *gift of God.* The divine initiative in the salva-
tion of believers is evident in several of Jesus' statements here. He says,
"All[13] that the Father gives me will come to me" (6:37). He says, "No one
can come to me unless the Father who sent me draws him" (6:44). He says,
"It is written in the Prophets: 'They will all be taught by God' " (6:45).[14]
Truly, as Jonah remarked, "Salvation comes from the LORD" (2:9).

Fifth, the heavenly food offered to mankind is an . . .

## Appropriated Bread (6:51, 53-58)

The provision for mankind of heavenly, life-giving, spiritual bread was not a simple thing. It necessitated Jesus' giving "his flesh" for the life of the world. He had to *die* a voluntary, vicarious death (6:51). On our part, it is necessary that we "eat [His] flesh" and "drink [His] blood" (6:51, 53-54). This means at least three things: (1) that we appropriate, through faith, the saving merit of His atoning death;[15] (2) that we participate, through faith, in His death to self and sin;[16] and (3) that we see, by faith, our living union with Christ (6:56). Jesus says this "feeding" on Him results in eternal life (6:57).

Jesus' words in 6:53-57 are primarily a teaching about spiritual realities. But we cannot help but sense how applicable they are to something as tangible as partaking of the Lord's Supper.[17] Our text adds a depth of meaning to all that the Table of the Lord signifies. In the Communion, believers appropriate by faith the Person and work of Christ Jesus.

Sixth, Jesus' discourse teaches us that He offers . . .

## Spirit-Given Bread (6:62-63)

Feeding on Jesus, the heavenly Bread of Life, is only possible through the indwelling Holy Spirit (6:63). It is He who makes experientially real the actual *presence* of Christ in the believer. And it is He who quickens to our hearts and minds the life-giving *words* of Christ (6:63). This indwelling, enlightening Holy Spirit is a gift to us from the exalted Jesus. He made the coming of the Spirit possible by His post-resurrection ascension to "where he was before"—heaven (6:62). We recognize that the Holy Spirit is the gift to believers of the exalted Jesus. How important that we receive Christ's Gift!

Finally, our text informs us that what is offered to us is a . . .

## Discriminating Bread (6:60, 64, 66, 68-69)

When the implications of our Lord's "hard teaching" (6:60) dawned upon His followers, many of them "turned back and no longer followed him"

(6:66). In spite of the miracles they had seen, many did not believe (6:36).[18] They were willing to follow Him for the physical food He provided. But they were not willing to meet the conditions of self-denial that would bring them spiritual food.

Jesus was not surprised (6:64). He knew that the response to His offer was ultimately in the hands of His sovereign Father (6:65).

He turned to His twelve disciples. "You do not want to leave too, do you?" Jesus asked (6:67).

Peter expressed the decision of the Twelve: "Lord, to whom shall we go? You have the words of eternal life. We believe and know that you are the Holy One of God" (6:68-69).[19]

May Peter's confession be ours!

## Conclusion

Our text has set before us the ability and willingness of Jesus to satisfy our heart hunger for spiritual reality. He alone is the heaven-sent, life-giving, fully satisfying Bread of God. Spirit-revealed, He waits to be assimilated into our lives through the God-given gift of faith. Therefore, it is Jesus Himself who is to be the object of our every quest! It is Jesus Himself who is to be the center of our heart's devotion! It is Jesus Himself for whom we must continually hunger and thirst.

How critical it is that this hunger for the true Bread be satisfied! And so our text teaches us also how to approach the Lord's Table whenever Communion is observed. Horatius Bonar's Communion hymn may well be your heart's expression:

> Here would I feed upon the bread of God,
>     Here drink with Thee the royal wine of heaven;
> Here would I lay aside each earthly load,
>     Here taste afresh the calm of sin forgiven.
>
> This is the hour of banquet and of song;
>     This is the heavenly table spread for me;
> Here let me feast, and feasting, still prolong
>     The brief bright hour of fellowship with Thee.

Too soon we rise; the symbols disappear;
  The feast, though not the love, is past and gone;
The bread and wine remove, but *Thou* art here,
  Nearer than ever; still my shield and sun.[20]

### Endnotes

1. The reference to the Father's seal of approval on the Son alludes to one particular event—the descent of the Holy Spirit upon Jesus (1:33).
2. The Greek verb here translated by the NIV "shall have" is, in fact, present tense. A better translation would be, "For my Father's will is that everyone who looks to the Son and believes in him *should have* eternal life. . . ."
3. Alfred C. Snead, "Fully Surrendered," *Hymns of the Christian Life* (Camp Hill, PA: Christian Publications, Inc., 1978), # 218, stanza 4.
4. See again John 5:28-29.
5. Here is the first of seven metaphors in John's Gospel where Jesus uses the expression, "I am" (Greek, *ego eimi*). They are reminiscent of God's identification of Himself to Moses at the burning bush (Exodus 3:14) and later. In addition to the Bread of Life (6:35), Jesus declares Himself to be the Light of the World (8:12), the Gate (for the sheep) (10:7, 9), the Good Shepherd (10:11, 14), the Resurrection and the Life (11:25), the Way (14:6) and the Vine (15:1, 5).
6. In 6:35, both Greek verbs are in the present tense, which implies a *continual* coming and believing.
7. Ray Palmer, trans., "Jesus, Thou Joy of Loving Hearts," *Hymns of the Christian Life, #* 35, stanza 3.
8. William Williams, "Guide Me, O Thou Great Jehovah," *Hymns of the Christian Life*, # 342, stanza 1.
9. Jesus' teaching here is parallel to Paul's doctrine of justification through faith. The noun *pistis,* "faith," is not used in John's Gospel. Rather the word *ergon,* "work," is used as a description of faith. In 6:29, *work* does not mean what Paul means by "works of the law" (Romans 3:28), i.e., works performed by human effort in order to be justified. It means, rather, what God requires of sinful human beings.
10. *Pisteo,* "believe," here and in 6:29, is in the present tense.
11. F.F. Bruce, *The Gospel of John* (Grand Rapids, MI: Eerdmans, 1983), 154.
12. As in the case of Abraham, who "believed" God (Romans 4:3). Believing God entailed trusting His promise, and obeying His command to leave Ur and proceed to "the land I will show you" (Genesis 12:1-3).
13. The word "all" is the neuter *pan,* denoting the sum total of believers. Verse 37 continues, "and whoever comes to me (literally, "the one coming to me," i.e., each individual believer) I will never drive away." Bruce, *The Gospel of John,* 153, has this comment: "In the work of salvation the Father and the Son are completely at one, the Father giving the believing community to the Son, the Son receiving and guarding those who come to him, because he is utterly devoted to the Father's will." C.K. Barrett, *The Gospel According to St. John* (London: S.P.C.K., 1955), 294, writes, "The verse sums up the universalism, the in-

dividualism, and the predestinarianism of the gospel. Jesus rejects no one who comes to him, but in coming to him God's decision always precedes man's."

14. The quotation is from Isaiah 54:13. See also Jeremiah 31:33-34. Barrett, *The Gospel According to St. John,* 296, explains, "The quotation is adduced in explanation of God's drawing men. This consists in teaching, the inward teaching which God gives to those whom he chooses and so directs to Jesus. For everyone who has heard . . . what the Father says, and learnt . . . from it, comes to Jesus."
15. Compare Paul's "through faith in his blood" (Romans 3:25).
16. Compare Paul's "we were baptized into his death" (Romans 6:3ff).
17. While we cannot agree with those who teach that these verses are totally fulfilled in the Communion Supper (as, for example, C.H. Dodd, *The Interpretation of the Fourth Gospel* [Cambridge: At the University Press, 1970], 338-339), yet we must agree with R.H. Lightfoot, *St. John's Gospel* (London: Oxford University Press, 1966), 162, when he says, "A reference to the eucharistic rite of the Church is inescapable." Compare First Corinthians 11:23-26.
18. The Greek equivalent of the English pronoun "me" (6:36) is not present in the most reliable manuscripts of John.
19. Noting that the word "holy" carries with it the thought of separation, Lightfoot, *St. John's Gospel,* 170, writes that Peter's confession "implies not only that the Lord is indeed by nature from above and not of this world, . . . but also that in this respect He stands unique. He alone has descended out of heaven. . . . He alone speaks words which bestow eternal life, . . . and of these truths St. Peter and his colleagues are assured."
20. Horatius Bonar, "Here, O My Lord," *Hymns of the Christian Life,* # 429, stanzas 2, 3 and 4, emphasis added.

## Part V

## *Questions for Reflection or Discussion*

1. Does the Church bear some responsibility to the physically hungry of the world? Why or why not?

2. What deeper-life truth is illustrated in Jesus' feeding of the 5,000?

3. Contrast the way Paul uses the word "works" in Romans 4 with the way Jesus uses it in John 6:29.

4. Besides being a sacrament of remembrance, what spiritual truth is illustrated in the Communion, or the Lord's Supper?

5. In what sense is eternal life both a present and a future possession?

# 15

# Opposition to the Teaching

John 7:1-52

*After this, Jesus went around in Galilee, purposely staying away from Judea because the Jews there were waiting to take his life. 2 But when the Jewish Feast of Tabernacles was near, 3 Jesus' brothers said to him, "You ought to leave here and go to Judea, so that your disciples may see the miracles you do. 4 No one who wants to become a public figure acts in secret. Since you are doing these things, show yourself to the world." 5 For even his own brothers did not believe in him.*

*6 Therefore Jesus told them, "The right time for me has not yet come; for you any time is right. 7 The world cannot hate you, but it hates me because I testify that what it does is evil. 8 You go to the Feast. I am not yet going up to this Feast, because for me the right time has not yet come." 9 Having said this, he stayed in Galilee.*

*10 However, after his brothers had left for the Feast, he went also, not publicly, but in secret. 11 Now at the Feast the Jews were watching for him and asking, "Where is that man?"*

*12 Among the crowds there was widespread whispering about him. Some said, "He is a good man."*

*Others replied, "No, he deceives the people." 13 But no one would say anything publicly about him for fear of the Jews.*

*14 Not until halfway through the Feast did Jesus go up to the temple courts and begin to teach. 15 The Jews were amazed and asked, "How did this man get such learning without having studied?"*

16 Jesus answered, "My teaching is not my own. It comes from him who sent me. 17 If anyone chooses to do God's will, he will find out whether my teaching comes from God or whether I speak on my own. 18 He who speaks on his own does so to gain honor for himself, but he who works for the honor of the one who sent him is a man of truth; there is nothing false about him. 19 Has not Moses given you the law? Yet not one of you keeps the law. Why are you trying to kill me?"

20 "You are demon-possessed," the crowd answered. "Who is trying to kill you?"

21 Jesus said to them, "I did one miracle, and you are all astonished. 22 Yet, because Moses gave you circumcision (though actually it did not come from Moses, but from the patriarchs), you circumcise a child on the Sabbath. 23 Now if a child can be circumcised on the Sabbath so that the law of Moses may not be broken, why are you angry with me for healing the whole man on the Sabbath? 24 Stop judging by mere appearances, and make a right judgment."

25 At that point some of the people of Jerusalem began to ask, "Isn't this the man they are trying to kill? 26 Here he is, speaking publicly, and they are not saying a word to him. Have the authorities really concluded that he is the Christ? 27 But we know where this man is from; when the Christ comes, no one will know where he is from."

28 Then Jesus, still teaching in the temple courts, cried out, "Yes, you know me, and you know where I am from. I am not here on my own, but he who sent me is true. You do not know him, 29 but I know him because I am from him and he sent me."

30 At this they tried to seize him, but no one laid a hand on him, because his time had not yet come. 31 Still, many in the crowd put their faith in him. They said, "When the Christ comes, will he do more miraculous signs than this man?"

32 The Pharisees heard the crowd whispering such things about him. Then the chief priests and the Pharisees sent temple guards to arrest him.

33 Jesus said, "I am with you for only a short time, and then I go to the one who sent me. 34 You will look for me, but you will not find me; and where I am, you cannot come."

35 The Jews said to one another, "Where does this man intend to go that we cannot find him? Will he go where our people live scattered among the Greeks, and teach the Greeks? 36 What did he mean when he said, 'You will look for me, but you will not find me,' and 'Where I am, you cannot come'?"

37 On the last and greatest day of the Feast, Jesus stood and said in a loud voice, "If anyone is thirsty, let him come to me and drink. 38 Whoever believes in me, as the Scripture has said, streams of living water will flow from within him." 39 By this he meant the Spirit, whom those who believed in him

*were later to receive. Up to that time the Spirit had not been given, since Jesus had not yet been glorified.*

*40 On hearing his words, some of the people said, "Surely this man is the Prophet."*

*41 Others said, "He is the Christ."*

*Still others asked, "How can the Christ come from Galilee? 42 Does not the Scripture say that the Christ will come from David's family and from Bethlehem, the town where David lived?" 43 Thus the people were divided because of Jesus. 44 Some wanted to seize him, but no one laid a hand on him.*

*45 Finally the temple guards went back to the chief priests and Pharisees, who asked them, "Why didn't you bring him in?"*

*46 "No one ever spoke the way this man does," the guards declared.*

*47 "You mean he has deceived you also?" the Pharisees retorted. 48 "Has any of the rulers or of the Pharisees believed in him? 49 No! But this mob that knows nothing of the law—there is a curse on them."*

*50 Nicodemus, who had gone to Jesus earlier and who was one of their own number, asked, 51 "Does our law condemn anyone without first hearing him to find out what he is doing?"*

*52 They replied, "Are you from Galilee, too? Look into it, and you will find that a prophet does not come out of Galilee."*

From now on, Jesus' life would be characterized by intensifying conflict. We saw the beginning of it when He healed the paralyzed man on the Sabbath at the pool of Bethesda (5:1ff). He had violated the rules of Jerusalem's religious establishment, and those leaders let Him know it. He was the brunt of their angry persecution (5:16). And when He went as far as to insinuate that He was equal with God, they began to consider His execution (5:18). Because Jesus knew it was not yet time for His death, He prudently left Judea for an itinerant ministry in Galilee.[1] While Jesus was in Galilee, John records, He fed the hungry multitude and discoursed on the Bread of Life in the Capernaum synagogue (chapter 6).

Now, six months later,[2] He returned to Jerusalem to take part in the Feast of Tabernacles (7:2).[3] The Sandhedrin, hearing again what they considered His "blasphemous" teaching, was increasingly intent on taking Jesus' life.[4] Opposition was mounting—ever more glaring, more threatening. Our text portrays this growing antagonism to Jesus in three ways. First, it appears mildly in . . .

## *Familial Misconception (7:1-10)*

It happens. People endeavoring to follow the Lord may run into opposition from those closest to them. Family members, other relatives, close friends misinterpret their motives or behavior. In his biography of Rees Howells, the Welsh intercessor, Norman Grubbs cites an example. Howells lived at a time and in a place where men wore caps. Yet he felt certain that God wanted him to go about with his head uncovered. Thus he would prove to himself and God that he was willing to be a fool for Christ's sake. This practice brought great embarrassment to the family. They could not understand why he would purposely go against the accepted social standards of the day.

Jesus found Himself in similar tensions with His unbelieving (7:5) brothers. They did not understand why Jesus chose to stay in Galilee. If He truly were the Messiah He professed to be, Jerusalem was the obvious focal point. Jerusalem was where He should be working His miracles. That was where the opinion-makers lived. If Jesus expected to vindicate His mission and authority (7:3-4), Jerusalem, not Galilee, was the place. As far as His brothers were concerned, Jesus was not living up to their preconception of Messiah.

Jesus' brothers knew nothing of living from moment to moment in "sensitive rapport with God's directing will."[5] They could not possibly have understood that Jesus must await His Father's "right time" (7:6).[6] Neither could they comprehend a Messianic mission that would begin with public hatred (7:7), not popular acclaim. Jesus, however, understood both the Father's timing and purpose. So He chose to remain in Galilee (7:8-9)[7] rather than to go with His brothers to the Feast. Midway in the Feast, however (7:14), He would make a "secret" (7:10) entry. Such would not be perceived as an official offer of Messiahship.[8]

Not only did Jesus experience familial misconception. Public opposition appeared in increasing . . .

## *Official Defamation (7:11-24)*

Both Jerusalem's religious leadership and the public at large would call Jesus demon-possessed (7:20). The Sanhedrin, who held executive authority over Jewish affairs in Jerusalem, hoped Jesus would be at the Feast. They wanted to arrest Him. When He failed to appear, they became concerned.

"Where is that fellow?"[9] they asked each other, hoping to get their hands on Him (see 7:11). The pilgrims crowding the city were also hoping for an opportunity to see and hear Jesus. Even in His absence He was the topic of excited conversation (7:12). No one, however, dared say anything positive about Him lest they feel the displeasure of the authorities (7:13).

Finally, Jesus made His way to the temple courts and began to teach (7:14).[10] Imagine the reaction of the crowd! Imagine the greater reaction of the doctors of theology as this "rustic prophet"[11] expounded the Scriptures! He spoke with power and authority like no others before Him,[12] yet He held no degree from Jerusalem Theological Seminary (7:15)! I am reminded of a pastor in Wheaton, Illinois, during my student days. He had no formal theological training. Yet Sunday after Sunday he held us spellbound as he expounded the Scriptures and applied them to our lives. A graduate school professor, learning of this man's call to that church, had remarked, "But what degrees does he have?" Did it matter?

Jesus knew, of course, that to be a teacher one must first be a learner. He laid no claim to formal instruction beyond what every Hebrew boy would receive. But he was not self-taught.[13] Just as the works He did were His Father's (5:36), so also the words He spoke were His Father's (7:16).[14] And if any were in doubt, they could be convinced of it by deliberately choosing the will of God (7:17).[15] What is the will of God? It is to believe on His Son.[16]

Jesus said His aim was to bring glory not to Himself but to the Father who sent Him (7:18).[17] For the sincere seeker, the origin of Jesus' message may readily be inferred from that objective. It is a message from God the Father, delivered with His authority.

Jesus then returned to His comments about Moses, made near the end of His previous debate with these opponents (5:45-47). He had told them that if they really believed Moses, they would believe Him. Because He perceived they sought to kill him, He charged them with breaking the very Law they so proudly defended (7:19).

His word prompted a character-smearing outburst from the people. "You are demon-possessed," they answered (7:20). Ignoring their accusation,[18] Jesus proceeded to defend His healing of the paralyzed man at Bethesda

Pool (7:21-24). His argument amounts to this: "If you circumcise on the Sabbath,[19] you should allow Me to heal on the Sabbath. Probe beneath the surface and you will see that My actions are consonant with the spirit and purpose of the Law."

Third, opposition to Jesus' teaching appeared in the midst of . . .

### *Popular Confusion (7:25-36)*

Speaking of our attitude toward Jesus, the old invitation song warns us clearly, "Neutral you cannot be."[20] How evident this was during the Feast of Tabernacles in Jerusalem! In rapid succession our text juxtaposes positive and negative things about this One sent from the Father. Some of the Jerusalemites were saying, "Is this the man our leaders are trying to kill? Why is He still teaching in the temple? Do our leaders now have evidence that He *is* the Messiah?" (see 7:25-26). *Positive!*

"But we know where this man is from; when the Christ comes, no one will know where he is from" (7:27). *Negative!* (The reference is to a Jewish belief that Messiah would be in hiding until the divinely appointed hour for His unveiling. As far as they were concerned, Jesus did not fit that criterion.) Jesus agreed on the natural level, but asserted that they really did not know His source in the Father (7:28-29).

Again, "At this they tried to seize him" (7:30). *Negative!* "Still, many in the crowd put their faith in him. They said, 'When the Christ comes, will he do more miraculous signs than this man?' " (7:31). *Positive!*

"Then the chief priests and the Pharisees sent temple guards to arrest him" (7:32). *Negative!* This dangerous faith movement must be crushed. But Jesus knows His fate is not to be determined by Jewish leaders, but by Himself in obedience to the will of the Father. In the Father's plan, there is still "a short time"[21] before His departure (7:33). *Positive!* The door to faith is still open. But when He finally does go to "the one who sent [Him]," those who rejected Him will have condemned themselves (7:33-34). *Negative!*

Once more, "Where does this man intend to go that we cannot find him? Will he go . . . and teach the Greeks?" (7:35). *Negative!* Yet indeed our Lord would evangelize the Greeks.[22] *Positive!* Little did those questioners know how prophetic their words were! Our Lord did indeed evangelize the

Greeks. But it was not because He fled from Jewish hostility. It was because in obedience to His Father He voluntarily accepted death resulting from that hostility. Within just a few years, Greek (Gentile) converts would number in the tens of thousands!

We come, finally, to . . .

## Jesus' Gracious Invitation (7:37-38)

Jesus' gracious invitation was delivered on the eighth day of the Feast of Tabernacles. It issued in a final display of conflicting responses. To grasp the poignancy of the Savior's words, we need first to see them in the context of the feast's daily morning ritual. At dawn on each of the first seven days, a ceremony was enacted which acknowledged God's goodness in sending rain. Rain, of course, ensured a plentiful harvest the following season. Led by a priest, the people went to the pool of Siloam. There they filled a golden pitcher, returning it to the temple amid the sound of cymbals, trumpets and joyful voices. As priests poured the water into a funnel at the west side of the altar, the temple choir began singing the great "Hallel" (Psalms 113-118).

On the eighth day, the ceremony apparently was not enacted.[23] Thus the words of Jesus had even greater spiritual significance. "If anyone is thirsty," Jesus shouted, "let him come to me and drink" (7:37).

He was saying, in effect, "Water from the Pool of Siloam will never quench your spiritual thirst. Only I can do that. Not only will I satisfy *your* thirst but, through you who believe on Me, the thirst of others will be satisfied" (see 7:38). John is constrained to explain Jesus' words. The living water that will flow out from within believers is the Holy Spirit Himself. He will be the gift of the crucified, risen and exalted Lord (7:39). According to Jesus' words (7:38), such an outflow of the Spirit had been promised in the graphic spiritual imagery of such prophetic Scriptures as Zechariah 14:8[24] and Ezekiel 47:1-11. There water is portrayed as flowing from the Jerusalem temple and bringing abundant life to everything it touches.[25]

And so once again, in response to Jesus' invitation, the judgments of the crowd are divided. *Positively,* some say, "Surely this man is the Prophet" (7:40); or, "He is the Christ" (7:41). But *negatively,* others counter with: "How can the Christ come from Galilee? Does not the Scripture say that the

Christ will come from David's family and from Bethlehem, the town where David lived?" (7:41-42). *Positively,* from the temple guards: "No one ever spoke the way this man does" (7:46). *Negatively,* from the Pharisees: "You mean he has deceived you also?" (7:47). And finally, we hear the curt interchange with Nicodemus: "Does our law condemn anyone," he asks, "without first hearing him to find out what he is doing?" (7:51). "Are you from Galilee, too? Look into it, and you will find that a prophet does not come out of Galilee" (7:52). Clearly at *this* Feast of Tabernacles, neutrality toward Jesus of Nazareth was not an option!

## Conclusion

What a compelling invitation comes to you and me from the lips of our Lord! He wants us to experience the kind of life that satisfies our innermost spiritual thirst. But beyond that, it overflows in life-giving ministry to other hungry hearts (7:37-39)! The Holy Spirit, about whom Jesus was speaking in these verses, is the "clothing with power" Jesus promised (see Luke 24:49 and Acts 2:33). Therefore, if you and I are to have an overflowing, effective ministry to a needy world, we *must* come in faith to the risen Christ. We must ask from Him the same baptism of the Holy Spirit that the first disciples received on the Day of Pentecost.

Let me share with you the testimony of the late Paris Reidhead, former missionary and pastor, my dear friend and mentor. As a missionary in Africa he came to the conviction that "my life woefully lacked the fruit of the Spirit.... As I studied the New Testament, I was amazed to discover that the very things that marked the ministry of our Lord and of the early Church were the things that I so desperately needed."

Reidhead went on to tell of his soul-searching, questioning and study of the Scripture. Finally he came to the conclusion that what he needed was to be filled with the Holy Spirit. He continued, "I was satisfied that [my quest] was in accord with the Word. I asked ... two brothers to pray for me.... My heart reached out in faith to take the promise of Luke 24:49. Gently, beautifully, wonderfully God met the need of my hungry heart. I knew that He had filled me with His own blessed Self."[26]

Reidhead's thirsty heart had been fully satisfied. But there came *official opposition* from the leaders of the Mission of which he was a member. When they heard what had happened to him, they demanded his resignation. In the years that followed, God gave Paris Reidhead a large and influential ministry with The Christian and Missionary Alliance. In addition to his pastorates, he was in demand as a conference speaker.

Christ's disciples must be prepared to expect the same kind of opposition that their Master experienced.[27] Family misunderstanding, official antagonism, popular exclusion—any or all of these may be the lot of one who seeks the deeper life. Yet the gains for one who experiences this crisis of the deeper life far outweigh any loss. Henry F. Lyte described it this way:

> Let the world despise and leave me—
> They have left my Saviour, too;
> Human hearts and looks deceive me—
> Thou art not, like man, untrue;
> And while Thou shalt smile upon me,
> God of wisdom, love, and might,
> Foes may hate, and friends may shun me;
> Show Thy face and all is bright.[28]

### Endnotes

1. In John 7:1, the verb "went around" is in the Greek imperfect tense, indicating continuous action.
2. Assuming that the "feast of the Jews" mentioned in 5:1 was the Passover, there would be six months between that feast and the Feast of Tabernacles (7:2).
3. The Feast of Tabernacles, also known as the Feast of Booths *(sukkoth),* celebrated the supernatural preservation of the nation during their forty-year desert wandering, when they lived in tents. It followed the safe gathering in of the harvest. See Leviticus 23:33-43.
4. John emphasizes the increasing opposition to Jesus by informing his readers seven times in chapter 7 and three times in chapter 8 about the Jews' intention to kill Jesus.
5. F.F. Bruce, *The Gospel of John* (Grand Rapids, MI: Eerdmans, 1983), 172.
6. The Greek word translated here as "time" is *kairos.* Kittel (Gerhard Kittel and Gerhard Friedrich, eds., *Theological Dictionary of the New Testament,* 10 vols. [Grand Rapids, MI: Eerdmans, 1964]), vol. III, 459, describes it as "the fateful and decisive point" ordained by God. He goes on to say, 460, "In accordance with the strict sense of *kairos,* it seems that Jesus does not know it in advance. He discerns it as such only at the moment when it comes. . . . He then decides in accordance with its divine claim." This scenario, of course, does not recognize the omniscience of Jesus, the God-Man.

7. F. Godet, *Commentary on the Gospel of St. John,* vol. II (Edinburgh: T. & T. Clarke, 1881), 270, interpreting 7:8, has Jesus saying, "You go up to the Feast as a pilgrim; I am not going up to this Feast as Messiah the King," implying that He would do so at another feast, His last Passover.

8. As was His "triumphal entry," recorded in 12:12ff.

9. This is how C.K. Barrett, *The Gospel According to St. John* (London: S.P.C.K., 1955), 314, renders *pou estiv ekeinos.* Neighbors of the healed blind man ask the same question in 9:12.

10. One is reminded of the prophecy of Malachi: "See, I will send my messenger, who will prepare the way before me. Then suddenly the Lord you are seeking will come to his temple" (3:1).

11. C.H. Dodd, *The Interpretation of the Fourth Gospel* (Cambridge: At the University Press, 1970), 351.

12. Compare Matthew 7:29.

13. Leon Morris, *The Gospel According to John* (Grand Rapids, MI: Eerdmans, 1971), 405, observes: "Had He said that He was self-taught, or that He needed no teacher, or the like, He would have been discredited immediately. The age did not prize originality. The Rabbinic method was to cite authorities for all important statements. So Jesus does not claim to be the originator of His message."

14. Compare John 3:34.

15. Morris, *The Gospel According to John,* 406, quotes Augustine's famous statement: "Understanding is the reward of faith. Therefore do not seek to understand in order to believe, but believe that thou mayest understand. . . ."

16. See Morris, *The Gospel According to John,* 406; Barrett, *The Gospel According to St. John,* 318; R.H. Lightfoot, *St. John's Gospel* (London: Oxford University Press, 1966), 178. On the other hand, B.F. Westcott, *Commentary on the Gospel According to St. John* (London: John Murray, Albermarle Street, 1967), 118, states: "The will of God is not to be limited to the Old Testament revelation, or to the claims of Christ, but includes every manifestation of the purpose of God."

17. See John 8:50. Godet, *Commentary on the Gospel of St. John,* vol. II, 278, says, "The messenger who seeks only the glory of the master who sends him and lets no personal interests intrude into his communications, gives by this very fact a proof of the faithfulness with which he delivers his message. As certainly as he says nothing with a view to himself, so certainly does he also say nothing of his own accord."

18. But see John 8:49, where Jesus denies their charge that He is demon-possessed.

19. The rabbis concluded that the law of circumcision overrode the law of keeping the Sabbath. One rabbi wrote: "If circumcision, which concerns one of a man's 248 members, overrides the Sabbath, how much more must his whole body (supposed in danger of death) override the Sabbath?" Quoted by Barrett, 320.

20. A.B. Simpson, "What Will You Do with Jesus?", *Hymns of the Christian Life* (Camp Hill, PA: Christian Publications, Inc., 1978), # 566.

21. See 12:35; 13:33; 14:19; 16:16-19 for similar expressions.

22. Not in person, but through His apostles at His command.

23. Bruce, *The Gospel of John,* 181.

24. According to Bruce, *The Gospel of John,* 182, this was the reading from the Prophets prescribed for the first day of the Feast of Tabernacles.

25. Bruce, *The Gospel of John,* 182, has this vital interpretive comment on these Scriptures: "The fulfillment of these and similar prophecies (cf. Joel 3:18; Isa. 33:21) is not to be

sought in twentieth-century schemes to cut a canal through Israeli territory to rival the Suez Canal or anything of that sort; it lies plain for all to read in John's description of 'the river of the water of life, bright as crystal, flowing from the throne of God and of the Lamb' (Rev. 22:1). It is from no earthly Jerusalem that the living waters go forth; it is from the dwelling-place of God in lives that are consecrated to him, in believing hearts where Christ has taken up his abode."

26. The quotations are taken from Reidhead's unpublished testimony, "That I May Know Him."

27. Compare John 15:18ff.

28. Henry F. Lyte, "Jesus, I My Cross Have Taken," *Hymns of the Christian Life,* # 260, stanza 2.

# 16

# *Opposition to the Light*

## John 8:12-59[1]

*12 When Jesus spoke again to the people, he said, "I am the light of the world. Whoever follows me will never walk in darkness, but will have the light of life."*

*13 The Pharisees challenged him, "Here you are, appearing as your own witness; your testimony is not valid."*

*14 Jesus answered, "Even if I testify on my own behalf, my testimony is valid, for I know where I came from and where I am going. But you have no idea where I come from or where I am going. 15 You judge by human standards; I pass judgment on no one. 16 But if I do judge, my decisions are right, because I am not alone. I stand with the Father, who sent me. 17 In your own Law it is written that the testimony of two men is valid. 18 I am one who testifies for myself; my other witness is the Father, who sent me."*

*19 Then they asked him, "Where is your father?"*

*"You do not know me or my Father," Jesus replied. "If you knew me, you would know my Father also." 20 He spoke these words while teaching in the temple area near the place where the offerings were put. Yet no one seized him, because his time had not yet come.*

*21 Once more Jesus said to them, "I am going away, and you will look for me, and you will die in your sin. Where I go, you cannot come."*

*22 This made the Jews ask, "Will he kill himself? Is that why he says, 'Where I go, you cannot come'?"*

*23 But he continued, "You are from below; I am from above. You are of* this world; I am not of this world. 24 I told you that you would die in your sins; if you do not believe that I am the one I claim to be, you will indeed die in your sins."

25 "Who are you?" they asked.

"Just what I have been claiming all along," Jesus replied. 26 "I have much to say in judgment of you. But he who sent me is reliable, and what I have heard from him I tell the world."

27 They did not understand that he was telling them about his Father. 28 So Jesus said, "When you have lifted up the Son of Man, then you will know that I am the one I claim to be and that I do nothing on my own but speak just what the Father has taught me. 29 The one who sent me is with me; he has not left me alone, for I always do what pleases him." 30 Even as he spoke, many put their faith in him.

31 To the Jews who had believed him, Jesus said, "If you hold to my teaching, you are really my disciples. 32 Then you will know the truth, and the truth will set you free."

33 They answered him, "We are Abraham's descendants and have never been slaves of anyone. How can you say that we shall be set free?"

34 Jesus replied, "I tell you the truth, everyone who sins is a slave to sin. 35 Now a slave has no permanent place in the family, but a son belongs to it forever. 36 So if the Son sets you free, you will be free indeed. 37 I know you are Abraham's descendants. Yet you are ready to kill me, because you have no room for my word. 38 I am telling you what I have seen in the Father's presence, and you do what you have heard from your father."

39 "Abraham is our father," they answered.

"If you were Abraham's children," said Jesus, "then you would do the things Abraham did. 40 As it is, you are determined to kill me, a man who has told you the truth that I heard from God. Abraham did not do such things. 41 You are doing the things your own father does."

"We are not illegitimate children," they protested. "The only Father we have is God himself."

42 Jesus said to them, "If God were your Father, you would love me, for I came from God and now am here. I have not come on my own; but he sent me. 43 Why is my language not clear to you? Because you are unable to hear what I say. 44 You belong to your father, the devil, and you want to carry out your father's desire. He was a murderer from the beginning, not holding to the truth, for there is no truth in him. When he lies, he speaks his native language, for he is a liar and the father of lies. 45 Yet because I tell the truth, you do not believe me! 46 Can any of you prove me guilty of sin? If I am telling the truth, why don't you believe me? 47 He who belongs to God hears what God says. The reason you do not hear is that you do not belong to God."

*48 The Jews answered him, "Aren't we right in saying that you are a Sa-*
*maritan and demon-possessed?"*

*49 "I am not possessed by a demon," said Jesus, "but I honor my Father*
*and you dishonor me. 50 I am not seeking glory for myself; but there is one*
*who seeks it, and he is the judge. 51 I tell you the truth, if anyone keeps my*
*word, he will never see death."*

*52 At this the Jews exclaimed, "Now we know that you are*
*demon-possessed! Abraham died and so did the prophets, yet you say that*
*if anyone keeps your word, he will never taste death. 53 Are you greater*
*than our father Abraham? He died, and so did the prophets. Who do you*
*think you are?"*

*54 Jesus replied, "If I glorify myself, my glory means nothing. My Fa-*
*ther, whom you claim as your God, is the one who glorifies me. 55 Though*
*you do not know him, I know him. If I said I did not, I would be a liar like*
*you, but I do know him and keep his word. 56 Your father Abraham re-*
*joiced at the thought of seeing my day; he saw it and was glad."*

*57 "You are not yet fifty years old," the Jews said to him, "and you have*
*seen Abraham!"*

*58 "I tell you the truth," Jesus answered, "before Abraham was born, I*
*am!" At this, they picked up stones to stone him, but Jesus hid himself, slip-*
*ping away from the temple grounds.*

The Feast of Tabernacles, as we have seen, was a time of great rejoicing in Jerusalem. It commemorated God's miraculous preservation of the nation during their forty-year wilderness wandering. Besides the water ceremony, which took place each morning during the feast, there was a second called "The Illumination of the Temple." This was an evening ceremony on the first day. It took place in the Court of the Women, where the temple Treasury was located.[2] Barclay describes it:

> The court was surrounded with deep galleries, erected to hold the
> spectators. In the center four great candelabra were prepared.
> When the dark came the four great candelabra were lit and, it was
> said, they sent such a blaze of light throughout Jerusalem that ev-
> ery courtyard was lit up with their brilliance. Then all night long,
> until cock-crow the next morning, the greatest and the wisest and
> the holiest men in Israel danced before the Lord and sang psalms
> of joy and praise while the people watched.[3]

The ceremony reminded people of the pillar of divine fire which lit Israel's nights in the vast Sinai Desert (Exodus 13:21f). That wilderness illumination and the ceremony which commemorated it were doubtless in Jesus' mind as He sat in the temple Treasury (John 8:20).

"I am the light of the world," Jesus declared. "Whoever follows me will never walk in darkness, but will have the light of life"[4] (8:12). His words in the temple Treasury are the second of His remarkable "I AM" declarations recorded by John. He was saying, in effect, "You have remembered the pillar of fire in the wilderness. You have seen the blazing candelabra in the temple lighting up Jerusalem. I alone am the true Light of the world. I shed light on the true nature, meaning and purpose of life. Those who follow Me[5] will be delivered from this world's black night of sin and spiritual ignorance. They will be freed from the devil's kingdom of darkness to walk all of life in union with Me."

Out of this astounding assertion of our Lord a fourfold opposition to the Light arises. First, we see . . .

## *Opposition to His Valid Testimony (8:12-20)*

The Pharisees would surely remember the many Old Testament Scriptures attributing light to God alone.[6] Thus they were immediately on the attack. But instead of addressing the primary question, they focused on a legal technicality. A lone person's testimony without corroborating witnesses was invalid (8:13).[7] Ostensibly, from a strictly legal point of view, the Pharisees had a point, as Jesus had earlier conceded (5:31ff). But that by no means meant His testimony was not in fact dependable. On the contrary, His witness to Himself was entirely trustworthy (8:14). Jesus' argument, in which He emphatically contrasted Himself with the Pharisees,[8] ran along these lines: *He* could bear witness to Himself, because *He* knew what *they* could not possibly know—that He had come from heaven to be the Light of the world. When He finished His work on earth, He would return to heaven (8:14). *He,* therefore, knew intuitively that He was the Light of the world. Moreover, His works and words substantiated His claim, despite the objections of the spiritually blind.

*Their* judgment of Him, based on appearances and insufficient knowledge, was superficial, weak and incomplete[9] (8:15). *He* never practiced the same sort of shortsighted judgment of others as *they* did (8:15). But were He to judge, His judgment would be right because of His intimate relationship with the Father. God the Father was the Source of truth and the One who sent Him (8:16). Furthermore, His Father was the second necessary witness required by their Law (8:17-18).

The Pharisees, predictably, refused to receive Jesus' testimony concerning His relationship to the Father. "Where is your father?" they asked with obvious skepticism. In reply our Lord made plain the truth so central to John's Gospel: *Only through Jesus can God the Father be known.* The refusal of the Pharisees to acknowledge Jesus as the Son of God was evidence that they knew neither Him nor His Father (8:19).

One may observe, as does Leon Morris,[10] that the Pharisees' reaction to Jesus' claim is still current. Simply put, they did not wish to be convinced of the truth. *"We* do not see it that way," they were saying. "The evidence, as far as *we* are concerned, is not sufficient to establish the claim." No amount of proof would change their minds! And that is still the case with many.

## *Opposition to His Divine Person (8:21-30)*

Jesus went on to issue a solemn warning to His opponents. It was a warning that needs to be sounded still. He declared that their sin[11]—their willful rejection of the Light, their refusal to believe in Him—would bring dire consequences. Their opposition to His divine Person was shutting them out of heaven, where He would be going shortly.[12] They were committing the sin of all sins—the rejection of the Son of God. They would therefore experience the supreme disaster—to be shut out from His presence forever (8:21).

The Jews were perplexed by Jesus' announcement that He was going away and they could not come where He was going. When He had made a similar assertion previously, they had wondered if He might be leaving Judea to teach the Greeks (7:35-36). This time, they sensed He was speaking about death. Although they could scarcely conceive of the possibility, they wondered if He might be considering suicide (8:22).[13] To a Jew, suicide was extremely repugnant.

Jesus made no direct comment on their thoughts, but continued His assessment of their lost condition. Their inability to understand Him and their refusal to receive Him had a logical explanation. They and He belonged to two entirely opposite kingdoms. *They* found their origin and nature in the realm of this fleeting, morally evil world. *He* was of an essentially separate and different order—"from above" (8:23). *They* insisted on living basically independent of God. *He* lived in total dependence on His Father God. Once more Jesus put the contrast in words that pronounced the fate of His opponents and affirmed His true identity. "If you do not believe that I am the one I claim to be, you will indeed die in your sins" (8:24).[14]

As though to obtain from Jesus a once-for-all, unequivocal identification, the Jews interrupted Him.

"*You*," they demand (literally), "who are you?"[15] In response, Jesus assured them that the claims He had been making all along still stood (8:25). And then He went back to all He had previously said concerning their worldly and lost condition (8:23-24). He told them, in effect, "As painful as this is to me,[16] I cannot fail to declare to you—yes, even to the whole world—the many more judgments concerning you which I have heard from my truthful Father" (8:26).

Finally, He looked ahead to Calvary: "When you have lifted up the Son of Man," He said, "then you will know that I am the one I claim to be" (8:28). At that point they would understand that the Father did indeed send Him. They would understand that He spoke what He had heard from His Father. And because He did only what pleased God, God the Father would never leave Him alone. These revelations would follow His being lifted up on the cross to die. But then it would be too late,[17] because they had rejected His *divine person* (8:27-29).

## Opposition to His Liberating Offer (8:31-47)

Our Lord had testified of His relationship to His Father. He had asserted that faith in Him was the only way to heaven. Not all who heard His words rejected them. Some of His hearers believed in Him (8:30). But their faith was still tentative and outward. They lacked an understanding of true discipleship. And the preponderance of His listeners were still skeptics.

Jesus proceeded to explain that *continuing* obedience to His teaching (the "truth") was the mark of genuine discipleship (8:31). The knowledge of such truth issued in true freedom (8:32).[18] Thus Jesus made to those who had just believed in Him a *liberating offer.*

As usual the majority of those listening misinterpreted and misapplied Jesus' words. They thought He was talking about political freedom. In a grand instance of self-deception,[19] they insisted they had been in political servitude to no one (8:33). They were descendants of Abraham. Did Jesus not know that to Abraham "the sovereignty of the world had been assured by an eternal and inalienable right"[20]? But Jesus was speaking not of political freedom. He was referring to liberation from slavery to sin; only He could procure that (8:36). In their spiritual blindness, most were not prepared to receive that freedom. They might call God their Father and proudly trace their *natural* lineage to Abraham. Yet their rejection of Jesus, whose word they did not believe, demonstrated no *spiritual* tie to Abraham (8:37-39). Their real father was none other than the father of lies, the devil. It was his murderous desires that they were intent to carry out (8:42-45). If they really were children of God, they would obey the word of God, as revealed in His Son Jesus (8:47). Thus they reject Jesus' offer of spiritual freedom.

## Opposition to His Bold Claim (8:48-59)

Jesus would go farther. He would claim to have existed before Abraham (8:58). For these contentious Jews, it was the last straw. And it came at the end of Jesus' interchange with them. Here is what led up to it.

The Jews' response to Jesus' comment about their devilish paternity was to accuse Him of being demon-possessed (8:48). Once before He had overlooked such a charge (see 7:20ff). This time Jesus denied it. He maintained instead that His entire purpose in life was to honor His Father (8:49-50). He went on to insist that whoever "keeps [His] word . . . will never see death" (8:51). This statement again provokes an accusation that He is demonized. After all, how could He say such a thing when people of old who had kept God's word had died? Abraham and the prophets were prime examples. Was He claiming superiority to Abraham (8:52-53)? Who did He think He was? What kind of self-glorification was this? To which Jesus replied that

He was not at all glorifying Himself. God, His Father, would do that (8:54)! But, yes indeed, He was claiming superiority to Abraham. The fact was that Abraham, whom they claimed as their father, had an entirely different view of Him. While they hoped to see Jesus dead, Abraham *joyfully* looked forward to a living Messiah through his progeny (8:56).

The Jews took Jesus to be saying He was a contemporary of Abraham. They failed to see how Someone as young as He could truthfully make such a claim (8:57). And so, the statement.

" 'I tell you the truth," Jesus answered, 'before Abraham was born, I am!' " (8:58).[21] The crowd was outraged at His supposed blasphemy. Emotions aroused, they were about to take the law into their hands and give Him a blasphemer's death (8:59). But the time for His death had not yet come, and He eluded them.

## *Conclusion*

There is so much in our text that we need to take to heart! The absolute necessity of believing on the Son if we would have eternal life. The ability of Jesus to free us from not only the *guilt* of sin but its *bondage*. The fact that only through God the Son can we know God the Father. But there is one particular truth not emphasized sufficiently in today's believing community. It needs to be brought home afresh to us.

We have seen in our text a Christ who knew intuitively where He had come from and where He was going. He possessed within Himself the witness that He was the Son of God and that His Father loved Him. His own people refused to accept His testimony concerning Himself. Yet this *inner witness* was, without a shred of doubt, a valid *testimony* to the truth (8:14). How, then, may this speak to us?

Our experience will by no means be the same as our Lord's. But it is possible for us, too, to know with the highest possible inner assurance that we are children of God. We can *know* God's love for us poured out into our hearts.[22] The Apostle Paul describes this witness of the Spirit in these words: "The Spirit himself *testifies* with our spirit that we are God's children" (Romans 8:16, emphasis added).

This is much more than a logical deduction from texts of Scripture, valuable though that is. In the words of Robert Haldane, it is "the Holy Spirit [witnessing] to our spirit in a distinct, . . . immediate . . . and . . . concurrent testimony. This testimony, although it cannot be explained, is nevertheless felt by the believer."[23]

It is an essential aspect of the baptism[24] of the Holy Spirit. It brings to the believer a very real sense of God's presence and overwhelming joy. It is the highest and best assurance of our place in God's family. It is given by the Spirit in answer to earnest desire and believing prayer. Consider these words from D. Martyn Lloyd-Jones:

> [This witness of the Spirit] is something that He does; it is the action of the Spirit. You cannot "take" the action of the Spirit; you can only desire it, you can only ask for it. Faith does not mean that you persuade yourself that you "take" something, that you have something; faith means that you believe the Word of God, that you believe in the possibility of this experience, that you believe the instruction which tells you to "ask" and to "seek" and to "knock," and that, if you keep on doing so, it will be "given unto you." Faith does not lay hold on the blessing itself, it lays hold on the One who gives the blessing and pleads with Him. . . . Faith is that which produces the urge and desire in us, and leads us to pray without ceasing until we receive the blessed gift.[25]

The prayer of anyone who has ever known this witness of the Spirit is the prayer that was so dear to the heart of Hudson Taylor, the founder of the China Inland Mission:

> Lord Jesus, make Thyself to me
> A living, bright reality;
> More present to faith's vision keen
> Than any outward object seen;
> More dear, more intimately nigh
> Than e'en the sweetest earthly tie.

May that be every believer's prayer!

### Endnotes

1. John 7:53 through 8:11 is not in the earliest (and many other ancient) manuscripts. I have chosen to treat it in a separate chapter entitled "A Vignette" which appears immediately before the Conclusion. See Table of Contents.
2. The Treasury area contained thirteen trumpet-shaped collection boxes. Each bore an inscription stating the use to which its contents would be put.
3. William Barclay, *The Gospel of John*, vol. II (Philadelphia: The Westminster Press, 1975), 11.
4. ". . . the light of life" means, most likely, "the light that gives life." The phrase could also mean "the light that *is* life" or "the light that springs from life" or "the light that illuminates life."
5. The tense of the Greek verb translated "follow" implies a continuous following, a wholehearted discipleship.
6. Such passages as Numbers 6:25; Psalm 27:1; 36:9; 119:105; Proverbs 6:23; Isaiah 60:20 are but a few of many.
7. As I noted in Chapter 11 of this commentary, the Old Testament passage in the mind of the Pharisees was Deuteronomy 19:15.
8. In the original of 8:14-16, "you" and "I" are emphasized more than our English translations indicate.
9. Literally, "according to the flesh."
10. Leon Morris, *The Gospel According to John* (Grand Rapids, MI: Eerdmans, 1971), 439.
11. The singular word "sin" indicates that here (8:21) Jesus has one particular sin in mind.
12. The phrase "going away" is used by Jesus in John to indicate His death, His resurrection and His ascension to the Father.
13. The Greek vocabulary of 8:22 demands a translation such as, "Surely he will not kill himself!" Josephus states the Jews' very severe attitude toward suicide: "But as for those who have laid mad hands upon themselves, the darker regions of the nether world receive their souls, and God, their father, visits upon their posterity the outrageous acts of the parents." Quoted by Morris, *The Gospel According to John*, 446.
14. Literally, Jesus says here, "If you do not believe that I AM, you will indeed die in your sins." As we have observed, this is no less than the Old Testament name of God. Jesus is clearly, unequivocally declaring His deity. The reader is left to complete the predicate. Our NIV text appropriately explains, "If you do not believe that I am *the one I claim to be.*" Other alternate readings could be ". . . that I am the Light of the World," ". . . that I am the Divine Name," or, ". . . that I am the promised Messiah." The statement is reminiscent of God's pronouncement recorded in Deuteronomy 32:39: "See now that I myself am He! There is no god besides me." The Septuagint translates it, "See now that I AM." In Isaiah 43:10, there is a similar statement.
15. Morris, *The Gospel According to John,* 448, I think incorrectly, has the Jews scornfully saying, "You, who are you to be saying such things?"
16. See F. Godet, *Commentary on the Gospel of St. John*, vol. II (Edinburgh: T. & T. Clarke, 1881), 328.
17. See C.K. Barrett, *The Gospel According to St. John* (London: S.P.C.K., 1955), 344. On the other hand, there is much to be said for Morris' comment, *The Gospel According to John,* 452: "There is a revelatory aspect to the cross, and after the crucifixion those who reflect on it will be in a position to appreciate that Jesus is indeed more than a man." And for Godet's, *Commentary on the Gospel of St. John,* vol. II, 330: "The conviction here pre-

dicted took place in the conscience of all the Jews without exception, when, after the sending of the Holy Spirit, the perfectly holy and divine nature of His person, work and teaching was manifested in Israel by the preaching of the apostles and the existence of the church."

18. To "know" truth in the biblical sense is to have more than an intellectual perception of it. One cannot be said to *know* the truth until, considering its implications and through its application, it becomes life-changing.

19. Comments B.F. Westcott, *Commentary on the Gospel According to St. John* (London: John Murray, Albermarle Street, 1967), 134, "The episodes of Egyptian, Babylonian, Syrian and Roman conquests were treated as mere transitory accidents, not touching the real life of the people, who had never accepted the dominion of their conquerors or coalesced with them."

20. Ibid.

21. Once again we see that divine name, *ego eimi*—I AM, which Jesus takes to Himself throughout this Gospel. Jesus is proclaiming His deity!

22. As stated in Romans 5:5.

23. Quoted by D. Martyn Lloyd-Jones, "Exposition of Chapter 8:5-17," *Romans* (Grand Rapids, MI: Zondervan, 1976), 295.

24. I am using the expression "baptism of the Holy Spirit" as it was used historically by Dr. A.B. Simpson to be synonymous with the experience of the "infilling of the Spirit." In more recent years, as explained by John Stott in his book *Baptism and Infilling of the Holy Spirit,* the term has come to be equated with conversion, as used by Paul in First Corinthians 12:13. I recognize that some today use the expression in both senses.

25. Ibid., 389.

# 17

# Opposition to the Healing

## John 9:1-41

*As he went along, he saw a man blind from birth. 2 His disciples asked him, "Rabbi, who sinned, this man or his parents, that he was born blind?"*

*3 "Neither this man nor his parents sinned," said Jesus, "but this happened so that the work of God might be displayed in his life. 4 As long as it is day, we must do the work of him who sent me. Night is coming, when no one can work. 5 While I am in the world, I am the light of the world."*

*6 Having said this, he spit on the ground, made some mud with the saliva, and put it on the man's eyes. 7 "Go," he told him, "wash in the Pool of Siloam" (this word means Sent). So the man went and washed, and came home seeing.*

*8 His neighbors and those who had formerly seen him begging asked, "Isn't this the same man who used to sit and beg?" 9 Some claimed that he was.*

*Others said, "No, he only looks like him."*

*But he himself insisted, "I am the man."*

*10 "How then were your eyes opened?" they demanded.*

*11 He replied, "The man they call Jesus made some mud and put it on my eyes. He told me to go to Siloam and wash. So I went and washed, and then I could see."*

*12 "Where is this man?" they asked him.*

*"I don't know," he said.*

*13 They brought to the Pharisees the man who had been blind. 14 Now* the day on which Jesus had made the mud and opened the man's eyes was a Sabbath. 15 Therefore the Pharisees also asked him how he had received his sight. "He put mud on my eyes," the man replied, "and I washed, and now I see."

16 Some of the Pharisees said, "This man is not from God, for he does not keep the Sabbath."

But others asked, "How can a sinner do such miraculous signs?" So they were divided.

17 Finally they turned again to the blind man, "What have you to say about him? It was your eyes he opened."

The man replied, "He is a prophet."

18 The Jews still did not believe that he had been blind and had received his sight until they sent for the man's parents. 19 "Is this your son?" they asked. "Is this the one you say was born blind? How is it that now he can see?"

20 "We know he is our son," the parents answered, "and we know he was born blind. 21 But how he can see now, or who opened his eyes, we don't know. Ask him. He is of age; he will speak for himself." 22 His parents said this because they were afraid of the Jews, for already the Jews had decided that anyone who acknowledged that Jesus was the Christ would be put out of the synagogue. 23 That was why his parents said, "He is of age; ask him."

24 A second time they summoned the man who had been blind. "Give glory to God," they said. "We know this man is a sinner."

25 He replied, "Whether he is a sinner or not, I don't know. One thing I do know. I was blind but now I see!"

26 Then they asked him, "What did he do to you? How did he open your eyes?"

27 He answered, "I have told you already and you did not listen. Why do you want to hear it again? Do you want to become his disciples, too?"

28 Then they hurled insults at him and said, "You are this fellow's disciple! We are disciples of Moses! 29 We know that God spoke to Moses, but as for this fellow, we don't even know where he comes from."

30 The man answered, "Now that is remarkable! You don't know where he comes from, yet he opened my eyes. 31 We know that God does not listen to sinners. He listens to the godly man who does his will. 32 Nobody has ever heard of opening the eyes of a man born blind. 33 If this man were not from God, he could do nothing."

34 To this they replied, "You were steeped in sin at birth; how dare you lecture us!" And they threw him out.

35 Jesus heard that they had thrown him out, and when he found him, he said, "Do you believe in the Son of Man?"

36 *"Who is he, sir?"* the man asked. *"Tell me so that I may believe in him."*

37 Jesus said, *"You have now seen him; in fact, he is the one speaking with you."*

38 Then the man said, *"Lord, I believe,"* and he worshiped him.

39 Jesus said, *"For judgment I have come into this world, so that the blind will see and those who see will become blind."*

40 Some Pharisees who were with him heard him say this and asked, *"What? Are we blind too?"*

41 Jesus said, *"If you were blind, you would not be guilty of sin; but now that you claim you can see, your guilt remains."*

S he walked around campus carrying her white cane and her tape recorder. She was totally blind, without any hope of gaining her sight. Fellow students were kind and helpful. A dorm mother had courageously prayed that she would be healed. In a morning chapel service of worship, we were offering Spirit-inspired praises to God. Suddenly, He who is the Light of the World sovereignly and unannounced opened her blind eyes.

"I can see! I can see!" she exclaimed as she turned to those around her. We had witnessed the gracious healing work of God in that young student's life![1]

Christ our Healer, the same "yesterday and today and forever" (Hebrews 13:8), had once again displayed His mercy mixed with power. It was a repetition of His miracle in Jerusalem when He opened the eyes of the man in our text. The man of John 9 was living in the physical darkness of congenital blindness. And, like the other miracles John recorded, this one too was a "sign" pointing to a grand truth concerning Jesus.[2] He is the *Light of the World* (9:5), delivering those who believe on Him from the darkness of sin and spiritual ignorance. Jesus is "a lamp to [their] feet and a light for [their] path" (Psalm 119:105). At the same time, He brings inevitable judgment upon all who reject the light (John 9:39). We will examine our text, noting first . . .

## *The Blind Man Healed (9:1-12)*

Evidently it was well-known in the community that the beggar whom Jesus came upon had been born blind. He at once became the focus of the disciples' theological inquisitiveness.

"Rabbi, who sinned, this man or his parents, that he was born blind?" (9:2). The question seems strange to modern ears. We are quite prepared to grant a *possible* connection between sin and sickness. Both experience and Scripture[3] indicate it. But we are not prepared to concede that blindness, for example, is *always* the punishment for someone's sin.[4] This was the belief and teaching of the rabbis of Jesus' day. Thus the disciples concluded that perhaps the sins of *the parents* were being visited upon their offspring. Or perhaps, as some supposed, the child might have sinned in the womb![5] From their contemporary viewpoint, their question was quite legitimate.

Jesus, however, corrected this error. He assured His disciples that in this instance the man's blindness was not a punishment for sin. Rather, it was a God-given occasion for Him who is *the Light of the World* (9:5) to manifest God's mighty work (9:3).[6] This kind of heaven-sent opportunity to glorify God *must* be seized whenever it presents itself. The relentless passing of time or some adverse circumstance could mean the loss of such an opportunity (9:4).[7] The Apostle Paul surely reflects this thought when he instructs the believers in Ephesus to "[make] the most of every opportunity, because the days are evil" (Ephesians 5:16).

With this explanation, Jesus now proceeds with the faith-building steps that will bring sight to the blind man. In the ancient world, it was commonly believed that saliva contained healing power. To gain the man's confidence, Jesus begins with the methods and customs of His time. He does what the man would expect any doctor to do—He puts His saliva on the man's eyes (9:6).[8]

Then, wisely, He gives the needy man something that he himself must do , necessitating the exercise of his faith. He commands him to go and wash off the muddy mixture in the Pool of Siloam. John observes that the name of the pool means "Sent."[9] When the blind man man obeyed, he could see (9:7)! It is an interesting play on words. The One who was *sent* to restore spiritual "sight" *sent* the man born blind to a pool called *"Sent."* There his physical eyes were opened!

The wonder of a once-blind beggar walking with joyfully steady step created no small sensation! People could scarcely believe what they were seeing, and the news spread like wildfire.

"Have you heard what happened to the blind beggar?"

"Yes, but I don't believe it!"

"It's true; I saw him myself."

"It must have been a look-alike."

"Well, let's find him and settle the matter."

"There he is!" So the arguers accost the well-known beggar. "You surely can't be the man who was blind?" they queried.

"I'm the man!" the healed man replied with obvious gratitude.

"What happened? How did you get your eyesight?" So the man told them the details.

"You mean to say mud and water gave you your eyesight?" There was skepticism in the question. "Where can we find this Man?" But the former beggar did not know. He had not once seen his Benefactor.

What happened next would be a playwright's dream! We notice, second, . . .

## The Healed Man Expelled (9:13-34)

SETTING: A synagogue court of law in Jerusalem

THE CAST:

A Sabbath-breaking Rabbi

A feisty, formerly blind beggar

The man's parents, who are reluctant witnesses

Biased Pharisees—examiners, judge, jurors—who take themselves far too seriously

Spectators—always eager to see the Pharisees bested

THE PLOT: A man born blind, who begs for a living, is given his sight by an itinerant Teacher. Because it happened on the Sabbath, the Teacher is arraigned before a religious inquiry. The court attempts to get the man born blind to change his testimony to suit its bias. When he refuses to comply and impudently questions the court's competence, he is expelled from the synagogue.

### Scene I

The Pharisees, upon hearing the former blind man's story, are chiefly concerned that the Healer broke the Sabbath.[10] But their opinion of the

Healer is not unanimous. Some argue, "Breaking the law (healing on the Sabbath) proves he is not a prophet of God." Others contend, "Performing such a miracle proves he is a prophet of God" (9:13-16). They decide that the formerly blind man may best be able to judge the character of his Benefactor. When they ask his opinion, he sides with those who consider Jesus a prophet (9:17).

### Scene II

Still unwilling to admit a miraculous healing, the court dismisses the man and subpoenas his parents. The parents identify the former blind man as their son. They affirm that he had indeed been blind from birth. When asked to explain how he had received his sight, they refuse to give an opinion. They fear that any semblance of belief in Jesus would mean their excommunication from the synagogue. To them that would be a fate worse than death.[11] Since their son was an adult, he could speak for himself (9:18-23).

### Scene III

The healed man returns to the witness stand. The court adjures him, under penalty of perjury, to reveal what he is hiding (9:24). The court's reasoning is that the man cannot be telling the truth.[12] They know Jesus to be a sinner because He worked on the Sabbath. Therefore, He could not possibly have performed a miracle (9:24). The defendant's reply (9:25) is the testimony of many a sinner saved by God's grace: "One thing I do know. I was blind, but now I see!"

### Scene IV

The inquiry continues. By this time, the man suspects that this court does not want the truth. It simply is trying to trip him up in order to nullify his positive testimony favoring Jesus. He refuses, therefore, to repeat his story, choosing rather to mock them. "Do you want to become his disciples, too?" he asks (9:26-27). Angry and realizing that they no longer make sense, the Pharisees hurl abuse at the man. It is a ploy not uncommon in such circumstances.

"We are much better informed than you are," the Pharisees declare. "We are disciples of Moses! We know that God spoke to Moses. But as for this fellow,[13] we don't even know where he comes from" (9:28-29).

At this, the feisty ex-beggar, displaying remarkable courage and insight, taunts them. It is an unassailable argument. He says, in effect, "You rabbis teach that God does not listen to sinners. But God listened to Jesus, and He opened my eyes, something unheard of. Therefore, Jesus must be a prophet from God" (9:30-33).

That does it! How dare a man blind because of his sinfulness presume to lecture *them*—scholars of Moses—on theology? So they expel the man from the synagogue (9:34). Now see, third, . . .

## The Expelled Man Believing (9:35-38)

The man who had received his sight was excommunicated from the synagogue. But he was not removed from the thoughts of Him who is the Light of the World. When word of the man's unceremonious expulsion got back to Jesus, our Lord looked him up. Jesus knew it was for His sake that he was being persecuted.

"Do you[14] believe in the Son of Man?" (9:35)[15] Jesus asks. It seems evident that Jesus believes the man was at least somewhat familiar with the Scriptures. For his part, the man senses that he *should* believe in this One.

"Who is he, sir?" the man wants to know. And Jesus immediately makes Himself known (9:37).[16] Whereupon the man, who had first regarded Jesus as only a "man" (9:11), then a "prophet" (9:17), receives Him as "Lord."[17] He falls at Jesus' feet, giving Him the loving adoration due to God (9:38).

Finally, see . . .

## The Opposers Judged (9:39-41)

It seems unlikely that Jesus' words of 9:39-41 were spoken in front of the worshiping man. Had there been Pharisees present as Jesus identified Himself, they would certainly have protested His statements. But Jesus enunciates a spiritual principle in terms appropriate to the healing of the blind man. He has come as the Light of the world to give spiritual sight to those willing to acknowledge their blindness. But there are others who proudly claim to have spiritual sight while blindly rejecting the true Light. They will be judged as those who know exactly what they are doing (9:39). Had the Pharisees truly been blind in their treatment of Jesus, their guilt would have been less. The judgment meted out to them would reflect their ignorance. But they rejected Him while claiming to know the Scripture that spoke of Him. Therefore they accrued to themselves the utmost guilt (9:41). The principle may be concisely stated: *People are judged on the basis of what they do with the light they have received.* The former beggar received the Light; the Pharisees rejected the Light.

## Conclusion

Our text speaks of light and sight. The episode appropriately illustrates the work of the Holy Spirit in opening spiritually blind eyes to the gospel. The Apostle Paul describes the unconverted as people living "in the futility of their thinking." He goes on to say, "They are *darkened* in their understanding and separated from the life of God" (Ephesians 4:17-18, emphasis added). To the Romans he describes those whose "thinking became futile and their foolish hearts were *darkened*" (Romans 1:21, emphasis added). It takes the power of the Holy Spirit to rescue "us from the dominion of darkness and [bring] us into the kingdom of the Son he loves" (Colossians 1:13). How thankful we should be that God opened our eyes to the truth!

But let us observe, second, that this sight-giving work of the Spirit must be continually desired. If God's truth is to have an ongoing effect on our lifestyle, we need the Spirit's activity throughout life. Paul's prayer for believers bears out this truth. It needs to be the heartfelt prayer of spiritually minded people today:

> I keep asking that the God of our Lord Jesus Christ . . . may give you the Spirit of wisdom and revelation, so that you may know him better. I pray also that the eyes of your heart may be enlightened in order that you may know the hope to which he has called you, the riches of his glorious inheritance in the saints, and his incomparably great power for us who believe. (Ephesians 1:17-19)[18]

Third, our text sets before us Jesus, *the* Light of the world. But His statement in 9:4 implies that *we*, too, by doing the works of God, are also to be light. As the Apostle Paul puts it, we must "shine like stars in the universe" (Philippians 2:15). To us our Lord says, "You are the light of the world. . . . Let your light shine before men, that they may see your good deeds and praise your Father in heaven" (Matthew 5:14, 16). As the moon reflects the light of the sun, so we are called to reflect the light of Jesus in a dark world. Paul says it this way: "For you were once darkness, but now you are light in the Lord. Live as children of light (for the fruit of the light consists in all goodness, righteousness and truth) and find out what pleases the Lord" (Ephesians 5:8-10).

We must allow the Holy Spirit to produce in us the fruit of the Spirit—*the fruit of the light,* we might say. Then this kind of shining is wonderfully possible.

> Shine brightly through me, Jesus,
> In a world as dark as night;
> Let my life reflect your nature,
> Let me radiate your light.

### Endnotes

1. This incident took place in Wheaton College chapel in the 1950s when my wife and I were in attendance.
2. The previous signs were: 1) The changing of the water into wine (chapter 2): the "old wine" of the Law is replaced with the "new wine" of the Spirit; 2) the healing of the official's son, and 3) the healing at the Bethesda pool (chapters 4 and 5): Jesus, the Giver of abundant life; 4) the feeding of the 5,000 (chapter 6): Jesus, the Bread of Life; 5) the walking on the water (chapter 6): showing Jesus' kingly power over nature.
3. James 5:15-16 seems to imply this possibility.
4. Job's friends were of the same mind (e.g., Job 4:7f).
5. Some rabbis inferred this from Jacob and Esau's prenatal conduct (Genesis 25:22) together with Psalm 58:3—"Even from birth the wicked go astray; from the womb they are wayward and speak lies"—an obvious hyperbole. It was also believed by some that it was possible for souls to sin before they took possession of human bodies.
6. The wording of the Greek of 9:3 makes possible more than one translation and interpretation. The NIV has it: "but *this happened* so that the work of God might be displayed in his life." The italicized words are supplied by the translator and could be interpreted to mean that God purposely ordained the man should be born blind in order that his healing might display God's power to heal. It is also possible to translate the sentence: "But this happened *with the result that* the work of God might be displayed." This would imply only

that God would use the man's condition as an occasion for displaying His work. This second interpretation seems to be closer to the truth than the first.

7. Jesus could be saying, "The time of My incarnation is limited. My stay in the world is short. Therefore I must work quickly and in accordance with My character as the world's light." See F.F. Bruce, *The Gospel of John* (Grand Rapids, MI: Eerdmans, 1983), 209, and Leon Morris, *The Gospel According to John* (Grand Rapids, MI: Eerdmans, 1971), 480.

8. William Barclay, *The Gospel of John*, vol. II (Philadelphia: The Westminster Press, 1975), 442f, for an excellent description of the ancient world's use of saliva for medical purposes.

9. This landmark in Jerusalem took its name from the fact that the waters that filled the pool were *sent* from the spring of Gihon in the Kidron Valley. They coursed through an underground conduit built during the reign of Hezekiah to ensure a constant supply of water should the city be besieged (2 Kings 20:20; 2 Chronicles 32:2-4, 30).

10. The "kneading" of a mud and spittle poultice would be considered work, as would the anointing of the blind man's eyes in a non-emergency situation.

11. Bruce, *The Gospel of John*, 215.

12. "Give glory to God" is a solemn charge to tell the truth. Compare Joshua 7:19, where the same thing is said to Aachan.

13. A free translation of the Greek *ekeinos*, "that one."

14. The original emphasizes the "you" as compared with the Pharisees who did not believe.

15. The man might very well have known that the expression, "Son of Man," found its Old Testament Messianic roots in Daniel. In one of the prophet's visions he reports: "There before me was one like a son of man.... He was given authority, glory and sovereign power; all peoples, nations and men of every language worshiped him. His dominion is an everlasting dominion that will not pass away, and his kingdom is one that will never be destroyed" (7:13-14).

16. Jesus uses the same expression here as He used when He made Himself known to the Samaritan woman (John 4:26).

17. The NIV, I think correctly, translates the designation, *kurie,* in 9:36 as "Sir" and then in 9:38 as "Lord."

18. In the New Testament, one cannot be said to know spiritual truth unless and until it has a practical effect on behavior.

## Part VI

## *Questions for Reflection or Discussion*

1. How does the Jewish Feast of Tabernacles illustrate the work of the Holy Spirit?

2. According to John 8:12-59, what fourfold opposition to Jesus arises from His claim to be the Light of the world?

3. What is meant by the "witness of the Spirit"? How does this assure believers of their salvation?

4. What ministry of the Holy Spirit is illustrated by Jesus' opening the eyes of the blind man in John 9:1-41? What is the ministry of the Holy Spirit according to First Corinthians 2:6-16?

5. In what sense are believers also lights in a dark world?

*Part VII*

# The People of the Son

John 10:1-42

# 18

# A Shepherded People

## John 10:1-21

*"I tell you the truth, the man who does not enter the sheep pen by the gate, but climbs in by some other way, is a thief and a robber. 2 The man who enters by the gate is the shepherd of his sheep. 3 The watchman opens the gate for him, and the sheep listen to his voice. He calls his own sheep by name and leads them out. 4 When he has brought out all his own, he goes on ahead of them, and his sheep follow him because they know his voice. 5 But they will never follow a stranger; in fact, they will run away from him because they do not recognize a stranger's voice." 6 Jesus used this figure of speech, but they did not understand what he was telling them.*

*7 Therefore Jesus said again, "I tell you the truth, I am the gate for the sheep. 8 All who ever came before me were thieves and robbers, but the sheep did not listen to them. 9 I am the gate; whoever enters through me will be saved. He will come in and go out, and find pasture. 10 The thief comes only to steal and kill and destroy; I have come that they may have life, and have it to the full.*

*11 "I am the good shepherd. The good shepherd lays down his life for the sheep. 12 The hired hand is not the shepherd who owns the sheep. So when he sees the wolf coming, he abandons the sheep and runs away. Then the wolf attacks the flock and scatters it. 13 The man runs away because he is a hired hand and cares nothing for the sheep.*

*14 "I am the good shepherd; I know my sheep and my sheep know me— 15 just as the Father knows me and I know the Father—and I lay down my life for the sheep. 16 I have other sheep that are not of this sheep pen. I*

*must bring them also. They too will listen to my voice, and there shall be
one flock and one shepherd. 17 The reason my Father loves me is that I lay
down my life—only to take it up again. 18 No one takes it from me, but I lay
it down of my own accord. I have authority to lay it down and authority to
take it up again. This command I received from my Father."*

*19 At these words the Jews were again divided. 20 Many of them said,
"He is demon-possessed and raving mad. Why listen to him?"*

*21 But others said, "These are not the sayings of a man possessed by a
demon. Can a demon open the eyes of the blind?"*

Our Israeli tour bus rounded a curve in the highway going south toward
Jerusalem. Suddenly we came upon a small flock of sheep crossing
the narrow road behind their dark-complexioned shepherd. We stopped and
waited, cameras in hand, until the last woolly animal had crossed. It was as
though we were back in the Judean uplands of Bible days. We were observing what Jesus must have seen often as He traversed the rough, stony pastoral countryside. And as we watched, we observed the shepherd's weather-
beaten yet tender face. We heard his almost-eerie voice calling his flock to
follow him. The above text was before our very eyes!

Both Old and New Testaments use the Palestinian shepherd and his sheep to
describe the relationship between God and His people. How familiar, for example, are the comforting words, "The LORD is my shepherd; I shall not want"
(Psalm 23:1, KJV). Or, "He tends his flock like a shepherd: He gathers the
lambs in his arms and carries them close to his heart; he gently leads those that
have young" (Isaiah 40:11).[1] Messiah too is prophetically described as "a ruler
who will be the shepherd of my people Israel" (Matthew 2:6, quoting Micah
5:2). And here our text sets before us in parable[2] and discourse Christ's relationship to His own people. He is, in the words of Hebrews 13:20, "that great
Shepherd of the sheep." Notice first the picture of . . .

## Palestine Shepherding (10:1-6)

Our Lord began His discourse with a true-to-life description of Palestine
shepherding. The "sheep pen" (10:1), where a flock would spend the night,
was usually a walled enclosure made of stone. Roughly square in shape and
open to the sky, it provided protection from wild beeasts and the worst of the

elements. The "gate" (10:1), or entry, might be guarded by the shepherd if his were the only flock in the pen. If, as in Jesus' reference, the pen was home to several flocks, an independent "watchman" would guard the entry. His job was to admit authorized personnel only—the true shepherds (10:3). He kept out sneak-thieves and brigands[3] who could enter the pen only by climbing over the wall (10:1).

In the morning the shepherd would come to pasture his flock. Standing at the entry, he called each of his sheep by its descriptive name (10:3). One might be Brown Leg, another Black Ear. Each recognized the shepherd's voice and went to him. Then he led his flock, encouraging them to follow him (10:4). The sheep followed no one but their own shepherd, whose voice they recognized. Should a stranger approach, they would flee in alarm (10:5).[4] Although the Pharisees were familiar with the activity Jesus described, they did not get the import of His message (10:6).

In reality, Jesus was continuing the severe rebuke which He had begun at the end of chapter 9.[5] Ezekiel spoke of "shepherds of Israel who only take care of themselves" and not the flock. He said they had "not strengthened the weak or healed the sick or bound up the injured." Neither had they "brought back the strays or searched for the lost." They had "ruled them harshly and brutally" (Ezekiel 34:2-4). The Pharisees claimed to be shepherds of God's flock. But they had tyrannically treated the blind man whose eyes Jesus opened. Instead of caring for him, as true shepherds should, they expelled him from the synagogue. They were more concerned for their burdensome traditions than for the man's well-being. Without doubt, they were the sneak-thieves and brigands of Jesus' parable. They were seeking, audaciously and hypocritically, to steal sheep from the True Shepherd. They had established within the theocratic fold of Israel an authority unsanctioned by God.[6]

But the time had come for Jesus to "lead *his own* sheep out" (see John 10:3)[7] of a theocracy doomed for destruction. A new flock, with a Shepherd sent from God the Father, was even then being formed. That was the meaning of the parable. The sheep were hearing the voice of their Shepherd!

Notice, second:

## *The Door of the Fold (10:7-10)*

With the words, "I tell you the truth," Jesus changed the metaphor. No longer was it the *shepherd* leading his sheep. Now it was the *gate* through which the sheep might enter the *fold*.[8] The meaning is not difficult to perceive. The fold represents God's kingdom—His great salvation, or eternal life. In this new parable our Lord Jesus is the "Gate." He was presenting Himself as the entry into that royal realm.

Through Jesus—*only* through Jesus—does a person partake of that ultimate salvation. "I tell you the truth," said Jesus, "I am[9] the gate for the sheep" (10:7). And as if to emphasize this truth, He repeated it: "I am the gate; whoever enters through me[10] will be saved." And then He added, "He will come in and go out, and find pasture" (10:9). Jesus was describing the inward peace and divine strength, the freedom and security that are ours in Christ. Those who comprised the Jewish hierarchy of that day were interested only in their own advantage. In contrast, Jesus offered to those who believed on Him life to the full (10:10).

What a gracious yet astonishingly bold claim Jesus was making! He was unequivocally asserting that He and no other is the way to eternal life. Contemporary minds regard as unacceptable this unruffled intolerance of all other purported "ways."

"How can one be so bigoted?" they demand.

"What insufferable narrow-mindedness!" they exclaim. "Are not all religions true?" They have rejected the biblical revelation of truth. They have abandoned rational thought. Confidently (yet illogically) they assert that every humanly devised way to heaven is a true way. As Bultman observes, when the true way is revealed, it is impossible to be tolerant of the various false ways. They lead only to error and disaster.[11]

Sir George Adam Smith tells how, while traveling, he came across a shepherd and his sheep. He fell into conversation with the man, who showed him the sheepfold. It consisted of four walls with an entryway.

Sir George asked, "That is where they go at night?"

"Yes," said the shepherd, "and when they are in there, they are perfectly safe."

"But there is no door," the visitor observed.

"I am the door," replied the shepherd. "When the light has gone and all the sheep are inside, I lie in that open space. No sheep ever goes out but across my body, and no wolf comes in unless he crosses my body. I am the door."[12] Without knowing it, the shepherd had spoken the words of Jesus.

Notice, third . . .

## The Good Shepherd (10:11-15)

The relationship of our Lord Jesus to believers is, first, a very *caring* relationship. He likens Himself to the good[13] shepherd who "lays down his life for the sheep" (see 10:11, 15). His relationship is not that of the hireling. The hired hand lacks the "pride of ownership and the care that proceeds from possession."[14] His only concerns are to save his skin and draw his pay. He does not expose himself to danger to protect the lives of the sheep (10:12-13). The good shepherd, on the other hand, is utterly devoted to his sheep. He will put his life on the line to protect them from death and destruction.

Surely the cross was in our Lord's thinking at that moment. He loved His people so sacrificially that He would voluntarily die to give them eternal life. The Apostle Paul reminds us, "Very rarely will anyone die for a righteous man, though for a good man someone might possibly dare to die. But God demonstrates his own love for us in this: While we were still sinners, Christ died for us" (Romans 5:7-8). It is wonderfully true that the atonement effected by Christ is sufficient for the sins of the whole world. Yet there is a very special sense in which He died for those who will become His sheep.

Second, the relationship between Christ and believers is a very *discriminating* one. It is based on a special "knowledge." Jesus says literally, "I know *mine* and *mine* know me" (John 10:14). How much biblical truth is wrapped up in that statement! If we ask, "How did they become *His*?" the biblical answer is that God the Father "foreknew" believers. He set His love upon them and chose them.[15] He gave them to His Son (see 17:2, 6), and they are the Shepherd's own precious possession.

Suppose we inquire, "What does He mean by saying that He *knows* these who are his own?" The answer is that the Shepherd as well has chosen them as His very own. He has called them to Himself, given them His Word and instructed them in His will. Suppose we ask, "What does it mean to say that they *know* Him?" The answer is that they have heard His call, believe His word and are doing His will.

Third, the relationship between Christ and believers is like the relationship between the Father and the Son. "I know my sheep and my sheep know me—just as the Father *knows* me and I *know* the Father" (10:14-15). The Father sent the Son, gave Him His Word and instructed Him in His will. The Son recognized His calling, heard the Father's Word and did the Father's will. So it is that Jesus later said to His disciples—and still says to us: "As the Father has sent me, I am sending you" (20:21).

Notice, third, . . .

## The Other Sheep (10:16-18)

Jesus has had much to say concerning His shepherding relationship to believers. It applied to those whom He had called to Himself from the Jewish fold. It will apply as well to those He later calls from the Gentile world. These are the "other sheep that are not of this sheep pen" (10:16). It was God's eternal purpose that His Church should be worldwide in scope. He chose Saul of Tarsus to be His special apostle to the Gentiles.[16] Saul (later renamed Paul) preached first to his own people, the Jews. When they hardened their hearts, he saw it as the God-ordained opportunity for Gentiles to hear and believe.[17] A large company of God-sent missionaries has followed Paul's lead. Through them, Christ the Shepherd has been in the process of bringing the "other sheep" into His *one* fold. Those who "listen to [His] voice," Jew and Gentile, are joined together as one people of God.[18]

Our Lord concludes His Good Shepherd discourse by affirming once more what lay ahead for Him. He would voluntarily give His life and rise again in accordance with the Father's command (10:17-18). As usual, His words produced a divided response among His hearers (10:19-21).

## Conclusion

What comfort, encouragement and motivation for believers is in our text! The people of the Son are indeed a *shepherded people*. Meditate long on the

Shepherd's deep, personal, unselfish *love* for His sheep. Love led Him to Calvary, where He gave His own life that we might have abundant life.

Think often of the *electing grace* of the Shepherd, who "called" His sheep by name. He "led them out" of the destructive realm of this evil world and made them His very own possession.

Consider well how this strong Shepherd *protects* His own. He guards them from the snarling "wolves" of demonic temptation, fear, loneliness, discouragement, despair, unbelief and fleshly desire.

Marvel at His personalized *care* for the sheep. He *feeds* them in the green pastures of His word and *waters* them at the fresh springs of His Spirit.

Let us take seriously the powerful *missionary imperative* implicit in this discourse. Christ's purpose is to bring the "other sheep" into His fold. It was this text that motivated the missionary statesman, Robert A. Jaffray, to go ever onward. As he evangelized Southeast Asia, the words of his Lord rang in his heart: "I have other sheep. . . . I must bring them also" (10:16). Among all of earth's people groups, Jaffray did not know whom Christ might sovereignly call into His fold. But he recognized, as must every missionary, that *his* part was to faithfully proclaim the good news. A.J. Gordon put it so well: "It is our work to bring Christ to the world; it is the Spirit's work to bring the world to Christ." Such an understanding of the missionary task would spare many servants of the Lord from discouragement. Results may be meager. The work can be hard. But having done everything, they stand.

John Piper comments appropriately:

> Since the eternal destiny of every individual hangs on knowing Christ and embracing him gladly as the highest value of life, is then the task of missions to maximize the number of people redeemed or the number of peoples reached? The biblical answer is that God's call for missions in Scripture *cannot* be defined merely in terms of crossing cultures to maximize the total number of individuals saved. Rather God's will for missions is that every people group be reached with the testimony of Christ and that a people be called out for his name from all nations.[19]

Our text makes it abundantly clear that the people of the Son are truly a *shepherded people.* We sing with understanding and love:

Saviour, like a shepherd, lead us,
    Much we need Thy tenderest care;
In Thy pleasant pastures feed us,
    For our use Thy folds prepare;
Blessed Jesus, blessed Jesus,
    Thou hast bought us, Thine we are.

We are Thine; do Thou befriend us,
    Be the guardian of our way;
Keep Thy flock, from sin defend us,
    Seek us if we go astray;
Blessed Jesus, blessed Jesus, . . .
    Hear, oh, hear us when we pray.[20]

### Endnotes

1. Other Old Testament references to God as the shepherd are Psalm 77:20; 79:13; 80:1; 95:7; 100:3; Jeremiah 23:1-4; Ezekiel 34. Some New Testament references are Matthew 9:36; 18:12-14; 26:31; Mark 6:34; Luke 12:32; 15:4; Hebrews 13:20; 1 Peter 2:25.
2. Whether our text is a parable, an allegory, a metaphor or just symbolic language (all these words are used by various commentators), is really unimportant.
3. The Greek *lestes* signifies someone ready to engage in violence.
4. William Barclay, *The Gospel of John*, vol. II (Philadelphia: The Westminster Press, 1975), 56ff, gives interesting accounts from various travelers of how the shepherd's voice attracts the sheep and strange voices alarm them. Leon Morris, *The Gospel According to John* (Grand Rapids, MI: Eerdmans, 1971), 503, writes: "It appears that strangers, even when dressed in the shepherd's clothing and attempting to imitate his call, succeed only in making the sheep run away."
5. Nowhere else are the words of 10:1, "I tell you the truth," used to begin a new discourse. Consequently, we may conclude that neither is there a chronological break between chapters 9 and 10. Verse 21, referring to the opening of the blind man's eyes, also connects our text with the previous chapter.
6. F. Godet, *Commentary on the Gospel of St. John*, vol. II (Edinburgh: T. & T. Clarke, 1881), 378.
7. Compare Jesus' words in 6:37: "all that the Father gives me will come to me." They are "his own" sheep.
8. We must not ask how one Person can be both "Shepherd" and "Gate" at the same time. These are two different illustrations, the "Gate" parable being a shorter parable within the larger.
9. Once again the divine name, *ego eimi,* appears.
10. The words translated "through me" are in an emphatic position in the sentence, emphasizing the unique position of our Lord.
11. Cited by Morris, *The Gospel According to John,* 508.
12. Ibid., 507, footnote 30.

13. The word is *kalos,* meaning, among other things, attractive, useful, noble, praiseworthy, contributing to salvation.
14. Morris, *The Gospel According to John,* 510.
15. See Romans 8:29, where believers are said to be "foreknown" by God. This foreknowledge is something more than mere prescience. It is God setting His love upon them and choosing them in Christ from before the creation of the world (Ephesians 1:4).
16. See God's word to Ananias in Acts 9:15.
17. See Paul's argument in Romans 9-11. There he explains that Israel's refusal to accept the gospel had opened a door for the Gentiles to be saved.
18. Perhaps the finest New Testament exposition of this truth is in Ephesians 2:11-22.
19. John Piper, *Let the Nations Be Glad!* (Grand Rapids, MI: Baker Books, 1993), 222.
20. Attributed to Dorothy A. Thrupp, "Saviour, Like a Shepherd, Lead Us," *Hymns of the Christian Life* (Camp Hill, PA: Christian Publications, Inc., 1978), # 344, stanzas 1 and 2.

# A Secured People

John 10:22-42

*22 Then came the Feast of Dedication at Jerusalem. It was winter, 23 and Jesus was in the temple area walking in Solomon's Colonnade. 24 The Jews gathered around him, saying, "How long will you keep us in suspense? If you are the Christ, tell us plainly."*

*25 Jesus answered, "I did tell you, but you do not believe. The miracles I do in my Father's name speak for me, 26 but you do not believe because you are not my sheep. 27 My sheep listen to my voice; I know them, and they follow me. 28 I give them eternal life, and they shall never perish; no one can snatch them out of my hand. 29 My Father, who has given them to me, is greater than all; no one can snatch them out of my Father's hand. 30 I and the Father are one."*

*31 Again the Jews picked up stones to stone him, 32 but Jesus said to them, "I have shown you many great miracles from the Father. For which of these do you stone me?"*

*33 "We are not stoning you for any of these," replied the Jews, "but for blasphemy, because you, a mere man, claim to be God."*

*34 Jesus answered them, "Is it not written in your Law, 'I have said you are gods'? 35 If he called them 'gods,' to whom the word of God came—and the Scripture cannot be broken— 36 what about the one whom the Father set apart as his very own and sent into the world? Why then do you accuse me of blasphemy because I said, 'I am God's Son'? 37 Do not believe me unless I do what my Father does. 38 But if I do it, even though you do not believe me, believe the miracles, that you may know and under-*

*stand that the Father is in me, and I in the Father." 39 Again they tried to*
*seize him, but he escaped their grasp.*
  *40 Then Jesus went back across the Jordan to the place where John had*
*been baptizing in the early days. Here he stayed 41 and many people came*
*to him. They said, "Though John never performed a miraculous sign, all*
*that John said about this man was true." 42 And in that place many be-*
*lieved in Jesus.*

"It was winter," says John in our text—winter, not only with reference to the coldness of the season. It was cold, cold winter in relational terms between the Jews and Jesus. This would be His last offer of salvation to official Jerusalem. Here Jesus defined the stark contrast between His "sheep" and those who, rejecting all He stood for, demonstrated they were not.

The interchange between our Lord and His antagonists took place in Solomon's Colonnade[1] during the "Feast of Dedication" (10:22-23). This was the latest of the great Jewish festivals to be established. Sometimes it was called the Festival of Lights; today it is known as Hanukkah. It commemorated the recapturing and rededication of the temple in 165 B.C. during the Maccabean era. Antiochus Epiphanes, the king of Syria, had desecrated the temple, turning its chambers into brothels. On the great altar he offered swine's flesh to pagan gods. In Jewish minds the Feast of Dedication symbolized their hope that God would again deliver His people. Thus it was an appropriate time for Jewish officials to "close in" on Jesus.[2]

"How long will you keep us in suspense?"[3] these Jewish leaders asked Him. "If you are the Christ, tell us plainly" (10:24).

Jesus very forthrightly told the Samaritan woman that He was the Messiah (4:26). But in Jerusalem, likely because of the political and military implications in that term, Jesus had avoided the title "Messiah." However, if the Jews had not been so faithlessly blind, they would have recognized His true identity. They had seen the many miracles He performed in the name of God His Father (10:25). But their insensitive hearts only became harder still.

Notice how our text characterizes . . .

## *Those Who Are Not Christ's Sheep (10:24-26)*

Jesus took up once again the shepherd/sheep theme that He had begun earlier. He went to the very root of the Jews' refusal to receive His offer of salvation through Himself. Put simply, they were "not [His] sheep" (10:26). They were not among those whom the Father had given to His Son. Proof of this lay in a) *their spiritual blindness.* To grasp Jesus' heavenly origin and divine nature required the Spirit of God. This Enlightenment they did not possess; their minds were darkened. It lay also in b) *their willful unbelief.* True saving faith is always the gift of God, and such faith they did not manifest. Finally, the proof lay in c) *their open hostility.* The very tone of their words (10:24) displayed belligerence. Rather than humbling themselves under Christ's searching probe, they proudly, angrily rebelled at His words. In attitude, speech and action they evidenced the absence of God's enlightening and saving power in their lives. Their blind unbelief demonstrated that they were not the sheep of Christ's fold.

In shimmering contrast, notice how our text describes . . .

## *Those Who Are Christ's Sheep (10:27-30)*

Each beautifully simple phrase in these verses is filled with momentous theological truth demanding our careful attention. Notice that Christ's sheep are a) a *chosen* people.

"My Father . . . has given them to me," Jesus said (10:29). In His "high-priestly" prayer, our Lord spoke of His disciples as "those you have given me" (17:9, 24). In His discourse on the Bread of Life, He declared, "All that my Father gives me will come to me" (6:37). The Apostle Paul wrote concerning "those God foreknew" (descriptive of His electing love). He went on to say, "[God] also predestined [them] to be conformed to the likeness of his Son" (Romans 8:29).[4] In his letter to the Ephesians, Paul praised God who "chose us in [Christ] before the creation of the world to be holy and blameless in his sight" (Ephesians 1:4). They are the ones whom Peter addressed as "chosen according to the foreknowledge of God the Father through the sanctifying work of the Spirit, for obedience to Jesus Christ and sprinkling by his blood" (1 Peter 1:2). Later Peter called them "a chosen people, a royal priesthood, a holy nation, a people belonging to God" (2:9).

These were the people in the heart of God from eternity past. In God's sovereignly amazing grace, He had chosen to give them to His Son as His Son's body.

Not only were they a *chosen* people, but they were b) a *called* people. "My sheep listen to my voice,' He said; "I know them" (John 10:27).[5] They heard Him calling them out of their former lives of bondage to sin, guilt, hopelessness and despair. They heard Him calling them from the man-made chains of external, "pharisaical" regulations. They heard His gracious call to "come to me, all you who are weary and burdened, and I will give you rest" (Matthew 11:28). This was the same call of which Paul wrote: "Those he predestined, he also called" (Romans 8:30). This call guaranteed the believing response of those whom God had chosen to hear it. It was that work of the Spirit of Christ whereby He awakened people to their spiritual need and a conviction of sin. At the same time He opened their minds to understand the gospel and believe it. It was the Shepherd calling the sheep to Himself.

Also, they were c) an *obedient* people: ". . . and they follow me" (John 10:27). The genuine sheep proved their relationship with God by continued obedience to the will of Christ. With Paul they recognized that they had been chosen "in [Christ] before the creation of the world *to be holy and blameless in his sight"* (Ephesians 1:4, emphasis added). They did not "go on sinning so that grace may increase" (Romans 6:1). They recognized that their baptism into Christ implied a death to sin and a life lived to God. They heeded Peter's admonition to "be all the more eager to make your calling and election sure" (2 Peter 1:10). If they strayed from the path, the Shepherd brought them back. By returning they demonstrated that they were truly "elect." When the "stranger" voices of the world, the flesh and the devil beckoned, they knew these were not the Shepherd's voice. They fled lest they fall into evil. They lived in confidence that God would enable them to persevere in holiness to the end. He did and they did.

I well recall a conversation I had with an elderly mother. Over the years she had imbibed a misleading and dangerous version of eternal security. Her son had made a profession of faith in Christ when he was a boy. As a grown man this son had totally forsaken his faith and the church. The mother, however, assured me that should her son die in his present state, he would "of course" go to heaven. The reason: He had made a profession of faith as a child. It was my duty as her pastor to warn her not to take her son's salvation for granted. Rather, she should pray that her son would return to the Lord and receive mercy lest he die in his sin. Bunyan observed in *Pilgrim's Progress,* "There is a road to hell from the very gate of Heaven." That mother had misinterpreted the truth concerning a believer's security in Christ. Eternal security is not a license to sin! It is the Shepherd's promise to the sheep who are following Him.

Fourth, they were d) an *eternally secure* people. "I give them eternal life, and they shall never perish; no one can snatch them out of my hand" (John 10:28). What a hope! Eternal life! A whole new quality of life that began in the here and now and would continue throughout eternity. John reflected this truth when he wrote: "And this is the testimony: God has given us eternal life, and this life is in his Son. He who has the Son has life; he who does not have the Son of God does not have life" (1 John 5:11-12). What security! Protected in the safety of the Savior's strong and loving hands!

Early in my ministry, I served a church whose members believed the commission of one sin or the omission of one duty cost them their salvation. They were at the opposite extreme from the mother I referred to above. Almost every Sunday, people were at the altar to "get saved" again. To them, salvation was a desperate struggle to maintain an acceptance with God. I began to preach often from texts which declared the security of the believer, including our present text. I well remember the relief of one worshiper as she met me at the door following a service. The woman had come to see that it was not she who held on to Christ, but He who held on to her! Our text gives both warning to the careless and comfort to the concerned.

But not only is the believer held in the loving, protecting hands of the Shepherd. He or she is held as well in the Father's strong hands (John 10:29). With Paul the children of God are "convinced that neither death nor life, neither angels nor demons, neither the present nor the future, nor any powers, neither height nor depth, nor anything else in all creation, will be able to separate us from the love of God that is in Christ Jesus our Lord" (Romans 8:38-39).[6] They are safe in the tender, sheltering guardianship of both Father and Son. To be secured by the Son is to be secured by the Father. "I and the Father are one" is our Lord's affirmation of the promise (John 10:30).

F.F. Bruce writes, "So responsive is the Son to the Father that he is one in mind, one in purpose and action with him. Where the eternal well-being of true believers is concerned, the Son's determination and pledge to guard them from harm is endorsed by the Father's word and confirmed by the Father's all-powerful act."[7]

Finally, notice . . .

### *The Shepherd's Claim to Deity (10:31-39)*

It was Jesus' declaration of His oneness with the Father that caused the Jews to prepare once again[8] to stone Him (10:31)—and this without a trial, which the law required. Jesus, in their eyes a "mere man," had committed the unpardonable sin of blasphemy. Therefore He must be put to death as their law required.[9] But see with what fearless courage and composure our Lord answered their charge.

Using a rabbinically styled argument appropriate for His opponents, Jesus quoted a somewhat obscure reference in Psalm 82:6. There mere men, by virtue of their offices as judges and recipients of the word of God, were called "gods." The Jews would have to admit the truth of the psalm. After all, it was part of their sacred Scriptures that could not be broken (10:35). Thus the force of our Lord's argument was this: "You must admit that these human judges were called 'gods.' I have been set apart by the Father for My mission in the world. I have demonstrated My oneness with the Father by the miracles I performed. Why, then, should you charge Me with blasphemy when I identify Myself as God's Son? You must take My words seriously. The Father is in Me, and I am in the Father" (see 10:35-38).

With that, Jesus slipped through their hateful hands back to the relative safety of Trans-Jordan. There God had prepared, through the prophetic ministry of Jesus' forerunner (10:40-42), a more receptive community to believe on Him.

### *Conclusion*

A person reading the Old Testament cannot help but notice how often ancient Israel reviewed God's mighty saving acts. Psalm 105 is an excellent example of this remembering. Such recollections preserved in them a spirit of praise and encouraged them to believe for the future. For similar reasons the Apostle Paul in the New Testament invited believers to remember. They were to regard with thanksgiving their transfer from the kingdom of darkness to the kingdom of God's dear Son. Ephesians 2 and Titus 3:3-8 are examples of such admonition and the praise to God it should produce.

If I am to maintain a deeper life in Christ, I must pause periodically to marvel at salvation's miracle. It is absolutely vital that I be "lost in wonder, love and praise" at God's great mercy to me. It will never do simply to say, "Praise God, I accepted Christ as my Savior," as true as that may be. I need to remember that there is something positively amazing about the fact that I am now a believer in Jesus.

I must consider, for example, that I was once alienated from God and hostile to Him. I was blind to spiritual reality, bound by self and sin. I was once a child of wrath, condemned to eternal death. So hopeless was my natural condition that, left to my own decision-making, I would never have believed in Christ. There was a time when I was *not* one of Christ's sheep.

But our text would have me remember that long before I was born, God chose me. Even before the universe was created, God Himself predestined me to be His. He set His love on me and purposed to give me to Christ, the Good Shepherd. And while I was still dead in sins, the voice of the Shepherd called and awakened in me a sense of need. The Holy Spirit saw to it that I heard the good news that Christ died for sinners and rose again, convicted me of sin. God brought spiritual understanding to my darkened mind. He gave me the gifts of repentance and faith. And the Shepherd Himself came to dwell within! Any decision I made was but an inevitable response to His divine conquest. Without question, from beginning to end, salvation is of the Lord!

John Bunyan knew this. In his less-familiar allegory, *War on the Soul,* he vividly describes the offensive made by the Spirit of God. The objective: to gain entrance into Mansoul. It is a kingdom so closed to the King of heaven that only an all-out frontal attack can break down the barriers. Thank God, the King's victory was never in doubt! And now, with Henry W. Baker, I sing:

> The King of love my Shepherd is,
>     Whose goodness faileth never;

I nothing lack if I am His
  And He is mine forever.

Where streams of living water flow
  My ransomed soul He leadeth,
And where the verdant pastures grow,
  With food celestial feedeth.

Perverse and foolish oft I strayed;
  But yet in love He sought me,
And on His shoulder gently laid,
  And home, rejoicing, brought me.

In death's dark vale I fear no ill
  With Thee, dear Lord, beside me;
Thy rod and staff my comfort still,
  Thy cross before to guide me.

Thou spreadst a table in my sight;
  Thy unction grace bestoweth;
And, oh, what transport of delight
  From Thy pure chalice floweth.

And so through all the length of days
  Thy goodness faileth never:
Good Shepherd, may I sing Thy praise
  Within Thy house forever.[10]

### Endnotes

1. There are two other New Testament references to this portico that ran along the east side of the outer court of Herod's temple. In Acts 3:11, it was where the crowd gathered to hear Peter's response to the healing of the blind beggar. In Acts 5:12 the early believers are said to have met together in Solomon's Colonnade. In our text Jesus may have gone there for protection from the cold of winter.

2. J.B. Phillips, *The New Testament in Modern English* (New York: Macmillan, 1957).

3. The question may also be translated, "Why do you plague us?" indicating their hostility; or "Why do you take away our life?" (that is, "Why are you seeking to bring an end to our

hold on the religious life of the nation?") Leon Morris, *The Gospel According to John* (Grand Rapids, MI: Eerdmans, 1971), 518.

4. See also Romans 9 for Paul's description of God's unconditional election of His people.
5. Compare John 10:3, 16.
6. Many interpret "eternal security" to mean that once a person professes faith in Christ, he is eternally secure, whether or not he walks in obedience to God's Word. Such a view is far from the teaching of our text. "They shall never perish" comes *after* the words, ". . . and they follow me."
7. F.F. Bruce, *The Gospel of John* (Grand Rapids, MI: Eerdmans, 1983), 232.
8. See John 8:58-59.
9. See, for example, Numbers 15:30-31. Some modern theologians use Jesus' expressions of oneness with the Father in John's Gospel to deny His deity. The fact remains that Jesus' contemporaries understood Him to be claiming equality with God—deity. And in fact this is exactly His claim!
10. Henry W. Baker, "The King of Love My Shepherd Is," *Hymns of the Christian Life* (Camp Hill, PA: Christian Publications, Inc., 1978), # 178.

## Part VII

## *Questions for Reflection or Discussion*

1. In what respects is the relationship of Jesus to His people like the relationship of a Palestinian shepherd to his sheep? Why is it appropriate to call Christ's people sheep?

2. What may we learn from Psalm 23 about our relationship with Christ?

3. How does John 10:16-17 motivate the program of world missions?

4. What does Romans 8:28-39 teach us about the relationship of Christ to His sheep?

5. Why is the grace of God so utterly amazing?

*Part VIII*

# The Popularity of the Son

John 11:1-12:19

# 20

# *A Graveside Resurrection*

John 11:1-54

*Now a man named Lazarus was sick. He was from Bethany, the village of Mary and her sister Martha. 2 This Mary, whose brother Lazarus now lay sick, was the same one who poured perfume on the Lord and wiped his feet with her hair. 3 So the sisters sent word to Jesus, "Lord, the one you love is sick."*

*4 When he heard this, Jesus said, "This sickness will not end in death. No, it is for God's glory so that God's Son may be glorified through it." 5 Jesus loved Martha and her sister and Lazarus. 6 Yet when he heard that Lazarus was sick, he stayed where he was two more days.*

*7 Then he said to his disciples, "Let us go back to Judea."*

*8 "But Rabbi," they said, "a short while ago the Jews tried to stone you, and yet you are going back there?"*

*9 Jesus answered, "Are there not twelve hours of daylight? A man who walks by day will not stumble, for he sees by this world's light. 10 It is when he walks by night that he stumbles, for he has no light."*

*11 After he had said this, he went on to tell them, "Our friend Lazarus has fallen asleep; but I am going there to wake him up."*

*12 His disciples replied, "Lord, if he sleeps, he will get better." 13 Jesus had been speaking of his death, but his disciples thought he meant natural sleep.*

*14 So then he told them plainly, "Lazarus is dead, 15 and for your sake I am glad I was not there, so that you may believe. But let us go to him."*

16 Then Thomas (called Didymus) said to the rest of the disciples, "Let us also go, that we may die with him."

17 On his arrival, Jesus found that Lazarus had already been in the tomb for four days. 18 Bethany was less than two miles from Jerusalem, 19 and many Jews had come to Martha and Mary to comfort them in the loss of their brother. 20 When Martha heard that Jesus was coming, she went out to meet him, but Mary stayed at home.

21 "Lord," Martha said to Jesus, "if you had been here, my brother would not have died. 22 But I know that even now God will give you whatever you ask."

23 Jesus said to her, "Your brother will rise again."

24 Martha answered, "I know he will rise again in the resurrection at the last day."

25 Jesus said to her, "I am the resurrection and the life. He who believes in me will live, even though he dies; 26 and whoever lives and believes in me will never die. Do you believe this?"

27 "Yes, Lord," she told him, "I believe that you are the Christ, the Son of God, who was to come into the world."

28 And after she had said this, she went back and called her sister Mary aside. "The Teacher is here," she said, "and is asking for you." 29 When Mary heard this, she got up quickly and went to him. 30 Now Jesus had not yet entered the village, but was still at the place where Martha had met him. 31 When the Jews who had been with Mary in the house, comforting her, noticed how quickly she got up and went out, they followed her, supposing she was going to the tomb to mourn there.

32 When Mary reached the place where Jesus was and saw him, she fell at his feet and said, "Lord, if you had been here, my brother would not have died."

33 When Jesus saw her weeping, and the Jews who had come along with her also weeping, he was deeply moved in spirit and troubled. 34 "Where have you laid him?" he asked.

"Come and see, Lord," they replied.

35 Jesus wept.

36 Then the Jews said, "See how he loved him!"

37 But some of them said, "Could not he who opened the eyes of the blind man have kept this man from dying?"

38 Jesus, once more deeply moved, came to the tomb. It was a cave with a stone laid across the entrance. 39 "Take away the stone," he said.

"But Lord," said Martha, the sister of the dead man, "by this time there is a bad odor, for he has been there four days."

40 Then Jesus said, "Did I not tell you that if you believed, you would see the glory of God?"

*41 So they took away the stone. Then Jesus looked up and said, "Father, I thank you that you have heard me. 42 I knew that you always hear me, but I said this for the benefit of the people standing here, that they may believe that you sent me."*

*43 When he had said this, Jesus called in a loud voice, "Lazarus, come out!" 44 The dead man came out, his hands and feet wrapped with strips of linen, and a cloth around his face.*

*Jesus said to them, "Take off the grave clothes and let him go."*

*45 Therefore many of the Jews who had come to visit Mary, and had seen what Jesus did, put their faith in him. 46 But some of them went to the Pharisees and told them what Jesus had done. 47 Then the chief priests and the Pharisees called a meeting of the Sanhedrin.*

*"What are we accomplishing?" they asked. "Here is this man performing many miraculous signs. 48 If we let him go on like this, everyone will believe in him, and then the Romans will come and take away both our place and our nation."*

*49 Then one of them, named Caiaphas, who was high priest that year, spoke up, "You know nothing at all! 50 You do not realize that it is better for you that one man die for the people than that the whole nation perish."*

*51 He did not say this on his own, but as high priest that year he prophesied that Jesus would die for the Jewish nation, 52 and not only for that nation but also for the scattered children of God, to bring them together and make them one. 53 So from that day on they plotted to take his life.*

*54 Therefore Jesus no longer moved about publicly among the Jews. Instead he withdrew to a region near the desert, to a village called Ephraim, where he stayed with his disciples.*

Our text describes the last, and by far the most amazing, of the seven "signs" in John's Gospel.[1] It is a miracle that lifts Jesus to the pinnacle of His popularity with the common people. At the same time it issues in the Sanhedrin's plot to put Him to death.

Notice first . . .

## *The Sisters' Report (11:1-3)*

Jesus was ministering in the comparative safety of Perea (10:40) when a message arrived from Mary and Martha in Bethany. Their brother, Lazarus,[2] was sick. It is evident from the context that their home was a quiet retreat to which our Lord went from time to time. Thus a strong bond of mutual affection had grown between Jesus and the three. Now, in a moment of crisis, the sisters did not hesitate to inform Jesus of Lazarus' condition.

It is interesting that they made no direct request that He come to them. But like Jesus' mother on an earlier occasion, they simply apprized Him of the situation.[3] They knew they could trust Jesus to do whatever was necessary for the one He loved (11:3).[4] In this they teach us that prayer is often just the laying of our needs before the God whom we trust to do what is best. Certainly Jesus did not betray their trust.

## The Savior's Response (11:4-44)

By the time word of Lazarus' illness arrived in Perea, he was dead. Jesus was aware of this (11:14), but He knew full well what He would do. He assured His disciples that death would not have the last word (11:4). His life-giving ministry to Lazarus would bring great glory to God. More than that, the Lazarus miracle would glorify God's Son as well (11:4). Only when we realize how often in John's Gospel the glorification of Jesus refers to His death[5] are we sobered. Jesus knew the journey to Bethany to cure Lazarus would be a giant step toward Calvary.

We might have imagined that Jesus, receiving the news about Lazarus' illness, would have set out at once. Not so. We can caption it *help postponed* (11:6). Why, we ask, did Jesus remain where He was for two more days? John makes sure we understand that the delay in no way indicated a lack of love for Mary, Martha and Lazarus (11:5). Neither is it likely that Jesus was waiting purposefully for Lazarus to die. As soon as He heard of Lazarus' illness, He knew by the Spirit that His friend was dead. Even if He left Perea at once, Lazarus' recovery would involve a resurrection. Nor is it probable that Jesus delayed His journey in keeping with some rabbinical thought that Lazarus was *irreversibly* dead.[6]

Surely the real reason Jesus delayed His departure lay in Himself. Guided by the Father, He acted on His own initiative, not the persuasion of others—even those closest to Him.[7]

Then we see *intervention proposed* (11:7-16). At the end of two days, Jesus proposed to His disciples that they now return to Judea (11:7). The disciples, quite naturally, were astounded at the suggestion. Judea would put

Jesus again at risk (11:8). Jesus' reply to their expressed concerns was simply to say, in effect, "My ministry is of limited duration. Therefore I must use the time left to Me to do God's will, regardless of the consequences" (11:9-10).[8]

Then, focusing His disciples' thoughts once again on Lazarus, He informed them, "Our friend Lazarus has fallen asleep;[9] but I am going there to wake him up" (11:11). Surprisingly, the disciples took His words literally[10] and commented on the restorative qualities of sleep (11:12-13). So Jesus made His meaning plain (11:14). He assured the disciples that what they saw would greatly strengthen their faith (11:15).

Thomas the Twin then interjected a courageous proposal. "Let us also go," he said, "that we may die with him" (11:16). Thomas thus expressed his utter devotion to Jesus—and his failure to grasp the significance of Lazarus' death. At the same time, and certainly without realizing it, he articulated a sobering truth. Dying with Christ would become the characteristic mark of Christian discipleship.[11]

Third, we see in our text *comfort proffered* (11:17-37). When Jesus arrived at Bethany, He discovered that Lazarus had been in the tomb four days (11:17). Bethany was really a suburb of Jerusalem (11:18). The sisters' many friends in the city would have been fulfilling the customary seven days of mournful consolation (11:19).[12]

When Martha, seemingly the more active of the two sisters,[13] learned that Jesus was approaching, she hurried to meet Him (11:20). She expressed her sorrow that, understandably, Jesus could not have been there in person to heal her brother. In a sweet expression of timid faith, she intimated that even yet it may not be too late (11:21-22).

"Your brother will rise again," Jesus reassured Martha (11:23). It is as though He wanted to set in motion the grand event to follow. Martha was scarcely able to believe this could happen before "the resurrection at the last day" (11:24). She interpreted Jesus' statement in the light of prevailing doctrine taught by the Pharisees.[14]

But Jesus desired to take Martha beyond mere endorsement of doctrinal truth to confidence in Himself alone. He spoke those wonderful words, repeated at every Christian funeral, that bring comfort and hope to every sorrowing Christian heart: "I am the resurrection and the life. He who believes in me will live, even though he dies; and whoever lives and believes in me will never die" (11:25-26).

Resurrection life is in Christ Jesus alone! Apart from Him there *is* no resurrection and no eternal life. But united to Him through faith, believers possess even now that eternal life. It will find its ultimate expression in the resurrection that accompanies His glorious appearing.

"Do you believe this?" Jesus asked Martha. In response she went beyond affirming the truth of Jesus' words to a full confession of her faith. Surely it was truth revealed to her by the Spirit of God. It was a statement encompassing Jesus' Messiahship, His deity and His mission to the world (11:27).

At Jesus' request, Mary, accompanied by her Jewish comforters, joined her sister. All were mourning, seemingly "like [those] who have no hope" (1 Thessalonians 4:13). Such a manifestation of despair filled our Lord's spirit with holy anger, and He became agitated (John 11:33).[15] Despite the Old Testament intimations of resurrection, despite His teaching, despite His miracles, they were mourning like pagans. Such behavior angered Him.[16]

But there is another emotion within Him as well. As He walks with the mourners to the tomb, Jesus Himself weeps (11:35). He beholds "the havoc created by sin and death, the tragedy of the human situation in which even God's people are engulfed."[17]

Fourth, see *the miracle performed* (11:38-44). Jesus felt another surge of anger (11:38) as He arrived at the tomb. He ordered the stone that covered the opening removed (11:39). In spite of Martha's protestations about unbearable odor, Jesus assured those present that they would see the glory of God (11:40).

So they moved the stone to one side. Then Jesus prayed— aloud and publicly. He wanted all to know He had been sent by God, that He had no authority independent of His Father. He prayed, affirming that what was about to take place was nothing less than the Father's answer to His prayer.

Then, with a loud shout, like the cry that all who are in the tombs will one day hear, He commanded, "Lazarus! Come out!" We can almost hear the gasps of the onlookers as this cloth-bound specter, dead four days, emerged!

"Take off the grave clothes and let him go," Jesus ordered (11:44).

## *The Sanhedrin's Reaction (11:45-57)*

Many eyewitnesses to Lazarus' resurrection were moved to believe on Jesus (11:45). Others set out to report the event to Jesus' enemies in Jerusalem (11:46). At once the Sanhedrin was summoned into emergency session (11:47). John reports their curious reasoning as they debated together: "Here is a man whose miracles are attracting ever-increasing popularity. He might spark off an uprising, which could bring down upon us Rome's heavy hand. Rome could strip us of our autonomy, our temple worship, even our national identity. What shall we do?" (see 11:47-48).[18]

Up spoke Caiaphas, the high priest.[19] In the apparently typical rude manner of the Sadducees,[20] he said, in effect: "If you ignorant Pharisees don't know what action to take, I do. Don't you understand that there is no room now for justice to takes its course? This man Jesus must be put to death. One man's death is better than the death of the nation" (11:49-50).

His words, spoken with cynicism and political realism, unconsciously pronounced the will of God. Christ Jesus would die for the whole nation of Israel. But His vicarious sacrifice would cover more than just Israel. He would die for the sins of the whole world. And through His death, believing Jew and Gentile would be brought together as one body in Christ (11:51-52).

The "Caiaphas Doctrine" prevailed, and the plot to put Jesus to death solidified that very day. But since His work was not yet finished, Jesus left with His disciples for the small, secluded town of Ephraim, north of Jerusalem, where they could be undisturbed. The hour of His death was drawing ever closer.

## *Conclusion*

The spectacular raising of Lazarus pales when we consider the resurrection that will accompany the return of *Christ, our Coming King.* Lazarus was raised, but he died again. Christ died and rose, never to die again. We who believe in Him are destined to share His resurrection glory eternally. There is coming "a great gettin'-up morning"! The Voice that awakened the brother of Mary and Martha from his "sleep" will be heard once more. This time Jesus will call forth the Lord's people the world over. And "we shall rise, hallelujah, we shall rise!"

Notice how the Lord's resurrection words of our text so beautifully parallel those of the Apostle Paul. In his first letter to the Thessalonians he wrote: "We believe that Jesus died and rose again and so we believe that God will bring with Jesus *those who have fallen asleep in him*" (4:14, emphasis added).

Similarly, our Lord announced: "He who believes in me will live, *even though he dies*" (John 11:25, emphasis added).

Paul wrote: "According to the Lord's own word, we tell you that we *who are still alive,* who are left till the coming of the Lord, will certainly not precede those who have fallen asleep. . . . The dead in Christ will rise first. After that, *we who are still alive* and are left will be caught up together with them in the clouds to meet the Lord in the air" (1 Thessalonians 4:15-17, emphasis added).

Likewise, our Lord declares: "And *whoever lives* and believes in me *will never die*" (John 11:26, emphasis added).

How comforting are these words of the apostle and of the Savior! How reassuring to know that He who weeps with His people at the graves of "sleeping" loved ones "will wipe every tear from their eyes. There will be no more death or mourning or crying or pain, for the old order of things has passed away" (Revelation 21:4). Indeed, how glorious to know that "if the Spirit of him who raised Jesus from the dead is living in you, he who raised Christ from the dead will also give life to your mortal bodies through his Spirit, who lives in you" (Romans 8:11).

### Endnotes

1.  To review, the other six signs in John's Gospel are:
    1) The changing of water into wine (2:1-11)
    2) The healing of the official's son (4:43-54)
    3) The healing at the pool (5:1-15)
    4) The feeding of the 5,000 (6:1-15)
    5) The walking on the water (6:16-24)
    6) The healing of the man born blind (chapter 9)
2.  The name "Lazarus" is a shortened form of Eleazar, which means "God helps."
3.  See John 2:3, where Mary says to Jesus, "They have no more wine."
4.  The word translated "love" here is *phileo.* F. Godet, *Commentary on the Gospel of St. John,* vol. III (Edinburgh: T. & T. Clarke, 1881), 6, thinks it a more suitably affectionate word than "the more dignified" and "nobler term," *agapao.* But in 11:5 John uses the word

*agapao* to describe Jesus' love for His three Bethany friends. It is likely that the two words are synonyms and can be used interchangeably.

5. See for example, John 7:39; 12:23.
6. C.K. Barrett, *The Gospel According to St. John* (London: S.P.C.K., 1955), 335, quotes G. Dalman as follows: "A state of death beyond the third day meant, from the popular Jewish point of view, an absolute dissolution of life. At this time the face cannot be recognized with certainty; the body bursts; and the soul, which until then had hovered over the body, parts from it." Jesus would hardly have concurred with such an idea and would therefore not have delayed His departure from Bethany on this account.
7. Review Jesus' actions in John 2:1-11 and 7:1-10.
8. See Barrett, 325. Calvin, *Commentary on the Gospel According to John*, I, 428, states what appears to me to be the meaning of 11:9-10: "Christ borrows a comparison from Day and Night. For if any man perform a journey in the dark, we need not wonder if he frequently stumble, or go astray, or fall; but the light of the sun *by day* points out the road, so that there is no danger. Now the calling of God is like the light of day, which does not allow us to mistake our road or to stumble. Whoever, then, obeys the word of God, and undertakes nothing but according to his command, always has God to guide and direct him from heaven, and with this confidence he may safely and boldly pursue his journey. . . . Relying on this protection, therefore, Christ advances boldly into Judea, without any dread of being stoned; for there is no danger of going astray when God, performing the part of the sun, shines on us, and directs our course."
9. The portrayal of death as "sleep" is common in the New Testament. See, for example, Matthew 9:24; Acts 7:60; 1 Corinthians 15:6; 1 Thessalonians 4:13.
10. We have seen a misinterpretation of Jesus' words elsewhere in John, as for example with Nicodemus (3:3-8) and with the woman at the well (4:10-15).
11. See Barrett, *The Gospel According to St. John,* 328.
12. See William Barclay, *The Gospel of John*, vol. II (Philadelphia: The Westminster Press, 1975), 88-90, for a graphic description of what would have been the atmosphere and the events surrounding Lazarus' funeral.
13. Cf. Luke 10:39f.
14. See Acts 23:8.
15. George R. Beasley-Murray, *Word Biblical Themes* (Dallas, TX: Word Publishing, 1989), 67, comments: "Virtually every English translation of the Bible waters down [11:33] to mean that Jesus was 'deeply moved' in spirit, but the lexicographers and the great commentators protest that that is not what John meant. Rudolf Schnackenburg, the greatest contemporary scholar on John's Gospel, wrote: 'The word . . . indicates an outburst of anger, and any attempt to reinterpret it in terms of an internal emotional upset by grief, pain, or sympathy is illegitimate.' " With this B.F. Westcott, *Commentary on the Gospel According to St. John* (London: John Murray, Albermarle Street, 1967), 170, agrees: "So much is clear that the general notion of antagonism, or indignation, or anger, must be taken."
16. Barrett, *The Gospel According to St. John,* 332, suggests, I think incorrectly, that Jesus is angry because the grief of the sisters and of the Jews is almost forcing Him to perform a miracle. If He does so, it cannot be hidden; it will be the immediate occasion of His death.
17. Beasley-Murray, *Word Biblical Themes,* 67.
18. Here is an example of the irony not uncommon in John's Gospel. The Jews had Jesus crucified in order to preserve their status quo with Rome. But the very takeover they sought to avoid came upon them. At the time John wrote his Gospel, the Romans had destroyed Je-

rusalem and the temple and subjugated the Jews. Moreover, throughout the Roman world, people were placing their faith in Jesus Christ.

19. Son-in-law of Annas (18:13) and high priest from about A.D.18-36. Cf. Matthew 26:57.

20. Leon Morris, *The Gospel According to John* (Grand Rapids, MI: Eerdmans, 1971), 567, quotes Josephus as saying: "The Sadducees . . . are, even among themselves, rather boorish in their behavior, and in their intercourse with their peers are as rude as to aliens."

# 21

# A Grateful Reception

John 11:55-12:19

55 When it was almost time for the Jewish Passover, many went up from the country to Jerusalem for their ceremonial cleansing before the Passover. 56 They kept looking for Jesus, and as they stood in the temple area they asked one another, "What do you think? Isn't he coming to the Feast at all?" 57 But the chief priests and Pharisees had given orders that if anyone found out where Jesus was, he should report it so that they might arrest him.

1 Six days before the Passover, Jesus arrived at Bethany, where Lazarus lived, whom Jesus had raised from the dead. 2 Here a dinner was given in Jesus' honor. Martha served, while Lazarus was among those reclining at the table with him. 3 Then Mary took about a pint of pure nard, an expensive perfume; she poured it on Jesus' feet and wiped his feet with her hair. And the house was filled with the fragrance of the perfume.

4 But one of the disciples, Judas Iscariot, who was later to betray him, objected. 5 "Why wasn't this perfume sold and the money given to the poor? It was worth a year's wages." 6 He did not say this because he cared about the poor but because he was a thief; as keeper of the money bag, he used to help himself to what was put into it.

7 "Leave her alone," Jesus replied. "It was intended that she should save this perfume for the day of my burial. 8 You will always have the poor among you, but you will not always have me."

9 Meanwhile a large crowd of Jews found out that Jesus was there and

*came, not only because of him but also to see Lazarus, whom he had raised from the dead. 10 So the chief priests made plans to kill Lazarus as well, 11 for on account of him many of the Jews were going over to Jesus and putting their faith in him.*

*12 The next day the great crowd that had come for the Feast heard that Jesus was on his way to Jerusalem. 13 They took palm branches and went out to meet him, shouting,*

*"Hosanna!"*

*"Blessed is he who comes in the name of the Lord!"*

*"Blessed is the King of Israel!"*

*14 Jesus found a young donkey and sat upon it, as it is written,*

*15 "Do not be afraid, O daughter of Zion;*

*see, your king is coming,*

*seated on a donkey's colt."*

*16 At first his disciples did not understand all this. Only after Jesus was glorified did they realize that these things had been written about him and that they had done these things to him.*

*17 Now the crowd that was with him when he called Lazarus from the tomb and raised him from the dead continued to spread the word. 18 Many people, because they had heard that he had given this miraculous sign, went out to meet him. 19 So the Pharisees said to one another, "See, this is getting us nowhere. Look how the whole world has gone after him!"*

What a Passover this was going to be! Two years earlier at Passover, our Lord had aroused the Jews' fury by purging the temple of its defilers (2:13-15). The next year, as Passover approached, He had miraculously fed a hungry crowd on the shores of the Sea of Galilee (6:1-15). But this year's commemoration of Israel's deliverance from Egypt would be different from the others.

Two years before, the "hour" of Jesus' death had not come. Now the fury of the Jewish leaders was about to reach its awful climax. Jesus would become the Paschal Lamb, of whom all other paschal lambs were but a symbol. One year before He had avoided the crowd's attempt to make Him King. Now He would join in their joyous celebration of His Messiahship.

Passover! Israel's greatest celebration! Jews from all over the nation—all over the Roman world—flocked to the Holy City. They came in advance of the Feast to carry out the ceremonial cleansing required by the law (11:55). These time-consuming purifications took place in the temple area. As groups of pilgrims waited their turn, conversation turned to the Man Jesus. They all knew He was engaged in mortal conflict with the Jewish authorities.

"What do you think?" they asked each other as they scanned the crowds for a glimpse of Jesus. "Will He come to the Feast or not? Surely, now that He is an outlaw, He will not be so foolish as to risk arrest by entering Jerusalem!" (see 11:56-57)[1]

But the crowds failed to understand the nature of the mission that would bring the Savior to this Passover. They underestimated the strong courage that would enable Him to carry out His mission. Even as they spoke, He was on His way from Ephraim to Jerusalem. On the Saturday preceding Passover[2] He arrived at Bethany, the site outside the city designated for overflow accommodation. There was no question where Jesus would stay. It would be at the home of Lazarus, whom he had so recently summoned from the grave (12:1). It was there in that home that Jesus received . . .

## A Woman's Adoration (12:2-11)

We can imagine the excitement among the people of Bethany when word spread that Jesus was in town! He who honored their village by raising Lazarus from the dead had returned with His disciples. They must do something to show their gratitude. Someone proposed a banquet in His honor. Simon the leper offered to host the dinner.[3] Martha, as might be expected, served. All agreed that Lazarus should be at the table with Jesus (12:2).

John offers no hint of the conversation. Perhaps the Savior discussed with the villagers His ministry. Surely He was grateful for those who had believed His word—and saddened by the unbelieving response of the Jewish leadership. He was now on His way to what would surely be His final Passover feast. But Lazarus must not feel that he was to blame for the official antagonism against Jesus. All that had happened—all that *would* happen—was in the plan of the Father for Him and for them.

As the meal and the conversation moved on, there came a *dramatic moment* Christ's followers would remember forever. Mary, Lazarus' sister, who by divine intuition felt the full significance of the moment, rose quietly. Carrying a costly alabaster jar of genuine[4] nard, she walked over to Jesus and stood next to Him. Deliberately breaking open the jar, she poured some of the nard on His head.[5] Then in an unusual act of humble adoration, she poured the rest on His feet, unself-consciously wiping them dry with the long tresses of her hair (12:3).[6] No sacrifice was too costly, no service too lowly for this woman who loved Jesus. Simon's house had never before been filled with such fragrance.

But alas, in *a dour meanness,* a lover of money censured this expression of love for Jesus. Judas could see only the wasteful extravagance of the act (12:4-5). He may have expressed what others were feeling,[7] but he also revealed the demonically inspired treachery of his own evil heart. In an insincere show of benevolence (12:5),[8] he demeaned his Master, mortified Mary and embarrassed the guests. Thief that he was, his true concern was not for the poor but for his own financial advantage (12:6). We may well wonder how he ever became treasurer for the disciples!

Jesus was not about to allow Mary, or her act of love, to be despised by this bitter outburst. He graciously offered *a defense of Mary.* He let Mary and all the guests know where His sympathies lay. "Why should you object," he said to Judas, "if Mary took the nard that might have anointed My dead body and poured it on Me while I can appreciate the love that prompted it? If you are really concerned for the poor, you will have ample opportunity to help them. But you will not always have opportunity to minister to me" (see 12:7-8).[9]

Meanwhile, crowds of Passover Jews were converging on Bethany to see Jesus and Lazarus, whom He had raised from the dead (12:9). Lazarus' visible presence bore witness to Jesus' power. And many people of Jerusalem and Judea were putting their faith in Jesus (12:11). Lazarus had become a political and theological threat to the Jewish hierarchy. He must be destroyed!

## A Crowd's Adulation (12:12-15)

Passover was less than a week away. It was time for Jesus to traverse the two miles from Bethany into Jerusalem. Accompanied by the excited crowd that had come to see Lazarus, He set out.

Those who believed that Jesus was the Messiah sensed that this could be the historic denouement. Until then, Jesus had resisted all such popular manifestations of His praise. Now, led by the Father, He joined in the crowd's jubilation, accepting the homage extended to Him. It was time to offer Himself to Israel as their true King!

Arriving at Bethphage, He deliberately entered the city in the kingly manner foretold by the Old Testament prophet Zechariah (12:15).[10] At His instruction, the disciples procured a young donkey, which He mounted for the ride into the heart of the Holy City (12:14).[11] The crowd began to swell as groups of Passover pilgrims from the city came out to join the incoming procession. In their hands they waved palm branches, spontaneously expressing their unbridled joy.[12] On their lips were words from the conqueror's psalm.[13] "Hosanna!" they shouted.[14] "Blessed is he who comes in the name of the Lord! Blessed is the King of Israel" (12:13).[15] They clearly declared that the Man on the donkey was none other than Messiah. And Jesus did not protest their adulation.

But if the crowd expected a political Savior, ready to overthrow Roman tyranny, they would be disappointed. Jesus' mount was not a horse, used by a king bent on war. It was a donkey, the mount of an emissary of peace. Neither the crowd nor Jesus' disciples comprehended the full meaning of this prophetic event.

## The Pharisees' Frustration (12:16-19)

If Jesus' disciples entered into the enthusiasm of the crowd, it was not because they clearly understood what was happening. Seemingly they did not grasp the connection between Zechariah's prophecy and Jesus' ride on the donkey. Nor did they realize that they themselves had assisted in the prophecy's fulfillment. That comprehension would have to await their Lord's death, burial, resurrection and ascension to glory. It would have to await the enlightening gift of the Holy Spirit (12:16).

If ignorance characterized Jesus' disciples, frustration characterized Jerusalem's hierarchy. The more the witnesses of Lazarus' resurrection spread the news about Jesus, the more were people inclined to abandon barren Judaism. They preferred the new life offered by Him who had raised Lazarus from the dead (12:17-18). In words marvelously descriptive of what would ultimately occur, the Pharisees lamented, "See, this is getting us nowhere. Look how the whole world has gone after him!" (12:19).

If there was to be an end to Jesus' popularity, it would be by the scheme of the unscrupulous Caiaphas. And so the days of *grateful reception* came to an end. Lazarus would continue to attract the curious. Mary's loving gift to the Savior would assure her a place in church history. And the crowd so ready to crown Jesus King would soon be calling for His crucifixion.

## *Conclusion*

What does our text say to us about living the deeper Christian life? First, let us look again at adoring Mary. Her story illustrates so beautifully the meaning of full consecration to Christ. When it came to her ointment, Mary was faced with alternatives. She could have used it on herself. She could have poured it on ordinary friends and loved ones. She could have dedicated it to Jesus (as she did). She could have divided it among all of the above. She could have sold it and given the money to the poor (the Judas Plan). She chose to devote it fully to Jesus. In entire surrender, she gave to Jesus alone the supreme love and devotion of her heart.

These multiple choices are options for our lives. Will we live for ourselves and the material baubles that we find attractive? Will we divide our loyalties among a number of categories? Or will we surrender ourselves completely and unreservedly to our Lord Jesus?

What prompted Mary to give to Christ her heart's full devotion? First, she was in *awe* of Christ. She knew the One before whom she knelt in worship was God incarnate. Second, while others were blind to Jesus' destiny, she had come to understand that her Savior would lay down His life for her and for the world. Hence, she was prompted by *gratitude*. Third, she was motivated by *faith*; she trusted in Jesus as the Son of God, her Savior and King. Fourth, above all, she was prompted by *love* for Jesus. Is it not true that entire consecration to Jesus must flow from worshiping, thankful, trustful, loving hearts?

How did Mary's consecration to Jesus demonstrate itself? Lip service was not enough; she gave what was very costly. Part was not enough; she must give all. The unbroken was not enough; it must be broken and poured out. Mary must humbly fall at her Savior's feet, lingering there like the lowest slave! While salvation is a free gift from our gracious God, full consecration to Jesus costs everything. As someone has said, "If He is not Lord of all, He is not Lord at all." In the words of Frances Havergal, it will require us to say:

> Take my life, and let it be
> Consecrated, Lord, to Thee.
> Take my moments and my days,
> Let them flow in ceaseless praise.
>
> Take my love; my Lord, I pour
> At Thy feet its treasure store.
> Take myself, and I will be
> Ever, only, all for Thee.[16]

Second, look again at that first Palm Sunday. An event took place in my boyhood which I shall never forget. The year was 1936, and word had come that King George VI and his queen were coming to Canada. They would be riding a royal train from coast to coast, stopping at selected stations along the way. My father, loyal Britisher that he was, made plans to drive to the designated stopping point nearest our home. Mother, not being as eager a monarchist as Father, made plans to stay home! In our 1933 Ford, Father and I arrived at the railway station. Then we parked and walked with thousands of others to where we thought we could best see the royal couple.

We waited for hours. Finally the train, bearing the royal insignia, slowly approached the depot. It stopped, and about ten minutes later, the door to the last car opened. Onto the small back platform stepped their majesties, George and Elizabeth—*our* king and queen. My father concluded immediately that we could get closer to them. Taking my hand, he pulled me forward, making an end run through what turned out to be a small shallow marsh (water up to our ankles), all the while cheering loudly with thousands of others who pushed to get closer to the train. In a burst of unquenchable patriotism, father threw his 1930s hard straw hat high into the sky. "God save the King!" we all cried, and the royal couple waved ever so gracefully.

With crowds cheering, another royal train, bearing another King, rode into Jerusalem on that first Palm Sunday. "God save the King!" they cried. "We *will* have this man to reign over us!" But alas, all too soon, their coronation cries turned to shouts of derision. Spurred on by hate-filled leaders, the fickle crowd called for this King's crucifixion. "We will *not* have this man to reign over us!"

Now this King who died and rose is exalted far above everyone and everything. He is no mere earthly king. He is King of kings and Lord of lords. We must choose whether we will bow to His sovereignty or let other lords control our lives. Let us cry out in loyal obeisance, "King of my life, I crown Thee now; Thine shall the glory be!"[17]

### Endnotes

1. This interpretation of the Greek wording of 11:56 seems to me to be closer to its meaning than that of the NIV.
2. See C.K. Barrett, *The Gospel According to St. John* (London: S.P.C.K., 1955), 342. But there is no real agreement among commentators as to what day of the week Jesus arrived in Bethany.
3. Cf. Matthew 26:6 and Mark 14:3.
4. The word used to describe the nard is *pistikes,* the meaning of which is uncertain. It may mean, as I have suggested, "genuine," or "liquid," or it may be a trade name, or a special kind of essence extracted from the pistachio nut. NIV translates it "pure."
5. See the Markan account. The general custom among ancient nations was to anoint the heads of guests on festal occasions.
6. In Bible-times Palestine, only an immoral woman would appear in public with her hair unbound. Mary did not concern herself with what others might think of her action.
7. Cf. Mark 14:4.
8. According to the Greek text, the nard was worth 300 denarii, a year's wages for a working man.
9. See F.F. Bruce, *The Gospel of John* (Grand Rapids, MI: Eerdmans, 1983), 257. The Greek text lends itself to several possible interpretations. Barrett, *The Gospel According to St. John,* 345, outlines some of them as follows: 1) "Let her remember what she has done now, on the day of my burial." 2) "Let her, when Joseph and Nicodemus anoint my body, remember that she has foreshadowed this act of piety and thus shared in it." 3) "Let her observe the last rite now, with a view to my burial." 4) "Let her alone; should she keep it till the day of my burial?" Matthew 26:12 has Jesus saying, "When she poured this perfume on my body, she did it to prepare me for burial." Mark 14:8, "She poured perfume on my body beforehand to prepare for my burial."
10. John has evidently cited Zechariah 9:9 from memory. This is a messianic quotation which Jesus applies to Himself. The context is one of peace (see 9:10). Zechariah 9:9 reads as follows:
    "Rejoice greatly, O daughter of Zion!

> Shout, Daughter of Jerusalem!
> See, your king comes to you,
>> righteous and having salvation,
>> gentle and riding on a donkey,
>> on a colt, the foal of a donkey."

11. John omits the account of how Jesus procured the donkey and its colt. See Matthew 21:1f.
12. See Leviticus 23:40 for the Mosaic instruction regarding the use of palm branches.
13. See William Barclay, *The Gospel of John,* vol. II (Philadelphia: The Westminster Press, 1975), 116, who informs us that Psalm 118 was sung by a Jerusalem crowd when they welcomed back the conqueror Simon Maccabaeus after he had captured Acra from Syrian dominion. Psalms 113-118, which were read as part of the Passover ritual, were called the "Egyptian Hallel." The crowd is shouting Psalm 118:25-26.
14. The word "Hosanna" is from the Hebrew, meaning, "Save now, we pray." Commentators like Barclay, *The Gospel of John,* 116, and F. Godet, *Commentary on the Gospel of St. John,* vol. III (Edinburgh: T. & T. Clarke, 1881), 60, equate it, in this context, with our modern expression, "God save the King."
15. Barrett, *The Gospel According to St. John,* 346, says that both phrases are Messianic titles.
16. Frances R. Havergal, "Take My Life, and Let It Be," Hymns of the Christian Life (Camp Hill, PA: Christian Publications, 1978), # 225, stanzas 1 and 6.
17. Jennie E. Hussey, "Lead Me to Calvary," ibid., #81, stanza 1.

## Part VIII

## *Questions for Reflection or Discussion*

1. Discuss the meaning of the concept of "firstfruits" as it applies to the doctrine of the resurrection (see 1 Corinthians 15:20ff).

2. Compare the raising of Lazarus to the resurrection of believers promised in such passages as First Thessalonians 4:13-18.

3. What deeper life lessons may we learn from the actions of Mary, who anointed the Lord's feet?

4. What message did Jesus send to Jerusalem when He rode in triumph into the city?

5. What did Jesus mean when He said, "The kingdom of God is within you"?

*Part IX*

# The Love of the Son

John 12:20-13:38

# 22

# *Love Lifted Up*

### John 12:20-36

*20 Now there were some Greeks among those who went up to worship at the Feast. 21 They came to Philip, who was from Bethsaida in Galilee, with a request. "Sir," they said, "we would like to see Jesus." 22 Philip went to tell Andrew; Andrew and Philip in turn told Jesus.*

*23 Jesus replied, "The hour has come for the Son of Man to be glorified. 24 I tell you the truth, unless a kernel of wheat falls to the ground and dies, it remains only a single seed. But if it dies, it produces many seeds. 25 The man who loves his life will lose it, while the man who hates his life in this world will keep it for eternal life. 26 Whoever serves me must follow me; and where I am, my servant also will be. My Father will honor the one who serves me.*

*27 "Now my heart is troubled, and what shall I say? 'Father, save me from this hour'? No, it was for this very reason I came to this hour. 28 Father, glorify your name!"*

*Then a voice came from heaven, "I have glorified it, and will glorify it again." 29 The crowd that was there and heard it said it had thundered; others said an angel had spoken to him.*

*30 Jesus said, "This voice was for your benefit, not mine. 31 Now is the time for judgment on this world; now the prince of this world will be driven out. 32 But I, when I am lifted up from the earth, will draw all men to myself." 33 He said this to show the kind of death he was going to die.*

*34 The crowd spoke up, "We have heard from the Law that the Christ will remain forever, so how can you say, 'The Son of Man must be lifted up'? Who is this 'Son of Man'?"*

*35 Then Jesus told them, "You are going to have the light just a little while longer. Walk while you have the light, before darkness overtakes you. The man who walks in the dark does not know where he is going. 36 Put your trust in the light while you have it, so that you may become sons of light." When he had finished speaking, Jesus left and hid himself from them.*

As the climactic Passover Feast approached, a small group of "Greeks" sought an audience with Jesus. These men were Hellenist[1] "god-fearers"[2]—Gentiles—like the Roman soldier Cornelius (Acts 10:1-2) and the Ethiopian eunuch (Acts 8:27). Judaism, with its one God and high moral standards, had attracted a number of non-Jews. Apparently these who sought to see Jesus were accustomed to joining in the annual Passover feast at Jerusalem (John 12:20). Their desire to talk personally with Jesus confirmed to Him that the hour of His death had indeed come. I call this desire for an audience . . .

## *An Interview Requested (12:20-22)*

These Hellenists who "would like to see Jesus" (12:21) were in sharp contrast to the Jewish Pharisees. The Pharisees had just decided to join forces with the Sadducees in seeking Jesus' death (11:47-50). But this small company in Jerusalem was sufficiently impressed with Jesus to desire a private conference.

What prompted these Hellenists to seek out Jesus? Perhaps they were drawn to Him by His forceful expulsion of the money changers from the Court of the Gentiles.[3] They may have interpreted Jesus' action as undertaken in the interests of Gentiles who desired to worship in quiet. Or perhaps their interest grew simply out of all they had heard about the words and works of this amazing Person. Whatever the reason, they were anxious for an interview. With due deference,[4] they made their request through the disciple with the Greek name—Philip. It is possible that he and they came from the same region (12:21).[5]

Philip appears reluctant to make a unilateral decision. He knew that Jesus, for the most part, had confined Himself to Jewish people. Perhaps he did not feel comfortable granting a request that would have interrupted Jesus' routine. So he engaged the help of his resourceful partner, Andrew,[6] and the two informed Jesus of the request (12:22). How would Jesus respond to the Greeks?

## A Death Required (12:23-26)

The approach of Hellenist inquirers appears to have made a profound impression on Jesus. Their coming must have reminded Him that He was the Savior not only of Israel but of the *whole* world. Now, symbolically, the request of these Greeks heralded the coming proclamation of the gospel to the Gentiles. The Savior knew, however, that this proclamation could take place only after His death, resurrection and ascension to glory. So His immediate response was to declare that the hour of His indispensable death had arrived. Doubtless He addressed the words to a wider audience than just the Greeks.[7] We might say Christ interpreted the coming of the Greeks as God's confirmation that His mission has reached its climax. The time had come for Him to lay down His life for the world.

See how poignantly He expresses this truth: "The hour has come for the Son of Man to be glorified" (12:23).[8] Such an announcement would have filled His Jewish listeners with great excitement. They would have understood Him to say He was about to set up His kingdom on earth![9] But His next words assuredly would have dashed their misdirected hopes. His glory resided, rather, in His impending death. He described it in familiar imagery. One kernel of wheat, left unplanted, remains forever a single kernel. But if it is buried in the dark earth, it can reproduce itself a hundredfold (12:24).[10] It is clear, as Augustine so beautifully put it, that "He spake of Himself. He Himself was the grain that had to die, and be multiplied; to suffer death through the unbelief of the Jews, and to be multiplied in the faith of many nations."[11]

Having described the saving necessity of His death, Jesus articulated the principle that ruled His life: The person who selfishly gives priority to His own life ("the man who loves his life") is even now destroying it.[12] The person who regards his life as secondary to kingdom interests ("the man who hates his life") inherits eternal life (12:25).[13]

Had Jesus attempted to avoid the cross by political or religious compromise, He would have perished (and taken the world with Him). Thankfully, that scenario would not happen. Because Jesus laid down His life in obedience to His Father, He was raised, never to die again. And we may share His eternal life.

But the principle by which Jesus ordered His life applies equally to all of us who would be His servants. We must follow Him, even to death! We must be where He is, whether in shame or glory (12:26). We too are called upon to voluntarily "take up [our] cross and follow [him]" (Mark 8:34). In dying to our personal ambitions, in rejecting every temptation to "save our skins,"[14] we inherit eternal life.

Over forty years ago, five young missionaries attempted to establish contact with the Aucas of Ecuador. From their small plane they dropped objects that they hoped the Indians would receive as tokens of friendship. But when they finally landed they were met with Auca spears. All five men were killed.

A crass world considered their deaths a waste, a useless tragedy. But not so their believing loved ones! They knew the truth of our text. They prayed that from the planting of these "seeds" there would spring forth an abundant harvest. *God answered prayer.* Today there is a Christian church among the Aucas. But it cost the lives of five young men.

Jesus has explained the necessity of His humiliating, painful death. He goes on to describe . . .

## A Temptation Resisted (12:27-28)

Even as Jesus affirmed the self-denial that would take Him to His death, the horror of what was ahead struck home (12:27).[15] He knew He was about to sense the shame of an illegal arrest and trial. He would be bound, slapped, mocked, beaten. There would be the heavy cross to carry, the nails ripping flesh and sinews, the thorns ringing His head. And beyond the physical suffering were the sins of the world and the apparent desertion by His Father God.

Must He *really* undergo all this? The struggle between the willing spirit and the natural flesh was as powerful for Jesus as it would be for us. In sincerity and utter candor He made no attempt to hide His inner battle from those around Him. This was a Man "tempted in every way, just as we are" (Hebrews 4:15). There was but one fleeting moment of hesitation (John 12:27). Shall He pray that He be saved from this hour?[16]

Of course not! He came into the world for this very purpose. *He was born to die!* His whole mission was to be a sin offering to God for all mankind! Resolutely, He was now prepared to resist the temptation to escape it all. And so He prayed, "Father, glorify your name!" (12:28).

## A Climax Revealed (12:29-33)

The enormous importance of this critical moment in our Lord's life calls forth an instant, audible response from God.[17] To most in the crowd, it was but the meaningless rumble of thunder or an angelic visitation (12:29). But to those who possessed the spiritual capacity, it was the voice of God. It was as though heaven was saying, "Let there be no doubt—the obedient life of the Son and the signs He wrought *have glorified* the name of the Father. The impending cross, the resurrection and the subsequent proclamation of the gospel to the world *will glorify* it again!" (12:28).

Jesus Himself did not need the Voice's objective assurance (12:30). But for the benefit of the crowd, the word from above presented the final, decisive evidence to those who "heard." Jesus was indeed the very Son of God. Furthermore, the Voice came as a drumroll heralding the most pivotal moment in world history. Three crucial consequences would *"now"* [18] issue from the Lord's being "lifted up from the earth" (12:32) on the cross:[19]

1) The cross would mean "judgment on this world" (12:31). In its final abhorrent reaction to Jesus, human society, secular and religious, revealed its rebellion and enmity against God. Thus it condemned itself.[20]

2) The cross would mean "the prince of this world will be driven out" (12:31). The cross and the resurrection spelled the total defeat of God's archenemy, Satan. Satan considered Calvary a coup. In fact, he had sealed his own ultimate destruction. Cast out of his usurped authority,

he is no longer "the prince." He continues to go about as a roaring lion seeking to devour the unwary (1 Peter 5:8). But he knows that in the name of Jesus, his power to enslave men and women has been broken. Now we can sing with Luther:

> The Prince of Darkness grim—
> We tremble not for him;
> His rage we can endure,
> For lo, his doom is sure,
>   One little word shall fell him.[21]

3) The cross will be the instrument through which Christ "will draw all men to [Himself]" (12:32). It will usher in a universally accessible salvation. People purchased by Christ's blood "from every tribe and language and people and nation" (Revelation 5:9) will be drawn to Him.

Finally, our text portrays . . .

## *A Multitude Reproved (12:34-36)*

The words of Jesus perplexed the crowd. Their Scriptures seemed to preclude the death of Messiah.[22] Yet here the one who called Himself the Son of Man was speaking of His impending death! How was this possible? Was this "Son of Man" the Messiah, or were the Messiah and Son of Man two distinct individuals? And if they were, what role did the Son of Man play in the final drama of Jewish history (12:34)? Those with Jesus right then were asking Him to resolve their dilemma.

But our Lord made no attempt to answer their question. Too much was at stake right then to spend time on unnecessary explanations. Instead, Jesus made one final effort to impress upon His listeners the urgency of the hour. He had come among them as the Light of the world. They had seen His works and heard His words and claims. Now the light was about to leave them. Unless they availed themselves of this one last opportunity to believe on Him, darkness would overtake them. They would be lost (12:35).

His words are yet a solemn warning. Only by putting their faith in Him who is the Light can people be delivered from spiritual night. Only by be-

lieving on Him can they reflect the light of His presence in them (12:36).[23]
Having made this last appeal, Jesus goes into hiding (12:36).

## *Conclusion*

Let us consider from our text one of the most important truths we can ever
apply in deeper-life living: If we would bear fruit in God's kingdom, we, like
kernels of wheat, must first die (12:24). Not literally die, like the five missionaries in Ecuador. But it is the dying that our spiritual forefathers called "death
to self." Jesus called it taking up our cross and following him (see Matthew
16:24). By that He meant following Him to the place of death. Paul describes it
as "put[ting] to death . . . whatever belongs to your earthly nature" (Colossians
3:5).[24] The painful truth is that by nature our choices are *self*-centered. We tend
to tolerate the "self-sins"—selfishness, self-confidence, self-righteousness,
self-indulgence, self-exaltation, self-defense, selfish ambition, self-pity.

If we are to follow Christ (John 12:26), we must consign "self" (the flesh)
to the cross. The Apostle Paul shows us the way in Romans 6. We discover,
first, that we are to *know* the objective truth that we have been "baptized into
[Christ's] death" (6:3). We are dead to sin. Second, we are to *"count* [our-
selves] dead to sin but alive to God in Christ Jesus" (6:11). Third, we are to
*"offer* [ourselves] . . . and . . . the parts of [our bodies] to [God] as instruments of righteousness" (6:13). All this we are enabled to do through the
power of the Spirit of Christ who dwells within us. It is not by self-effort that
"self" is put to death; it is by our surrendering to the Spirit (see 8:13). As we
invite Christ to live His life in us, "self" is crucified. As a result, we bring
forth the lovely Christlike fruit of the Holy Spirit (see Galatians 5:22-23).

Dr. A.B. Simpson has captured this deeper life truth in his poem, "Let
Yourself Alone":

> Vain and fruitless is the struggle
>   Self to sanctify;
> God alone can cleanse and keep you,
>   Wherefore should you try?
>
> Oh, the needless cares and conflicts
>   You had never known,

If you'd learned the simple lesson—
    Let yourself alone.

Let your eyes keep looking upward;
    Cease to look within;
All your introspection cannot
    Cleanse a single sin.

You will find your best self effort
    Vain, and worse than vain,
As the touch of soilèd fingers
    Only leaves a stain.

It is life you need, not labor—
    Life that springs from Him;
If you'd have your cup run over,
    Fill it to the brim.

All the springs of power and blessing
    Flow from yonder throne;
If you'd have them fill and flood you,
    Let yourself alone.[25]

### Endnotes

1. The word "Greeks" is literally "Hellenists"—not necessarily persons of Greek origin, but cultured Gentiles who spoke the Greek language.
2. Called God-fearers because they had not gone as far as to become proselytes to the Jewish faith through circumcision.
3. The Synoptic Gospels have the cleansing of the Temple at the close of Jesus' ministry. See Mark 11:15-17.
4. These Hellenists address Philip "Sir"—*kurie.*
5. Bethsaida (12:21) was actually across the river from Galilee in Gaulanitis.
6. "Andrew" is also a Greek name.
7. B.F. Westcott, *Commentary on the Gospel According to St. John* (London: S.P.C.K., 1955), 180, and F. Godet, *Commentary on the Gospel of St. John*, vol. II (Edinburgh: T. & T. Clarke, 1881), 68, believe that the Greeks must have heard Jesus' words, too. They disagree with those who suggest that Jesus ignored the Greeks' request. It would not be like Him, they maintain, to disregard sincere seekers.

    On the other hand, C.K. Barrett, *The Gospel According to St. John* (London: S.P.C.K.,

1955), 352, thinks that Jesus is not replying to the Greeks but "to the situation created by [their] wish to see him." He observes that the evangelization of the Gentiles does not belong to the earthly ministry of Jesus. The way to it lies through Jesus' crucifixion and resurrection and the mission of the Church.

8. In John's Gospel, the glorification of the Son of Man encompasses His death, burial, resurrection and ascension to the Father. Here in our text it may very well include also His "draw[ing] all men to [himself]" (12:32) by means of His death.

9. Willliam Barclay, *The Gospel of John,* vol. II (Philadelphia: The Westminster Press, 1975), 122, writes: "When [Jesus] said that [i.e., "The hour has come for the Son of Man to be glorified"], the listeners would catch their breath. They would believe that the trumpet call of eternity had sounded, that the might of heaven was on the march, and that the campaign of victory was on the move. But Jesus did not mean by *glorified* what they understood. They meant that the subjected kingdoms of the earth would grovel before the conqueror's feet; by *glorified,* he meant *crucified.*"

10. One is reminded of Jesus' parable of the seed and the sower in Luke 8:1-15.

11. Cited by Leon Morris, *The Gospel According to John* (Grand Rapids, MI: Eerdmans, 1971), 593.

12. The verb translated "lose," *apolluo,* has in it the thought of destruction. The tense of the verb in the original would indicate that the process of destruction had already begun.

13. I encourage you to meditate on the following parallel Scriptures: Matthew 13:1-9, 18-23; Mark 4:3-9, 13-20; Luke 8:5-8, 11-15.

14. Barrett's phrasing, *The Gospel According to St. John,* 353.

15. These verses are evidently parallel to the Synoptic Gospels' accounts of Jesus' struggle in the Garden of Gethsemane.

16. Interpreters are divided over Jesus' meaning. Some understand it as the NIV reads: "What shall I say? 'Father, save me from this hour'?" Others think it is a petition: "Father, save me from this hour!" Westcott, page 182, comments that if the latter is true, then we must translate his prayer as "Father, bring me safely *out of* (Greek *ek,* as in Hebrews 5:7) the conflict," and not "Keep me from entering it." At face value, Jesus is experiencing great agony of soul and is tempted to seek deliverance from the cross.

17. Compare the voice from heaven at two other crisis moments in Jesus' life: His baptism (Matthew 3:17) and His transfiguration (Matthew 17:5).

18. The NIV correctly follows the Greek emphasis on "now" by making it the first word in each of the two statements of 12:31. If the time for the death of Christ had not previously arrived, *now* it most certainly had.

19. That Jesus' being "lifted up from the earth" (12:32) refers to the cross is made unequivocally clear by 12:33. His death was not to be by stoning but by crucifixion.

20. John Calvin, *Commentary on the Gospel According to John,* vol. II (Edinburgh: The Calvin Translation Society, 1847), 36, takes the unusual position that "judgment" means reformation. He observes that the Hebrew *mishpat* (judgment) means "a well ordered state." The death of Christ was therefore the commencement of a well-regulated condition and the full restoration of the world.

21. From Martin Luther's Reformation hymn, "A Mighty Fortress Is Our God," *Hymns of the Christian Life* (Camp Hill, PA: Christian Publications, Inc., 1978), # 11, stanza 3.

22. The "Law" here is not to be limited to the Pentateuch but is indicative of the whole Old Testament. Such passages as Psalm 89:36; 110:4; Isaiah 9:7; Daniel 7:14 may have been in the people's minds.

23. In the expression, "sons of light," the word "sons" is a Hebraic way of saying "like the light."
24. See also Colossians 3:6-11 and Galatians 5:19-21.
25. From A.B. Simpson, *Songs of the Spirit* (New York: The Christian Alliance Publishing Co., 1920), 25.

# Love Refused

John 12:37-50

*37 Even after Jesus had done all these miraculous signs in their presence, they still would not believe in him. 38 This was to fulfill the word of Isaiah the prophet:*

*"Lord, who has believed our message*
*and to whom has the arm of the Lord been revealed?"*

*39 For this reason they could not believe, because, as Isaiah says elsewhere:*

*"He has blinded their eyes*
*and deadened their hearts,*
*so they can neither see with their eyes,*
*nor understand with their hearts,*
*nor turn—and I would heal them."*

*41 Isaiah said this because he saw Jesus' glory and spoke about him.*
*42 Yet at the same time many even among the leaders believed in him. But because of the Pharisees they would not confess their faith for fear they would be put out of the synagogue; 43 for they loved praise from men more than praise from God.*
*44 Then Jesus cried out, "When a man believes in me, he does not believe in me only, but in the one who sent me. 45 When he looks at me, he*

*sees the one who sent me. 46 I have come into the world as a light, so that no one who believes in me should stay in darkness.*

*47 "As for the person who hears my words but does not keep them, I do not judge him. For I did not come to judge the world, but to save it. 48 There is a judge for the one who rejects me and does not accept my words; that very word which I spoke will condemn him at the last day. 49 For I did not speak of my own accord, but the Father who sent me commanded me what to say and how to say it. 50 I know that his command leads to eternal life. So whatever I say is just what the Father has told me to say."*

Jesus' public ministry ended disappointingly. The text before us chronicles that disappointing end. Jesus had been sent from the Father to a chosen people as their Messiah. He had authenticated His claim to be the Son of God by numerous signs, seven of which John has recorded. He had offered Himself to the people as the Fulfiller of all their spiritual needs and longings. To all who would believe in Him, He had held out the gift of eternal life. Surely such a privileged people would have lifted grateful hands to the Lord. From the highest echelons of authority to the lowliest peasants, they would have received God's Son with joy.

But it did not happen. Instead, they rejected Him! "He came to that which was his own, but his own did not receive him."[1] Though He had done[2] so many and such great[3] miracles, most people had refused to believe in Him (12:37). How could this be? His holy character and the wisdom of His words also should have created faith in their hearts. And there were the clear predictions of Scripture. Why did they persist in unbelief? Godet says the unbelief of the Jewish people was "the great apologetic question of the Apostolic age."[4] Paul, for example, in anguish tries to explain how his racial kinsmen, with all their spiritual privilege, could have rejected their Messiah.[5] In his Gospel, John likewise thinks it necessary to present his readers with . . .

## The Explanations (12:38-41)

John's explanations of Israel's unbelief are two. First, their rejection of Jesus was *predicted* in Isaiah 53:1. Like all Old Testament prophecies, this one also must be fulfilled (12:38). Under the Spirit's inspiration, the apostle interprets Isaiah as foretelling this outcome. Both Christ's God-given *words* ("our message") and His Spirit-empowered *signs* ("the arm of the Lord")[6] would be met with stubborn unbelief. And such was indeed the case.

Second, not only was Israel's unbelief predicted, it was *willed* by God. John points his readers to another Isaiah passage. In Isaiah 6, the prophet, John says, "saw Jesus' glory and spoke about him (12:41).[7] The holiness of the Lord caused Isaiah to bemoan his own uncleanness. Whereupon God pardoned his guilt and anointed him for ministry. Isaiah then heard God ask, "Whom shall I send? And who will go for us?" His immediate response was, "Here am I. Send me!" (Isaiah 6:8). But the task to which God commissioned him was not easy. God called Isaiah to proclaim His word to an unbelieving Judah and Jerusalem. But his efforts would only make people worse. Because of their willful disobedience, God would render them more thoroughly blind and plunged into an ever deeper darkness.

John changes the quotation from a message to be declared to a statement of what God, in judgment, has done. Israel, says the apostle, could not believe because God "has blinded their eyes and deadened their hearts." The result: "They can neither see with their eyes, nor understand with their hearts, nor turn" for healing (John 12:40). Israel had persisted in unbelief. Therefore God, in His sovereign purpose (yet not against their wills), deprived them of the light necessary to bring them to faith. Like a callous on the skin, their hearts were hardened against Christ. Had they but turned from their unbelief, they would have been saved.

God pronounced a similar sentence on Pharaoh, king of Egypt. In the face of repeated plagues, he continued to "harden his heart" (Exodus 8:32). As he persisted in resisting the voice of God, "the LORD hardened Pharaoh's heart" (Exodus 9:12, emphasis added). Similarly, Paul describes God's judgment on people who willfully rejected the light He had given them. Paul says "God gave them over" to the sins in which they chose to indulge (see Romans 1:24, 26, 28). As Augustine put it, "God thus blinds and hardens, simply by letting [people] alone and withdrawing his aid."[8] And it is thus even today. Sadly, we may refuse God's grace so persistently as to destroy our power to accept it. "I will not" eventually leads to "I cannot."

There is, however, one supreme overriding purpose in Israel's unbelief. For it, we who are Gentiles must be eternally grateful to God. We discern it in Paul's assertion to the unbelieving Jews who called on him in Rome. After quoting the very same Isaiah passage that John quotes, Paul declared, "Therefore I want you to know that God's salvation has been sent to the Gentiles, and they will listen!" (Acts 28:28). In his letter to the Romans, he informs his readers that it was precisely "because of [Israel's] transgression [that] salvation has come to the Gentiles" (Romans 11:11). How wonderfully God makes His wrath against men to bring Him praise! (See Psalm 76:10). How marvelously He is able to bring great good out of evil![9]

Our text has been reporting Israel's refusal to believe on Jesus. But now John turns to a more hopeful aspect. In spite of the general unbelief in Israel, there were . . .

## The Exceptions (12:42-43)

We might have concluded from what John has said that Jewish opposition to Jesus was total. But such was not the case. John informs us that "many[10] even among the leaders believed in him" (12:42). Furthermore, his words indicate that their belief was genuine.[11] Though most chose to reject Christ, deep within these comparatively few was the conviction that the majority was wrong.

But they were secret believers. So great was their fear of excommunication from the synagogue that they drew back from a public confession of faith (12:42). To openly declare themselves would have meant an end to the place, the profit and the prestige in which they gloried. Alas! they valued these passing earthly treasures more than the eternally valuable approval of God (12:43).

What shall we say about the "faith" of such people? Barclay reasons that secret discipleship is a contradiction of terms. "Either the secrecy kills the discipleship or the discipleship kills the secrecy."[12] Westcott asserts that their refusal to confess Christ publicly was a "fatal defect."[13] Calvin, on the other hand, is of the opinion that though their faith was real, it was "not a lively faith, or a faith so vigorous as it ought to have been." But he goes on to say, "I do not think that they were altogether silent; but as their *confession* was not sufficiently open, [John] . . . simply declares that they did not make profession of their faith."[14] It is obvious that we must leave the judgment of the weak and fainthearted to God. He has perfect insight into the thoughts and motives of all people. Might it not be that some of these same leaders were among those baptized in water (a public confession) and the Spirit fifty days after Jesus' resurrection?[15] We can only hope that such might have been the case. Our text, however, does make clear that outright rejection of Jesus brings with it . . .

## *The Condemnation (12:44-50)*

Beginning with chapter 13, Jesus' words will be devoted to the private instruction and encouragement of His disciples. But before John takes us into the seclusion of the Upper Room, he acquaints us with Jesus' final public utterances. John uses them to review for his readers the important truths he has emphasized throughout his Gospel.[16] Let us look again at these vital themes.

First, we are reminded of what is affirmed over and over in this Gospel: Jesus was *sent from the Father* (12:44).[17] God sent Him from the glory which He had with the Father into the created world of time and space. He became "flesh" and lived among human beings (1:14). He was not here on His own. He was an ambassador with the authority of His Father upon Him.

Second, Jesus was *the revelation of the Father*. As He will say later, "Anyone who has seen me has seen the Father" (14:9). To believe in Jesus is to believe in the Father (12:44). To steadily contemplate[18] the Son is to behold the Father (12:45). If one asks, "What is God like?" the answer of John's Gospel is, "He is just like Jesus!"[19]

Third, we are reminded again that Jesus is *the Light of the World* (12:46).[20] It is He who has rescued believers out of Satan's kingdom of darkness (Colossians 1:13). It is He who enlightens minds darkened by the night of willful sin (Ephesians 4:18). It is Christ, by His Spirit, who enlightens the spiritual eyes of believers to know God. He reveals the hope to which they are called, His inheritance within them and His power available to them (see Ephesians 1:17-19).

Fourth, Jesus is *the Savior of the World* (12:47). Through our Lord's perfect obedience, atoning death, triumphant resurrection and glorious ascension He purchased eternal salvation for the human race. All who believe on Him (12:44) are freed from the guilt and power of sin and from eternal death.

Finally, Jesus' words *judge the disobedient* (12:47-48). Our Lord spoke only what the Father told Him to speak (12:50). Those who willfully persist in disobeying His words (12:47) bring judgment upon themselves.[21] Jesus is the One sent from the Father, the Revealer of the Father, the Light of the world. People who obey the Father's command to believe on the Son receive eternal life (12:50).

## *Conclusion*

Sadness mixed with hope permeates our text. And there are warnings to which we must give heed. This text speaks to us of a people whose eyes were clouded by the cataracts of willful unbelief. The lust of their leaders for earthly power, prestige and popularity had robbed them of heaven's praise. Their rejection of the Light of the world has spelled their eternal condemnation. Is that not also descriptive of the world in which *we* live? It is our world that we are to warn, as Jesus warned His world. *Flee from the inevitable and deserved wrath of God upon rebellious sinners!* It is to this world that we are called to bring the saving message of God's love manifested in Christ. Not all will receive our message; we know this full well. But we may expect a remnant from whose eyes God dispels the darkness. Our Savior's example encourages us to evangelize—whether our message is believed or rejected.

And there are warnings here in our text for all who desire to live the deeper life in Christ. The path of holiness is beset with dangers along the way. None of us is immune to them. In a previous chapter we observed the peril of loving the praise of people more than the praise of God.[22] What spiritual blessings have been forfeited through the fear of man!

Second, the words of Isaiah 6:10, though spoken in a different situation, should alert us. There is danger when we fail to resist the temptations that assail us. Victory over the alluring seductions of sin is won or lost in the first moments of battle. Did not the Christian leader who yielded to immoral passions begin by nurturing the first unclean thought? Did not the person enchained by pornography begin with a first salacious look?

Hengstenberg has rightly observed, "God has so constituted man that when he does not resist the first beginnings of sin, he must obey to the end the power to which he has surrendered himself."[23] Sin, if not resisted, be-

comes binding. Not one of us is exempt from temptation. Therefore we need
to be always on guard. Perhaps George Heath's ever-appropriate exhortation should be sung once again by Christian people:

> My soul, be on thy guard;
>     Ten thousand foes arise;
> The hosts of sin are pressing hard
>     To draw thee from the skies.

> Oh, watch, and fight, and pray;
>     The battle ne'er give o'er;
> Renew it boldly every day,
>     And help divine implore.

> Ne'er think the victory won,
>     Nor lay thy armor down;
> The work of faith will not be done
>     Till thou obtain the crown.

> Fight on, my soul, till death
>     Shall bring thee to thy God;
> He'll take thee, at thy parting breath,
>     To His divine abode.[24]

### Endnotes

1. Well in advance John prepared his readers for this outcome. In the prologue to his Gospel
   he indicates the rejection Jesus experienced (see 1:11).
2. The permanent character and abiding quality of Jesus' actions are indicated by the Greek
   perfect tense of the verb translated "had done" (12:37).
3. According to Leon Morris, *The Gospel According to John* (Grand Rapids, MI: Eerdmans,
   1971), 603, the word *tosauta* can be used either of quantity ("so many") or quality ("so
   great"). The NIV's "all these" (12:37) is too weak.
4. F. Godet, *Commentary on the Gospel of St. John*, vol. III (Edinburgh: T. & T. Clarke,
   1881), 82.
5. Romans 9-11 is devoted to Paul's explanation for Jewish unbelief.
6. "The arm of the Lord" describes the mighty power of God in action. See, for example,
   Psalm 89:13; 98:1; Isaiah 40:10; 62:8; 63:12.
7. As Abraham saw Jesus (John 8:56), so does the prophet Isaiah see Him.
8. Quoted by Morris, *The Gospel According to John*, 605.

9.  See this principle enunciated, for example, in the life of Joseph (Genesis 50:20).

10. By the use of the word "many" in 12:42, John lets us know that even amid unbelief God's grace was powerfully at work. Compared with the many who did not believe, the believers were few in number.

11. The statement, "Many . . . believed in him" (*episteusan eis auton*) would seem to indicate that their faith was genuinely saving faith. See 12:44-45 for the same construction.

12. William Barclay, *The Gospel of John,* vol. II (Philadelphia: The Westminster Press, 1975), 133.

13. B.F. Wescott, *Commentary on the Gospel According to St. John* (London: John Murray, Albermarle Street, 1967), 186. He does not define "fatal."

14. John Calvin, *Commentary on the Gospel According to John*, vol. II (Edinburgh: The Calvin Translation Society, 1847), 46.

15. See Acts 6:7 for such a suggestion.

16. Morris, *The Gospel According to John,* 607, thinks it probable, because of what is said in 12:36, that 12:44-50 contains an earlier message spoken by Jesus. John inserts it here as a fitting summary of Jesus' teaching. Godet, 90, takes the more controversial position that the words in 12:44-50 were composed by John to recap the whole of Christ's teaching. The phrase, "Jesus cried out" (12:44), emphasizes the extreme importance of what He will say.

17. That this is no unimportant theme is seen by the fact that it is stated nearly forty times in John's Gospel.

18. Such is the meaning of the word *theoreo,* translated "look at." Jesus is not speaking about physical sight but about Spirit-given inner sight.

19. Cf. Colossians 1:15, 19; Hebrews 1:3.

20. Review again John 1:4, 7, 9; 3:19; 8:12; 9:5; 12:35-36. The Greek construction of John 12:46 might more properly be translated "I (emphatic), Light, have come into the world, and will remain Light."

21. There is a very real sense in which Christ both judges and does not judge. He judges, but only indirectly through His words that men refuse to believe. In that sense He does not judge, but people bring judgment upon themselves. As Barclay observes, *The Gospel of John,* 135, "By his attitude to Jesus, a man shows what he is and therefore judges himself." See John 5:22, 27, 30; 8:16, 26; 9:39. Cf. 3:18f.

22. See the conclusion to Chapter 11 of this book.

23. Quoted by Godet, *Commentary on the Gospel of St. John,* 86.

24. George Heath, "My Soul, Be on Thy Guard," *Hymns of the Christian Life* (Camp Hill, PA: Christian Publications, Inc., 1978), # 368.

# 24

# Love Modeled

John 13:1-38

*It was just before the Passover Feast. Jesus knew that the time had come for him to leave this world and go to the Father. Having loved his own who were in the world, he now showed them the full extent of his love.*

*2 The evening meal was being served, and the devil had already prompted Judas Iscariot, son of Simon, to betray Jesus. 3 Jesus knew that the Father had put all things under his power, and that he had come from God and was returning to God; 4 so he got up from the meal, took off his outer clothing, and wrapped a towel around his waist. 5 After that, he poured water into a basin and began to wash his disciples' feet, drying them with the towel that was wrapped around him.*

*6 He came to Simon Peter, who said to him, "Lord, are you going to wash my feet?"*

*7 Jesus replied, "You do not realize now what I am doing, but later you will understand."*

*8 "No," said Peter, "you shall never wash my feet."*

*Jesus answered, "Unless I wash you, you have no part with me."*

*9 "Then, Lord," Simon Peter replied, "not just my feet but my hands and my head as well!"*

*10 Jesus answered, "A person who has had a bath needs only to wash his feet; his whole body is clean. And you are clean, though not every one of you." 11 For he knew who was going to betray him, and that was why he said not every one was clean.*

*12 When he had finished washing their feet, he put on his clothes and returned to his place. "Do you understand what I have done for you?" he asked them. 13 "You call me 'Teacher' and 'Lord,' and rightly so, for that is what I am. 14 Now that I, your Lord and Teacher, have washed your feet, you also should wash one another's feet. 15 I have set you an example that you should do as I have done for you. 16 I tell you the truth, no servant is greater than his master, nor is a messenger greater than the one who sent him. 17 Now that you know these things, you will be blessed if you do them.*

*18 "I am not referring to all of you; I know those I have chosen. But this is to fulfill the scripture: 'He who shares my bread has lifted up his heel against me.'*

*19 "I am telling you now before it happens, so that when it does happen you will believe that I am He. 20 I tell you the truth, whoever accepts anyone I send accepts me; and whoever accepts me accepts the one who sent me."*

*21 After he had said this, Jesus was troubled in spirit and testified, "I tell you the truth, one of you is going to betray me."*

*22 His disciples stared at one another, at a loss to know which of them he meant. 23 One of them, the disciple whom Jesus loved, was reclining next to him. 24 Simon Peter motioned to this disciple and said, "Ask him which one he means."*

*25 Leaning back against Jesus, he asked him, "Lord, who is it?"*

*26 Jesus answered, "It is the one to whom I will give this piece of bread when I have dipped it in the dish." Then, dipping the piece of bread, he gave it to Judas Iscariot, son of Simon. 27 As soon as Judas took the bread, Satan entered into him.*

*"What you are about to do, do quickly," Jesus told him, 28 but no one at the meal understood why Jesus said this to him. 29 Since Judas had charge of the money, some thought Jesus was telling him to buy what was needed for the Feast, or to give something to the poor. 30 As soon as Judas had taken the bread, he went out. And it was night.*

*31 When he was gone, Jesus said, "Now is the Son of Man glorified and God is glorified in him. 32 If God is glorified in him, God will glorify the Son in himself, and will glorify him at once.*

*33 "My children, I will be with you only a little longer. You will look for me, and just as I told the Jews, so I tell you now: Where I am going, you cannot come.*

*34 "A new command I give you: Love one another. As I have loved you, so you must love one another. 35 By this all men will know that you are my disciples, if you love one another."*

*36 Simon Peter asked him, "Lord, where are you going?"*

*Jesus replied, "Where I am going, you cannot follow now, but you will follow later."*

*37 Peter asked, "Lord, why can't I follow you now? I will lay down my life for you."*

*38 Then Jesus answered, "Will you really lay down your life for me? I tell you the truth, before the rooster crows, you will disown me three times!"*

For several of my teen years, our family attended a church that practiced foot washing. I think my father doubted that foot washing was something Jesus intended His followers to perpetuate literally. But because there was no other church in the community that preached the gospel so clearly, we went along with it. Once a month, at the close of the morning service, the adherents actually washed each others' feet! On that Sunday every mother made sure the family's feet were spotless and the family's socks were "holeless"!

Whatever our family's attitude toward the custom, the church leaders felt the rite would advance practical holiness and self-abasing love. Whether the foot washing translated into better interpersonal relationships was open to debate. And, besides, you could choose whose feet you would wash—and who would wash yours!

Certainly, however, in the context of Bible lands and Bible times, what Jesus did was a beautiful picture of . . .

## Servant Love (13:1-17)

The decisive Passover feast, Jesus' last, was upon Him. The voice of the Holy Spirit witnessed in His spirit that the time for His return home was very near. Soon He would rejoin His Father God in the glory that He had known before the creation of the world. It would not be an easy transition. He would go by way of a Roman cross—one of the most cruel and shameful deaths ever devised by mankind.

Although He was about to leave this world, Jesus' disciples—a gift from the Father—must remain for now. They would experience the world's unwarranted hostility without His physical presence to encourage them. Such an hour called forth redoubled tenderness on Jesus' part. He deeply loved these men who had shared His ministry for more than three years. He must in some way demonstrate to them the extent of His love (13:1).[1]

See, first, *the act of love* (13:4-5). The scene was an evening meal.[2] The Twelve, including Judas, were at the table with their Master, reclining on couches according to Eastern custom. The traitor's scheme, instigated by the devil, had already been conceived in his heart (13:2).[3]

Customarily in such a situation, a servant with water and towel would have met the group at the door. His first duty would be to wash off the dust that their sandaled feet had picked up. But evidently there was no servant to perform that ignoble task. Nor was any of the competitive disciples willing to take the servant's place. So they proceeded with the meal, their feet unwashed.

Jesus was well aware of His sovereignty, His heavenly origin and His pending return to His Father (13:3). By this point, His disciples, too, were convinced of His deity. Jesus deemed it important to exemplify in the presence of these proudly ambitious men[4] the servant nature of true greatness.[5] He would do the unthinkable: He would perform the duty of the lowly household slave. Had one of the disciples done such a thing, the others would have perceived it as an admission of inferiority.

Silently, their Teacher and Lord left His place at the table. He deliberately removed His upper garment[6] and wrapped a slave's towel around His waist (13:4). Suddenly all eyes were fixed on the Lord. All conversation ceased. The disciples could not believe their eyes. Then from one of the large pots just inside the door, He poured water into a basin. To the amazement of the twelve, He proceeded to wash and dry their feet (13:5). How must they all have felt? Doubtless Peter expressed the feelings of all of them.

"Do *you* wash *my* feet?" he asked (13:6).[7]

How must Judas have felt? Some have suggested that Jesus deliberately gave Judas the seat of honor on His left.[8] What a battle must have been raging in his treacherous heart! There he was, hypocritically playing the role of loyal disciple! He must have known Jesus was appealing to him, even at that late hour, to turn from the treason that would destroy him.

Notice next *the meaning of the act* (13:6-17). This loving ministry symbolized 1) the need for daily cleansing from sin and 2) the humility that should mark Christ's followers. Washing with water symbolized *cleansing*

(13:6-11). As Jesus advanced around the table, He came to Simon Peter. Peter expressed his dismay that Jesus should be washing His feet (13:6). Surely it should be the other way around! But the Lord reassured Peter. At the moment, washing Peter's feet was hard to comprehend. But after His death and resurrection and the descent of the Spirit, Peter would indeed perceive its significance (13:7).[9]

Even these words did not satisfy the strong-willed Peter, who began actually to dictate to his Master. Peter was certain that absolutely nothing would alter his position on the matter (13:8).[10] But Jesus warned him that if he refused, he would have no part in Christ's ministry,[11] Whereupon Peter, ever impetuous, asked Jesus to wash his hands and head as well (13:9). But that was not necessary. Having previously bathed, now only his feet were dirty (13:10).

Jesus' words obviously had a double meaning. The "bath" of which He spoke symbolized for believers the initial "washing of rebirth" (Titus 3:5). This "washing" cleansed from all past sin and guilt through Jesus' atoning death on the cross. The washing of feet represented believers' need for continued cleansing from moral defilement. This cleansing comes as we confess whatever sins we may have committed along the way.[12]

With respect to the disciples, all of them except Judas were clean through the word of Christ (John 13:10; see also 15:3). The betrayer was "not . . . clean" (13:11). The other disciples were not yet aware of Judas' impending betrayal of Jesus, but Judas knew Jesus referred to him (13:11). It was as though Jesus was extending to him a further opportunity to change his mind.[13]

Second, Jesus' washing the disciples' feet was a lesson in humble *service* one to the other (13:12-17). It was the mark of true greatness. He, their Teacher and Lord, had not thought it beneath Him to take the lowest place (13:13-14). Neither, therefore, should they (13:15). This demanded more than mental assent to His counsel. It demanded action. They should imitate the spirit of His actions. In His kingdom, the blessing of rising was through descending; the way to the highest position was to choose the lowest (13:17).[14]

Furthermore, our text describes the grace of . . .

## *Unrequited Love (13:18-30)*

A dramatic evening unfolded around the supper table that ever-so-crucial night! We will follow the movement step by step. *We* know what the disciples did not yet know—that Jesus was about to be betrayed by one of their own. Throughout their years together, Judas had displayed loyal friendship (13:18).[15] Jesus may have feared that the other disciples would see Jesus as the helpless victim of Judas' treachery. If so, they might lose faith in Him. To assure them that He knew what lay ahead, Jesus hinted mysteriously of an impending disaster (13:19).

Then as He sensed in His pure heart the ramifications of Judas' crime, Jesus finally named it. Betrayal. By one of His own (13:21). Bewildered, the disciples reacted in silent amazement, doubting each other and their own hearts (13:22). Finally Peter, unable to repress his concern, entreated John,[16] reclining next to Jesus (13:23), to ask who it was (13:24).[17]

"Lord, who is it?" John asked in a whisper (13:25). And Jesus replied that the traitor was the disciple to whom He would give a small morsel of bread from the dish.[18] Such an action, according to Eastern custom, was a sign of special friendship. It was a mark of honor. And He gave the morsel to Judas Iscariot, son of Simon (13:26).[19] What else could this have been but a final gracious appeal to the man's conscience? Judas was no puppet held on the strings of a fate he could not control. He acted freely and willfully. How different the story could have been had Judas, upon receiving the bread, bowed in contrite repentance!

But that was not the case. In that moment, the son of Simon inexorably and tragically rejected the divine love Jesus extended to him. At the very moment he took the bread, Satan, to whom he had given place, took control of his will (13:27). Repentance was no longer possible. The conflict was decided! Judas became the embodiment of unmixed evil—evil that must be purged from the group. In a voice that all could hear, Jesus ordered him to do, as quickly as possible,[20] what he was bent on doing.

It is strange that not even John understood the nature of Jesus' command. The disciples thought perhaps Jesus was putting into action preparations for the Passover meal (13:29). But Judas went out into the dark Judean night, into the dark night of the soul, to his eternal doom.

Third, and finally, our text presents us with Jesus' exhortation to . . .

## Mutual Love (13:31-38)

With Judas' departure, the dialogue between Jesus and His disciples took on an affectionate, intimate nature.[21] He was preparing them for His departure. With the symbolic washing of the disciples' feet and the dismissal of Judas behind them, *now* the Son of Man was glorified.[22] Jesus had now freely accepted the consequences of Judas' work. For all intents and purposes, His passion, graphically expressed in the foot washing, was accomplished and His glory revealed.

Not only was the Son glorified, but by His offering of perfect obedience, God was glorified[23] in Him (13:31). His own ultimate glorification awaited[24] His fast-approaching resurrection and ascension to heaven. At that time God would restore to Him the glory which He had in eternity past (13:32). By then the disciples would no longer enjoy His physical presence nor yet participate in His glory. Rather, their part would be to remain behind to continue His work in the world until His return (13:33, 36).

The world in which they would minister would be pervaded by bitterness, selfishness and hatred. Such a ruinous spirit could destroy them. They would need an entirely opposite power controlling their close associations with one another. Furthermore, to communicate His love to a loveless world, they would need to model it in their interpersonal relationships. If they were to be identified as Christ's people, they would need to evidence the love that characterized His life (13:35). And so the Lord gave to these men the "new"[25] command: *Love one another.*

"As I have loved you," Jesus said, "so you must love one another" (13:34).

Peter, always self-confident, was more interested in learning where Jesus was going and why he could not immediately follow Him. If it involved martyrdom, he was quite prepared (13:36-37). His intentions were excellent, but Jesus knew Peter better than Peter knew himself. Peter had yet to discover that following Jesus was not a human possibility born from a human decision. Discipleship required ability available only through the power of the Holy Spirit. This enablement Peter did not yet have. Given the opportunity to be identified with his suffering Lord, he would deny Him three times (13:38). But unlike Judas, Peter would repent with bitter tears.

## Conclusion

Our text teaches us the nature and importance of true Christian love. As to its *nature,* it is a love that is willing to "wash the disciples' feet," even the feet of a Judas! Down the centuries some have perpetuated the practice as a religious rite.[26] But it is unlikely that Jesus intended His object lesson to be that. Rather, washing others' feet is an attitude, a spirit. It says we do not proudly covet a place of honor but unpretentiously take a servant's place—the lowest place.

How needful is this posture of humility in the Church today! And how often it is missing. Barclay's words are sadly to the point:

> So often, even in churches, trouble arises because someone does not get his place. So often even ecclesiastical dignitaries are offended because they did not receive the precedence to which their office entitled them. . . . The world is full of people who are standing on their dignity when they ought to be kneeling at the feet of their brethren. In every sphere of life, desire for prominence and unwillingness to take a subordinate place wreck the scheme of things. A player is one day omitted from the team and refuses to play any more. . . . A member of a choir is not given a solo and will not sing any more. . . . Someone is given a quite unintentional slight and either explodes in anger or broods in sulkiness for days afterwards. When we are tempted to think of our dignity, our prestige, our rights, let us see again the picture of the Son of God, girt with a towel, kneeling at his disciples' feet.[27]

Jesus said, "Whoever wants to become great among you must be your servant, and whoever wants to be first must be your slave—just as the Son of Man did not come to be served, but to serve, and to give his life as a ransom for many" (Matthew 20:26-27). That is the nature of Christian love.

Our text also presents us with the *importance* of such love. Jerome recounts that John's disciples grew weary of his constant exhortation, "Little children, love one another." It was all he would say as they carried the feeble apostle into their assembly. When they asked him why he always said this, he replied, "Because it is the Lord's commandment; and if it only be fulfilled it is enough."[28] Therein lies its importance: It is the Lord's command!

But not only that, love is the fundamental mark of a Christian. In his first letter, the Apostle John reminds us, "We know that we have passed from death to life, because we love our brothers. Anyone who does not love remains in death" (1 John 3:14). How needful it is for the penetrating light of this word to shine into our contemporary church life. Too often bitterness, discord, jealousy, dissension, factions and selfish ambition hold sway. Love is absent.

Again, love is the mark by which the world may recognize Christ's disciples. Tertullian observed, "The heathen are wont to exclaim with wonder, 'See how these Christians love one another!' for they [the heathen] hate one another; and, 'How they are ready to die for one another!' for they are more ready to kill one another."[29]

May my church and yours, in that sense, be a foot washing church!

### Endnotes

1. The NIV expression "the full extent" (13:1) is a translation of the Greek *telos,* which may be rendered either "to the end [of his life]," "to the uttermost" or "completely."

2. B.F. Westcott, *Commentary on the Gospel According to St. John* (London: John Murray, Albermarle Street, 1967), 195, concludes that this could not have been the Passover meal since, according to 13:29, supplies for the Feast had not yet been purchased.

3. F. Godet, *Commentary on the Gospel of St. John,* vol. III (Edinburgh: T. & T. Clarke, 1881), 118, speculates on what brought Judas to this decision. He had anticipated that joining Jesus would advance his political agenda and open up a brilliant career. When he saw that Jesus' way was opposite to what he expected, he became ever more irritated and exasperated. By being Jesus' disciple, he saw himself deceived concerning Jesus and seriously compromised in the eyes of the chief priests. So his treason proceeded both from resentment and a desire to regain favor with the rulers.

4. The disciples had been arguing about which of them was the greatest. See Luke 22:24-27.

5. Cf. Philippians 2:6-8.

6. C.K. Barrett, *The Gospel According to St. John* (London: S.P.C.K, 1955), 366, sees the laying aside of Jesus' outer garment as a foreshadowing of the laying down of His life.

7. The Greek construction sharply contrasts the "you" and the "my."

8. See, for example, William Barclay, *The Gospel of John,* vol. II (Philadelphia: The Westminster Press, 1975), 145. He makes this assumption from the fact that Jesus could speak privately to him without the others overhearing. Leon Morris, *The Gospel According to John* (Grand Rapids, MI: Eerdmans, 1971), 626, also thinks it not unlikely that because he was the treasurer of the group, Judas was in a place of honor on Jesus' left. This too would be a part of Jesus' last appeal to the traitor.

9. The NIV translates *meta tauta* ("after these things") as "later." Most commentators interpret this as meaning after the cross and resurrection or after Pentecost. On the other hand, F. Godet, *Commentary on the Gospel of St. John,*103, thinks that here *meta tauta* means "soon," i.e., after the explanation of 13:13-17.

10. Peter's words are exceedingly emphatic. He uses two Greek negatives, *ou* and *me,* before the verb "you shall wash," and *eis ton aiona,* "forever," after the verb. To get the force of his words, we might translate 13:8, "There is just no way you will ever, ever get to wash my feet."

11. This is the interpretation that commentators like F.F. Bruce, *The Gospel of John* (Grand Rapids, MI: Eerdmans, 1983), 281, give to the words "no part in me." Westcott, *Commentary on the Gospel According to St. John,* 191, interprets Jesus as saying, "You have no share in my kingdom as a faithful soldier in the conquests of his captain." On the other hand, Barrett, *The Gospel According to St. John,* 367, has Jesus meaning, "You will have no share in the benefits of my passion, and no place among my people."

   Barclay, *The Gospel of John,* vol. II, 141, interprets Jesus' words as a "baptismal" figure. "Unless you pass through the gate of baptism, you have no part in the church." Although water baptism pictures the washing away of sins, most evangelicals would be somewhat uncomfortable with this sacramental interpretation. Barrett (*The Gospel According to St. John* [London: S.P.C.K., 1955]), has this to say: "John has penetrated beneath the surface of baptism as an ecclesiastical rite, [and] seen it in its relation to the Lord's death, into which converts were baptized (cf. Rom. 6:3), and thus integrated it into the act of humble love in which the Lord's death was set forth before the passion."

12. This corresponds with what John wrote in First John 1:8. Morris, *The Gospel According to John,* 618, quotes a lexical source as follows: "[H]e whose inmost nature has been renovated does not need radical renewal, but only to be cleansed from every several fault into which he may fall through intercourse with the unrenewed world."

   Bruce, *The Gospel of John,* 281, correctly observes that some manuscripts of 13:10 read, "A person who has had a bath does not need to wash." If this is what Jesus said, the text would mean, according to Bruce, "When a person has received the cleansing benefits of Christ's death, he cannot receive them all over again. Salvation is complete."

13. Godet, *Commentary on the Gospel of St. John,* 105, considers Jesus' words, "though not every one of you," as a last effort to bring Judas to repentance.

14. Commenting on 13:20, which he connects to 13:14, 16, Morris, *The Gospel According to John,* 623, writes: "To serve Jesus is to take the way of the cross and it necessarily leads men into lowly paths. But it is not to be lightly esteemed. It has a high and holy dignity. Those sent by Christ are brought close to God."

15. Psalm 41:9, quoted by Jesus, equates a close friend as "he who shares my bread" and betrayal as "[lifting] up his heel against me." According to Morris, *The Gospel According to John,* 622, "lifting the heel" is a metaphor derived from the horse's habit of lifting up its hoof preparatory to kicking. To see how Jesus would have felt under these circumstances, read Psalm 55:12-14.

16. I think we may rightly conclude with the majority of Bible scholars that the "disciple whom Jesus loved" (13:23) was, in fact, the Apostle John, author of this Gospel.

17. A person taking part in such a meal would recline on his left side, his left arm supporting his body, his right arm free to eat. Thus the disciple to the right of Jesus would find his head immediately in front of Jesus and would be in a position to lean back against Him and speak confidentially.

18. It would seem that John was the only disciple to hear Jesus' words. The identity of the betrayer was thus kept secret for the time being. Perhaps if the other disciples had known what Judas was about to do, he would never have left the room alive!

19. The use of Judas' full name adds solemnity to the action.

20. The word "quickly" *(tacheiov)* (13:27) is best rendered, according to Barrett, *The Gospel According to St. John,* 374, "more quickly." That is, "What you are about to do, do more quickly than you are presently doing it."
21. "My children" *(teknia)* (13:33) expresses a deeply affectionate kinship and is descriptive of the tenderness with which Jesus now spoke.
22. The tense and voice of the verb "glorified" *(edoxasthe)* (13:31) is aorist passive, translated literally, "was glorified."
23. Again, the voice and tense indicate a past action.
24. The tense of the verb "glorify" changes in 13:32 from aorist to future. It needs to be noted that the words, "If God is glorified in him" (13:32), do not appear in the best manuscripts of John's Gospel. Verses 31 and 32 would then read, "Now was the Son of Man glorified and God was glorified in him; then God will glorify the Son in himself, and will glorify him at once."
25. The command to love is not "new" in the time sense (cf. 1 John 2:7). The first and greatest commandment from the beginning was to love God and one's neighbor (Leviticus 19:18; Deuteronomy 6:5). But Jesus' command was "new" in several senses: 1) It was delivered in and for the new age which was inaugurated by His life and death; 2) It corresponded to the command that regulated the relation between Jesus and the Father (John 10:17-18; 12:49f); 3) It could only be fulfilled through the power of the Holy Spirit; 4) It involved the same kind of self-sacrifice that was manifested at Calvary.
26. For a brief history of the practice of foot washing, see Westcott, 192.
27. Barclay, *The Gospel of John,* vol. II, 139f.
28. Quoted by Westcott, *Commentary on the Gospel According to St. John,* 198.
29. Ibid.

# Part IX

## *Questions for Reflection or Discussion*

1. What is the New Testament teaching about "death to self"? How is it akin to Jesus' teaching in John 12:24-26?

2. How does John 12:27 illustrate the real humanity of Jesus?

3. Compare and contrast John's description of God's judgment on unbelieving Israel in John 12:37-41 with Paul's doctrine of the judgment of God upon the heathen world according to Romans 1:18-32.

4. How would you define true humility?

5. How does Jesus' washing the disciples' feet illustrate the truth of First John 1:9?

# The Promises of the Son

## John 14:1-16:33

# 25

# The Way to the Father

John 14:1-14

*"Do not let your hearts be troubled. Trust in God; trust also in me. 2 In my Father's house are many rooms; if it were not so, I would have told you. I am going there to prepare a place for you. 3 And if I go and prepare a place for you, I will come back and take you to be with me that you also may be where I am. 4 You know the way to the place where I am going."*

*Thomas said to him, "Lord, we don't know where you are going, so how can we know the way?"*

*6 Jesus answered, "I am the way and the truth and the life. No one comes to the Father except through me. 7 If you really knew me, you would know my Father as well. From now on, you do know him and have seen him."*

*8 Philip said, "Lord, show us the Father and that will be enough for us."*

*9 Jesus answered: "Don't you know me, Philip, even after I have been among you such a long time? Anyone who has seen me has seen the Father. How can you say, 'Show us the Father'? 10 Don't you believe that I am in the Father, and that the Father is in me? The words I say to you are not just my own. Rather it is the Father, living in me, who is doing his work. 11 Believe me when I say that I am in the Father and the Father is in me; or at least believe on the evidence of the miracles themselves. 12 I tell you the truth, anyone who has faith in me will do what I have been doing. He will do even greater things than these, because I am going to the Father. 13 And I will do whatever you ask in my name, so that the Son may bring glory to the Father. 14 You may ask me for anything in my name, and I will do it."*

Recently our morning newspaper, *The Hamilton Spectator,* contained the following remarks by the newly elected moderator of Canada's largest Protestant denomination. In response to his interviewer's questions, he replied:

> I don't believe Jesus was God, but I'm no theologian. I don't believe Jesus is the only way to God. I don't believe He rose from the dead as a scientific fact. I don't know whether those things happened. It's an irrelevant question. I have no idea if there is a hell. I don't think Jesus was that concerned about hell. He was concerned about life here on earth. Is heaven a place? I have no idea. I believe that there is a continuity of spirit in some way, but I would be a fool to say what that is. We've got enough problems trying to live ethically and well here to have any . . . understanding of what happens after we die.

Remarkably, the man went on to affirm that Jesus was central to his beliefs. Jesus motivated his compassion for others. But he did not accept the Bible as a valid historical record. Nor did he accept the traditional Christian concept of Jesus as the Son of God. "I believe," he said, "that Christ reveals to us as much of the nature of God as we can see in a human being."

How tragic! The Jesus of this church moderator is not the Jesus of the text we now approach with reverence and faith.

We can well imagine the mental and emotional state of the disciples at this point. Jesus had made some unthinkable disclosures during the pre-Passover supper He shared with His disciples. He had revealed that He would be betrayed (13:21). He told them He would be leaving them, and this time they could not accompany Him to wherever He was going (13:33). He predicted Peter would disown Him three times (13:38). Altogether the future looked uncertain and full of trouble. Why would their Master have to leave them? How could they survive without Him? Would they ever see Him again? They were a shocked, distressed, confused, fearful band.

And there was more. Jesus would be disgraced and humiliated before the world—arrested, unjustly tried, condemned to a criminal's death. He would be buried in a guarded, sealed tomb. This whole scenario was exactly opposite to what they had anticipated. Their secure, comfortable world was about to crash over their heads.

It is within, and because of, this atmosphere of gloom that Jesus speaks the beautifully simple yet profound words of our text. Ever sympathetic, He speaks words calculated to bring comfort, courage and hope to His disheartened disciples. And down through the centuries His words have continued to bring peace to countless troubled people. He makes four promises to His followers: 1) a future place in His Father's house; 2) a true knowledge of His Father's nature; 3) a greater ministry than His own; and 4) the privilege of answered prayer. We will look at those promises in that order.

## *The House of the Father (14:1-3)*

The disciples were troubled because Jesus told them He would be leaving. But the tumult in their hearts could be stilled[1] if they would but pay careful attention to His words. They could trust Him to tell them the truth about what lay ahead (14:1).[2] After all, their past three years of experience with Him offered no basis to doubt His word.[3]

The facts were these: 1) He was on His way back to the "Father's house" (14:2).[4] 2) There would be plenty of room for all of them.[5] 3) He would be getting things ready for them to join Him (14:2). 4) He would eventually return to take them with Him to heaven (14:3). Thus, their separation from Him was only temporary and would result in an eternity with Him in heaven.

We need to linger a little longer over certain words and phrases of our text, so pregnant with meaning. Consider, for instance, that phrase "my Father's house." How descriptive of heaven! It suggests the dwelling place of God's glory—like the tabernacle and temple of old. It suggests, as well, security against all harm and evil. It is a place where all needs are fully supplied. It is a home where loving family relationships are forthright and enduring.

Or take that word "rooms." The Greek *monai* was used of the highway resting places where road-weary travelers would find refreshment and renewed strength. Its corresponding verb is *meno,* meaning "to remain" or "abide." Thus the term suggests that heaven is the believer's long-range dwelling place. There the pilgrim will find welcome rest from the weariness of life's long journey.

> I've wrestled on towards heaven,
>     'Gainst storm and wind and tide;
> Now, like a weary traveler
>     That leaneth on his guide,
> Amid the shades of evening,
>     While sinks life's lingering sand,
> I hail the glory dawning
>     From Emmanuel's land.[6]

And what wealth we may discern in those reassuring words, "I am going there to prepare a place for you!"[7] They speak of the whole process of Jesus' passion and glorification—His "going away." Jesus' death and resurrection opened heaven's doors wide to all believers.[8] The words John uses here remind us as well of that passage where He "who went before us"[9]—Jesus—entered the sanctuary on our behalf (Hebrews 6:20). He became "a high priest forever, in the order of Melchizedek."

And what are we to make of Jesus' promise, "I will come back and take you to be with me" (John 14:3)? We who speak of "Christ, our Coming King" hold very strongly to the literal meaning of that promise. We believe Him to be saying precisely what the Apostle Paul says: "For the Lord himself will come down from heaven, with a loud command, with the voice of the archangel and with the trumpet call of God" (1 Thessalonians 4:16).

Others over the years have understood Jesus to be speaking of Pentecost,[10] conversion or death. Some merely say Christ is "ever coming to the world and to the Church, and to men as the Risen Lord."[11] Granted, each of these is in some sense a "coming" of Christ. Nevertheless, the hope of the glorious appearing of our Lord and Savior shines brightly in our text.

### The Way to the Father (14:4-6)

Jesus' suggestion that His disciples already know "the way" (14:4) does not satisfy "doubting Thomas." His is an honest perplexity. He and his colleagues do know Jesus, but they have not yet realized that He Himself is "the way" (14:5). And Thomas is not going to pretend that he understands something when, in fact, he does not. His frank admission of ignorance prompts from our Lord one of His greatest statements ever.

"*I* am[12] the *way* and the *truth* and the *life*," Jesus declares. "No one comes to the Father except through me" (14:6, emphasis added). What depth of meaning is in those words of our text! Jesus has taken three great Old Testament truths and claimed to fulfill all three.

1) The Old Testament speaks much about the *way* in which men must walk and the *ways* of God. For example, God told Moses to "walk in all the *way* that the LORD your God has commanded you" (Deuteronomy 5:33, emphasis added). Moses said to Israel: "I know that after my death you are sure to become utterly corrupt and to turn from the *way* I have commanded you" (31:29, emphasis added). Isaiah said: "Your ears will hear a voice behind you, saying, 'This is the *way;* walk in it' " (Isaiah 30:21, emphasis added). The Psalmist prayed: "Teach me your *way,* O LORD" (Psalm 27:11, emphasis added). Now Jesus was saying, "I am the *way*" (John 14:6). What did He mean?

Several years ago when my wife and I were ministering in Chile, we took a bus north from Santiago to the city of Viña del Mar. The missionary had instructed the bus driver to let us off at the terminal. For some unexplainable reason, he let us off at an earlier stop downtown. It soon dawned on us "gringos" that we were hopelessly lost. We had no idea where the bus depot was and no way of asking for directions. We explained our situation to the Lord and entered the foyer of a nearby hotel. There, in the providence of God, we found the one man who spoke English.

"Could you tell us how to get to the bus terminal?" we asked. The man began to describe the way but soon decided it was too complex for us to remember.

"I will take you there myself," he volunteered. What sweet words those were to us! He walked us all the long way from the hotel to the bus terminal, where we were met by another waiting missionary. Is that not what Jesus does for us? He not only gives advice and directions but He takes us by the hand and leads us to the Father. He does not just *tell* us about the way; He *is* the way.

2) The Old Testament speaks of *truth*. For example, the Psalmist says, "Teach me your way, O LORD, and I will walk in your *truth*" (Psalm 86:11,

emphasis added). And again, "I have chosen the way of *truth*" (119:30, emphasis added). And now Jesus boldly affirms, "I am the *truth*" (John 14:6). What is He saying? Bultmann puts it well: "Truth is not the teaching about God transmitted by Jesus but is God's very reality revealing itself—occurring!—in Jesus."[13] Most wonderfully is God's truth seen in the cross, where both the justice and the mercy of God are revealed.

3) Again, the Old Testament speaks of *life*: "For these commands are a lamp, this teaching is a light, and the corrections of discipline are the way to *life*" (Proverbs 6:23, emphasis added). And this: "He who heeds discipline shows the way to *life*" (10:17, emphasis added). And again: "You have made known to me the path of *life*" (Psalm 16:11, emphasis added). But the source of eternal life is to be found only in Jesus, who said, "I am the *Life*" (John 14:6).[14]

Not only did Jesus say He was the embodiment of these Old Testament truths. He went further and claimed to be the *only* way to the Father and to His house. "No one comes to the Father except through me," He said (14:6). Present-day thinking does not assign such exclusivity to Jesus Christ. Are there not other ways to God? What about the other world religions? Will they be left out? Cannot people devise their own ways to heaven? Jesus' claim does not sit well with the inclusivism of our day. Even some alleged evangelicals are climbing on the universalist bandwagon. But we who genuinely follow Christ and His Word must gently, albeit firmly, reject the modern viewpoint. Jesus is not one of many possible ways to heaven. *Jesus is the one and only way to God the Father, who is in heaven.* The testimony of our text and the testimony of John's entire Gospel affirm just one Way. And Jesus is that Way.

## *The Nature of the Father (14:7-11)*

But what is the Father in heaven like? What is His disposition? His nature? Jesus' disciples wanted to know. People today want to know. And the answer of our text is straightforward: The Father has revealed Himself in the Person of Jesus Christ, His one and only Son. Jesus made this clear in four positive affirmations to His disciples: 1) "If you really knew me, you would know my Father as well. From now on, you do know him and have seen him" (14:7).[15] 2) "Anyone who has seen me has seen the Father" (14:9). 3) "Don't you believe that I am in the Father, and that the Father is in me?" (14:10).[16] 4) "Believe me when I say that I am in the Father and the Father is in me; or at least believe on the evidence of the miracles themselves" (14:11).

God is just like Jesus! He, too, is forgiving, tender, compassionate, transparent, truthful. Know what Jesus is like and you will know what God is like.

## The Power of the Father (14:12)

Jesus had assured His disciples that they would be reunited with Him in His Father's house. He had revealed Himself as both the Way to the Father and the carbon copy of the Father's nature. He continued by outlining the ministry they would have between His departure and His return. He promised them that the power which enabled Him to perform His mighty works would be theirs, too. In fact, it would be given to "anyone who has faith in [Him]" (14:12). Moreover, He promised that believers would do "even greater things" than He had done. This ability would be due to His ascension to the Father (14:12). Doubtless, Jesus was speaking here about the great numbers who would believe on Him through the preaching of the gospel.[17] Signs would follow that preaching as a result of the Pentecostal outpouring of the Holy Spirit. The Holy Spirit would be a special gift to the Church from the Father and the ascended Son.[18]

## The Glory of the Father (14:13-14)

Last, our text sets before us the glory of the Father. Jesus now shows His disciples their ongoing privilege of prayer in His name. To pray "in Jesus' name" is not to tack on to the end of our prayers a kind of magic formula. Rather, it is prayer that flows from our union with Christ in His purposes and desires. It is prayer that is consistent with His character. It seeks, first and foremost, the glory of God. To pray in Jesus' name means that our request is for something that He, himself, would present to the Father. "Anything" having these qualities is a fit subject for prayer and will bring Jesus' own response (14:14).

## *Conclusion*

What a comforting, revealing, challenging text! It presents to us, first, *the cure for a troubled heart.* In a world haunted by past failures, present misgivings and future uncertainties, the person without Christ could be greatly distressed. But to the believer there comes the quieting word of Jesus: "My child, trust your faithful, all-wise Father; trust your caring Savior." Nothing will ever happen to you that God has not pre-approved. Nothing!

> Peace, perfect peace, with sorrows surging round?
> On Jesus' bosom naught but calm is found.
>
> Peace, perfect peace, our future all unknown?
> Jesus we know, and He is on the throne.[19]

Our text assures us, second, of our Savior's *coming again* in glory. This is the believer's blessed hope—the glorious appearing of our God and Savior Jesus Christ. It is this hope that promotes faithful missionary endeavor (Matthew 24:14). It inspires courage amid trials (Romans 8:18-25). It promotes holiness of life (1 John 3:2-3). It is the hope expressed by Almeda J. Pearce:

> When He shall come, resplendent in His glory,
>     To take His own from out this vale of night,
> Oh, may I know the joy at His appearing,
> Only at morn to walk with Him in white!
>
> When I shall stand within the court of heaven
>     Where white-robed pilgrims pass before my sight—
> Earth's martyred saints and blood-washed overcomers—
>     These then are they who walk with Him in white!
>
> When He shall call, from earth's remotest corners,
>     All who have stood triumphant in His might,
> Oh, to be worthy then to stand beside them,
>     And in that morn to walk with Him in white![20]

Third, our text holds out to believers the responsibility of *continuing His work. We are* empowered by that One who is the gift of the ascended Christ—the Holy Spirit Himself. Our Lord Jesus has gone back to the Father in heaven, preparing a place for us, interceding for us. He has sent the Holy Spirit to encourage and enable. He has promised to come again to receive us to Himself. In the interim, He has commissioned us to prayerfully engage in taking His gospel to the ends of the world.

> Lord, Thou hast given to me a trust,
>   A high and holy dispensation,
> To tell the world, and tell I must,
>   The story of Thy great salvation;
> Thou might'st have sent from heaven above
>   Angelic hosts to tell the story,
> But, in Thy condescending love,
>   On men Thou hast conferred the glory.
>
> Let me be faithful to my trust,
>   Telling the world the story;
> Press on my heart the woe;
>   Put in my feet the go;
> Let me be faithful to my trust
>   And use me for Thy glory.[21]

May this be our heartfelt prayer!

### Endnotes

1. Leon Morris, *The Gospel According to John* (Grand Rapids, MI: Eerdmans, 1971), 636 translates the Greek *me taressestho,* "Stop being troubled."
2. The words "Trust in God; trust also in me" (14:1) may also be translated, "You are trusting God; trust *me* also." This appears to be the better translation and follows the KJV.
3. This is the significance of "If it were not so, I would have told you" (14:2).
4. The picture here, according to F. Godet, *Commentary on the Gospel of St. John,* vol. III (Edinburgh: T. & T. Clarke, 1881), 129, is derived from the vast oriental palaces in which there is room not only for the sovereign and his heir, but also for all the sons of the king, no matter how numerous. C.K. Barrett, *The Gospel According to St. John* (London: S.P.C.K., 1955), 381, and B.F. Westcott, *Commentary on the Gospel According to St. John* (London: John Murray, Albemarle Street, 1967), 200, see the Father's house with its many

rooms as the heavenly, spiritual antitype of the Jerusalem temple with its many rooms (see John 2:20).

5. This is obviously the import of the word "many" (14:2).

6. From *The Last Sayings of Samuel Rutherford*, adapted by Anne R. Cousin, "The Sands of Time Are Sinking," *Hymns of the Christian Life* (Camp Hill, PA: Christian Publications, Inc., 1978), # 390, stanza 4.

7. Unlike the KJV translation, the NIV incorrectly inserts the word "there," making Jesus say, "I am going *there* to prepare a place for you."

8. See Barrett, *The Gospel According to St. John,* 381.

9. The Greek is *prodromos,* a "forerunner," used by the Roman armies to describe the function of reconnaissance troops. They went ahead of the main army to blaze the trail and to ensure that it was safe for the rest to follow. See William Barclay, *The Gospel of John,* vol. II (Philadelphia: The Westminster Press, 1975), 155.

10. See Godet, *Commentary on the Gospel of St. John,* 132. He understands the words "and take you to be with me" (14:3) to describe "the close and indissoluble union contracted between the believer and the Person of the glorified Savior from the time he receives the gift of the Holy Spirit."

11. Westcott, *Commentary on the Gospel According to St. John,* 210. This last thought is suggested by the fact that the verb translated by the NIV, "I will come back" (14:3), is actually in the present tense, "I am coming."

12. Once again there appears the *ego eimi* ("I am"), which John uses frequently in his Gospel.

13. Quoted by Morris, *The Gospel According to John,* 294. It should also be noted that when "truth" is ascribed to God, it means His faithfulness, reliability and trustworthiness.

14. Think again of the many times in John's Gospel that *Life* is said to be in Jesus. Cf. 1:4; 3:15-16; 4:14; 5:24, 26, 29; 6:35, 40, 47; 10:10, 28; 11:25; 17:2; 20:31.

15. Barrett, *The Gospel According to St. John,* 382-383, prefers the rendering of two early manuscripts and has Jesus saying, in effect: "If you have come to know Me, as you have, you shall know My Father also." Verse 7 bears out the correctness of this interpretation.

16. The Greek makes clear that the question expects an affirmative answer.

17. This is the sole interpretation of most of the commentators on this passage. See, for instance, Westcott, *Commentary on the Gospel According to St. John,* 204; Barclay, *The Gospel of John,* vol. II, 164; Barrett, *The Gospel According to St. John,* 384; F.F. Bruce, *The Gospel of John* (Grand Rapids, MI: Eermans, 1983), 300; and Morris, *The Gospel According to John,* 645.

18. The book of Acts recounts the fulfillment of Jesus' promise.

19. Edward H. Bickersteth, "Peace, Perfect Peace," *Hymns of the Christian Life,* # 318, stanzas 3 and 5.

20. Almeda J. Peerce, "When He Shall Come," ibid., # 134.

21. A.B. Simpson, "My Trust," ibid., # 583, stanza 1 and chorus.

# 26

# The Gift of the Spirit

John 14:15-31; 16:5-15

*15 "If you love me, you will obey what I command. 16 And I will ask the Father, and he will give you another Counselor to be with you forever— 17 the Spirit of truth. The world cannot accept him, because it neither sees him nor knows him. But you know him, for he lives with you and will be in you. 18 I will not leave you as orphans; I will come to you. 19 Before long, the world will not see me anymore, but you will see me. Because I live, you also will live. 20 On that day you will realize that I am in my Father, and you are in me, and I am in you. 21 Whoever has my commands and obeys them, he is the one who loves me. He who loves me will be loved by my Father, and I too will love him and show myself to him."*

*22 Then Judas (not Judas Iscariot) said, "But, Lord, why do you intend to show yourself to us and not to the world?"*

*23 Jesus replied, "If anyone loves me, he will obey my teaching. My Father will love him, and we will come to him and make our home with him. 24 He who does not love me will not obey my teaching. These words you hear are not my own; they belong to the Father who sent me.*

*25 "All this I have spoken while still with you. 26 But the Counselor, the Holy Spirit, whom the Father will send in my name, will teach you all things and will remind you of everything I have said to you. 27 Peace I leave with you; my peace I give you. I do not give to you as the world gives. Do not let your hearts be troubled and do not be afraid.*

*28 "You heard me say, 'I am going away and I am coming back to you.' If you loved me, you would be glad that I am going to the Father, for the*

*Father is greater than I. 29 I have told you now before it happens, so that when it does happen you will believe. 30 I will not speak with you much longer, for the prince of this world is coming. He has no hold on me, 31 but the world must learn that I love the Father and that I do exactly what my Father has commanded me.*

*"Come now; let us leave."*

*16:5 "Now I am going to him who sent me, yet none of you asks me, 'Where are you going?' 6 Because I have said these things, you are filled with grief. 7 But I tell you the truth: It is for your good that I am going away. Unless I go away, the Counselor will not come to you; but if I go, I will send him to you. 8 When he comes, he will convict the world of guilt in regard to sin and righteousness and judgment: 9 in regard to sin, because men do not believe in me; 10 in regard to righteousness, because I am going to the Father, where you can see me no longer; 11 and in regard to judgment, because the prince of this world now stands condemned.*

*12 "I have much more to say to you, more than you can now bear. 13 But when he, the Spirit of truth, comes, he will guide you into all truth. He will not speak on his own; he will speak only what he hears, and he will tell you what is yet to come. 14 He will bring glory to me by taking from what is mine and making it known to you. 15 All that belongs to the Father is mine. That is why I said the Spirit will take from what is mine and make it known to you."*

The ever-so-great redemption graciously provided by our Lord has secured for believers two saving benefits. First, through His *death and resurrection* He has obtained for us free justification "through faith in his blood" (Romans 3:25; see also 4:25). That is to say, on the merits of the "finished" work of Calvary (John 19:30), our past sins are fully forgiven. We have standing with God as though we had never sinned!

Second, and just as important, through our Lord's post-resurrection *ascension to the Father,* He has procured for us the gift of the Holy Spirit. In describing the Pentecostal outpouring, the Apostle Peter proclaims, "God has raised this Jesus to life, and we are all witnesses of the fact. Exalted to the right hand of God, he has received from the Father the promised Holy Spirit, *and has poured out* what you now see and hear" (Acts 2:32-33, emphasis added).

"Everything we need for life and godliness" (2 Peter 1:3) has been purchased for us by our Lord Jesus. *Pardon* from the guilt of sin, *power* for holy
living and effective ministry, a guiding divine *presence*—everything has
been secured for us through Jesus' death, burial, resurrection and ascension.
Everything!

In the two passages that constitute our present text, the Lord promised to
His disciples the gift of the Holy Spirit. He described the ministry which He
would fulfill both in their lives and in the world. For seekers after the deeper
life, without doubt these sections are among the most important in John's
spiritual Gospel.

To begin, we notice the title Jesus gave this Third Person of the Trinity.
Jesus called Him the "Counselor"[1] (John 14:16). The word is a translation
of the Greek *parakletos*,[2] and means, literally, "one called alongside" as a
helper, an advocate or defender—a friend in court.[3] As such, He would always be within reach. He was ready to come to the disciples' assistance in
their conflict with the world. He would be their support in weakness and
their counselor in the difficulties of life. He would console them in afflic-
tion. In every situation, He would replace their Master who was about to
leave them.[4] He was, as A.B. Simpson put it, "God for everything. God at
hand under all circumstances and equal to all demands."[5]

In our two texts are seven vital truths concerning the person and work of
the Holy Spirit. Observe, first, that His presence in our lives is . . .

## The Fruit of Loving Obedience (14:15, 21, 23, 24)

"If you love me," said Jesus, "you will obey what I command. And I will
ask the Father, and he will give you another Counselor" (14:15-16). The
Apostle Peter spoke of the Holy Spirit as the One "whom God has given to
those who obey him" (Acts 5:32). *Obedience* is both the evidence and the
definition of our love for Christ and the condition for receiving the Holy
Spirit. We demonstrate our love not simply in an intellectual comprehension
of Christ's teachings but by applying them to our lives.

A young married man once called on me expressing a desire to be filled
with the Spirit. Prompted by the Spirit, I said, "Go and do the next thing God
tells you to do!" He left my study hurt that I had not taken more time with

him. For several weeks I did not see the fellow. When he called again, I knew by looking that God had fulfilled the desire of his heart. He confided that at the time he had called on me, he and his wife were estranged. The "next thing God told [him] to do" was to go to the city where his wife was staying and be reconciled to her. He obeyed the voice of God, and his obedience resulted in the indwelling of the Holy Counselor. As one preacher put it, "Obedience is always followed by blessing!"

Second, our text informs us that the Holy Spirit is . . .

## The Gift of the Father (14:16, 26)

"I will ask the Father, and *he will give* . . ." (14:16). "But the Counselor . . . whom the Father *will send* . . ." (14:26). Centuries before, through the prophet Joel, God had said, "I will pour out my Spirit on all people. . . . Even on my servants, both men and women, I will pour out my Spirit in those days" (Joel 2:28-29). This was the Father's promise. Luke informs us that just before Jesus' ascension to heaven, He said, "I am going to send you what my Father has promised; but stay in the city until you have been clothed with power from on high" (Luke 24:49). In our present text, Jesus promised that the Father would send the Holy Spirit in answer to His request. As we noted above, on the day the request was fulfilled, Peter explained it to the onlookers in these words: "Exalted to the right hand of God, [Jesus] has received from the Father the promised Holy Spirit and has poured out what you now see and hear" (Acts 2:33). The Holy Spirit is God's *gift*—as are His other blessings that He bestows on His believing children.

Third, the Holy Spirit is . . .

## The Revealer and Reminder of Truth (14:17, 26)

He is called "the Spirit of truth" (14:17). We can say, first, that it is the Holy Spirit who anoints a preacher or a missionary. The Spirit enables him or her to communicate the truth of the gospel. The Spirit opens the hearts of hearers to receive the truth that is proclaimed.[6] Second, it is the Holy Spirit who takes the written Scriptures and illuminates them. The Spirit gives the Word a reality within us, making the Word *the truth* to us. How often a familiar verse suddenly leaps from the  page with a freshness and meaning hitherto unrealized![7]

Again, our Lord promised His followers that the Holy Spirit would "teach [them] all things" (14:26). Everything they needed to know the Holy Spirit would teach them. He would bring to their memories Jesus' very words so that they, in turn, could pass them on to others. We have the written New Testament Scriptures because God fulfilled that promise.

Fourth, the Holy Spirit is . . .

## The Life of the Church (14:17, 19)

Mankind generally—the people Jesus referred to in John 14:17 as "the world"—live in opposition to God. They are quite unaware of the Holy Spirit and, therefore, cannot receive Him (14:17). They are dead to God, "dead in . . . transgressions and sins" (Ephesians 2:1). Jesus' disciples, on the other hand, already knew the Holy Spirit through His enlivening presence in the Lord Jesus.[8] In their not-too-distant future, upon Jesus' exaltation, they would know the Spirit's permanent residence *within* them (John 14:17).[9] His indwelling presence would bring to each of them that quality of life called "eternal." As well, it would constitute the empowering spiritual life of the whole Church. Furthermore, just as the Spirit raised Jesus from the dead (Romans 8:11), so too He would raise the disciples from physical death (John 14:19).

Fifth, the Holy Spirit is . . .

## The Real Presence of Christ (14:18, 20, 23)

A.J. Gordon, a contemporary of A.B. Simpson, spoke of the Holy Spirit as "Jesus' other self." It was his unique way of saying the Holy Spirit within believers is the Spirit of Christ Himself. To affirm that the Holy Spirit lives within us is to affirm that *Christ* lives within us. A.W. Tozer used to say that when the Holy Spirit fills us, Christ seems real enough to reach out and touch!

The disciples were grieving the soon-departure of their Master. How would they survive without Him? Earlier He had sought to quiet their troubled hearts by promising to return for them. They would then be with Him permanently in His Father's house (14:1-3). Now He assures them that between His departure and His return they would not be left as fatherless children.[10] They would know His personal, permanent presence within them through the indwelling Spirit (14:18). The Spirit would make real to them their union with the Father and the Son. He would also make them conscious of Jesus' union with them and His Father (14:20, 23).[11]

How kind was our Lord to bequeath His peace to His troubled disciples! It was a peace that would stabilize them in moments of peril and distress, removing fear and cowardice (14:27). How gracious of Jesus to replace their sadness with deep-down joy! As for Jesus, within little more than hours, He would fulfill the mission that had brought Him to earth. He would lay down His life and return to the One who, being greater than He,[12] had commissioned Him to do so (14:28).

Sixth, the Holy Spirit is . . .

## The "Convicter" of the World (16:8-11)

Not only does the Holy Spirit have a ministry to believers, but He has a ministry to the unbelieving world. To believers, He is their advocate, their helper, their defender. To the "world" He is the "convicter" (16:8).[13] He will convict the world of its sin in rejecting Jesus (16:9). Sin is no longer merely the transgression of laws. It is the refusal of the Savior. He will also convict the world concerning the perfection of Christ's "righteousness." Jesus demonstrated total obedience to God in His laying down His life. God's approval of what Jesus did was demonstrated in Jesus' exaltation. God has "exalted him to the highest place" and given Him "the name that is above every name" (Philippians 2:9).

The Spirit has one other "convicting" job. He will convict the world concerning "judgment." The death of Jesus brought about the judgment of Satan, "the prince of this world." On the basis of that historical event, the Holy Spirit convinces people of their own judgment by God (John 16:11).

"How," one may ask, "does the Holy Spirit convict the world of sin, righteousness and judgment?" The convicting comes primarily through the Spirit-enabled witness of the Church, individually and corporately. Spirit-anointed preachers proclaim the necessity of faith in Christ. They proclaim the nature of true righteousness as it was displayed in Christ's passion. They proclaim the fact of God's final judgment on evil. Such a proclamation of truth is calculated to call sinners to repentance and warn them if they harden their hearts.

Finally, the Holy Spirit is . . .

## The Glorifier of Jesus (16:12-15)

Like the artist who points viewers to his art, not himself, so the Holy Spirit points believers to Jesus. We please the Spirit by honoring the Savior, whom the Spirit came to exalt. The Holy Spirit reveals to us the life-changing person, work and teaching of Jesus (16:14-15). As well, it is His work to disclose to our hearts and minds the Father's future plans for Christ's Church—us. Those plans are set out in the Revelation—one of the most Christ-centered books of the Bible. There we see Jesus, exalted to the throne of the universe. Our Lord Jesus Christ is all and in all![14]

## Conclusion

The gift of God the Father to our fallen world was, and is, His only begotten Son. The gift of the Father and the Son to the Church was, and is, the Holy Spirit. Our text sets before us the Spirit's absolute indispensability. He convicts sinners of their need of a Savior. He opens their hearts to believe on Jesus. The Spirit brought the Church into being, uniting believers in one body in Christ. It is the Holy Spirit who fulfills Jesus' promise to be present wherever and whenever the Church assembles.

It is the Spirit who brings to the believer's consciousness the awesomely sweet reality of that presence. It is the Holy Spirit who makes real to the believer all that Jesus has done in His great atonement. It is the Spirit who casts the light of understanding upon all that Jesus spoke. It is the Holy Spirit who, by filling His people, enables believers to display Christlikeness in their dispositions. It is the same Spirit who enables the various ministries necessary for the life of the Church.

It is the Spirit's anointing that empowers believers to bear convincing witness of Christ to the world. It is the Holy Spirit who endows the Church's individual members with gifts that edify the whole body. It is the Holy Spirit who enables believers to reverently worship and joyfully praise the Father and the Son. It is the Spirit who, in our weakness, comes to our aid, praying through us His prayers to the Father. It was the Holy Spirit who inspired prophets and apostles to write the holy Scriptures. It is the same Spirit who enables the readers of that Book to understand what God has said.

Therefore, let us be careful to honor the Holy Spirit. In our assemblies, let us submit to our Triune God. Let us seek His fullness and obey His gentle promptings in our daily lives. Let us never quench His power nor grieve His holy heart. Let us put to death in us all that is of the world and the flesh and the devil. Let us live day by day, hour by hour, moment by moment, in union with the Spirit. Only in that way will we please God!

Some verse by A.B. Simpson makes a fitting finish to this chapter:

> O Comforter, gentle and tender,
>     O holy and heavenly Dove,
> We are yielding our hearts in surrender,
>     We're waiting Thy fullness to prove.
>
> Come, strong as the wind o'er the ocean,
>     Or soft as the breathing of morn,
> Subduing our spirit's commotion
>     And cheering when hearts are forlorn.
>
> Oh, come as the heart-searching fire,
>     Oh, come as the sin-cleansing flood;
> Consume us with holy desire
>     And fill with the fullness of God.
>
> Anoint us with gladness and healing;
>     Baptize us with power from on high;
> Oh, come with Thy filling and sealing
>     While low at Thy foot-stool we lie.[15]

### Endnotes

1. The KJV translation, "Comforter," is unfortunate. It was due to the influence of the Latin Vulgate.

2. Rather than attempting to translate *parakletos,* some prefer to transliterate the Greek: "Paraclete."

3. See F.F. Bruce, *The Gospel of John* (Grand Rapids, MI: Eerdmans, 1983), 301; Leon Morris, *The Gospel According to John* (Grand Rapids, MI: Eerdmans, 1971), 648, 662; and F. Godet, *Commentary on the Gospel of St. John,* vol. III (Edinburgh: T. & T. Clarke, 1881), 143. C.K. Barrett, *The Gospel According to St. John* (London: S.P.C.K, 1955), 385, acknowledges that the primary meaning of *parakletos* is a "legal assistant" or "advocate." But he thinks that here the word has in it the thought of exhorting (from *parakalein,* as in Romans 12:1), and refers to "prophetic Christian preaching" (Acts 2:40; 1 Corinthians 14:3). He notes that "the main burden of the *paraklesis* [prophetic exhortation] is that men should enter, or accept, the messianic salvation which has been brought into being through the work of Jesus." *Parakletos* is also used of Jesus in First John 2:1—"We have one who speaks to the Father in our defense—Jesus Christ, the Righteous One."

4. In describing the Spirit as "another" Counselor, Jesus is implying that up to now He has fulfilled that function, which the Holy Spirit will now take over.

5. A.B. Simpson, *The Holy Spirit: Power from on High,* ed. Keith M. Bailey (Camp Hill, PA: Christian Publications, Inc., 1994), 353.

6. See also John 15:26-27.

7. Cf. First Corinthians 2:10-14, where Paul describes this ministry of the Holy Spirit.

8. See, for example, B.F. Westcott, *Commentary on the Gospel According to St. John* (London: John Murray, Albermarle Street, 1967), 206.

9. Some manuscripts have 14:17 reading as follows: ". . . for he lives *(menei)* with you and *is* [instead of "will be"] in you." Barrett, *The Gospel According to St. John,* 386-387, believes this to be the better reading. He observes that the words "he lives with *(para)* you" reflect the presence of the Spirit in the Church, and the words "he is in *(en)* you" speak of His indwelling of the individual believer. Westcott, *Commentary on the Gospel According to St. John,* 206, has a similar interpretation. I find the concept attractive.

10. Barrett, *The Gospel According to John,* 387, states that though the word *orphanous,* translated "orphans," means children left without a father, it was also used by the Greeks (e.g., in the writings of Plato) to describe disciples left without a master. With Socrates' death, his disciples felt like *orphanous.* So Jesus is saying here, "I will not leave you like disciples without a master. By the Spirit I will be your permanent teacher."

11. Commentators are not agreed as to the meaning of Jesus' words, "I will come to you," (literally, "I am coming to you"). Some, such as Barrett, *The Gospel According to John,* 387, and Morris, *The Gospel According to St. John,* 651, take Him to be speaking about His resurrection. Others, like Bruce, *The Gospel of John,* 303, and Godet, *Commentary on the Gospel of St. John,* vol. III, 145, think He is speaking about the event of Pentecost. This, I think, is correct, although Bruce has this insightful comment, "In this Gospel, the distinction between the various phases of Jesus' promised coming is a vanishing distinction. Every phase of his promised coming is embraced in this assurance, 'I am coming to you.' "

12. "Greater" not in essence but in function.

13. The word is *elegzei,* "to expose," "to bring to light," "to show a thing in its true colors," "to convince," "to convict."

14. See how Paul puts this final destiny in Ephesians 1:9-10.

15. A.B. Simpson, "O Comforter, Gentle and Tender," *Hymns of the Christian Life* (Camp Hill, PA: Christian Publications, Inc., 1978), # 142.

# 27

# *Lasting Fruit*

## John 15:1-17

*"I am the true vine, and my Father is the gardener. 2 He cuts off every branch in me that bears no fruit, while every branch that does bear fruit he prunes so that it will be even more fruitful. 3 You are already clean because of the word I have spoken to you. 4 Remain in me, and I will remain in you. No branch can bear fruit by itself; it must remain in the vine. Neither can you bear fruit unless you remain in me.*

*5 "I am the vine; you are the branches. If a man remains in me and I in him, he will bear much fruit; apart from me you can do nothing. 6 If anyone does not remain in me, he is like a branch that is thrown away and withers; such branches are picked up, thrown into the fire and burned. 7 If you remain in me and my words remain in you, ask whatever you wish, and it will be given you. 8 This is to my Father's glory, that you bear much fruit, showing yourselves to be my disciples.*

*9 "As the Father has loved me, so have I loved you. Now remain in my love. 10 If you obey my commands, you will remain in my love, just as I have obeyed my Father's commands and remain in his love. 11 I have told you this so that my joy may be in you and that your joy may be complete. 12 My command is this: Love each other as I have loved you. 13 Greater love has no one than this, that he lay down his life for his friends. 14 You are my friends if you do what I command. 15 I no longer call you servants, because a servant does not know his master's business. Instead, I have called you friends, for everything that I learned from my Father I have made known to you. 16 You did not choose me, but I chose you and appointed*

*you to go and bear fruit—fruit that will last. Then the Father will give you*
*whatever you ask in my name. 17 This is my command: Love each other.*

**M**y wife and I live in Ontario's gorgeous grape-growing region. It is
known as the "Golden Horseshoe" because of its natural beauty, cli-
mate and geographic shape. Traveling down the highway east of our home,
we pass mile upon mile of vineyards. Row after row of skillfully tended
vines, supported by networks of strong cords, bear clusters of luscious
grapes. Often as we pass the vineyards, I cannot help but think of the above
text.

It is possible that Jesus and His disciples, when they left the upper room
(14:31), also passed a vineyard. And the Master-Teacher, ever looking for
illustrations, saw one in the connection between branch and vine. It was a
picture of the union that must exist between the disciples and Him if they
were to bear spiritual fruit. Consider, first . . .

## The Vineyard (15:1, 5)

Without grape vines, a vineyard would be poorly named. So we will start
with the *vine*.[1] The Lord Jesus called Himself "the true vine" (15:1). It is not
unlikely that He would have been contrasting Himself with that other vine,
Israel. Throughout much of the Old Testament, the nation of Israel is described as a "corrupt, wild vine" (Jeremiah 2:21). Even though it had been
planted by Yahweh (Isaiah 5:1-7) of "sound and reliable stock" (Jeremiah
2:21), it "yielded only bad fruit" (Isaiah 5:2). Intended by God to be the con-
veyor of His truth to the nations, Israel had failed to be "the son you have
raised up for yourself"(Psalm 80:15).[2] Thus, not the nation of Israel, but "the
*true* vine"—Jesus, the Son of Man—revealed to the world the *true* salvation
of God.

"The *branches*" were the second element in our Lord's vineyard metaphor. These were the shoots that sprouted from the vine (John 15:5).[3] They
are a picture of those who believe in Jesus Christ. They derive their life and
their fruitfulness from the Lord Jesus, to whom they are organically united
by the Spirit.[4]

The third element in the metaphor is *"the gardener."*[5] It is He who purposed and planned the vineyard. His hand cultivated the soil. He planted the vines and carefully, faithfully promoted their growth and fruitfulness.

God the Father is the Gardener (15:1). It was He who in eternity past purposed for Himself this vineyard (Christ and the Church). He "planted" the true Vine (His Son) in the soil of a world prepared for His coming. He brought into being the "branches" (believers united to Christ). He caused the branches to be fruitful (15:16).

Consider, second, . . .

## *The Culture (15:2, 6)*

Two procedures named by Jesus in our text comprised the culture of the vineyard. First, there was the *pruning* of fruit-bearing branches. I mentioned that my wife and I live in vineyard country. Here the vines are so severely pruned that, to the untaught eye, there appears to be scarcely any foliage left. But this drastic pruning ensures a bountiful harvest of grapes. Jesus used this pruning imagery to portray a spiritual counterpart. If His disciples are to be fruitful for God, whatever would hinder fruit-bearing must be cut away (15:2). This cutting process had already begun in their lives through His spoken word. As His word remained in their hearts and minds, it would be an instrument of daily discipline (15:3).[6]

For us, too, it is the word of Christ "dwelling in us richly" (see Colossians 3:16) that acts to cut away those things that hinder our fruitfulness. That same word warns us against the selfish spirit of this age (1 John 2:15-17). The word of Christ alerts us to the schemes of the devil (Ephesians 6:10ff). It defines for us the works of the flesh, which by the Spirit we must put to death (Galatians 5:19-21). And if it should be that our meditation in the Word is too little, "God," as Godet observes, "will use other and more painful means which will, like a sharp pruning knife, cut to the quick of the natural affections and the carnal will."[7]

A second process in the vineyard culture is the *burning* of unfruitful branches. The Vinedresser—in this case, the Father God—will not tolerate unproductive branches. They are expending vitality that might better go to the fruit-bearing branches. They must be pruned away. When they are pruned—severed from the vine by the Gardener (John 15:2)—they soon wither and are of no use but to be removed from the vineyard[8] and burned (15:6). Commentators tend to follow their theological bias when they interpret this declaration of Jesus.[9] We need to mark it as a warning and regard it, as all of Jesus' teaching, with utmost seriousness. If a person does not remain in Jesus, "he is like a branch that is thrown away and withers; such branches are picked up, thrown into the fire and burned" (15:6).

Having examined the vine and its culture within the vineyard, we need to consider the fruit that the vine produces.

### The Fruit (15:4-5, 7-17)

In the natural world, it is obvious that the productive life of a branch severed from the vine or the tree has ended. Only as it remains a part of the whole can it produce (15:4). So it is in the spiritual world. Only through our vital union with Christ, the Vine, can there be fruit. Two questions beg answers: 1) What does it mean to "remain" in the Vine (15:4)? And 2) What is the fruit which results from remaining in Jesus (15:4)?

We may say that to *remain in Christ* is to maintain that living union with Him that comes when the Holy Spirit indwells God's child through faith (see Galatians 2:20). Andrew Murray writes:

> You know what abiding in Him is. It is to consent with our whole soul to His life being our life, to reckon upon Him to inspire us in all that goes to make up life, and then to give up everything most absolutely for Him to rule and work in us. It is [resting in] the full assurance that He does, each moment, work in us what we are to be, and so Himself enables us to maintain that perfect surrender in which He is free to do all His will.[10]

And what is the *fruit* that Jesus promised to those who remain in Him? He is surely speaking, first, about those lovely *Christian characteristics* that He sets forth in 15:9-13. There he mentions self-sacrificing love (15:9-10, 12), joy (15:11), obedience (15:10). Paul calls these and six additional items "the fruit of the Spirit"—"love, joy, peace, patience, kindness, goodness, faithfulness, gentleness and self-control" (Galatians 5:22-23). Few of these Christlike traits are ours through natural heredity. Neither are they traits that we can acquire through the will. They are, rather, the *effect* of our yielding moment by moment to the Christ who dwells within us. They are *His* qualities manifest in us. "Apart from me you can do nothing," said our Lord (John 15:5). And the positive implication of those words is that we "can do everything through him who gives [us] strength" (Philippians 4:13).

Again, the harvest that results from remaining in Christ is surely the fruit of loving and faithful *service* for Him.[11] This service flows out of a *friendship* with Christ. Through that friendship we have an understanding of His plans and purposes (John 15:14-15). It is service willing to "go" (15:16) into the world and bear witness to God's saving power. It is service that results in lasting conversions (15:16).

Finally, we can say that remaining in Christ produces the fruit of *answered prayer.* A person living in vital union with Christ will be enabled to "ask in [His] name" (15:16). To pray in the Father's will is to receive the Father's answer. What happens when you put together a Christlike disposition, self-sacrificial love, devoted service and answered prayer? God the Father is glorified and the world sees a demonstration of true discipleship (15:8).

## Conclusion

Consider again that statement of Jesus: "Apart from [separated from] me, you can do nothing" (15:5). Nothing! Absolutely nothing! The *fruit of the Spirit* does not result from a heavenly injection that lasts—hopefully—until the next revival meeting! The fruit our text speaks results from constant attachment to the Source of spiritual life—Jesus Himself. The branch draws its life from the vine, producing fruit corresponding to its species. So, by faith, we believers must draw from our life in Christ, in the process bearing fruit corresponding to our new nature.

A.B. Simpson writes:

> We are not supplied in a moment for a lifetime. We have no store of grace for tomorrow. The manna must fall each day afresh; the life must be inhaled breath by breath; we must feed upon the living bread day by day. It is not at our command, but all derived from Him.
>
> We must abide in Him, and He in us, for "apart from [Him, we]

can do nothing" (John 15:5). Our store of grace is not a great res-
ervoir, but just a little water pipe carrying enough for the moment
and ever passing [it] on. And so we must learn to live in constant
communion with Jesus and constant fellowship with the Holy
Spirit.[12]

We must not think of our *service for God* as the fruit of our own wise
planning, talent, strength or ingenuity. Such work will be "wood, hay or
straw" when "the fire will test the quality of each man's work" (1 Corinthians 3:12-13). The work that stands will be that service done through the
Spirit's gifting, by His anointing and in union with Christ.

Nor is the fruit of *answered prayer* the product of our human perspective
as to what God should or should not do. The late R.R. Brown observed that
true prayer is born in heaven and sent by the Spirit into the hearts of God's
people. From there it rises again to heaven, where it is heard and answered.
The Apostle Paul says it this way: "We do not know what we ought to pray
for, but the Spirit himself intercedes for us with groans that words cannot express. And he who searches our hearts knows the mind of the Spirit, because
the Spirit intercedes for the saints in accordance with God's will" (Romans
8:26-27).

Christlikeness, anointed ministry and prayer in the will of God all
find their source in Christ, the true vine. Since the daily increase of this
fruit comes only through maintaining union with Him, how vital that union is! At all cost, this faith-union with Christ must be nurtured. We
maintain the connection in several ways: through daily prayer and meditation on and submission to His Word. We do so through a continual
spirit of praise and thanksgiving. We do so through the immediate confession of any sin that interrupts our fellowship with Him.

We must let no worldly pleasure, no fleshly lust, no self-centered indul-
gence sever our lifeline. At stake is intimate fellowship with Him who is our
life. At stake is fruitfulness that brings glory to God.

"Oh, the heartfelt blessedness arising from a conscious union with the
Son of God!" William Carvosso, who penned those words, was a Cornish
Wesleyan who could neither read nor write until he was past fifty. May the
Spirit of God be pleased to reveal to you and me this vital blessedness!

Frances Ridley Havergal must have been thinking of that vital union with Christ when she composed this prayer:

> Jesus, Master, whose I am,
>> Purchased Thine alone to be
> By Thy blood, O spotless Lamb,
>> Shed so willingly for me,
>>> Let my heart be all Thine own,
>>> Let me live to Thee alone.

> Other lords have long held sway;
>> Now Thy name alone to bear,
> Thy dear voice alone obey,
>> Is my daily, hourly prayer;
>>> Whom have I in heaven but Thee?
>>> Nothing else my joy can be.

> Jesus, Master, I am Thine;
>> Keep me faithful, keep me near;
> Let Thy presence in me shine,
>> All my homeward way to cheer.
>>> Jesus, at Thy feet I fall;
>>> O be Thou my all in all.[13]

### Endnotes

1. The "vine," technically, is the wood stem or trunk from which the fruit-bearing shoots or branches spring.
2. Psalm 80:8 describes Israel as "a vine [God brought] out of Egypt."
3. The word *klema*, according to Gerhard Kittel and Gerhard Friedrich, eds., *Theological Dictionary of the New Testament*, vol. III (Grand Rapids, MI: Eerdmans, 1964), 757, denotes not "branch" in the usual sense of the word, but a "shoot," a "young twig," a "slip" coming out of a vine.
4. The Pauline counterpart to the imagery of the vine and the branches is that of the "head" and the "body" (e.g., Ephesians 4:12-16).
5. The Greek word is *georgos*—literally "a farmer who tills the soil." In the present context a good translation would be "vinedresser."
6. The perfect tense of the words "I have spoken" conveys the thought that Christ's word remained in their hearts and minds long after they first heard it.

7.  F. Godet, *Commentary on the Gospel of St. John*, vol. III (Edinburgh: T. & T. Clarke, 1881), 162.

8.  This seems to be the force of "thrown away" *(exo)*, literally "thrown out."

9.  Commentators have made valiant attempts to interpret 15:2 and 15:6. On 15:2, C.K. Barrett, *The Gospel According to St. John* (London: S.P.C.K., 1955), 395, comments: "The interpretation of the unfruitful branches may be twofold. The original branches in God's vine were the Jews; these, being unfruitful (unbelieving), God removed. . . . This seems to have been the earliest Christian interpretation of the vine-symbolism . . . but the *en emoi* ["in me"] shows that [Jesus'] primary thought was of apostate Christians." Godet, 161, explains 15:6 as follows: "[Christ] is thinking of those professors of the gospel, who, while externally united to Him, nevertheless live in a state of internal separation from Him, through neglect to maintain the spiritual tie which unites them to Him." John Calvin, *Commentary on the Gospel According to John*, vol. II (Edinburgh: The Calvin Translation Society, 1847), 108, thinks Jesus is referring to those who, in the opinion of men, are in the vine, but who actually have no root in it. He explains 15:6 as follows: "Not that it ever happens that any one of the elect is *dried up,* but because there are many hypocrites who, in outward appearance, flourish and are green for a time, but who afterwards, when they ought to yield fruit, show the very opposite of that which the Lord expects and demands from his people." R.H. Lightfoot, *St. John's Gospel* (London: Oxford University Press, 1966), 282, sees in Jesus' words "perhaps an indirect reference to the defection of Judas, as being typical of all faithless discipleship."

10. Andrew Murray, *Like Christ* (Three Hills, Alberta, Canada: Prairie Book Room, n.d.), 17.

11. See Barrett, *The Gospel According to St. John,* 393.

12. A.B. Simpson, *The Holy Spirit: Power from on High*, ed. Keith M. Bailey (Camp Hill, PA: Christian Publications, Inc., 1994), 503.

13. Frances R. Havergal, "Jesus, Master, Whose I Am," *Hymns of the Christian Life* (Camp Hill, PA: Christian Publications, Inc., 1978), # 234.

# 28

# Persecution

## John 15:18-16:4

18 "If the world hates you, keep in mind that it hated me first. 19 If you belonged to the world, it would love you as its own. As it is, you do not belong to the world, but I have chosen you out of the world. That is why the world hates you. 20 Remember the words I spoke to you: 'No servant is greater than his master.' If they persecuted me, they will persecute you also. If they obeyed my teaching, they will obey yours also. 21 They will treat you this way because of my name, for they do not know the One who sent me. 22 If I had not come and spoken to them, they would not be guilty of sin. Now, however, they have no excuse for their sin. 23 He who hates me hates my Father as well. 24 If I had not done among them what no one else did, they would not be guilty of sin. But now they have seen these miracles, and yet they have hated both me and my Father. 25 But this is to fulfill what is written in their Law: 'They hated me without reason.'

26 "When the Counselor comes, whom I will send to you from the Father, the Spirit of truth who goes out from the Father, he will testify about me. 27 And you also must testify, for you have been with me from the beginning.

"All this I have told you so that you will not go astray. 2 They will put you out of the synagogue; in fact, a time is coming when anyone who kills you will think he is offering a service to God. 3 They will do such things because they have not known the Father or me. 4 I have told you this, so that when the time comes you will remember that I warned you. I did not tell you this at first because I was with you.

S *uffering. Persecuted. Underground.* Those words describe the Church of Jesus Christ in many parts of today's world. Thousands who bear Christ's name are unjustly imprisoned, tortured and tormented. Large numbers are being martyred. Calls go out to North American believers to uphold in prayer their oppressed brothers and sisters.

A few concerned Western leaders actively protest the inhumane treatment of Christians in China or the Sudan, but not many. In fact, even in our so-called "civilized West," overt hostility toward the Christian faith is steadily increasing. Our popular media mock the godly and scornfully caricature ministers of the gospel. If the Bible is mentioned at all, it is belittled; the name of Jesus is derided. How long will it be before being a Christian is "politically incorrect" in North America? Will outright persecution become the lot of North American disciples of Christ?

Of course, none of this is new. By the time John wrote his Gospel, Christianity was already illegal. Those who confessed "Jesus is Lord" were regarded by Rome as disloyal insurrectionists.[1] Slanderous rumors circulated that Christians were cannibalistic,[2] immoral,[3] arsonists[4] and family wreckers.[5] And everyone knows how Nero blamed Christians for the fire that burned Rome. Much of the New Testament was written to people being persecuted for their faith in Christ.[6] The Apostle Paul, who himself once hounded God's Church, makes clear that "everyone who wants to live a godly life in Christ Jesus will be persecuted" (2 Timothy 3:12).[7] And here in our text, the Lord Jesus Himself promised His disciples that after He left, they would be the brunt of the world's[8] hatred.

## *The Hostile World's Hatred Is Inevitable (15:18-21)*

There was no doubt in our Lord's mind that the world would hate His disciples.[9] This should not have surprised them when they remembered the world had first hated their Lord.[10] It was a persistent, abiding hatred.[11] The Jewish leaders hated Christ for His sheer goodness, which condemned their selfishness and greed. They hated His penetrating insight into their innermost duplicity. They hated His gracious teaching, which so contradicted their hypocritical legalism. They hated His claim that God was His Father, with whom He had unbroken fellowship.

Inevitably, once Jesus was off the scene, these persecutors transferred their animosity to His representatives. They sensed in them the same other-worldly spirit so unlike their own (15:19). Without even trying, these believers had a spirit very like their Master's. They were unselfish, loving, gracious. They deported themselves well. Their sheer goodness condemned the world. As Bishop Ryle observed, "It is not the weaknesses and inconsistencies of Christians that the world hates, but their grace."[12]

Furthermore, the disciples had good news to proclaim. A loving Father God offered free, unmerited forgiveness to all who would believe in Jesus Christ. As it had been with Jesus' ministry, some would believe and obey this teaching (15:20); many more would reject it.[13] Calvin shrewdly observed, "The Gospel cannot be published without instantly driving the world to rage."[14] Church history amply testifies to the truth of his statement.

This proved itself true on a bright Sunday afternoon I well remember. My father was guest preacher at a small country church. He was declaring the liberating truth of justification through faith in Christ. But the congregation had been taught to trust in their own righteousness. When he mentioned Christ's blood as the atonement for sin, one man in the audience jumped to his feet.

"We do not believe that around here," he shouted at my father. "Sit down!" Sensing that the man spoke for many others, father quietly left the pulpit and the building. Mother and I followed him out. But a few hearers were grateful to know they could be saved through faith apart from their own efforts. They invited my father to a home, where he continued his teaching.

At the core of the Jews' persecution of Jesus was their refusal to acknowledge that the Father God had sent Him—that Jesus was the Son of God. The Jews believed, so they thought, in the God of Abraham, Isaac and Jacob. But in denying the deity of Jesus (His "name"), they betrayed their ignorance of Him *and* His Father (15:21, 23). Today too many profess "faith in God." But by rejecting Jesus, the Son sent by God, they demonstrate that theirs is a god of their own manufacture. He is not the God who is really there. The truth concerning Jesus negates the validity of their pseudo-god. It declares them to be misled. And so they turn against those who proclaim the true God—the Father of Jesus Christ. If they could, they would rid the world of them.

Notice, second, that Jesus declares that . . .

## The Enlightened Sinner's Unbelief Is Inexcusable (15:22-25)

The Jews' hatred toward Jesus and His disciples, though inevitable, was *inexcusable*. Revivalist Charles Finney used to say that God's judgment on unbelievers would be proportionate to the light they had and what they did with it.[15] He maintained—I believe rightly—that God's wrath toward a "gospel-hardened sinner" will be much more severe than upon one who has never heard the good news about Jesus.[16]

Jesus' words demonstrate this truth. Without question, the Jews who rejected Christ's claims and teachings were callous-hearted. Their guilt would have been less had Jesus not revealed God to them (15:22). They had seen His perfect life,[17] heard His claims to Messiahship and witnessed His authenticating miracles. Because His life and ministry were unlike any other, they were without excuse (15:24-25).[18] As with the enemies of David, the enemies of Jesus hated Him "without reason" (see Psalm 35:19; 69:4). Consciously, deliberately, they had rejected the Light God gave them.

There is a third point. Our text teaches that . . .

## The Persecuted Disciples' Testimony Is Imperative (15:26-27)

Following His resurrection, the Lord would commission His disciples to proclaim His gospel to all nations. Although they would experience the world's hatred, no persecution must stop their faithful witness to the risen Christ. Let them be the object of demonic rage. Let them be arrested and flogged. The Holy Spirit, whom Jesus would send on an enabling mission from the Father,[19] would witness to Jesus through them (15:26).[20] The disciples, having been with Jesus from the beginning, would testify to the historical facts of His ministry (15:27). The Holy Spirit would reveal the true meaning of those facts.[21] No power on earth would or could keep them silent!

Not infrequently, times of great persecution have been times of great church growth. "I will build my church," said Jesus, "and the gates of Hades will not overcome it" (Matthew 16:18). Every attempt of ruthless tyrants to stamp out Jesus' Church has failed. Every force created to withstand its advance has been driven back.

There is a related important observation. Times of persecution have sometimes been preceded by seasons of powerful revival and fresh outpourings of the Holy Spirit. It is as if the Lord is preparing His Church for the suffering that lies immediately ahead. So it was, for instance, in Vietnam before the 1975 communist takeover. Missionaries reported remarkable manifestations of the Spirit's presence and power. And throughout those years—and since—the Church has multiplied.

Finally, our text teaches us that . . .

## The Concerned Savior's Warning Is Preventive (16:1-4)

Our Lord wanted His disciples forewarned concerning the tribulation that would mark their identification with Him (John 16:4). Not all opposition would come from the pagans. They would see the gospel they preached rejected by their own people. If anyone should have received their message with eager joy, it should have been the Hebrews.[22] Instead, Jewish authorities would vent their rage by excommunicating Jesus' followers from their synagogues.[23] The very execution of Christians would be regarded as an act of devotion, pleasing to God (16:2).[24]

Our Lord does not want His disciples' faith to be shaken when they see the impenitence of their fellow Jews.[25] Nor would He want them to renounce their faith under persecution—something He evidently considered a real possibility (16:1).[26] Therefore He alerts them to what they may anticipate. In this, He is quite unlike some contemporary preachers. They give their hearers the impression that coming to Christ will mean the end of all their troubles. Our Lord was forever honest in His teaching. In effect, He was offering His disciples the hardest task in the world. And, filled with the Holy Spirit, they responded with unflinching loyalty.

## *Conclusion*

In 1849, as Garibaldi appealed for recruits at the siege of Rome, he announced: "I offer neither pay nor quarters nor provisions. I offer hunger, thirst, forced marches, battles and death. Let him who loves his country in heart, and not with his lips only, follow me."[27] Young men, drawn by such an appeal, joined him by the hundreds. They were willing to suffer for an earthly cause.

Our Lord calls us to suffer for a heavenly cause. In Bible times, when Jesus called for volunteers to follow Him, He said, "If anyone comes to me and does not hate his father and mother, his wife and children, his brothers and sisters—yes, even his own life—he cannot be my disciple. And anyone who does not carry his cross and follow me cannot be my disciple. . . . [A]ny of you who does not give up everything he has cannot be my disciple" (Luke 14:26-27, 33). This is far from the so-called "easy believism" that continues to dominate contemporary North American evangelicalism. Jesus did not make discipleship easy. When Jesus said "take up *your cross,"* disciples of His day visualized death by the most agonizing method known to mankind. They thought of condemned criminals hanging on crosses by the roadside. They understood full well that He was calling them to suffer and to die for Him. They knew He was asking of them the ultimate sacrifice. It was unconditional surrender. He was Lord.

True discipleship will—yes, must—by its very nature entail some degree of persecution. It is necessary, as Peter tells his readers, to expose insincere believers and identify and strengthen those who are true (1 Peter 5:10).

Dietrich Bonhoeffer, the Lutheran pastor imprisoned by the Nazis for his opposition to their regime, wrote:

> Suffering, then, is the badge of true discipleship. The disciple is not above his master. Following Christ means suffering, because we have to suffer. . . . If we refuse to take up our cross and submit to suffering and rejection at the hands of men, we forfeit our fellowship with Christ, and have ceased to follow him. But if we lose our lives in his service and carry our cross, we shall find our lives again in the fellowship of the cross of Christ.[28]

The words of Philip Lloyd sound an appropriate note with which to conclude our study of this text:

> How good it would be for us sometimes, when we are worrying about our feelings and about our "prayer life," if an angel were to appear to us and say, "Don't waste time worrying about these things. What you need to do is to get on with the business of being persecuted"![29]

Not that we should purposely invite persecution. But should not we who desire the deeper life examine ourselves from time to time? Should we not make sure we are free from worldly compromise that avoids what Jesus promised—the world's hatred?

Isaac Watts put it well:

> Am I a soldier of the cross,
>    A follower of the Lamb?
> And shall I fear to own His cause,
>    Or blush to speak His name?
>
> Must I be carried to the skies
>    On flowery beds of ease,
> While others fight to win the prize
>    And sail through bloody seas?
>
> Are there no foes for me to face?
>    Must I not stem the flood?
> Is this vile world a friend to grace
>    To help me on to God?
>
> Since I must fight if I would reign,
>    Increase my courage, Lord;
> I'll bear the toil, endure the pain,
>    Supported by Thy Word.[30]

## Endnotes

1. Christians would not speak the words, "Caesar is Lord."
2. Christians "ate flesh" and "drank blood" at their Communion observances.
3. Christians greeted one another with a kiss and conducted "love feasts."
4. Christians foretold a day when "the elements will be destroyed by fire, and the earth and everything in it will be laid bare" (2 Peter 3:10).
5. There would be inevitable division in homes where one spouse was a Christian and the other a pagan or where children became Christians and their parents did not.
6. See, particularly, First Peter and Revelation, both of which were written to suffering churches.
7. It is interesting to note that when the risen Lord intercepted Saul of Tarsus, Christ said to him, "Why do you persecute *me?*" Jesus was being persecuted in His people.
8. By the "world," John means mankind in opposition to Christ and all He stands for.
9. "If the world hates you" (15:18) is the kind of conditional statement in Greek which demands the thought, "If, as is the case, the world hates you, . . ." or "Since the world hates you. . . ."
10. The words in the original, translated by the NIV as "me first" (literally "me before you"), might also be translated, "me, ranking above you." John Calvin, *Commentary on the Gospel According to John*, vol. II (Edinburgh: The Calvin Tranlation Society, 1847), 123, so understands them. In keeping with this translation, he comments, ". . . Christ, who is far exalted above them, was not exempted from the hatred of the world, and therefore his ministers ought not to refuse the same condition."
11. The perfect tense of the Greek word for "hated" implies the thought of continuing hatred.
12. Quoted by Leon Morris, *The Gospel According to John* (Grand Rapids, MI: Eerdmans, 1971), 679.
13. It was the same with the Old Testament prophets. The nation of Israel as a whole rejected their message, but a "remnant" remained faithful to God.
14. Calvin, *Commentary on the Gospel According to John,* vol. II, 123.
15. Christ's words in Matthew 11:20-24 clearly bear this out.
16. This truth, however, does not contradict Paul's teaching in Romans 1 that there is indeed sufficient light in creation to render the heathen lost, whether or not they have heard the gospel.
17. Morris, *The Gospel According to John,* 681, interprets "what no one else did" (15:24) as including not only His miracles, but His entire life—everything about Him that they saw and heard.
18. F. Godet, *Commentary on the Gospel of St. John,* vol. III (Edinburgh: T. & T. Clarke, 1881), 173, explains: "Their long resistance to God through the whole course of their history would certainly have been forgiven, as well as their individual transgressions, if they had at least surrendered in the presence of this supreme manifestation. But rejection of Jesus characterized their state as one of invincible estrangement, as *hatred of God,* which is by its nature the unpardonable sin."
19. This, according to B.F. Westcott, *Commentary on the Gospel According to St. John* (London: John Murray, Albermarle Street, 1967), 224, and C.K. Barrett, *The Gospel According to St. John* (London: S.P.C.K, 1955), 402, is the meaning of the phrase, "who goes out from the Father."
20. The Spirit bore this witness through Peter and the 120 disciples on the Day of Pentecost. Compare, also, Matthew 10:16-20.

21. See Godet, *Commentary on the Gospel of St. John,* 174.
22. We sense Paul's pain over this in Romans 9-11.
23. It had happened to the man born blind, whom Jesus healed (John 9:22, 34). At the time of John's writing, the synagogue prayer included a curse on the Nazarenes, which was intended to ensure that they would take no part in the service. See F.F. Bruce, *The Gospel of John* (Grand Rapids, MI: Eerdmans, 1983), 317.
24. See, for example, the martyrdom of Stephen (Acts 7:57ff). Consider also Paul's description of his pre-Christian behavior as a Pharisee toward believers (26:9-11). G. Venn Pilcher, quoted by Morris, *The Gospel According to John,* 693, observes, by way of illustrating this thought, that "a sermon was preached at the burning of Archbishop Cranmer, and the horrors of the Inquisition were carried out with a perfectly good conscience."
25. See Westcott, *Commentary on the Gospel According to St. John,* 225 and Godet, *Commentary on the Gospel of St. John,* 176.
26. See Barrett, *The Gospel According to St. John,* 403. Both these concerns are expressed in the word *skandalidzomai,* "go astray" (16:1). Gerhard Kittel and Gerhard Friedrich, eds., *Theological Dictionary of the New Testament,* vol. II (Grand Rapids, MI: Eerdmans, 1964), 345ff, observe that the *skandalon* in the New Testament is any obstacle in coming to faith and any cause of going astray from faith. *Skandalidzo* is the causing of a fall from the faith and *skandalidzomai* (the word in our text) is the actual taking place of the fall. He suggests that in this verse, it means "to be unsettled in faith."
27. Quoted by William Barclay, *The Gospel of John,* vol. II (Philadelphia: The Westminster Press, 1975), 191.
28. Dietrich Bonhoeffer, *The Cost of Discipleship* (London: SCM Press, 1959), 80.
29. Quoted by Morris, *The Gospel According to John,* 679.
30. Isaac Watts, "Am I a Soldier of the Cross?" *Hymns of the Christian Life* (Camp Hill, PA: Christian Publications, Inc., 1978), # 367.

# Fullness of Joy

John 16:16-33

*16 "In a little while you will see me no more, and then after a little while you will see me."*

*17 Some of his disciples said to one another, "What does he mean by saying, 'In a little while you will see me no more, and then after a little while you will see me,' and 'Because I am going to the Father'?" 18 They kept asking, "What does he mean by 'a little while'? We don't understand what he is saying."*

*19 Jesus saw that they wanted to ask him about this, so he said to them, "Are you asking one another what I meant when I said, 'In a little while you will see me no more, and then after a little while you will see me'? 20 I tell you the truth, you will weep and mourn while the world rejoices. You will grieve, but your grief will turn to joy. 21 A woman giving birth to a child has pain because her time has come; but when her baby is born she forgets the anguish because of her joy that a child is born into the world. 22 So with you: Now is your time of grief, but I will see you again and you will rejoice, and no one will take away your joy. 23 In that day you will no longer ask me anything. I tell you the truth, my Father will give you whatever you ask in my name. 24 Until now you have not asked for anything in my name. Ask and you will receive, and your joy will be complete.*

*25 "Though I have been speaking figuratively, a time is coming when I will no longer use this kind of language but will tell you plainly about my Father. 26 In that day you will ask in my name. I am not saying that I will ask the Father on your behalf. 27 No, the Father himself loves you because you have loved me and have believed that I came from God. 28 I came from the Father and entered the world; now I am leaving the world and going back to the Father."*

*29 Then Jesus' disciples said, "Now you are speaking clearly and without figures of speech. 30 Now we can see that you know all things and that you do not even need to have anyone ask you questions. This makes us believe that you came from God."*

*31 "You believe at last!" Jesus answered. 32 "But a time is coming, and has come, when you will be scattered, each to his own home. You will leave me all alone. Yet I am not alone, for my Father is with me.*

*33 "I have told you these things, so that in me you may have peace. In this world you will have trouble. But take heart! I have overcome the world."*

In the previous four chapters we have been meditating on the *promises* of the Son. We have seen that in the last days before His departure by way of the cross, our Lord promised His disciples access to the Father (14:1-14), the gift of the Holy Spirit (14:15-31; 16:5-15), lasting fruit (15:1-17)—and persecution by the world (15:18-16:4). Now in our present text He promises *fullness of joy.*

When revival (a fresh outpouring of the Holy Spirit) touches a church or a nation, one of its hallmarks is *joy.* Whether personal or corporate renewal, there springs from Spirit-filled hearts spontaneous rejoicing. A new hymnody is born. Songs of gladness fill the house. This was true of that first Pentecost (Acts 2:1-13). It has been true of later revivals, such as the great Welsh revival.

"Oh, how they sang!" remember the eyewitnesses. It was true as well in the Canadian revival in the early 1970s. We could say with Pascal, "Joy, joy, joy, tears of joy."

But it must be admitted that before joy came great sorrow of heart. "The first effect, always, of a revival," wrote the late Martin Lloyd-Jones, "is to humble people and to convict them. [It is] to cast them into an agony of soul, to make them wonder whether they have ever been Christians at all."[1] In the Canadian revival, we learned that not until there had been deep repentance did there come rejoicing. "Blessed are those who mourn," reads the Beatitude, "for they will be comforted" (Matthew 5:4). "Weeping may remain for a night" cried the psalmist, "but rejoicing comes in the morning" (Psalm 30:5). Such is the way of the Lord!

## The Disciples' Sadness (16:16-20)

The sorrow that the disciples were feeling—and that they would feel yet more deeply—would accentuate their joy. While their sorrow did not spring from a conviction of sin, *all* sorrow sharpens joy. Their sorrow was due to their *bewilderment* at what Jesus had told them. They could not understand his enigmatic words: "In a little while you will see me no more, and then after a little while you will see me" (16:16). They were reluctant to inquire of the Lord as to what He meant. So they began to deliberate His meaning among themselves (16:17-18). "What is this 'in a little while'?" "What does He mean, 'You will see me no more, and then after a little while you will see me' "? Where is He going? If—as they still hoped—His intention was to found an earthly kingdom, why should He leave? And if this was not His intention, why should He return? That which from our vantage point is perfectly clear was for the disciples a complex puzzle. And yet, even for us who look back, Jesus' words seem to have a double meaning. He could be speaking about His death and resurrection. Or He could be referring to His ascension to the Father and His coming to them again at Pentecost. Or He could be thinking of both.[2] We, at least, have greater perspective than Jesus' disciples had. They were suffering the pain of perplexity.

But a yet *future* sorrow would envelop these men. They would indeed "weep and mourn" as they beheld their beloved Master hanging helplessly upon a Roman cross. They would gaze with grief upon His guarded grave. Somehow they could not bring themselves to believe He would rise again. They would huddle hopelessly as they contemplated an empty future without His guiding presence. And their sorrow would be compounded as they saw, in contrast to their anguish, the sadistic joy of those who had condemned Him to death (16:20). Theirs was the anguish of abandonment. Perplexity now! More sorrow to come! Yet Jesus assured them that all of this would but enhance the joy that followed.

## The Disciples' Joy (16:20-28)

A mother's joy as she holds her newborn baby erases the memory of the pain she has just been through. So the gladness the disciples were soon to experience would erase the memories of these wrenching hours (16:21-22).[3] They would have the joy of seeing, hearing and actually touching their risen Lord! (cf. 1 John 1:1). They would experience the even greater and unending joy of Jesus' presence within them. This would be a joy totally independent of outward circumstances (16:22). Furthermore, the Holy Spirit, their teacher,[4] would reveal to them the meaning of the cross. He would help them understand the saving implications of Christ's resurrection and ascension. They would rejoice that their perplexities were dispelled and all their questions answered (16:23).[5] The pain of ignorance would give place to the joy of *knowledge*.

But there was still more! The disciples would experience the *power of prayer in the name of Jesus* (16:23-24).[6] That is to say, prayer from now on would be on the ground of Jesus' person and work. Because of all Jesus is and has done for their salvation, the disciples may approach the Father directly. In prayer they may ask and the Father will answer. They will not need to enlist Christ's intercession, as though He were more merciful and more ready to hear (16:26). The Father does not need to be persuaded to be gracious. He loves them with a very special love because they love His Son. They believe Jesus' heavenly origin (16:27-28) and destination (16:28). And so He delights to hear and answer their prayers. The pain of ignorance would be replaced by the joy of knowledge. And the grief of helplessness would be replaced by the joy of power with God through prayer.

Finally, our text presents to us . . .

## The Disciples' Inadequacy (16:29-33)

Jesus has now explained His statement that so perplexed the disciples (16:29). That He was able to perceive their unexpressed uncertainties and anticipate their questions strengthened their belief that He came from God (16:30). Yet He warned them that their faith was not yet adequate to stand firm through the trying days just ahead (16:32).[7] In the face of Jesus' imminent arrest, trial and crucifixion, they would take refuge in their own homes.

They would leave Him without earthly, though not without heavenly, support (16:32).

Although Jesus' grave words might trouble the minds of His disciples, He assured them that they need not lose heart. True, they would experience tribulation at the hands of the world. But through Jesus' death and resurrection He would triumph over the world, and so could they (16:33).[8]

## Conclusion

The Apostle Paul writes, "The kingdom of God is . . . a matter of . . . righteousness, peace and *joy* in the Holy Spirit" (Romans 14:17, emphasis added). That is to say, wherever God reigns in a human life, the fruit of His Spirit is joy (Galatians 5:22). It is the joy that Jesus promised His disciples. This is not the kind of human happiness dependent on life's beneficent circumstances. It is a joy that wells up in the spirit despite the circumstances, even amid very trying situations. It was the joy that motivated Paul and Silas to sing praises to God in their prison cell (Acts 16:25). It was the *"joy given by the Holy Spirit"* (1 Thessalonians 1:6, emphasis added) with which the Thessalonians welcomed the gospel message. It was the joy that filled the hearts of the Macedonian believers. "Out of the most severe trial" they demonstrated their *"overflowing joy"* through "rich generosity" (2 Corinthians 8:2, emphasis added). We are looking at joy in the midst of persecution, joy in the midst of poverty. This is joy given by the Holy Spirit, joy that marks spiritual revival.

In Acts 19 there is an interesting account of a visit the Apostle Paul made to Ephesus. There he met a dozen or so people whom the record calls "disciples" (Acts 19:1). Samuel Chadwick, the noted Methodist preacher, suggests in one of his sermons that Paul sensed immediately a lack in their lives. These good, moral, upright people, sternly religious, were bona fide believers in Jesus.[9] But Chadwick sees them with sad countenances, burdened down with the weight of having to be righteous! It was this, thinks Chadwick, that caused Paul to ask them, "Did you receive the Holy Spirit when you believed?" (19:2). Paul sensed in their lives the absence of the Holy Spirit.

Startled by his question, this small band of disciples admitted they had "not even heard that there is a Holy Spirit" (Acts 19:2). With their baptism in the Spirit, their whole demeanor changed. The sadness left their hearts. The minor key left their worship. Their self-imposed righteousness was turned into life in the Spirit. They began to offer uninhibited praise to God. As Christ's joy entered their lives, rejoicing came forth from their mouths. Joy is a distinguishing mark of the Spirit's infilling.[10]

Our world will not pay much attention to a sad, stern, somber Christianity. But it will notice when people are filled with a genuine spirit of joy. It was this amazing joy of the early Christians that conquered the ancient world. They went to prison rejoicing. They sang as the lions roared toward them. They rejoiced that they could "participate in the sufferings of Christ" (1 Peter 4:13). As A.B. Simpson put it:

> The joy of the Lord is the strength of His people,
>     The sunshine that banishes sadness and gloom;
> The fountain that bursts in the desert of sorrow,
>     And sheds o'er the wilderness gladness and bloom.
>
> The joy of the Lord is our strength for life's burdens,
>     And gives to each duty a heavenly zest;
> It sets to sweet music the task of the toiler,
>     And softens the couch of the laborer's rest.
>
> The joy of the Lord is our strength for life's trials,
>     And lifts the crushed heart above sorrow and care;
> Like the nightingale's notes, it can sing in
>         the darkness,
>     And rejoice when the fig tree is fruitless and bare.
>
> The joy of the Lord is the hope of our calling,
>     And, oh, for His coming how fondly we pray!
> When we shall return with rejoicing to Zion,
>     And sorrow and sighing shall vanish away.[11]

Peter described his persecuted readers as those "filled with an inexpressible and glorious joy" (1 Peter 1:8). Joy is a mark of the deeper life. Does it mark your.life? Does it mark mine?

### *Endnotes*

1. D. Martyn Lloyd-Jones, *Joy Unspeakable* (Wheaton, IL: Harold Shaw Publishers, 1984), 101.
2. F. Godet, *Commentary on the Gospel of St. John,* vol. III (Edinburgh: T. & T. Clarke, 1881), 186, believes the former. Leon Morris, *The Gospel According to John* (Grand Rapids, MI: Eerdmans, 1971), 704, the latter. C.K. Barrett, *The Gospel According to St. John* (London: S.P.C.K., 1955), 410, thinks that *opsestha me* ("you will see me") may rightly be interpreted as referring to His resurrection, His second coming and the in-between coming of the Spirit at Pentecost. John's readers are at liberty to see all three meanings in Jesus' words.
3. The metaphor of the pain of childbirth is not uncommon in the Old Testament. See, for example, Isaiah 26:17f; 66:7 and Hosea 13:13.
4. See John 14:26 and 16:13.
5. The verb *erotesete* means "to ask a question."
6. Here the word for "ask" is *aitesete.* As Morris, *The Gospel According to John,* 707, explains, it means to ask for something in prayer.
7. According to B.F. Westcott, *Commentary on the Gospel According to St. John* (London: John Murray, Albemarle Street, 1967), 236, the expression "You believe at last!" (literally, "Do you now believe?") is half question and half exclamation. It brings the force and permanence of their faith into doubt. The question does not deny the existence of some measure of faith, but its inadequacy is shown in the next verse.
8. Cf. 1 John 5:4f.
9. F.F. Bruce, in *Commentary on the Book of the Acts* (Grand Rapids, MI: Eerdmans, 1954), 385, says this about these men of Ephesus: "[T]hat these men were Christians is certainly to be inferred from the way in which Luke describes them as 'disciples'; this is a term which he commonly uses for Christians, and had he meant to indicate that they were disciples not of Christ but of John the Baptist (as has sometimes been deduced from v.3), he would have said so explicitly."
10. Cf. Ephesians 5:18ff., where the filling of the Spirit is accompanied by outward and inward singing and praise to God.
11. A.B. Simpson, "The Joy of the Lord," *Hymns of the Christian Life* (Camp Hill, PA: Christian Publications, Inc., 1978), # 280.

## Part X

## *Questions for Reflection or Discussion*

1. Evaluate this statement: "If you want to know what God is like, study the words and actions of Jesus."
2. Compare the ministry of the Holy Spirit in the Old Testament with His ministry in the Gospels and His ministry in the Book of Acts.
3. What does it mean to be "filled with the Spirit"?
4. How is obedience connected to the filling of the Holy Spirit?
5. Is there a difference between joy and happiness? If so, what is it?

# The Passion of the Son

John 17:1-19:42

# 30

# The Prayer of Consecration

John 17:1-26

*After Jesus said this, he looked toward heaven and prayed:*

*"Father, the time has come. Glorify your Son, that your Son may glorify you. 2 For you granted him authority over all people that he might give eternal life to all those you have given him. 3 Now this is eternal life: that they may know you, the only true God, and Jesus Christ, whom you have sent. 4 I have brought you glory on earth by completing the work you gave me to do. 5 And now, Father, glorify me in your presence with the glory I had with you before the world began.*

*6 "I have revealed you to those whom you gave me out of the world. They were yours; you gave them to me and they have obeyed your word. 7 Now they know that everything you have given me comes from you. 8 For I gave them the words you gave me and they accepted them. They knew with certainty that I came from you, and they believed that you sent me. 9 I pray for them. I am not praying for the world, but for those you have given me, for they are yours. 10 All I have is yours, and all you have is mine. And glory has come to me through them. 11 I will remain in the world no longer, but they are still in the world, and I am coming to you. Holy Father, protect them by the power of your name—the name you gave me—so that they may be one as we are one. 12 While I was with them, I protected them and kept them safe by that name you gave me. None has been lost except the one doomed to destruction so that the Scripture would be fulfilled.*

*13 "I am coming to you now, but I say these things while I am still in the world, so that they may have the full measure of my joy within them. 14 I have given them your word and the world has hated them, for they are not of the world any more than I am of the world. 15 My prayer is not that you take them out of the world but that you protect them from the evil one. 16 They are not of the world, even as I am not of it. 17 Sanctify them by the truth; your word is truth. 18 As you sent me into the world, I have sent them into the world. 19 For them I sanctify myself, that they too may be truly sanctified.*

*20 "My prayer is not for them alone. I pray also for those who will believe in me through their message, 21 that all of them may be one, Father, just as you are in me and I am in you. May they also be in us so that the world may believe that you have sent me. 22 I have given them the glory that you gave me, that they may be one as we are one: 23 I in them and you in me. May they be brought to complete unity to let the world know that you sent me and have loved them even as you have loved me.*

*24 "Father, I want those you have given me to be with me where I am, and to see my glory, the glory you have given me because you loved me before the creation of the world.*

*25 "Righteous Father, though the world does not know you, I know you, and they know that you have sent me. 26 I have made you known to them, and will continue to make you known in order that the love you have for me may be in them and that I myself may be in them."*

With this text we listen—with great reverence—as our Lord, having addressed His disciples (17:1),[1] now addresses His Father. It has long been known as Jesus' high priestly prayer. In it He consecrates Himself to the sacrifice of the cross. It can also appropriately be called the Lord's Prayer. Jesus Himself prayed it, as distinguished from the prayer He taught His disciples to pray (see Matthew 6:9-13 and Luke 11:2-4).

What an awe-inspiring prayer it is! Milligan and Moulton remark, "No attempt to describe the prayer can give a just idea of its solemnity, its pathos, its touching yet exalted character, its tone of tenderness and triumphant expectation."[2] It seems to encompass all the truth relative to the work of Christ set forth in John's Gospel. There is Jesus' obedience to the Father as He faces a death that will make visible God's glory. There is the choosing of the disciples out of the world. There is the ultimate unity of disciples and Lord, bonded as they are in divine love. There is the eternal continuity of that relationship in God's very presence.[3]

Offered audibly and perhaps, as Westcott suggests, in the temple courts,[4] it divides itself rather easily into three parts. Notice first that . . .

## Jesus Prays for Himself (17:1-5)

Our Lord's gaze was heavenward (17:1), the accepted posture for confident prayer.[5] He addressed His heavenly Father as intimately as any earthly child would address an earthly father.[6] He began by affirming that now at last the hour of His death had arrived. He asked His Father to honor His act of obedient suffering by raising Him from the dead and exalting Him to glory. But only so that He, the Son, through His obedience might bring glory to the Father (17:1).[7]

Jesus reminded His Father that He had been invested with authority over humanity, and this for the express purpose of giving[8] eternal life to all[9] whom the Father had chosen (17:2).[10] Now He was about to exercise that authority. He would do so by completing the sacrificial work that would make possible this new quality of life (17:4). He deemed it appropriate to ask His Father to restore the preincarnate glory He had selflessly relinquished (17:5).

Before we proceed to Jesus' petitions for His disciples, it is important that we look at Jesus' definition of eternal life (17:3). It seems at first almost parenthetical. Was Jesus seeking to instruct the disciples and all who might hear or read His prayer? Whatever His reason, He makes it clear that the essence of eternal life is *knowing God* and Jesus Christ.[11] This "knowing" has in it an element of intellectual knowledge. We are to know and believe the truth *about* God's person and acts (8:32). But primarily it involves our growing, personal experience with God.[12] It entails an immediate awareness of Him—an awareness that affects our ethical behavior and issues in worship.[13] It is a knowledge only possible through Jesus Christ, the Mediator (1 Timothy 2:5), who has reconciled us to the Father (2 Corinthians 5:18) and given us the Spirit of sonship that cries out, "Father" (Romans 8:15).

## Jesus Prays for His Disciples (17:6-19)

We are struck by the tender affection Jesus evidenced for these disciples whom He had chosen. He saw them not only as they were right then but as they would be in answer to His prayer. We are accorded a sevenfold portrait of the disciples and a threefold request on their behalf.

First, Jesus described them as those to whom He had revealed the *charac-ter of God* (literally, His "name," 17:6). To the Hebrew mind, people's names were indicative of their personality,[14] the circumstances of their birth[15] or their destiny.[16] The "name" of God, therefore, spoke of His nature and His character, both revealed in the person of Jesus Christ. Remember what Jesus said? "Anyone who has seen me has seen the Father" (14:9). The disciples were *knowledgeable*.

Second, Jesus saw His disciples as those upon whom God had set His love. Having been in the heart of the Father from before the foundation of the world, they were God's own *special possession*. And He had given them to Jesus (17:6, 9). No one could snatch them from the hand of the Father (10:29). Of them the Lord said, "You did not choose me, but I chose you . . . to go and bear fruit—fruit that will last" (15:16). They were *chosen*.

Third, Jesus reminded the Father that the disciples had accepted His words as God's words; they were to be taken seriously (17:6-8). It could be said of them, "My sheep listen to my voice; I know them, and *they follow me*" (10:27, emphasis added). They were *obedient*.

Fourth, because like Himself the disciples were "not of the world" (17:14), the godless world hated them. They were of an entirely different spirit from the craving, lustful, boasting spirit of this world (see 1 John 2:15-17). The spirit of this world, the Apostle John warned his readers, is destined to "pass away." Jesus' disciples were *other-worldly*.

Fifth, Jesus described them as men who would bring glory to Him (John 17:10). Based on their performance to that point, this was surely a faith statement! But Jesus looked beyond the actual to the potential. Although un-distinguished in the eyes of the world and weak in themselves, they would yet prove the world wrong. They would bring glory to their Savior through the power of the Holy Spirit. They were *Christ-glorifying*.

Sixth, Jesus had kept them from evil and apostasy by the divine authority resident in Him (17:12).[17] Only one of their number, Judas Iscariot—"the one doomed to destruction" (17:12)—had lost out.[18] And this was so the Scriptures would be fulfilled.[19] All the others would remain faithful because they were *secured*.

Seventh, Jesus in His prayer portrayed the disciples as people with a mission (17:18). *He* had been sent into the world by the Father. Likewise Jesus would send His disciples into the world to bear witness to Him and to the gospel. They were *commissioned.*

These were the disciples for whom Jesus was praying: disciples who had seen the Father in His Son. They were chosen, obedient, other-worldly, Christ-exalting. They were secured disciples, commissioned to bear witness to Christ and the gospel. In due time the Father would answer His Son's prayer. In spite of their apparent weaknesses, these disciples would become, through the Holy Spirit, the people Jesus envisioned.

Not only did Jesus thus characterize His disciples, but He made three requests to the Father on their behalf. First, He prayed for their continued *protection.* Until now, He had been their Protector. But He was about to return to His Father, leaving them without visible support (17:11). Hence, they would need God's protection from two dangers: 1) the ever-present danger of *disunity,* and 2) the lurking danger of the *evil one.* So He prayed that the disciples might be one, the way He and the Father were one (17:11). Leon Morris describes it as a unity in which "all wills [bow] in the same direction, all affections [burn] with the same flame, all aims are directed to the same goal—one blessed harmony of love."[20]

Furthermore, they would need protection from *"the evil one"* (17:15).[21] Jesus did not pray that the disciples would be taken out of the world. That would be contrary to their mission. But they would be remaining in territory dominated by the "god of this world" (see 2 Corinthians 4:4, KJV). Therefore it was essential that they not fall prey to Satan's schemes. He would tempt them to renounce their faith when persecuted, abdicate their mission when discouraged, compromise their message when opposed. But temptation was not sin; the Father who protected them would make a way of escape.

Second, our Lord prayed that they might have "the full measure of [His] *joy* within them" (John 17:13, emphasis added). He had promised them lasting joy (16:20, 22) which no circumstance could quench nor suffering suppress. He asked that the Holy Spirit fill their hearts with the same heavenly joy that He knew.

Third, Jesus prayed that His disciples might be *sanctified* as they permitted the *truth* to take effect in their lives (17:17). But just as the Old Testament priests first consecrated themselves,[22] He too, the Great High Priest, must set Himself apart (17:19).[23] In this way, His disciples could experience the inward holiness and power that would be theirs through the Holy Spirit. The Holy Spirit would apply the truth of the *Word of God* to their lives (17:17). Like their Master, they too "must deny [themselves] and take up [their] cross daily and follow [him]" (Luke 9:23).

We come at last to the final section of Jesus' high priestly prayer. In it . . .

## *Jesus Prays for All Believers (17:20-24)*

What our Lord prayed for His immediate disciples He now prayed for believers in distant lands and future times (17:20). With the eyes of faith, He saw His followers, endued with power, making disciples of all nations. He saw His Church comprised of every ethnic group on earth. For His Church He has two petitions.

He prayed, first, that the Church would be truly *unified* (17:21-23). This was not union brought about by organizational unanimity and administrative skill. It was, rather, a living, organic union, analogous to the union between the Father and the Son (17:21). M.J. Lagrange describes it in these words:

> The Son is in the faithful, He is in the Father: it is thus by Him
> that the faithful are united with the Father: not that they pass from
> the one to the other, but because they find the Father in the Son.[24]

Furthermore, the unity for which Christ prayed was one that came from the "glory" the Father gave Him. That glory He would give to the Church (17:22). Christ's glory was the cross; believers would be united in their mutual participation in His sufferings. Christ's perfect obedience to His Father's will was His glory; believers were to be united as they did God's will.

Again, it was a union accomplished by the indwelling of the Holy Spirit. *He* would unite believers to the Father and the Son, and thereby unite them to one another. It was to be a union characterized by divine love, the love the Father and the Son had for each other. It was to be a supernatural,

Spirit-enabled love (17:23, 26). And it demanded a supernatural explanation: God sent His son, Jesus, into the world (17:23).

Truth is, Christ's prayer for the Church's unity is even now being answered. Yes, denominational differences exist. Yes, the people of God do not see eye to eye on every point of polity and practice. Yet there exists in this world a living, vital, body of believers who are "one in the bond of love."

Second, Christ prayed that the Church would "see [His] glory" (17:24). God glorified Jesus as a reward for His sufferings. So we, if we suffer with Him here, will share in His glory. Paul says "our present sufferings are not worth comparing with the glory that will be revealed in us" (Romans 8:18). Christ's prayer for believers will be answered!

## Conclusion

We cannot read John 17 without being conscious that, like Moses before the burning bush, we are on holy ground. We take great comfort in knowing that other believers are praying for us. But how very encouraging to be reminded that Jesus Himself is ever interceding for us (Hebrews 7:25)!

Surely this prayer brought great comfort and strength to the original disciples. But it has brought direction, hope and assurance to believers down through the centuries as well. John Knox, the great Scottish preacher, on his deathbed in 1572, asked his wife to read John 17 to him. It was *there,* he commented, "where I cast my first anchor!"

What strength and encouragement our Lord's prayer brings to believers yet today! Here, knowing God, we are assured of eternal life. Here, trusting God, we are assured of His powerful protection from Satan's power. Here, chosen by God, we are secure in His love. Here, obeying God, we bring glory to His name. Here, indwelt by God, we are sanctified through His Word. Here, joined to the Father and the Son, we are united in loving fellowship with one another. Here, hoping in God, we anticipate ultimate glory. Here, we too learn how to pray for our fellow believers.

From this prayer, Jesus would go out to be betrayed, tried and crucified. How wonderful to remember that before those terrible hours just ahead, His words were not of despair but of glory!

### Endnotes

1. The Greek text reads, "These things spoke Jesus, and lifting up his eyes to heaven said . . ." The phrase "these things" doubtless refers to the entire content of chapters 14-16. His prayer (chapter 17) seems to follow immediately.
2. W. Milligan and W.F. Moulton, quoted in Leon Morris, *The Gospel According to John* (Grand Rapids, MI: Eerdmans, 1971), 716.
3. C.K. Barrett, *The Gospel According to St. John* (London: S.P.C.K., 1955), 417.
4. B.F. Westcott, *Commentary on the Gospel According to St. John* (London: John Murray, Albermarle Street, 1967), 237. He suggests that chapters 15 and 16, as well as chapter 17, were spoken in a temple court. "[I]t is inconceivable," he writes, "that chapter 17 should have been spoken anywhere except under circumstances suited to its unapproachable solemnity."
5. Cf. John 11:41. We remember that the tax collector in Jesus' parable, conscious of his own sinfulness, "would not even look up to heaven" (Luke 18:13).
6. The Greek *Pater* presupposes an Aramaic *Abba,* which some would translate by the modern term of endearment, "Daddy." Cf. Romans 8:15.
7. We are reminded of Paul's declaration in Philippians 2:5-11. Because of Christ's obedience to death on a cross, "God exalted him to the highest place and gave him the name that is above every name [i.e., God glorified Jesus], that at the name of Jesus every knee should bow . . . and every tongue confess that Jesus Christ is Lord, *to the glory of God the Father"* (italics added).
8. Morris, *The Gospel According to John,* 718-719, draws attention to the ten instances in this chapter where the thought of "giving" is used. He comments, "What *grace* is in the Pauline Epistles, *giving* is in the Fourth Gospel."
9. The word "all" in 17:2 is the Greek *pan* (neuter singular), emphasizing the assumed unity, the wholeness, of the one body of believers.
10. Jesus will come back to this thought of the Father's choice in 17:6 and 17:9.
11. The importance of *knowing* God is rooted in the Old Testament. See such passages as Proverbs 11:9; Jeremiah 9:23-24; Hosea 4:6; 6:2-3; Amos 5:4; Habakkuk 2:14.
12. Paul prays that the Ephesians will *know* God better through the revelation given by the Spirit (Ephesians 1:17).
13. True worship is only possible when a person has an immediate sense of the presence of God or the memory of having had such a sense.
14. As, for example, Jacob, who grasped his twin brother's heel and was named "heel holder" or "supplanter."
15. As, for example, Moses, whose name refers to his being taken out of the water.
16. As, for example, Jesus (Hebrew Yeshua, "Jehovah is salvation"), who would "save his people from their sins" (Matthew 1:21).
17. Bear in mind that the "name" reveals the character of the person (see note 16 above). This evidently is the meaning of the words, "by that name you gave me." God's revealed character has been committed to Jesus. He Himself has kept the disciples and in doing so has acted in the character and with the authority of God.
18. Morris, *The Gospel According to John,* 728-729, believes the description "the one doomed to destruction" ("the son of perdition" KJV) refers to Judas' character rather than to his destiny. It is likely that both are in view.
19. "That the Scripture would be fulfilled" may possibly be a reference to Psalm 41:9 or 109:4-13.

F.F. Bruce, *The Gospel of John* (Grand Rapids, MI: Eerdmans, 1983), 332, is right in observing: "Despite the predestinarian flavor of the language, Judas was not lost against his will, but with his consent. He might have responded to Jesus' last appeal to him in his gesture of fellowship at the supper table, but he chose to respond instead to the great adversary."

20. Morris, *The Gospel According to John,* 727.
21. The word translated "evil one" (*ponerous*) can be translated simply "evil." However, *ponerous* clearly means "evil one" in First John 2:13; 3:12; 5:18-19.
22. See Exodus 28:41 and 29:1, for example.
23. "To set apart" is the meaning of the word "sanctify." The context makes it clear that Jesus is consecrating Himself to a sacrificial death. He is both Sacrifice and Priest.
24. Quoted by Morris, *The Gospel According to John,* 735.

# 31

# The Arrest in the Garden

John 18:1-12

*When he had finished praying, Jesus left with his disciples and crossed the Kidron Valley. On the other side there was an olive grove, and he and his disciples went into it.*

*2 Now Judas, who betrayed him, knew the place, because Jesus had often met there with his disciples. 3 So Judas came to the grove, guiding a detachment of soldiers and some officials from the chief priests and Pharisees. They were carrying torches, lanterns and weapons.*

*4 Jesus, knowing all that was going to happen to him, went out and asked them, "Who is it you want?"*

*5 "Jesus of Nazareth," they replied.*

*"I am he," Jesus said. (And Judas the traitor was standing there with them.)*

*6 When Jesus said, "I am he," they drew back and fell to the ground.*

*7 Again he asked them, "Who is it you want?"*

*And they said, "Jesus of Nazareth."*

*8 "I told you that I am he," Jesus answered. "If you are looking for me, then let these men go." 9 This happened so that the words he had spoken would be fulfilled: "I have not lost one of those you gave me."*

*10 Then Simon Peter, who had a sword, drew it and struck the high priest's servant, cutting off his right ear. (The servant's name was Malchus.)*

*11 Jesus commanded Peter, "Put your sword away! Shall I not drink the cup the Father has given me?"*

*12 Then the detachment of soldiers with its commander and the Jewish
officials arrested Jesus.*

His hour had finally come! For three years Jesus had faithfully performed Spirit-empowered signs authenticating His divine Person. For
three years He had declared the gracious words that revealed His Father's
will to mankind. For three years He had faithfully taught the twelve disciples who would carry on His work. He had offered up to the Father His High
Priestly Prayer, consecrating Himself again to the sacrifice just ahead. He
had prayed for His disciples and for the Church yet to be. Now there was
nothing left to accomplish but the sacrifice He had been sent to offer.

And so, leaving Jerusalem,[1] Jesus and His disciples crossed the Kidron
Valley that ran along the east side of the city.[2] They entered a privately
owned,[3] enclosed olive grove—Gethsemane—to which they had often gone
for seclusion and rest (18:1).

## The Betrayal (18:2-3)

Judas had already concluded the agreement by which he would lead the
Jewish authorities to Jesus. Thirty pieces of silver was the settled-upon price
(Matthew 26:15). He surmised that Jesus and the other disciples would
spend the night in the olive grove. So he led the arresting authorities to the
place where he had so often spent time with his Master. What an eerie sight
the moonlit night must have afforded (John 18:3)! Two hundred armed Roman soldiers[4] with their commanding officer. Temple police, sent by the
chief priests and Pharisees—the real instigators of the arrest. Weapons,
torches, lanterns. All to apprehend one lone "conspirator" who, they were
sure, would resist arrest. Hatred and jealousy, hoarded for three years,
goaded the pursuers of Jesus.

In his classic volume, *The Suffering Savior,* F.W. Krummacher describes
the motivations for the hostility of priests who instigated this atrocious arrest in the olive grove:

> [Jesus] is undermining their proud hierarchy, stripping them of
> their false glory, snatching from their hands the scepter of despo-
> tism over the consciences of the poor people, diminishing their

tithes and resources, and intimating to them that they ought to place themselves in the ranks of publicans and sinners.[5]

And of the Pharisees, also represented in the garden, Krummacher writes:

Near the priests we behold the Pharisees, those blind leaders of the blind, the representatives of the delusive idea of individual merit, and hence, also of repugnance to a doctrine which affords a hope of salvation only by grace, and even to the most pious leaves nothing but the freely bestowed righteousness of Another. It is easy to understand how these men were offended at a Teacher who set up regeneration as a vital condition for all.[6]

The military and the temple guard were prepared for whatever force would be necessary to take Jesus into custody. Instead of force, our text describes . . .

## The Surrender (18:4-9)

The soldiers and officials arrived at the grove prepared to search behind every tree and in every hillside cranny. Instead, the Man they sought came voluntarily! Demonstrating complete mastery of the situation, Jesus asked, "Who is it you want?" (18:4).

"Jesus of Nazareth,"[7] they replied.

Jesus responded with those powerful words that reflected the name of Israel's God: "I AM" (18:5).[8] Did Judas, standing there on the side of Jesus' persecutors (18:5), flinch when he heard those words? Did they smite His conscience?[9] The effect on them all was utterly astounding. John reports that "they drew back and fell to the ground" (18:6).

What energy is being manifested here? Is this, as Westcott would have us believe, an exaggeration "utterly alien from [sic] the solemn majesty of the scene"?[10] Or was it the unperturbed majesty of Jesus' presence that filled them with awe? Did His fearless pronouncement of the name of God produce in them a moment of terror? Did God Himself overthrow them in order to expose their complete impotence before His divine superiority? Did God want them to know that it was not through compulsion or weakness that His

Son would go to the cross? No physical force at that moment could have prevented Jesus from departing triumphantly from the garden.

Instead, with His disciples now gathered around Him, He let the troops regroup. Then He repeated His question.

"Who is it you want?" As though unaffected by their earlier disarray, they again answered, "Jesus of Nazareth" (18:7). Once more, with the same unnerving poise, He identifies Himself. Then, like the Good Shepherd caring for His sheep, He submits that since He is the one they have come to arrest, there is no point in detaining "these men."[11] The disciples were in fact allowed to withdraw. John saw their freedom as a fulfillment of Jesus' words, "I have not lost one of those you gave me" (18:9).[12] It is clear that Jesus, when He originally spoke those words, was referring to eternal salvation. John therefore must have felt that had the disciples been arrested, they would have renounced their faith with eternal consequences. Whatever the case, we cannot help but sense the compassionate heart of the Shepherd. He was prepared to lay down His life for His "sheep." The entire narrative here graphically displays Jesus' courage, authority, protective love and self-surrender.

## The Defense (18:10-12)

Jesus may have been ready to surrender to the authorities without resistance. But the disciple who had sworn to lay down his life for his Master (13:37) was not prepared to let that happen. He who, later this very same night, would cringe at the allegation of a maiden now sprung into action. Drawing a dagger from his belt, he severed the right ear of Malchus, the high priest's servant (18:10).[13] Peter was ready to take on the entire Roman army! What he failed to realize was that such brave behavior could thwart the very purpose of that hour. Jesus was poised to procure the world's salvation.

Jesus would not allow the well-meaning actions of Peter to hinder the plan of salvation. The Son must not shrink from the cup that the Father has given Him (18:11).[14] In a poignant passage, Krummacher describes the content of that cup. It was a cup whose contents would have been measured out to us by divine justice on account of our sin:

In the cup was the entire curse of the inviolable law, all the horrors of conscious guilt, all the terrors of Satan's fiercest temptations, and all the sufferings which can befall both body and soul.
It contained likewise the dreadful ingredients of abandonment by
God, infernal agony, and bloody death, to which the curse was attached—all to be endured while surrounded by the powers of
darkness.[15]

And so the Lord of glory surrendered His divine rights. He willingly allowed Himself to be placed under arrest, bound and led away.[16]

## *Conclusion*

What lessons of eternal value may we discover from our text? Let us
learn, first, from Christ's *unselfish conduct* in the olive grove. In a beautiful
Christological hymn, the Apostle Paul describes the self-emptying of our
blessed Lord:

Who, being in very nature God,
   did not consider equality with God something to be grasped,
but made himself nothing,
   taking the very nature of a servant,
   being made in human likeness.
And being found in appearance as a man,
   he humbled himself
   and became obedient to death—
      even death on a cross! (Philippians 2:6-8)

We see the first evidence of the Savior's willing abasement in His refusal
to summon angels to rescue Him. He assured Peter of their availability.[17] Although He would be unfairly accused and cruelly treated, because this was
His Father's will, He bowed to it. He permitted political and religious representatives to treat Him meanly.

This, says Paul, is to be the believer's attitude (2:5). "Bless those who persecute you," he writes in his Romans letter (12:14). "Do not take revenge,
my friends, but leave room for God's wrath, for it is written: 'It is mine to
avenge; I will repay,' says the Lord" (12:19).

Instead of lashing out in vengeance, we are to "love [our] enemies and pray for those who persecute [us], that [we] may be sons of [our] Father in heaven" (Matthew 5:44-45). (Saying "sons of [our] Father" is the Hebrew way of saying "like our Father.") Though it may be difficult to surrender our rights, this is often God's way of advancing our holiness.

Second, we may learn from Peter's impetuous interference with the will of God. Our natural impulses, though with altruistic motive, can stand in the way of God's purposes. The parent who protects his or her child from the sanctions of the law may be opening the door to a worse crime. The sympathizer who seeks to rescue a friend from unfair treatment may be thwarting God's teaching purposes through the experience. John Calvin wisely observed:

> In the person of Peter, Christ condemns everything that men dare to attempt out of their own fancy. This doctrine is eminently worthy of attention; for nothing is more common than to defend, under the cloak of zeal, everything that we do, as if it were of no importance whether God approved, or not, what men suppose to be right, whose prudence is nothing else than mere vanity.[18]

God has said, "My thoughts are not your thoughts, neither are your ways my ways. . . . As the heavens are higher than the earth, so are my ways higher than your ways and my thoughts than your thoughts" (Isaiah 55:8-9). Let us, like our Lord, willingly surrender to the Father's will, whatever the cost. Let us, unlike Peter, refuse to interfere with the Father's will, even though its outworking seems wrong to us.

### Endnotes

1. The Greek says simply, "Jesus went out *(exelthen)* with His disciples." It is not precisely clear from where He went out. John 14:31 would seem to indicate that the group had already left the room where they had dined and were somewhere in Jerusalem. If that is so, 18:1 indicates that now Jesus left the city.
2. The Brook Kidron ("dark," "gloomy") ran through the valley. It was dry most of the year. Other Bible references to the Kidron Valley are Second Samuel 15:23; First Kings 2:37; 15:13; Nehemiah 2:15.
3. B.F. Westcott, *Commentary on the Gospel According to St. John* (London: John Murray, Albermarle Street, 1967), 251, suggests that perhaps the owner of the olive grove was an open or secret disciple of Jesus.

4. The word "detachment" is *speira,* literally a cohort, normally 600 men, or a maniple of 200 men. The Jewish authorities would not have arrested Jesus without first having communicated with Pilate, the Roman governor. Since it was the Passover time, when trouble might be expected, Pilate would not have hesitated to order a detachment of soldiers to accompany the temple representatives.

5. F.W. Krummacher, *The Suffering Saviour* (Chicago: Moody Press, 1948), 116.

6. Ibid.

7. Literally, "Jesus, the Nazarene." For other instances of this title, see Acts 2:22; 3:6; 4:10 and 6:14.

8. Literally, "I am" (*ego eimi*).

9. There is an ancient but likely untrue tradition that Judas was blinded or paralyzed and unable to move when Jesus uttered these words.

10. Westcott, *Commentary of the Gospel According to St. John,* 253. Leon Morris, *The Gospel According to John* (Grand Rapids, MI: Eermdans, 1971), 743, observes the possibility that those in front recoiled from Jesus' unexpected advance so that they bumped into those behind them, causing them to stumble and fall.

11. By not using the word "disciples," Jesus may be attempting to disassociate them from Himself to further procure their safety.

12. See John 6:39. The same thought is expressed in 17:12.

13. John does not record the fact that Jesus miraculously reattached the ear (see Luke 22:51). He is, however, the only writer to name the servant.

14. Although John does not specifically mention Jesus' agonizing prayer in Gethsemane, 18:11 clearly indicates his familiarity with it.

15. Krummacher, *The Suffering Savior,* 134.

16. At this point, Matthew informs us (26:56), "all the disciples deserted him and fled."

17. See Matthew 26:53—words that John does not record.

18. John Calvin, *Commentary on the Gospel According to John*, vol. II (Edinburgh: The Calvin Translation Society, 1847), 194.

# 32

# *Injustice and Denial*

John 18:12-27

*They bound him 13 and brought him first to Annas, who was the father-in-law of Caiaphas, the high priest that year. 14 Caiaphas was the one who had advised the Jews that it would be good if one man died for the people.*

*15 Simon Peter and another disciple were following Jesus. Because this disciple was known to the high priest, he went with Jesus into the high priest's courtyard, 16 but Peter had to wait outside at the door. The other disciple, who was known to the high priest, came back, spoke to the girl on duty there and brought Peter in.*

*17 "You are not one of his disciples, are you?" the girl at the door asked Peter.*

*He replied, "I am not."*

*18 It was cold, and the servants and officials stood around a fire they had made to keep warm. Peter also was standing with them, warming himself.*

*19 Meanwhile, the high priest questioned Jesus about his disciples and his teaching.*

*20 "I have spoken openly to the world," Jesus replied. "I always taught in synagogues or at the temple, where all the Jews come together. I said nothing in secret. 21 Why question me? Ask those who heard me. Surely they know what I said."*

*22 When Jesus said this, one of the officials nearby struck him in the face. "Is this the way you answer the high priest?" he demanded.*

> *23 "If I said something wrong," Jesus replied, "testify as to what is wrong. But if I spoke the truth, why did you strike me?" 24 Then Annas sent him, still bound, to Caiaphas the high priest.*
>
> *25 As Simon Peter stood warming himself, he was asked, "You are not one of his disciples, are you?"*
>
> *He denied it, saying, "I am not."*
>
> *26 One of the high priest's servants, a relative of the man whose ear Peter had cut off, challenged him, "Didn't I see you with him in the olive grove?" 27 Again Peter denied it, and at that moment a rooster began to crow.*

On His way to the cross, our Lord would undergo three trials. Two of these were before Jewish authorities—first before Annas[1] and then before Caiaphas and the Sanhedrin. The third was before Pilate, the Roman governor.

## Annas: The Cunning High Priest (18:13-14)

Annas was waiting for Jesus! This wealthy, wily, domineering man had been appointed high priest at age thrity-seven in A.D. 6 by Quirinius, governor of Syria. He was deposed some nine years later by Valerius Gratus, governor of Judea. Annas had made a fortune by extorting money from temple worshipers. He forced them to purchase their sacrificial animals in expensive temple bazaars. Prices on the outside, of course, would have been much less.[2] In cleansing the temple, Jesus had attacked Annas's vested interests and hit him where it hurt most—in the purse. It was not surprising that this crafty ex-high priest wanted to be *first* to gloat over Jesus' capture (18:13).[3]

Under Old Testament law, the high priest was appointed for life. When Roman governors ruled Israel, the office of high priest became a matter for contention, intrigue, bribery and corruption. The appointment went to the highest bidder—or to whoever was most willing to carry out the governor's wishes. When Annas was deposed, his five sons became successive high priests. The current high priest, Caiaphas, was Annas's son-in-law (18:13). John reminds us that he was the very same high priest who had advocated the death of Jesus (18:14).[4] Clearly, Jesus could not expect an unbiased decision from Caiaphas.

So Jesus was first arraigned before Annas. Whatever the legal technicalities, Annas still had power and prestige. As high priest emeritus,[5] he exercised considerable authority through his sons and son-in-law.

As we shall soon see, this before-dawn trial would be a mockery of justice. But before John allows us into the hearing, he returns to the disciple who bravely defended his Master in the olive grove.

## Peter: The Wavering Disciple (18:15-18)

Given the opportunity, most of the disciples fled the olive grove (see Matthew 26:56). Peter, however, accompanied by "another disciple," was courageous enough to follow Jesus to the door of Annas' courtyard. Perhaps the two wanted to ascertain the outcome of the trial (John 18:15).[6] The unnamed disciple was "known to the high priest" (18:15)[7] and was able to go with Jesus into the courtyard. This left Peter outside the gate awaiting permission to enter (18:16). When it came, the girl on gate duty could hardly believe he, too, was one of Jesus' disciples.

"*You* aren't one of the disciples of this man, too, are you?"[8] she exclaimed. Fear gripped Peter's pounding heart. *She isn't sure,* he thought. *Why not simply go along with her and avoid trouble?*

"You're right; I am not," replied the man who had sworn unfailing allegiance to his Lord (18:17).

Passing by the girl, Peter stepped warily into the courtyard of the high priest's palace. The night was unusually cold. In the center of the courtyard members of the temple guard and servants were talking and joking around a charcoal fire. Ill at ease but cold, Peter found a place among them and warmed himself over the glowing embers (18:18).

Meanwhile, inside the house, Jesus was the object of . . .

## Injustice: An Illegal Interrogation (18:19-23)

As if to contrast the cringing cowardice of Peter against the calm confidence of Jesus, John takes us into the house. The Lord was being examined by Annas. Annas was concerned as to the size of Jesus' following and what He was privately teaching them (18:19).[9]

Jesus knew that rabbinic law regarded it as improper to attempt to make an accused person convict himself.[10] He was under no obligation to demonstrate His innocence. Rather, it was Annas' responsibility to bring into the court witnesses who could speak in His defense. So the Lord advised the "out-of-order" inquisitor that he would have no difficulty procuring such testimony. There had been nothing secretive about His ministry. He had said nothing to His disciples privately that He did not say in synagogues and the temple (18:20).

"Secure your evidence about Me in the proper and legal way," Jesus was saying, in effect, to Annas. "Examine your witnesses, which you have every right to do; stop examining Me, which you have no right to do."

Jesus' refusal to incriminate Himself and His implicit correction of Annas' illegal procedure provoked a temple guard. He slapped Jesus in the face (18:22).[11] Barrett comments that "truth is always objectionable to those who are concerned to establish their case at all costs. It is easier and more effective to answer it with blows than with arguments."[12] But Jesus had used no insulting language.[13] He spoke nothing but the truth. Therefore He protested the officer's rude action (18:23). If He had spoken amiss, a formal charge of contempt of court should have been lodged against Him. If there was nothing wrong with what He said, the slap on the face was an unjustified assault.[14] But it was obvious that Jesus would not secure justice in Annas' court.

If Jesus were to be charged before Pilate, the Roman governor, an indictment must come from the reigning high priest. As leader of the nation and president of the Sanhedrin, Israel's supreme court, Caiaphas was the man to see. Annas, therefore, sent[15] the Lord to stand trial before him.[16]

Our text concludes with another scene in the courtyard, where a faltering Peter is still warming himself by the charcoal fire. Sadly, we see fulfilled . . .

## The Lord's Prediction: The Rooster's Crow (18:25-27)

Exactly who put the second challenge to Peter's identity John does not say. It may have been the same maid as before (18:17),[17] another maid[18] or some man in the crowd.[19] John is not interested in the details. A third challenge comes from a servant of the high priest, a relative of the man whose ear Peter severed (see 18:10). He had been in the olive grove, and he thought he had seen Peter with Jesus (18:26).[20] Poor Peter! Having once taken the line of least resistance, he could not lose face by confessing that he had lied at the courtyard door. Krummacher's description of Peter's plight is vivid:

> Peter now finds himself completely entrapped. How is he to act? Two ways are open to him, either to reveal his disgraceful denials by a candid acknowledgment, or else to act his lamentable part completely through, in which case he must carry his barefaced falsehoods to the utmost. In a state bordering on desperation he decides upon the latter. In the confusion of the moment, he is quite the old fisherman, the rough sailor again—nay, even much worse than he had ever been before, and heaps oath upon oath, and curse upon curse, to confirm his assertion that he knew not the Man.[21]

And then, just as His Master had predicted, no sooner was the third denial out of his mouth than somewhere nearby a rooster crowed.[22] And the enormity of what he had done dawned on Peter. Another Gospel tells us that Jesus "turned and looked straight at Peter. . . . And he went outside and wept bitterly" (Luke 22:61-62).

## Conclusion

Think with me about how Peter's *failure* worked for his ultimate good. He loved the Lord. He was courageous. The word of Christ had powerfully changed his life. He felt strong. There was nothing he couldn't face successfully. He had what it takes! But he did not know himself. Before he could become the man God could use, he had to feel his own great weakness. He had to know that he could not trust in his natural strengths and abilities. His future success would have to come through failure—a failure that would stay in his memory the rest of his life.

The story of Peter's failure contains a vital principle that Christian workers must learn if we are to "succeed." The principle is this: The path to success must often lead through failure.

Before Moses could be Israel's great savior, he had to fail in his personal attempt to rescue Israel from Egypt. He spent the next forty years as a shepherd in Midian. Wesley's failure in Georgia caused him to see his own need of conversion. Brainard's failure in his eyes and Yale's made him the prayer warrior God used to bring Indians to Christ. Each of these failures ultimately worked for God's glory and the manifestation of His power. The same principle held true in the life of A.J. Gordon of Boston. In his spiritual autobiography, *How Christ Came to Church,* this contemporary of A.B. Simpson recounts the process:

> Well do we remember those days when drudgery was pushed to the point of desperation. The hearers must be moved to repentance and confession of Christ; therefore more effort must be devoted to the sermon, more hours to elaborating its points, more pungency put into its sentences, more study bestowed on its delivery. And then came the disappointment that few, if any, were converted by all this which had cost a week of solid toil.
>
> And now attention was turned to the prayer meeting as the possible seat of difficulty—so few attending it and so little readiness to participate in its services. A pulpit scourging must be laid on next Sunday, and the sharpest sting which words can effect put into the lash. Alas, there is no increase in the attendance, and instead of spontaneity in prayer and witnessing there is a silence which seems almost like sullenness!
>
> Then the administration goes wrong and opposition is encountered among officials, so that caucusing must be undertaken to get the members to vote as they should. Thus the burdens of anxiety increase while we are trying to lighten them, and should-be helpers become hinderers, till discouragement comes and sleepless nights ensue; these hotboxes on the train of our activities necessitating a stop and a visit of the doctor, with the verdict overwork and the remedy absolute rest.[23]

Out of this consciousness of failure there came to A.J. Gordon, in the mercy of God, another consciousness: "There stands One among you, whom you know not." When all self-effort had failed, Gordon had nowhere else to turn but to the strong Son of God. And there He was: standing quietly in the Holy Spirit, waiting to be trusted to do His work as Head of the Church. Success came out of failure.

It appears that failure is necessary even though not to be sought. Why is this so? First, a consciousness of failure is necessary to show us the insufficiency of human ability and plans. The body of Christ cannot be nurtured on the same principles that succeed in a business corporation. When these business principles prove failures, we turn to the sovereign Holy Spirit and rest while we work!

Second, an awareness of failure is also necessary to humble us. When we have been humbled before others and God, we become vessels through whom God will minister life.

Third, a sense of failure is necessary in order to transfer glory from us to the Lord. Christ is the Head of the Church. Any "success" in ministry must be attributed to the Mighty One—not to us. In his hymn, "The Everlasting Arms," A.B. Simpson has a stanza hammered out of personal experience in ministry:

> Underneath us—oh, how easy!
> We have not to mount on high,
> But to sink into His fullness
> And in trustful weakness lie.
> And we find our humbling failures
> Save us from the strength that harms;
> We may fail, but underneath us
> Are the everlasting arms.[24]

That is it! "Our humbling failures save us from the strength that harms." Let this be our prayer:

> O Lord, Head of the Church: I do not want to fail. Yet You know that without a sense of my own weakness and failure I will not trust Your Holy Spirit. Lord, do in me and in my ministry all that is necessary to cast me fully on You. For Jesus' sake. Amen.

## Endnotes

1. Annas is Greek for Hanan, a contraction of Hananiah, meaning "merciful, gracious." He appears not to have lived up to his name.

2. For a fuller treatment of the practices that so angered our Lord, see again chapter 6 of this commentary.

3. Furthermore, the inquiry before Annas would impart the appearance of legality to the trial before the Sanhedrin. According to F. Godet, *Commentary on the Gospel of St. John*, vol. III (Edinburgh: T. & T. Clarke, 1881), 233, a capital sentence could not be pronounced by that body until the day following the appearance of the accused. In Jesus' case the time line had been shortened. And to preserve the appearance of legality, a semblance of a first preliminary hearing, followed by a second at which judgment should be given, was held.

4. See John 11:49ff.

5. In 18:15-23, Annas is spoken of as the high priest. Just as a former president of the United States is always referred to as "Mr. President," so a former high priest was called high priest as long as he lived. To make Caiaphas the high priest before whom Jesus is arraigned in these verses necessitates a rearrangement of some verses and a different translation of the verb "sent" (to "had sent") in 18:24. Such an endeavor is quite unnecessary.

6. C.K. Barrett, *The Gospel According to St. John* (London: S.P.C.K, 1955), 439, thinks it quite unlikely that Peter's purpose in following Jesus was to perpetuate the violence described in 18:10. It may have been because he expected a divine intervention.

7. The word translated "known" is the Greek *gnostos* and suggests something more than a mere acquaintance. C.H. Dodd, *The Interpretation of the Fourth Gospel* (Cambridge: At the University Press, 1970), 86, thinks that this other disciple was a member of the high priest's circle of friends, possibly a relative or of priestly birth—one who stood in an intimate relationship with the high priestly family (see Leon Morris, *The Gospel According to John* [Grand Rapids, MI: Eerdmans, 1971], 751). We are not given his identity, but William Barclay, *The Gospel of John*, vol. II (Philadelphia: The Westminster Press, 1975), 229, speculates that it was John. John, whose father's flourishing salt fish business supplied the fish for Annas' household, would be well-known to the high priest. Others suggest Nicodemus or Joseph of Arimathea, or as F.F. Bruce, *The Gospel of John* (Grand Rapids, MI: Eerdmans, 1983), 344, suggests, some Jerusalem disciple who had entrance into top society.

8. The NIV translators have correctly interpreted the Greek form of the question as expecting the answer "No." Usually the Greek negative *me* does anticipate that answer, but sometimes *me* can be the "*me* of cautious assertion" (Barrett, *The Gospel According to St. John*, 439). If that is the case, the girl is asking, in a nonhostile manner, "In addition to the man I recognize as being a disciple and friend of the high priest, are you not also a disciple of Christ?" Or, "You have come with Christ whom we know; perhaps you too are a disciple?" She expected the answer "Yes."

9. William Hendriksen, quoted by Morris, *The Gospel According to John*, 755, noting the word order in 18:19 ("disciples" precedes "teaching"), remarks: "This is exactly what one can expect from Annas! He was far more interested in the 'success' of Jesus—how large was his following?—than in the truthfulness or untruthfulness of that which he had been teaching. That is ever the way of the world."

10. See Barrett, *The Gospel According to St. John*, 440.

11. As though to say, "Are you trying to teach the high priest how to conduct a trial?"

12. Barrett, *The Gospel According to St. John*, 441.

13. As had Paul (Acts 23:2-5), and for which he apologized.
14. Those who misunderstand Jesus' teaching in Matthew 5:39 may accuse Him of violating His own dictum. When, however, our Lord spoke of turning the other cheek, He was not speaking of a literal action of the body. Rather, He was admonishing His disciples to refrain from having a vindictive spirit. The action of the official who struck Jesus was totally uncalled for, and therefore Jesus, who always insisted on living in truth, called the official to account.
15. According to Barrett, *The Gospel According to St. John,* 441, the move from Annas to Caiaphas need not have involved going from one building to another. It may have been simply a transfer into another courtroom.
16. John's is the only Gospel that records the appearance of Jesus before Annas. On the other hand, John omits any details of Jesus' trial before the Sanhedrin. Apparently he considered that the details of that trial were already sufficiently well-known.
17. See Mark 14:69-70. John has the exact same wording of the question in 18:25 as in 18:17.
18. See Matthew 26:69-72.
19. See Luke 22:57-60.
20. John's is the only Gospel that has a relative of Malchus challenging Peter. As might be expected, the details of Peter's denials are somewhat different in each of the Gospels. See Matthew 26:69ff; Mark 14:66ff; Luke 22:56ff.
21. F.W. Krummacher, *Our Suffering Saviour* (Chicago: Moody Press, 1948), 158-159.
22. Barclay, *The Gospel of John,* vol. II, 229, identifies the rooster's crow as a 3:00 a.m. trumpet, called in Greek an *alektorophonia,* "cockcrow." It marked the end of a military watch.
23. A.J. Gordon, *How Christ Came to Church* (Philadelphia: American Baptist Publication Society, 1985), 12.
24. A.B. Simpson, "The Everlasting Arms," *Hymns of the Christian Life* (Camp Hill, PA: Christian Publications, Inc., 1978), # 323, stanza 3.

# 33

# The Trial before Pilate

John 18:28-19:16

28 Then the Jews led Jesus from Caiaphas to the palace of the Roman governor. By now it was early morning, and to avoid ceremonial uncleanness the Jews did not enter the palace; they wanted to be able to eat the Passover. 29 So Pilate came out to them and asked, "What charges are you bringing against this man?"

30 "If he were not a criminal," they replied, "we would not have handed him over to you."

31 Pilate said, "Take him yourselves and judge him by your own law."

"But we have no right to execute anyone," the Jews objected. 32 This happened so that the words Jesus had spoken indicating the kind of death he was going to die would be fulfilled.

33 Pilate then went back inside the palace, summoned Jesus and asked him, "Are you the king of the Jews?"

34 "Is that your own idea," Jesus asked, "or did others talk to you about me?"

35 "Am I a Jew?" Pilate replied. "It was your people and your chief priests who handed you over to me. What is it you have done?"

36 Jesus said, "My kingdom is not of this world. If it were, my servants would fight to prevent my arrest by the Jews. But now my kingdom is from another place."

37 "You are a king, then!" said Pilate.

Jesus answered, "You are right in saying I am a king. If fact, for this reason I was born, and for this I came into the world, to testify to the truth. Everyone on the side of truth listens to me."

38 "What is truth?" Pilate asked. With this he went out again to the Jews and said, "I find no basis for a charge against him. 39 But it is your custom for me to release to you one prisoner at the time of the Passover. Do you want me to release 'the king of the Jews'?"

40 They shouted back, "No, not him! Give us Barabbas!" Now Barabbas had taken part in a rebellion.

1 Then Pilate took Jesus and had him flogged. 2 The soldiers twisted together a crown of thorns and put it on his head. They clothed him in a purple robe 3 and went up to him again and again, saying, "Hail, king of the Jews!" And they struck him in the face.

4 Once more Pilate came out and said to the Jews, "Look, I am bringing him out to you to let you know that I find no basis for a charge against him." 5 When Jesus came out wearing the crown of thorns and the purple robe, Pilate said to them, "Here is the man!"

6 As soon as the chief priests and their officials saw him, they shouted, "Crucify! Crucify!"

But Pilate answered, "You take him and crucify him. As for me, I find no basis for a charge against him."

7 The Jews insisted, "We have a law, and according to that law he must die, because he claimed to be the Son of God."

8 When Pilate heard this, he was even more afraid, 9 and he went back inside the palace. "Where do you come from?" he asked Jesus, but Jesus gave him no answer. 10 "Do you refuse to speak to me?" Pilate said. "Don't you realize I have power either to free you or to crucify you?"

11 Jesus answered, "You would have no power over me if it were not given to you from above. Therefore the one who handed me over to you is guilty of a greater sin."

12 From then on, Pilate tried to set Jesus free, but the Jews kept shouting, "If you let this man go, you are no friend of Caesar. Anyone who claims to be a king opposes Caesar."

13 When Pilate heard this, he brought Jesus out and sat down on the judge's seat at a place known as the Stone Pavement (which in Aramaic is Gabbatha). 14 It was the day of Preparation of Passover Week, about the sixth hour.

"Here is your king," Pilate said to the Jews.

15 But they shouted, "Take him away! Take him away! Crucify him!"

"Shall I crucify your king?" Pilate asked.

"We have no king but Caesar," the chief priests answered.

16 Finally Pilate handed him over to them to be crucified.

B efore us is the most moving, the most powerful, yet one of the saddest events recorded in John's Gospel. We are about to see imperial Rome's law outwitted by Jerusalem's conniving conspirators. We are about to see a judge, convinced of an accused's innocence, set aside justice to save his own skin. We are about to see a nation allegedly under God's rule abolish its theocracy to swear allegiance to their hated enemy. We are about to see Jesus, King of the Jews, Son of God, condemned to an unjust and horrible death.

John sets before us seven scenes. In them the Roman governor vacillates between Jesus and the Jews. Scene One is . . .

## The Bogus Charge (18:28-32)

From the hearing before Annas (18:12f), Jesus had been taken to the high priest Caiaphas (18:24). With the Sanhedrin as jury, Jesus affirmed His identity as Son of God. Rather than to investigate His claim, they condemned Him to death for blasphemy (Matthew 26:65).[1] But under Roman occupation, they lacked authority to exercise capital punishment (John 18:31). The Jews, therefore, would have to transfer Jesus to the Roman prefect (18:28) for a civil trial. They would ask Rome to do what they were not permitted to do. Our text takes up the story.

It was now early morning (18:28).[2] To have entered the prefect's praetorium[3] would have made the Jews ceremonially unclean (18:28).[4] This, in turn would have disbarred them from eating Passover that evening. Religious punctilios took priority over the life of an innocent Man. Ever concerned for ritual cleanness, they missed the true Paschal Lamb who that day would fulfill the meaning of the feast.

Pilate,[5] the governor, was wise enough to accommodate such Jewish proscriptions. In this case he condescended to move his *bema*[6] outside into the colonnade (18:29).[7] As was his duty, he opened the judicial proceedings by asking the Jewish authorities to present a formal charge (18:29). He was not about to rubber-stamp the sentence the Sanhedrin wanted. On their part, the Jews realized they had no charge that would stand up in a Roman court of law. So they insinuated that Pilate should trust their judgment and order Jesus' execution (18:30).

Pilate knew that they were bringing a capital charge against Jesus.[8] But since they had not said so formally thus far, he pretended not to know. He suggested they deal with the prisoner according to their own laws—that is, to stone Him for blasphemy (18:31).[9] But the chief priests wanted Jesus crucified. In this way they could connect Him to the curse pronounced on anyone hanged on a tree.[10] Thus it would be obvious that He was not Messiah but a blasphemous impostor whom God was judging. So they persisted to press for a Roman verdict (18:31), in the process revealing their true wishes.

John, however, saw divine significance in this insistence that Jesus be crucified. He interrupts the narrative to remind us of the Lord's own spoken words, "But I, when I am lifted up from the earth [i.e., crucified], will draw all men to myself" (12:32). The authorities' pressing was in fact a fulfillment of these words. Quickly John returns to Scene Two of the story.

### The "Kingdom" Interchange (18:33-38)

If the Jews were charging Jesus with rebellion against Caesar, punishable by crucifixion, Pilate must determine His guilt. He therefore brought Jesus *inside* the praetorium and proceeded to examine Him privately.[11] One close look at his prisoner convinced Pilate that it was highly unlikely Jesus was a king. With incredulity he asked, "Are *you*[12] the king of the Jews?" (18:33, emphasis added). Doubtless he expected a frank "No." But the answer would not be that simple. In the Roman political sense, the answer was "No." But in the religious sense of every believing Jew, Jesus *was* a king—*the* King. The answer depended on whether the charge came from Jewish or Gentile lips. So Jesus asked the governor, "Is that your own idea, or did others talk to you about me?" (18:34).

Pilate could not see the point of this distinction, and rather contemptuously asked, "I am not a Jew, am I?" (see 18:35). That is to say, "What have I to do with all your Jewish subtleties?[13] How do you expect me to know about such things? What difference does it make where the question came from? Let's get to the bottom of this. It was *your* people and *your* chief priests who handed you over to me. You must have done something to offend them.

What is it you have done?" (see 18:35). Pilate is only interested if Jesus has done something contrary to Roman law.

In answer, Jesus wants it clear that He has no designs on Caesar's throne. It is true that He is a King. But the origin of His kingship,[14] unlike Caesar's or Herod's, is not "of this world"—a world organized against God. As proof, His "servants"[15] did not resist his arrest. Christ's kingship has its source in heaven (18:36). He is therefore not guilty of sedition. Of that Pilate may be sure.

But Pilate is somewhat confused at this point. Is Jesus a king or is He not? His reply is half question and half exclamation—"Very well; so you are a king?" (18:37).[16] To which Jesus replies in effect, "King is *your* word. But if that is the word to use, then I am speaking of the kingdom of *truth.*[17] I was born into this world[18] for no other purpose than to bear witness to the truth. Everyone who stands for truth listens to my words, for I am the only one qualified to so testify" (18:37).

What a moving moment! Jesus challenged Pilate to listen to the voice of truth. But Pilate, for all his interest in fair play and open-mindedness, was not interested in eternal truth. Abruptly he dismissed the subject with a wistful, "What is truth?" (18:38).[19] We who are John's believing readers, however, know the answer to the governor's question. In Christ we have received the *true revelation* of God's being and nature. We know His love and justice manifested at Calvary. We have experienced God's power that raised Jesus from the dead. We are partakers of His salvation offered to all who believe. We follow His commands set forth in His Son's living words. All of that is eternal "truth"!

Then John sets Scene Three in "Rome vs. Heaven."            i 4 : 6

## *The Proposed Compromise (18:38-40)*

The prefect now moved *outside* once again to face a waiting Jewry. Whatever the nature of Jesus' kingdom, Pilate was convinced that He had committed no offense against Caesar. Pilate was disposed to acquit the prisoner (18:38), but he knew the Jews would not agree to that. So he decided on a compromise. Rome had a standing custom of releasing a prisoner at Passover. Pilate proposed that this year it be Jesus, "the king of the Jews"

(18:39).[20] If they accepted his proposal, he could set Jesus free while still technically "convicting" Him. This ought to please the high priests.

But the high priests angrily rejected his proposal. Instead they called for the release of Barabbas,[21] a popular hero who had dared to stand up against Rome (18:40). How ironic that the man whose release was granted (see Luke 23:25) had been convicted of the same crime with which Jesus was now charged!

Once more the scene changes. For Scene Four John takes us once again *inside* the Praetorium. There we will watch . . .

## *The Cruel Coronation (19:1-3)*

Convinced of Jesus' innocence, the politically clever Pilate attempted again to avoid crucifying Jesus. He would lay on Him a punishment which he hoped would satisfy the Jews: he had our Lord flogged (19:1). Normally this brutal and painful torture was a prelude to crucifixion.[22] The prisoner would be tied to a whipping post with his back fully exposed. The whip, composed of long leather thongs, studded at intervals with pieces of metal and sharpened bone, would literally tear a man's back to shreds. Few remained conscious throughout the ordeal. Some died; many went mad. Such were the "stripes" our Lord endured.

The words "king of the Jews" had evidently caught the attention of the Roman soldiers present in the praetorium. They had likely gone up from Caesarea with Pilate and were ready for some diversion. *If this man is the king of the Jews, let's make him look the part.* So they placed on Jesus' head a thorny wreath.[23] Over His deeply lacerated body they draped a cast-off scarlet military cloak (19:2).[24] Then, in repeated acts of mock obeisance, they knelt before Him, proclaiming, "Hail, king of the Jews!" And instead of a dutiful kiss or a present, they struck Him in the face (19:3).

We turn as quickly as possible from that wrenching sight to Scene Five. . .

## *The Royal Presentation (19:4-9)*

What a pathetic spectacle the disfigured and disabled Jesus, dressed in mockery, must have made as Pilate brought Him outside!

"*Ecce homo!* Here is the man!" Pilate called out in words that have rung through the centuries. "Here He is, poor fellow!" his announcement seemed to say (19:5). Pilate had found no basis in Roman law for a charge against Jesus (19:4). He hoped that the sight of this sad figure would persuade the Jews that He had learned His lesson. Obviously Jesus was no rebel with political ambitions!

But the chief priests would not accept Pilate's verdict of innocence. They sensed that Pilate was exposing them to public ridicule for bringing a charge of sedition against Jesus.

"Crucify! Crucify!" they shouted angrily (19:6). Pilate's taunting rejoinder throws the whole business into their hands. "*You* take him and crucify him—if you can. *I* want nothing to do with His death" (see 19:6). He knew full well that they could not execute a capital sentence. And even if they could, crucifixion was not a form of execution authorized by Jewish law.

Whatever the case with Roman law, the Jews had a law of their own.[25] And the governors of Judea undertook the responsibility of respecting and (where necessary) enforcing Jewish religious law. Pilate might be persuaded to look at the situation from their point of view. It was worth a try!

"He claimed to be the Son of God," they said. "Therefore He must die" (19:7). *The Son of God!*[26] This new piece of information sent fear into the heart of the superstitious prefect. Once more Pilate took Jesus into the praetorium in order to speak privately with Him (19:8-9). It is Scene Six.

## The "Deity" Interchange (19:9-11)

Incredulously Pilate asked Jesus, "Where do you come from? Are you a man or a god?" Every Roman knew stories of the gods or their offspring appearing in human form. To claim to be the Son of God was no blasphemy to a Roman. Furthermore, the prefect sensed something about Jesus that seemed to verify His claim. *Could He possibly be divine? Who knows in what guise the deity might meet me!* Jesus knew that Pilate, unlike the Samaritan woman, was not prepared to understand any true answer to His question. So Jesus remained silent. There was no point in even trying to explain (19:9).

"Don't you appreciate my authority?" Pilate exclaimed. "Don't you real-ize that your life is in my hands? I can say, 'Crucify' or 'Release.' You would be well advised to answer my question" (see 19:10).

"You would have no power over me if it were not given to you from above" (19:11), the regal Son of God replied. Jesus' life was not in Pilate's hands, but in the hands of heaven. Pilate was but heaven's instrument for the outworking of God's eternal purpose. He could only act with heaven's con-sent.[27] Pilate would bear guilt for the crucifixion of Jesus. But his sin was less heinous than that of Annas and Caiaphas. They criminally made use of Pilate's lawful authority (19:11).[28]

On that note Scene Six ends, and John goes on to the terrible Scene Seven.

## The Sentencing (19:12-16)

The Jews had one remaining move, but it was effective. It was the what-will-Caesar-say? move: "If you let this man go, you are no friend of Caesar," they said. "Anyone who claims to be a king opposes Caesar" (19:12). It was blackmail, pure and simple, but it tipped the scales.

Pilate was well aware of the consequences of such a report. And so, on that fateful Friday of Passover week, he took his place on his seat of judg-ment.[29] For the final time he presented to the Jews their king (19:14).

"Take him away! Take him away! Crucify him!" they shouted (19:15).

Pilate made one more effort.

"Shall I crucify your king?" he asked.

"We have no king but Caesar" (19:15). It was a tragically fateful avowal. In that awful confession, the nation that hated Caesar confessed him as their king. They rejected the sovereign reign of God and condemned His Son to death by crucifixion (19:16).

And the proud Roman governor who presided over this drama? He would go down in history as the vacillating, weak-willed Roman who, to save his own skin, sent Jesus to the cross.

## Conclusion

In seven poignant scenes our text has set before us the life-and-death struggle between two opposite kingdoms. It was a struggle between the kingdom of this world and the kingdom of heaven. Organized religion (the jealously blind priests) combined forces with the secular state (the weak and self-serving Pilate) to overthrow the rule of the Christ. It was the kingdom of darkness against the kingdom of light. Satan versus God! The battle took place in and outside Pilate's visible judgment hall. But not all the engaged principals were visible. It was warfare that continues to this day to engage Christ's followers.

See the *humility* of Jesus Christ, who "offered [His] back to those who beat [Him], [His] cheeks to those who pulled out [His] beard" (Isaiah 50:6). The innocent Son of God was flogged as a criminal. The King of heaven was mocked by sadistic soldiers. The meek Savior was slapped by wicked men. The Lord of glory paraded bruised, bleeding and innocent before a blood-thirsty crowd. But John the apostle would have us remember that this was "all for sinners' gain." It is by His stripes that we are healed.

See also the *glory* of Jesus Christ even as He faces the angry shouts, the false accusations and the collapse of justice. See His pure goodness, His quiet magnificence, His stately kingliness and His divine authority. These stand in gleaming contrast to the angry petulance and jealous hatred of Jewry. They stand pure and holy against the vacillations and manipulations of Pilate.

Unwittingly, Pilate, the man of this world, enthroned the Man whose kingdom is not of this world. Peter would remind us that, in this, Jesus has shown us how to suffer unjustly. Jesus has left us "an example that [we] should follow in his steps" (1 Peter 2:21).

See, finally, the *decision* which this trial requires of every person. A.B. Simpson described it in these words:

> Jesus is standing in Pilate's hall—
> Friendless, forsaken, betrayed by all:
> Harken! What meaneth the sudden call?
>    What will you do with Jesus?
>
> Jesus is standing on trial still,
> You can be false to Him if you will,
> You can be faithful through good or ill:
>    What will you do with Jesus?

Will you evade Him as Pilate tried?
Or will you choose Him, whate'er betide?
Vainly you struggle from Him to hide:
 What will you do with Jesus?

Will you, like Peter, your Lord deny?
Or will you scorn from His foes to fly,
Daring for Jesus to live or die?
 What will you do with Jesus?

"Jesus, I give Thee my heart to-day!
Jesus, I'll follow Thee all the way,
Gladly obeying Thee!" will you say:
 "This will I do with Jesus!"[30]

### Endnotes

1. We will rely on Matthew's Gospel here. John records none of these proceedings, probably because he deemed them sufficiently well-known.
2. According to Leon Morris, *The Gospel According to John* (Grand Rapids, MI: Eerdmans, 1971), 762, likely sometime between 6 and 7 o'clock.
3. The praetorium was the official residence of the governor (prefect) of the province, who normally lived in the praetorium at Caesarea. Pilate came to Jerusalem for the great feasts, probably in order to quell any possible disturbance. The exact location of the Jerusalem praetorium is debated. Some think it was in Herod's palace on the western wall of the city. Others place it in the fortress of Antonio, northwest of the temple area. For another reference to the building, see Acts 21:35, 40.
4. Rudolph Schnackenburg, *The Gospel According to St. John,* vol. III, trans. David Smith and G.A. Kon (New York: Crossroad, 1982), 244, suggests that "contact with the gentiles, as such, did not make one unclean; but the opinion is demonstrable from early times, that entering a gentile house makes one unclean because it is to be supposed that premature children were buried in it [uncleanness through dead bodies]." It could have been the presence of leavened bread in the praetorium that would cause ceremonial uncleanness (see Exodus 12:19; 13:7).
5. Pontius Pilate, a member of Roman nobility, though not a senator, had been appointed governor of Judea by Tiberius Caesar and occupied that position from A.D. 26 to 37. He has been described as a mercilessly hard man who despised the Jews. Because of his brutal treatment of the Samaritans, he was deposed by Vitellius, the legate of Syria, and sent to Rome to account for his actions. He was at heart a weak man who tried to cover up his weakness by a show of obstinacy and violence.
6. "Judge's seat" (see 19:13).

7. C.K. Barrett, *The Gospel According to St. John* (London: S.P.C.K., 1955), 443, informs us that the rules about the houses of gentiles did not apply to colonnades.

8. According to Luke's account (23:2), they accused Jesus of "[opposing] payment of taxes to Caesar and [claiming] to be Christ, a king." In other words, they were charging Him with sedition, which under Roman law was punishable by crucifixion.

9. According to Sir Edwyn Hoskyns, cited by Morris, *The Gospel According to John*, 787, the Jews could have stoned Jesus without Roman interference upon the charge of blasphemy.

10. Compare Deuteronomy 21:22-23 with Galatians 3:13.

11. Usually, according to Schnackenburg, *The Gospel According to St. John*, vol. III, 247, Roman procedure called for a prisoner's examination to be done in public. But to examine Jesus privately was Pilate's prerogative.

12. The pronoun "you" is emphatic in the original.

13. See F. Godet, *Commentary on the Gospel of St. John*, vol. III (Edinburgh: T. & T. Clarke, 1881), 246.

14. The word *basileia* here means "reign, rule or kingship" rather than "realm."

15. The word is *huperetai*, a "helper" or "assistant" who serves a master or a superior. It is the same word used in 18:3 to describe the Temple police. Here it describes "a king's retinue." See William F. Arndt and F. Wilbur Gingrich, *A Greek-English Lexicon of the New Testament* (Chicago: The University of Chicago Press, 1957), 850.

16. See Barrett, *The Gospel According to St. John*, 447. B.F. Westcott, *Commentary on the Gospel According to St. John* (London: John Murray, Albemarle Street, 1967), translates his words, *"So then, after all, thou art a king?"*

17. F.F. Bruce, *The Gospel of John* (Grand Rapids, MI: Eerdmans, 1983), 353, offers this interpretation of Jesus' words.

18. The words "I was born" and "I came into the world" speak of incarnation and preexistence.

19. Schnackenburg, *The Gospel According to St. John*, vol. III, 241, comments that Pilate's question is neither the product of a philosophical skepticism nor a cold irony nor a serious search for truth. It is clearly an avoidance of the subject and thus a rejection of Jesus' witness.

20. The release of a prisoner at Passover was, perhaps, intended by the Jews to commemorate the theme of release from Egypt, of which the Passover was a memorial.

21. Barabbas' name in Hebrew means "son of the father." Morris, *The Gospel According to John*, 773, observes with others that Barabbas, "son of the father," was released, while Another, who may well be called "the Son of the Father," was condemned.

22. Matthew's account (27:27f) has the flogging take place after the sentence of crucifixion is pronounced. He gives us other details omitted by John, e.g., Pilate's wife's dream; the staff in Jesus' right hand with which they repeatedly struck His head; and the removal and replacement of His clothes before and after the scarlet robe.

23. Hart, cited by Morris, *The Gospel According to John*, 790, footnote 3, argues that the wreath was a caricature of the "radiate" crown, in which spikes radiate outwards, and which might be made from the palm tree. It was a form of crown which pointed to the ruler as divine.

24. See Richard Chenevix Trench, *Synonyms of the New Testament* (Grand Rapids, MI: Eerdmans, 1948), 186.

25. *"We* [as well as you] have a law." The "we" is emphasized in the original.

26. Verse 19:7 reads literally, "because *son of God* he claimed to be." The Greek emphasizes the qualitative nature of Jesus' claim.
27. Cf. Romans 13:1, where Paul speaks similarly.
28. See Godet, *Commentary on the Gospel of St. John,* 256.
29. Barrett, *The Gospel According to St. John,* 452-453, and others observe that the verb translated "sat down" can, for grammatical reasons, also be construed to mean that Pilate had *Jesus* sit down on the judge's seat. In using a word subject to a double meaning, John means that although Pilate was sitting on the judge's seat, believers with the eyes of faith see the Son of Man, to whom all judgment has been committed, seated upon His throne.
30. A.B. Simpson, "What Will You Do with Jesus?" *Hymns of the Christian Life* (Camp Hill, PA: Christian Publications, Inc., 1978), # 566.

# 34

# Death on a Cross

### John 19:16-42

*16 So the soldiers took charge of Jesus. 17 Carrying his own cross, he went out to the place of the Skull (which in Aramaic is called Golgotha). 18 Here they crucified him, and with him two others—one on each side and Jesus in the middle.*

*19 Pilate had a notice prepared and fastened to the cross. It read: JESUS OF NAZARETH, THE KING OF THE JEWS. 20 Many of the Jews read this sign, for the place where Jesus was crucified was near the city, and the sign was written in Aramaic, Latin and Greek. 21 The chief priests of the Jews protested to Pilate, "Do not write 'The King of the Jews,' but that this man claimed to be king of the Jews."*

*22 Pilate answered, "What I have written, I have written."*

*23 When the soldiers crucified Jesus, they took his clothes, dividing them into four shares, one for each of them, with the undergarment remaining. This garment was seamless, woven in one piece from top to bottom.*

*24 "Let's not tear it," they said to one another. "Let's decide by lot who will get it."*

*This happened that the scripture might be fulfilled which said,*

>    *"They divided my garments among them*
>       *and cast lots for my clothing."*

*So this is what the soldiers did.*

*25 Near the cross of Jesus stood his mother, his mother's sister, Mary the wife of Clopas, and Mary Magdalene. 26 When Jesus saw his mother there, and the disciple whom he loved standing nearby, he said to his mother, "Dear woman, here is your son," 27 and to the disciple, "Here is your mother." From that time on, this disciple took her into his home.*

*28 Later, knowing that all was now completed, and so that the Scripture would be fulfilled, Jesus said, "I am thirsty." 29 A jar of wine vinegar was there, so they soaked a sponge in it, put the sponge on a stalk of the hyssop plant, and lifted it to Jesus' lips. 30 When he had received the drink, Jesus said, "It is finished." With that, he bowed his head and gave up his spirit.*

*31 Now it was the day of Preparation, and the next day was to be a special Sabbath. Because the Jews did not want the bodies left on the crosses during the Sabbath, they asked Pilate to have the legs broken and the bodies taken down. 32 The soldiers therefore came and broke the legs of the first man who had been crucified with Jesus, and then those of the other. 33 But when they came to Jesus and found that he was already dead, they did not break his legs. 34 Instead, one of the soldiers pierced Jesus' side with a spear, bringing a sudden flow of blood and water. 35 The man who saw it has given testimony, and his testimony is true. He knows that he tells the truth, and he testifies so that you also may believe. 36 These things happened so that the scripture would be fulfilled: "Not one of his bones will be broken," 37 and, as another scripture says, "They will look on the one they have pierced."*

*38 Later, Joseph of Arimathea asked Pilate for the body of Jesus. Now Joseph was a disciple of Jesus, but secretly because he feared the Jews. With Pilate's permission, he came and took the body away. 39 He was accompanied by Nicodemus, the man who earlier had visited Jesus at night. Nicodemus brought a mixture of myrrh and aloes, about seventy-five pounds. 40 Taking Jesus' body, the two of them wrapped it, with the spices, in strips of linen. This was in accordance with Jewish burial customs. 41 At the place where Jesus was crucified, there was a garden, and in the garden a new tomb, in which no one had ever been laid. 42 Because it was the Jewish day of Preparation and since the tomb was nearby, they laid Jesus there.*

Christ's faithful forerunner called Him the One whose sandal thongs "I am not worthy to untie" (John 1:27). When our Lord actually appeared at the Jordan, John exclaimed, "Look, the Lamb of God, who takes away the sin of the world!" (1:29). That was then. And now, three years later, it was happening. All that the prophets had foretold in minute detail was being played out, detail by detail. Jesus was sacrificing His life to atone for mankind's sin. Our text bids us look with deepest reverence upon that heaven-sent Lamb of God. We look, first, at . . .

## The Brutal Crucifixion (19:16-18)

As was customary with those condemned to this barbaric death, the soldiers placed upon the shoulders of Jesus the crosspiece to which His hands would be nailed. He was led along the "via dolorosa" to a site outside the city called "the place of the Skull" (19:17).[1] John does not wish to bring needless pain to those who love Jesus. He therefore spares us any graphic description of the cruel torture that was a Roman crucifixion. "Here they crucified him," he says simply (19:18).[2]

In front of curious onlookers, the horizontal piece was fastened to a vertical stake, and the Lord's hands and feet were nailed to the resulting cross so that His feet were off the ground. His body straddled a horn-like projection which bore some of the weight of his frame and prevented the flesh tearing loose from the nails. Of all means of execution, this was the most cruel. Pilate added to the shame by centering Jesus between two known criminals (19:18).

Second, we notice above Jesus' head . . .

## The Kingly Inscription (19:19-22)

Criminals on their way to crucifixion were preceded by someone bearing an official inscription noting the nature of the crime. This notice would then be affixed to the cross above the victim's head where all could see it. It is not hard to imagine Pilate's thoughts as he pondered the wording he would place over Jesus.

*Here's my opportunity to insult those hypocrites who forced my hand. I'll show the world what these despicable Jews do to their king.* And so he ordered written, JESUS OF NAZARETH, THE KING OF THE JEWS (19:19). The statement may have been done in spite. But it proclaimed truth—in three principal world languages: Aramaic, Latin and Greek (19:20).[3] Our Lord, crucified like a common criminal, had been proclaimed

King! The cross, an instrument of inhumane torture, became a throne of glory.

Pilate's inscription aroused the indignation of the chief priests. The One they had condemned to death was being touted as Messianic King of the Jews. And had they not declared only a brief time before, "We have no king but Caesar!"? So they sought to persuade Pilate to alter his inscription (19:21). But this time Pilate found his backbone, even if it was on a relatively unimportant matter.

"What I have written, I have written," he responded curtly (19:22).

John next directs our attention to . . .

## *The Gambling Soldiers (19:23-24)*

By Roman practice, the clothes of an executed man were the legal property of his executioners. The four soldiers comprising the military unit that crucified Jesus publicly divided up His personal attire.[4] But what about His seamless tunic? To tear it would render it valueless. So they elected to gamble for the tunic (19:24).

John, ever quick to observe the fulfillment of Old Testament prophecies,[5] remembers a verse from a Messianic Psalm: "They divide my garments among them and cast lots for my clothing" (Psalm 22:18). Unwittingly, the soldiers had brought to pass an Old Testament prediction. And John, for his part, wants his readers to know that Jesus is, indeed, the true Messianic King of Israel. John may have had another purpose in drawing attention to the seamless tunic. The garments of the Levitical priests were likewise woven and seamless (Exodus 28:39; 39:27). Jesus would be the great High Priest of the heavenly sanctuary.[6]

But John hurries over those details in order to direct our attention to another group of people at the cross. We marvel at . . .

## *The Loving Concern (19:25-27)*

Even amid His intense suffering, our Lord was concerned for the future well-being of His mother. In a society with little esteem for women, Jesus' pure love and respect was notable. Many women followed Him—and ministered to His material needs. They had come now to Jerusalem and were watching His suffering from a distance.[7] Four women—Jesus' mother; her sister,[8] another Mary, the wife of Clopas;[9] and Mary of Magdala[10]—were evidently closer. They were near enough to hear what Jesus said (19:25). John stood with them.[11]

Jesus may have felt His brothers were still too unsympathetic to be entrusted with their mother's care. He cast a loving gaze upon His mother Mary and said,[12] "Dear woman, here [turning His eyes to John] is your son" (19:26). And then, "Here [turning His eyes back to Mary] is your mother." John understood his Lord's intent. From that time until Mary's death (19:27), John took her into his home and provided for her.

Fifth, John describes Jesus' voluntary surrender of His life:

## The Finished Work (19:28-30)

As Jesus was about to be crucified, someone offered Him a sedative composed of wine mixed with myrrh. This would have dulled Jesus' senses and relieved, to an extent, His pain. Jesus, however, having resolved to die with an unclouded mind, had refused the drink (Mark 15:23). Now, approaching the end, His throat parched from hours of physical torture, He begged for something to quench His thirst. Was His request born, as well, from a purposeful desire to fulfill Messianic Scripture? Once again, John seems to imply that such was the case (John 19:28). Nearby was some sour wine, put there for the soldiers' use. Someone accommodatingly soaked a sponge in the liquid and, by means of a hyssop stalk,[13] lifted it to Jesus' lips (19:29). Did John think of the use of hyssop to sprinkle the blood of the sacrificed lamb in the Old Testament Passover rite (see Exodus 12:21-22)?

Having fulfilled the Scriptures, the Savior announced the glorious finale—"It is finished"—and with bowed head, died (John 19:30). "It is finished—*Tetelestai*."[14] How much that single word encompasses! The Old Testament prophecies concerning Jesus' death were now fulfilled. The Levitical ceremonies that typified His atoning sacrifice found at last their antitype. The Father's purpose for the Son's incarnation was accomplished. The work of redemption was completed. Eternal salvation was finally and freely available to all who believe. We can now restfully trust in "the finished work of Christ." We can now joyfully join in song with thousands upon thousands of heaven's angels: "Worthy is the Lamb, who was slain, to receive power and wealth and wisdom and strength and honor and glory and praise!" (Revelation 5:12).

But now two other Old Testament Scriptures are about to be fulfilled, as we contemplate . . .

### *The Pierced Side (19:31-37)*

It was getting late on Friday afternoon. In Jewish homes preparations were underway for the celebration of the Sabbath. Mosaic law specified that the body of an executed person not remain hanging overnight (Deuteronomy 21:22ff). Since the upcoming Sabbath marked the Passover, it was doubly important to hasten the deaths and burials of the three crucified men. To accomplish this, the Jewish leaders asked Pilate to order his soldiers to break the legs of the three victims (19:31).[15] It was Roman custom to leave the bodies of crucified criminals on their crosses as a warning to others. But in this case Pilate agreed to the Jews' request. But the soldiers discovered that Jesus was already dead, making it unnecessary to break His legs (19:32-33).

One soldier, however, took no chances. As if to say, "Just in case, here is a coup de grace to finish You!" he speared Jesus' side. The wound produced "a sudden flow of blood and water" (19:34). What are we to make of this amazing phenomenon? There are almost as many interpretations of it as there are Bible expositors![16] For John the poured-out blood certainly spoke of the *forgiveness* of sins. And the water signified *new life* made possible through our union with Christ. Surely we are justified in praying with Augustus M. Toplady,

> Let the water and the blood,
> From Thy riven side which flowed,
> Be of sin the double cure;
> Save from wrath and make me pure.[17]

However we interpret John's statement, the phenomenon made a powerful impression on him. He emphasizes in a most solemn manner that what he has just told us is the testimony of a reliable witness (himself). Moreover, his testimony should result in his readers' believing on Jesus (19:35). The water and the blood are the clearest evidence of Christ's humanity, counter to those who denied His human reality.[18] And once again, he connects what the soldiers did to the Old Testament Scriptures: "Not one of his bones will be broken";[19] and "They will look on the one they have pierced" (John 19:36-37).[20]

Godet graphically captures John's thoughts as he saw these two prophecies fulfilled:

> To understand what John felt at the moment which he here recalls, we must suppose a believing Jew, familiar with the Old Testament, seeing the soldiers approach who are to break the legs of the three victims. He asks himself anxiously what is to be done to the body of the Messiah, which is still more sacred than the Paschal lamb. And lo! simultaneously and in the most unexpected manner this body is rescued from the brutal operation which threatened it, and receives the spear-thrust, thereby realizing the spectacle which repentant Israel is one day to behold! After such signs, with what feelings will this man leave the cross? Will not what he has *seen* strengthen his faith, and soon also that of the whole Church? Such is the meaning of John.[21]

## The Garden Grave (19:38-42)

The rapid approach of the Sabbath dictated that Jesus' body be buried immediately. It so happened that a man of influence, Joseph from Arimathea, was apparently present at the crucifixion. Until then a secret disciple, Joseph nevertheless had disagreed with the Sanhedrin's decision to put Jesus to death (Luke 23:51). Securing Pilate's permission, Joseph removed Jesus' body from the cross (John 19:38). He had high level help in the person of Nicodemus (19:39), whose earlier caution seems to have metamorphosed into full discipleship. Nicodemus' considerable wealth enabled him to prepare an expensive mixture of myrrh[22] and aloes,[23] about seventy-five pounds in weight. This the two men spread on the linen strips with which they wrapped Jesus' body (19:40). Fortuitously, near Golgotha Joseph recently had prepared a tomb for his personal use (Matthew 27:60). This the two men pressed into immediate service. Tenderly, lovingly, they laid the body of Jesus to rest in the yet unused garden grave (Luke 23:53).

## *Conclusion*

Through the eyes of a faithful witness, we have beheld what took place at Golgotha on the fourteenth of Nisan. Soul-stirring events they were. But we must also reflect on their significance. Consider, first, therefore, what *attributes of God* are portrayed at Calvary. There we see both God's *justice* and His *mercy*. In the words of Annie Cousin,

> Jehovah lifted up His rod;
>    O Christ, it fell on Thee.
> Thou wert fierce smitten of Thy God;
>    There's not one stroke for me![24]

"Fierce smitten of Thy God." A holy God pours out His just wrath against sinners upon His own dear Son. God's justice is fully satisfied. "Now there's no rod for me." At Calvary God's mercy on sinners is clearly demonstrated. And thus, "If we confess our sins, he is faithful and just and will forgive us our sins and purify us from all unrighteousness" (1 John 1:9). God's justice and mercy have been marvelously joined together at the cross.

Consider, second, what *saving work* was *accomplished* at Calvary. There, through the shedding of the Savior's blood, He made nothing less than *full* atonement for sin. The Apostle Peter writes, "[Christ] himself bore our sins in his body on the tree" (1 Peter 2:24). Now, therefore, on the basis of that atonement, the believing sinner is "justified freely by [God's] grace" (Romans 3:24). The sinner is fully forgiven and treated as though he or she had never sinned! The Passover lamb's sprinkled blood on the doorframe protected the obedient Israelite household from the angel of death (Exodus 12:13, 22). So the shed blood of the crucified Christ saves from eternal death all who believe on Him. We can now sing with Edward Mote:

> My hope is built on nothing less
> Than Jesus' blood and righteousness;
> I dare not trust the sweetest frame
> But wholly lean on Jesus' name.[25]

Meditate, third, on the *sanctifying truth* that is *implied* in Calvary. When we interpret the cross as God does, there "our old self was crucified with [Christ]" (Romans 6:6). That being true, we are called upon to "count [ourselves] dead to sin but alive to God in Christ Jesus" (Romans 6:11). And reckoning this to be true, we are exhorted, "Therefore do not let sin reign in your mortal body so that you obey its evil desires. Do not offer the parts of your body to sin, as instruments of wickedness, but rather offer yourselves to God" (Romans 6:12-13).

God's holy and merciful character displayed. Full atonement for sin accomplished. The believer's co-crucifixion with Christ implied. All of this is the meaning of the justifying, sanctifying event that our text has set before us. With Paul let us affirm, "May I never boast except in the cross of our Lord Jesus Christ, through which the world has been crucified to me, and I to the world" (Galatians 6:14).

> There is a green hill far away,
>> Without a city wall,
> Where the dear Lord was crucified,
>> Who died to save us all.

> We may not know, we cannot tell
>> What pains He had to bear;
> But we believe it was for us
>> He hung and suffered there.

> He died that we might be forgiven,
>> He died to make us good,
> That we might go at last to heaven,
>> Saved by His precious blood.

> There was no other good enough
>> To pay the price of sin;
> He only could unlock the gate
>> Of heaven, and let us in.[26]

### Endnotes

1. So named, likely, because of the shape of the topography. Visitors to the traditional site of the crucifixion are still able to see what seems to resemble a skull.
2. A. Reville describes crucifixion this way: "It represented the acme of the torturer's art; atrocious physical sufferings, length of torment, ignominy, the effect on the crowd gath-

ered to witness the long agony of the crucified. Nothing could be more horrible than the sight of this living body, breathing, seeing, hearing, still able to feel, and yet reduced to the state of a corpse by forced immobility and absolute helplessness. We cannot even say that the crucified person writhed in agony, for it was impossible for him to move. Stripped of his clothing, unable even to brush away the flies which fell upon his wounded flesh, already lacerated by the preliminary scourging, exposed to the insults and curses of people who can always find some sickening pleasure in the sight of the tortures of others, a feeling which is increased and not diminished by the sight of pain—the cross represented miserable humanity reduced to the last degree of impotence, suffering, degradation." Quoted by Leon Morris, *The Gospel According to John* (Grand Rapids, MI: Eerdmans, 1971), 805.

3. Aramaic, the vernacular of the Palestinian Jews; Latin, the official language of the Roman conquerors and the language of government; Greek, the universally understood language of trade and commerce.

4. F.F. Bruce, *The Gospel of John* (Grand Rapids, MI: Eerdmans, 1983), 369, posits *two* main garments worn by Jesus: the outer garment, which he suggests the soldiers possibly divided along the seams, and the inner garment for which they gambled. William Barclay, *The Gospel of John*, vol. II (Philadelphia: The Westminster Press, 1975), 253, on the other hand, explains: "Every Jew wore five articles of apparel—his shoes, his turban, his girdle, his tunic, and his outer robe. There were four soldiers, and there were five articles. They diced for them, each had his pick and the inner tunic was left . . . and so they diced again to see who would possess it."

5. John cites four such prophecies in his crucifixion account: 19:24, 28, 36 and 37.

6. See this theme set forth in the letter to the Hebrews.

7. See Matthew 27:55; Mark 15:40; Luke 23:49.

8. Perhaps this is Salome, mentioned in Mark 15:40 and called in Matthew 27:56 "the mother of Zebedee's sons."

9. Likely Mary the mother of James the younger and of Joseph (Mark 15:40). According to a second-century Palestinian writer, Clopas (Cleophas) was the brother of Joseph the carpenter and father of Simeon, who became leader of the Jerusalem church after the stoning of James the Just.

10. The woman out of whom Jesus cast seven demons (Mark 16:9).

11. It is most certainly John, who is described here as "the disciple whom [Jesus] loved."

12. The Gospels record seven words spoken from the cross:

    1) "Father, forgive them, for they do not know what they are doing" (Luke 23:34).

    2) "I tell you the truth, today you will be with me in paradise" (Luke 23:43).

    3) "Dear woman, here is your son. . . . Here is your mother" (John 19:26-27).

    4) "My God, my God, why have you forsaken me?" (Matthew 27:46; Mark 15:34).

    5) "I am thirsty" (John 19:28).

    6) "It is finished" (John 19:30).

    7) "Father, into your hands I commit my spirit" (Luke 23:46).

13. Described in Merrill C. Tenney, ed., *The Zondervan Pictorial Bible Dictionary* (Grand Rapids, MI: Zondervan, 1967), 664, as "a sorghum cane reaching a height of over six feet." In the Old Testament it was "the Egyptian marjoram, a member of the mint family."

14. The Greek verb, *tetelestai*, is in the perfect tense, signifying a completed event which has ongoing results. The thought is that the work of redemption is forever complete.

15. F. Godet, *Commentary on the Gospel of St. John*, vol. III (Edinburgh: T. & T. Clarke, 1881), 273, suggests that the breaking of the legs would result in gangrene, making death

inevitable. This is not as satisfactory an explanation as Bruce's, 375, in which he suggests that death by asphyxiation would be the result.

16. From a purely *natural* viewpoint, B.F. Westcott, *Commentary on the Gospel According to St. John* (London: John Murray, Albemarle Street, 1967), 279, quotes one writer as attributing the immediate cause of Jesus' death to a rupture of the heart, which was followed by a large effusion of blood into the pericardium. This blood rapidly separated into its more solid and liquid parts which flowed out in a mingled stream when the spear pierced Jesus' side. Another interpreter maintains that the flow of blood and water lies beyond the laws of common physiology and is *miraculously* related to the exceptional nature of the body which sin had never tainted and which was destined to immediate resurrection. See Godet, *Commentay on the Gospel of St. John,* 274. Other commentators, like C.K. Barrett, *The Gospel According to St. John* (London: S.P.C.K., 1955), 463, see John's statement as entirely *figurative,* symbolizing, for example, "those living streams by which men are quickened and the church lives."

17. "Rock of Ages," *The Methodist Hymnal* (New York: The Methodist Publishing House, 1939), # 204, stanza 1.

18. These were the so-called "Docetists" (from the Greek *dokei,* "to seem"; "to appear," referring to Jesus' physical body).

19. See Exodus 12:46 and Numbers 9:12, referring to the Passover lamb; and the Messianic Psalm 34:20.

20. The quotation is from Zechariah 12:10 and is descriptive of repentant Israel.

21. Godet, *Commentary on the Gospel of St. John,* 279.

22. An odoriferous gum.

23. A scented wood which, when pounded together with the myrrh, became a mixture which was spread over the strips of linen with which the body was wrapped.

24. Annie R. Cousin, "O Christ, What Burdens Bowed Thy Head!" *Hymns* (Chicago: InterVarsity Press, n.d.), # 126, stanza 3.

25. Eduard Mote, "My Hope Is Built on Nothing Less," *Hymns of the Christian Life* (Camp Hill, PA: Christian Publications, Inc., 1978), # 306, stanza 1.

26. Cecil F.H. Alexander, "There Is a Green Hill," ibid., # 89.

# Part XI

## *Questions for Reflection or Discussion*

1. In what sense are believers the gift of the Father to the Son?

2. What does First Peter 2:18-25 tell us we may learn from observing the trial of Jesus? Does Paul write anything similar in his letters?

3. How do you think Peter's denial of his Lord affected his future ministry? Discuss the principle of success through failure.

4. How would you characterize Pilate, the Roman governor?

5. How do Peter and Paul interpret the historical event of the crucifixion of Christ?

*Part XII*


# The Triumph of the Son

John 20-21

# 35

# A Resurrection Confirmed

John 20:1-31

*Early on the first day of the week, while it was still dark, Mary Magdalene went to the tomb and saw that the stone had been removed from the entrance. 2 So she came running to Simon Peter and the other disciple, the one Jesus loved, and said, "They have taken the Lord out of the tomb, and we don't know where they have put him!"*

*3 So Peter and the other disciple started for the tomb. Both were running, but the other disciple outran Peter and reached the tomb first. 5 He bent over and looked in at the strips of linen lying there but did not go in. 6 Then Simon Peter, who was behind him, arrived and went into the tomb. He saw the strips of linen lying there, 7 as well as the burial cloth that had been around Jesus' head. The cloth was folded up by itself, separate from the linen. 8 Finally the other disciple, who had reached the tomb first, also went inside. He saw and believed. 9 (They still did not understand from Scripture that Jesus had to rise from the dead.)*

*10 Then the disciples went back to their homes, 11 but Mary stood outside the tomb crying. As she wept, she bent over to look into the tomb 12 and saw two angels in white, seated where Jesus' body had been, one at the head and the other at the foot.*

*13 They asked her, "Woman, why are you crying?"*

*"They have taken my Lord away," she said, "and I don't know where they have put him." 14 At this, she turned around and saw Jesus standing there, but she did not realize that it was Jesus.*

15 "Woman," he said, "why are you crying? Who is it you are looking for?"

Thinking he was the gardener, she said, "Sir, if you have carried him away, tell me where you have put him, and I will get him."

16 Jesus said to her, "Mary."

She turned toward him and cried out in Aramaic, "Rabboni!" (which means Teacher).

17 Jesus said, "Do not hold on to me, for I have not yet returned to the Father. Go instead to my brothers and tell them, 'I am returning to my Father and your Father, to my God and your God.' "

18 Mary Magdalene went to the disciples with the news: "I have seen the Lord!" And she told them that he had said these things to her.

19 On the evening of that first day of the week, when the disciples were together, with the doors locked for fear of the Jews, Jesus came and stood among them and said, "Peace be with you!" 20 After he said this, he showed them his hands and side. The disciples were overjoyed when they saw the Lord.

21 Again Jesus said, "Peace be with you! As the Father has sent me, I am sending you." 22 And with that he breathed on them and said, "Receive the Holy Spirit. 23 If you forgive anyone his sins, they are forgiven; if you do not forgive them, they are not forgiven."

24 Now Thomas (called Didymus), one of the Twelve, was not with the disciples when Jesus came. 25 So the other disciples told him, "We have seen the Lord!"

But he said to them, "Unless I see the nail marks in his hands and put my finger where the nails were, and put my hand into his side, I will not believe it."

26 A week later his disciples were in the house again, and Thomas was with them. Though the doors were locked, Jesus came and stood among them and said, "Peace be with you!" 27 Then he said to Thomas, "Put your finger here; see my hands. Reach out your hand and put it into my side. Stop doubting and believe."

28 Thomas said to him, "My Lord and my God!"

29 Then Jesus told him, "Because you have seen me, you have believed; blessed are those who have not seen and yet have believed."

30 Jesus did many other miraculous signs in the presence of his disciples, which are not recorded in this book. 31 But these are written that you may believe that Jesus is the Christ, the Son of God, and that by believing you may have life in his name.

Fifty days after he had witnessed an empty garden tomb, the Apostle Peter stood before an amazed crowd in Jerusalem. Addressing the several thousand gathered people, he declared:

> Men of Israel, listen to this: Jesus of Nazareth was a man accredited by God to you by miracles, wonders and signs, which God did among you through him, as you yourselves know. This man was handed over to you by God's set purpose and foreknowledge; and you, with the help of wicked men, put him to death by nailing him to the cross. *But God raised him from the dead, freeing him from the agony of death, because it was impossible for death to keep its hold on him.* (Acts 2:22-24, emphasis added)

Peter had seen the resurrected Jesus. And on the day the Spirit came in power, he boldly proclaimed Christianity's central truth: Jesus Christ rose from the dead! It is the historical fact that believers the world over affirm every Easter morning: "Christ is risen! He is risen indeed!"

Hallelujah! This thrilling story of our Lord's resurrection from the dead is the focus of our present text.

## *The Abandoned Tomb (20:1-9)*

Very early Sunday morning Mary Magdalene approached the tomb where the Lord she deeply loved had been laid to rest. Mary owed her very life to Jesus (Luke 8:2). She was coming, with a few other Galilean women, to add to the spices that embalmed Jesus' body. The women wondered how they could gain entrance to the sealed tomb (Mark 16:2). Approaching closer, she could see that the stone sealing the entrance had already been removed. And as she reached the tomb, she was distressed to discover it empty (John 20:1).

*Whatever has happened to the body?* Mary wondered. *I must tell His disciples! They will know what to do.* By now frantic, Mary Magdalene ran to inform Peter and John (20:2).

When Peter and John heard Mary Magdalene's account, they had to see for themselves. There was no time to lose! John, the younger of the two men, outran Peter, but, unlike Peter, he could not immediately bring himself to enter. What they discovered were the linen strips lying there just as though a body had passed through them, and a head cloth folded neatly by itself.

In an instant, what all this meant flashed through John's mind. Neither he nor Peter had yet been taught to expect the resurrection on the basis of their Scriptures. But his eyes told him that Jesus must be alive (20:3-9).[1] Peter had yet to be fully assured.

## *The Convincing Appearances (20:10-29)*

The *first appearance* of Jesus following His resurrection was to Mary Magdalene. How like Him to honor one so unimportant in the eyes of the world! After Peter and John left the scene, she had stayed behind. In her grief, she looked again into the tomb and saw two angels in white.[2] They asked the reason for her grief (20:13).

"They have taken my Lord away," Mary responded, "and I don't know where they have put him" (20:13).

Just then, sensing movement behind her,[3] she turned around and saw Jesus, whom she failed to recognize (20:14). There must have been something different about His resurrected body.[4] Jesus also asked Mary why she was crying. "Who is it you are looking for?" He inquired (20:15). Mary assumed this Man must be the gardener. If He had transferred Jesus' body (again she faced the tomb) to some other location, would He please tell her where—"and I will get him" (20:15). That she could not possibly carry the body seems not to have occurred to this grief-stricken woman!

No matter. For just then the "Gardener" spoke her name, and instantly she recognized the voice of her Lord.[5] Turning again to Him, she exclaimed "Teacher!" (see 20:16) and rushed to clasp His feet. Mary had always known Jesus as her Teacher. Probably she felt that this old relationship must never, never be lost again. But in truth Jesus would now be more to her than Teacher. With His ascension to His Father, there would be a whole new relationship between Him and all the disciples. No longer would He be the rabbi who walked the roads of Galilee with them. He would now be the *glorified, exalted* Lord who would remain with them forever.[6] Furthermore, by His Spirit He would bring them into a whole new relationship with God. They would receive the Spirit of sonship (Romans 8:15). Just as He called God "Father," they too would call Him "Father."[7] So Mary must not continue to hold to Him. Her immediate responsibility was to inform His "brothers"[8] of this new relationship (John 20:17). This she did, excitedly reporting, "I have seen the Lord!" (20:18).

Jesus' *second* post-resurrection *appearance* recorded by John[9] was on that same evening to His disciples. All of them (excluding Thomas and, of course, Judas Iscariot), were together behind locked doors. It was a precautionary measure lest the Jewish authorities attempt to round up Jesus' followers. Suddenly Jesus stood there among them!

First, lifting His hands, He *blessed* them with His "Peace be with you!" (20:19).[10] His identity could not be in doubt. His hands bore the nail wounds, His side the spear entry (20:20). One is constrained to ask what mysterious power is this that enables His resurrection body to be "at once sufficiently corporeal to show his wounds, yet sufficiently immaterial to pass through close doors."[11] Needless to say, the disciples were overjoyed to see and recognize their risen Lord.

Next, Jesus *commissioned* His disciples. "As the Father has sent me, I am sending you" (20:21). Jesus was "sent" by the Father.[12] His mission was to reveal in His sinless character, His words and His deeds the true nature of God the Father. He would be entirely dependent upon and obedient to His Father. He would minister entirely in the power of the Spirit of God resting upon Him. As Jesus stood before His disciples, He "sent" them (and in them His Church). Their relationship to Him would be like His relationship to the Father. As He revealed the nature of God, so they would reveal the Person and do the work of Jesus. As He was dependent upon and obedient to the Father, so they would depend on and obey Jesus by character, word and deed. As He ministered in the power of the Spirit, so they would minister in that same power.

Third, He *quickened* them. "He breathed on them and said, 'Receive the Holy Spirit' " (20:22). In the first creation, God breathed physical life into humanity (Genesis 2:7). So the Lord breathed into His disciples the regenerating life of the Spirit. Thus He united them savingly to Himself.

And then, fourth, He *conferred authority* upon them. "If you forgive anyone his sins, they are forgiven; if you do not forgive them, they are not forgiven" (John 20:23). Morris correctly explains Jesus' words as follows:

> The meaning of this is that the Spirit-filled church can pronounce with authority that the sins of such-and-such men have been forgiven or have been retained. If the church is really acting under the leadership of the Spirit it will be found that her pronouncements on this matter do but reveal what has already been determined in heaven.[13]

The *third appearance* of Jesus one week later was specifically for Thomas, who had been absent before (20:24). Thomas insisted on the same empirical proof the other disciples had received (20:25). Appearing again as He had on the previous Lord's day, Jesus offered to this doubting disciple the evidence which he needed in order to believe (20:26-27). "Seeing is believing," and Thomas was immediately convinced. My Lord and my God!" (20:28). It is the grand Christological pronouncement that John intended for his Gospel to produce.

Then, without any intention of reproaching Thomas, Jesus confirmed the condition of future believers: "Blessed are those who have not seen and yet have believed" (20:29). They are of whom Peter writes:

> Though you have not seen him, you love him; and even though you do not see him now, you believe in him and are filled with an inexpressible and glorious joy, for you are receiving the goal of your faith, the salvation of your souls. (1 Peter 1:8-9)

## The Unrecorded Signs (20:30-31)

In a most appropriate conclusion, John defines his ultimate purpose in writing this Gospel. He did not intend to record all the miraculous signs which Jesus had performed (20:30).[14] Rather he has presented us with carefully selected miracles. These not only validate the Lord's claims to deity, but they portray profound spiritual truth concerning His person and work. John's deep desire is that believers will find their faith strengthened and unbelievers come to faith. As these latter believe in Jesus Christ, the Son of

God, they will receive the gift of eternal life (20:31).[15] Like the Apostle Paul, John is convinced that "faith comes from hearing the message, and the message is heard through the word of Christ" (Romans 10:17).

## *Conclusion*

The excommunicated Roman Catholic theologian Hans Kung was asked if a camera could have recorded the resurrection of Jesus Christ. He replied that it could not have, for there was nothing visible to record. For Kung, the resurrection of Jesus Christ did not happen. The terminology was a symbolic way for early Christians to express their faith in Jesus.

In contrast to Kung, evangelicals believe the accounts of the resurrection are to be taken literally. A photographer that first Easter morning could have snapped the most important pictures of his career!

Our Christian faith is rooted in a historical event. That is an important statement. Paul writes, "If Christ has not been raised, our preaching is useless and so is [our] faith" (1 Corinthians 15:14). As we verbally confess "Jesus is Lord" and believe in our hearts that God raised Jesus from the dead we are saved (Romans 10:9). The tomb was indeed empty. Mary Magdalene, John, Peter, Thomas and a host of others *saw* the risen Jesus. In fact, He appeared to more than 500 believers at the same time (1 Corinthians 15:6). No event in history is better attested! We are compelled to say with Thomas, "My Lord and my God!" (John 20:28).

For seekers after the deeper life, Jesus' appearance to His disciples that first Sunday evening is of particular interest. John says our Lord "breathed"[16] on them and said, "Receive the Holy Spirit" (20:22). Was this simply in anticipation of the Day of Pentecost? Or was there a real impartation of the Spirit at that moment different from the Pentecostal outpouring? The evidence of the text points to the latter. The Greek imperative translated "receive" *(labete)* is in the aorist tense. It implies an immediate and actual impartation of the Spirit to the disciples at that very time. Interpreting the verse, Westcott writes:

> The presence of this new life of humanity in the disciples communicated to them by Christ was the necessary condition for the descent of the Holy Spirit on the day of Pentecost. The Spirit

which the Lord imparted to them was His Spirit, or as it may be
expressed, the Holy Spirit as dwelling in Him. By this he first
quickened them, and then sent them, according to his promise,
the Paraclete to be with them, and to supply all power for the exercise of their different functions. *The relation of the Paschal to
the Pentecostal gift is therefore the relation of quickening to en-
dowing.* (italics added)[17]

In the regenerating work of the Holy Spirit, He savingly unites believers
to Christ in "new birth." And there is a second anointing of the Spirit in
which He clothes believers with power from on high (Luke 24:49). I firmly
believe that. We may safely say that every genuine believer has dwelling in
him or her the Holy Spirit.[18] But there is a *filling* of (some say *baptism* with)
the Spirit which every believer has not necessarily experienced. But God
wills and intends it for everyone.[19] Have you, reader, been filled with the
Spirit? A.W. Tozer used to observe you *can* be filled, and you will know
*when* you are filled, and it will happen *suddenly.* May this be both your
heart's desire and your experience.

R. Kelso Carter's prayer is appropriate for the Church in these days:

Breathe upon us, Lord, from heaven,
    Fill us with the Holy Ghost;
Promise of the Father given,
    Send us now a Pentecost.

While the Spirit hovers near us,
    Open all our hearts we pray;
To Thine image, Lord, restore us;
    Witness in our souls today.

Lift us Lord, oh, lift us higher,
    From the carnal mind set free;
Fill us with refining fire;
    Give us perfect liberty.[20]

## Endnotes

1. Originally, John's faith was grounded simply in what he had seen at the tomb. By the time John wrote his Gospel, the Church's faith in the resurrection was supported by the conviction that it had been foretold in the Old Testament.
2. Matthew speaks of "an angel of the Lord" (28:2). Mark reports "a young man dressed in a white robe" (16:5). Luke writes of "two men in clothes that gleamed like lightning" (24:4).
3. Or perhaps, as some have suggested, the angels made some motion toward Jesus.
4. According to Luke 24:13ff, the two travelers on the road to Emmaus "were kept from recognizing him" until the moment when He broke bread in their home.
5. We are reminded of John 10:3, 27. The Good Shepherd calls His own sheep by name and they recognize His voice.
6. There are some, like C.E. Stuart, cited in F.F. Bruce, *The Gospel of John* (Grand Rapids, MI: Eerdmans, 1983), 389, who interpret 20:17 quite differently. They suggest that Jesus had to enter the heavenly Holy of Holies in order to complete the antitype of the Day of Atonement, initiated by His sacrifice on the cross. Sometime between 20:17 and 20:19 He is said to have ascended to the Father for this purpose.
7. Cf. Romans 8:15ff.
8. "Brothers" because they are sons of the same Father.
9. Luke 24:13ff records a previous appearing.
10. The Greek *eirene* is a translation of the Hebrew *shalom,* a conventional greeting, meaning no more than, "May all be well with you." But it had acquired a fuller sense in Christian usage. The peace that Christ gives is genuine heart serenity, independent of outward circumstances.
11. C.K. Barrett, *The Gospel According to St. John* (London: S.P.C.K., 1955), 472. This may very well be the nature of the "spiritual body" of which Paul speaks in First Corinthians 15:44.
12. See, for example 3:17, 34; 5:36, 38; 6:29, 57; 7:29; 8:42, together with at least twenty-five other passages.
13. Leon Morris, *The Gospel According to John* (Grand Rapids, MI: Eerdmans, 1971), 849. With this agrees Bruce, 392, who explains that the church's role is declaratory, but it is God who effectively remits or retains sins. B.F. Westcott, *Commentary on the Gospel According to St. John* (London: John Murray, Albemarle Street, 1967), 296, affirms that the exercise of this power to remit or retain sins must be placed in the closest connection with the faculty of spiritual discernment, a gift of the Holy Spirit.
14. In 21:25, John will hyperbolically allege that if all that Jesus did had been recorded, "the whole world would not have room for the books that would be written."
15. Some manuscripts of 20:31 would call for the translation, "But these are written that you may *continue to believe* that Jesus is the Christ." Others would indicate, "These are written that you may *come to the point of believing.*" As I observed in the Introduction, it is likely that John had both the strengthening of believers and the converting of unbelievers in mind when he set out to write his Gospel.
16. It is significant that in both Old and New Testaments, the word for breath, wind and spirit is the same. So the hymn writer correctly prayed, "Breathe on me, breath [Spirit] of God."
17. Westcott, *Commentary on the Gospel According to St. John,* 295. With this interpretation of the text Bruce, 391-392, agrees. He writes, "What John records is no mere anticipation of Pentecost, but a real impartation of the Spirit for the purpose specified." F. Godet, *Commentary on the Gospel of St. John,* vol. III (Edinburgh: T. & T. Clarke, 1881), 317, writes

in a similar vein, as does A.B. Simpson, *The Holy Spirit: Power from on High,* ed. Keith M. Bailey (Camp Hill, PA: Christian Publications, Inc., 1994), 316 and 385.

18. An experience corresponding to that of the disciples in John 20:22 and confirmed by Romans 8:9.

19. Corresponding to the Pentecostal gift of the Spirit, recorded in Acts 2. Although it is usually said that Acts 2 records the birth of the New Testament Church, might it not be thought that in reality the Church was born on the evening when Christ said to His disciples, "Receive the Holy Spirit"? If that be so, then Acts 2 records the event in which the gathered "Church" was filled with the Holy Spirit, an experience that God intended to be perpetuated throughout the ongoing history of the Church in the lives of believers.

20. Russell K. Carter, "Breathe Upon Us," *Hymns of the Christian Life* (Camp Hill, PA: Christian Publications, Inc., 1978), # 250.

# 36

# A Ministry Conferred

John 21:1-25[1]

*Afterward Jesus appeared again to his disciples, by the Sea of Tiberias. It happened this way: 2 Simon Peter, Thomas (called Didymus), Nathanael from Cana in Galilee, the sons of Zebedee, and two other disciples were together. 3 "I'm going out to fish," Simon Peter told them, and they said, "We'll go with you." So they went out and got into the boat, but that night they caught nothing.*

*4 Early in the morning, Jesus stood on the shore, but the disciples did not realize that it was Jesus.*

*5 He called out to them, "Friends, haven't you any fish?"*

*"No," they answered.*

*6 He said, "Throw your net on the right side of the boat and you will find some." When they did, they were unable to haul the net in because of the large number of fish.*

*7 Then the disciple whom Jesus loved said to Peter, "It is the Lord!" As soon as Simon Peter heard him say, "It is the Lord," he wrapped his outer garment around him (for he had taken it off) and jumped into the water. 8 The other disciples followed in the boat, towing the net full of fish, for they were not far from shore, about a hundred yards. 9 When they landed, they saw a fire of burning coals there with fish on it, and some bread.*

*10 Jesus said to them, "Bring some of the fish you have just caught."*

*11 Simon Peter climbed aboard and dragged the net ashore. It was full of large fish, 153, but even with so many the net was not torn. 12 Jesus said to them, "Come and have breakfast." None of the disciples dared ask him,*

"Who are you?" They knew it was the Lord. 13 Jesus came, took the bread and gave it to them, and did the same with the fish. 14 This was now the third time Jesus appeared to his disciples after he was raised from the dead.

15 When they had finished eating, Jesus said to Simon Peter, "Simon son of John, do you truly love me more than these?"

"Yes, Lord," he said, "you know that I love you."

Jesus said, "Feed my lambs."

16 Again Jesus said, "Simon son of John, do you truly love me?"

He answered, "Yes, Lord, you know that I love you."

Jesus said, "Take care of my sheep."

17 The third time he said to him, "Simon son of John, do you love me?"

Peter was hurt because Jesus asked him the third time, "Do you love me?" He said, "Lord, you know all things; you know that I love you."

Jesus said, "Feed my sheep. 18 I tell you the truth, when you were younger you dressed yourself and went where you wanted; but when you are old you will stretch out your hands, and someone else will dress you and lead you where you do not want to go." 19 Jesus said this to indicate the kind of death by which Peter would glorify God. Then he said to him, "Follow me!"

20 Peter turned and saw that the disciple whom Jesus loved was following them. (This was the one who had leaned back against Jesus at the supper and had said, "Lord, who is going to betray you?") 21 When Peter saw him, he asked, "Lord, what about him?"

22 Jesus answered, "If I want him to remain alive until I return, what is that to you? You must follow me." 23 Because of this, the rumor spread among the brothers that this disciple would not die. But Jesus did not say that he would not die; he only said, "If I want him to remain alive until I return, what is that to you?"

24 This is the disciple who testifies to these things and who wrote them down. We know that his testimony is true.

25 Jesus did many other things as well. If every one of them were written down, I suppose that even the whole world would not have room for the books that would be written.

Our text records a third appearance of Jesus to His immediate disciples. This time seven of them are present (21:2). It occurred in Galilee where they were awaiting Jesus' arrival.[2]

## *The Disciples' Amazement (21:3-14)*

They had gathered at the Sea of Tiberius (Galilee), the place so familiar to the ex-fishermen among them. The sight of the water, the boats and the drying nets called forth the old fishing instinct in Peter. He proposed that rather than just to sit around, they should find his old boat and spend the night fishing. They all agree. But their fishing expedition proved fruitless. Dawn found them nearing the shore, their nets empty (21:3).

As they approached land, they saw in the misty dawn a figure they did not recognize standing on the shore. He shouted out to them, somewhat teasingly, "Well boys,[3] haven't you any fish?" He knew very well that they had none,[4] for the mysterious person standing on the shore was Jesus. With sheepish disappointment in their voices, the weary fishermen shouted back a curt, "No!" (21:5). But they were about to see a most amazing reversal of their fortune!

Upon hearing their answer, the man on the beach advised them to cast their net on the right side of the boat. Assuming the man was a local who had some expertise in fishing the lake, they complied. The result was utterly astounding: a net so full of fish that they could not bring it on board (21:6)![5] And yet the net was unbroken by the weight of the catch (21:11).

Something about the stranger's demeanor alerted John that their benefactor was Jesus, whom they had been expecting.

"It is the Lord!" he exclaimed to Peter. And Peter, as might be expected,[6] impulsively decided to swim the hundred yards to shore. Making his appearance more presentable,[7] he leaped into the lake (21:7) and apparently beat the boat to the beach. His companions, including John, were content to stay aboard and help bring in the heavy net (21:8).

Upon beaching the boat, they were surprised to see that Jesus was preparing a fish-and-bread breakfast over hot coals (21:9). He invited them to add to it from their own catch (21:10). Under Peter's direction the disciples brought the net ashore. While breakfast cooked, the impressed fishermen tallied the size of their take—153 large fish (21:11)![8]

"Come and have breakfast," Jesus invited (21:12). They approached with awe. As had Mary Magdalene at the tomb, they sensed something different about Jesus' resurrected image. Yet they knew for certain that He was the

Lord (21:12). In an almost sacramental fashion, Jesus served first the bread and then the fish (21:13). And together they ate.

## Peter's Appointment (21:15-19)

The meal was over. The hungry disciples, weary from the night of toil, had eaten their fill. A hushed solemnity fell upon the eight men gathered around the fire's dying embers. Something of immense importance was about to take place. Jesus was about to call Peter to pastor His Church. Ever since Peter denied his Lord, the other disciples had questioned, though not openly, his right to a place of leadership. That cloud of suspicion needed to be lifted. Jesus must reaffirm Peter's position. This, in a gentle yet specific way, the Lord did.

Looking directly at Peter, Jesus asked him, "Simon son of John, do you love e more than *these men* do?"[9] As He put the question to Peter, Jesus gestured toward the other disciples in the circle. All of them well remembered Peter's boastful words, "Even if all fall away on account of you, I never will" (Matthew 26:33). Humbled now, his brash self-confidence gone, Peter no longer compared himself to the others. His reply was a simple, "Yes, Lord, *you* [who alone can read my heart] know that I love you" (John 21:15, emphasis added).[10] The cloud was beginning to lift! An important ministry was being conferred upon the penitent Peter. "Feed my lambs" was Jesus' charge (21:15).

A second time Jesus asked the question: "Simon son of John, do you love me?" (21:16). Once more, Peter made the same response, "Yes, Lord, *you* know that I love you." And again Jesus admonished, "Take care of my sheep" (21:16). By this time Peter was beginning to feel uncomfortable. Might he have remembered that he had denied his Lord *three* times?

A third time Jesus posed the question, "Simon son of John, do you love me?" By now Peter's spirit was grieved. *Doesn't Jesus believe me? Does He really have to extract an expression of love for each of my denials? Ah, yes, I know He must, if I am to feel fully restored.* And so, "Lord," he replied, in effect, "I could not fool You. You know everything there is to know about me. *You* know, even better than I do that I love You." With that confession, Peter's future ministry was confirmed.

"Feed my sheep,"[11] Jesus responded (21:17). The cloud had lifted! Whatever the mistakes of the past, Peter was fully restored! He would pastor Christ's people.[12]

But Peter's appointment would involve more than a pastoral ministry. There would be a darker side to Peter's future. As Jesus and Peter began to walk together on the beach, the Savior outlined that future to Peter. Like his Master, Peter would stretch out his hands upon a cross that he did not desire (21:18).[13] This apostle who once disavowed Jesus would, in the end, glorify God through a martyr's death (21:18-19).

"Follow me!" Jesus said to Peter. How far? All the way to the cross!

### John's Destiny (21:20-24)

Because of his closeness to Peter,[14] the "disciple whom Jesus loved" felt free to follow the two men as they walked and talked together on the shore. Peter turned and saw John coming toward them. He felt great affection for his friend. He was aware of John's more sensitive nature. Full of emotion, Peter asked Jesus, "Will my friend be forced to suffer a fate like mine?" (21:20-21). The Lord replied, "What my plans are for John must not concern you. . . . *If* I want him to remain alive until I return, what is that to you? You must follow me" (21:22, emphasis added). Jesus is saying to Peter, in effect, "My plan for John *could* be different from My plan for you. You must leave these matters to Me. You are responsible only for your own obedience to Me."

Peter may have missed the "if" in Jesus' question. The rumor spread that John would be alive at Christ's return (21:23). John seeks to correct that misconception (21:23).[15]

The apostle concludes his Gospel by assuring his readers that the record he has provided is true (21:24). At the same time, it is far from complete. There would not be room on all the world's bookshelves if *every* word and action of Jesus were preserved (21:25). Delightful hyperbole!

### Conclusion

Our text contains two narratives. They are related in their temporal context, but unrelated in their actual content. The first, though by no means an allegory, takes us back to Jesus' words to Peter and Andrew on an earlier occasion: "Come, follow me . . . and I will make you fishers of men" (Matthew 4:19). This time, although they fished all night, their work was futile. Jesus was not with them in the boat. We are reminded of Jesus' words in John 15:5, "Apart from me you can do nothing."

How fruitless are our efforts to evangelize if we are without the empowering presence of Christ in our ministry boat! It is only when "the Holy Spirit comes on [us]" (Acts 1:8) that we will be effective witnesses to Christ's saving power.

But observe the difference that Christ makes! When the disciples obeyed His command, their failure turned to success. He knew where the fish were. He could see where the net should be cast. So in the spiritual realm. By His Spirit, Christ wants to direct our witness. He desires to lead His witnesses to those He has prepared to receive the gospel. If we allow ourselves to be led by His Spirit, we find that obedience to His direction brings success in ministry.

Consider the second story. There are ministry lessons here, too. Just as the Lord forgave and restored Peter to a place of usefulness, so He can restore us despite past failures. Our text sets before us three indispensable qualifications for Christian service. The first is *love for Christ.* Three times Jesus asks Peter, "Do you love me?" Everything hinged on the answer to that question. And so with us. The first qualification of a Christian worker is not training or education. It is not eloquence, wisdom, organizing ability or a pleasing personality. It is not even a so-called "passion for souls." The first qualification is a deep love for Jesus Himself. Nothing can take the place of that.

The second qualification for true ministry is *a sense of call.* We must know that this is what Christ ordained us to do. Jesus responded to Peter's avowal of love by saying, "Feed my lambs. Take care of my sheep. Feed my sheep."

Sam Hadley for many years was the leader of Water Street Mission in New York City. Earlier, he had staggered into that mission as a drunken criminal. Three times he had suffered delirium tremens. His list of crimes was long enough to jail him for life. But that night, in Water Street Mission, he was wonderfully converted to Christ. The craving for drink and the lust for crime were plucked right out of him in one tremendous deliverance. That very night Christ gave him his commission to preach. Sam Hadley wrote: "I went out into the street, and looked up to the sky. . . . That night, right on the corner of Broadway and Thirty-Second Street, I was ordained to preach the everlasting Gospel, and have never doubted it for an instant. I have never stood before an audience without that vision inspiring me."[16] How necessary for ministry is a sense of Christ's call!

The third indispensable in Christian ministry is *obedience*. We must willingly follow Christ. After our Lord had heard Peter's confession of love, after He had conferred a ministry on Peter, He added, "Follow me!" (John 21:19). It is the servant who "follows" who receives the daily anointing and is endued with power from on high. How often this willingness to follow is assailed by the "self" within us. We will yield up anything else—money, time, comforts—if only we can hold onto self-management and self-direction. But there is no substitute for yielding totally and following fully. Nor is there anything that brings such a realization of oneness with our Lord.

> "Wilt thou follow Me?" the Savior asked.
>     The road looked bright and fair.
> And aflame with eager hope and zeal,
>     I replied, "Yes; anywhere!"
>
> "Wilt thou follow Me?" I almost blanched;
>     The road now fearsome grew;
> But I felt His love-grip on my hand;
>     And I answered, "Yes, right through."
>
> "Dost thou follow still?" His tender tone
>     Mid the storm-clash thrilled my heart;
> And I knew in a way before unknown,
>     We should never, never part![17]

**Endnotes**

1. Whether or not chapter 21 was written by the apostle John will have no bearing on my exposition of this text. Some, for example, C.K. Barrett, *The Gospel According to St. John* (London: S.P.C.K., 1955), 479-480, think that its vocabulary and style preclude a Johannine authorship. On the other hand, B.F. Westcott, *Commentary on the Gospel According to St. John* (London: John Murray, Albemarle Street, 1967), 299, is quite certain that John is the author.

2. Cf. Matthew 28:16.

3. The word Jesus uses is *paidia,* "children," which is likely nothing more than a familiar salutation.

4. The Greek wording shows that Jesus expected the answer "No."

5. Some expositors, for example, William Barclay, *The Gospel of John,* vol. II (Philadelphia: The Westminster Press, 1975), 281, do not see a miracle in the full net of fish. Barclay cites H.V. Morton, who saw two men fishing on the shore. One had waded out and was casting a bell net into the water. His partner on shore could see a shoal which the man in the water could not see and instructed him where to cast the net. Says Barclay, "Jesus was acting as guide to his fishermen friends, just as people still do today." Barclay's illustration, however, overlooks not only the number and size of the fish caught but the fact that the net remained intact. Reason compels us to recognize the episode as miraculous.

6. Not only because of Peter's impetuous nature, but because he might be seeking to demonstrate that he was genuinely sorry for having previously denied his Lord.

7. Presumably he had taken off much of his clothing in order to facilitate net casting. To greet someone was a religious act and could only be done if fully clothed.

8. Many suggestions have been made as to why John recorded the size of the catch and whether or not there was a symbolic significance to the number 153. Some, like Barrett, *The Gospel According to St. John,* 484, observe that the number 153 is the total of all the numbers between 1 and 17; 17 being the total of 10 and 7, both of which represent the complete complement of the Gentile Church. Others see Israel or the Trinity in the symbolism. Likely the disciples were simply doing what any good fishermen would do—totaling the quantity in order to divide the catch equally.

9. The word "truly" is not called for in the translation of 21:15, 16 (as in the NIV), unless there really was a difference in depth between the love Jesus solicited and the love Peter was willing to confess. It is clear from 21:17 that Peter loved Jesus fully.

   Some have thought that the "these" in Jesus' question referred to the boat, the fish, the nets and Peter's career as a fisherman. But this is unlikely. Peter had already left all that for Jesus' sake.

10. Much has been made of the supposed difference in meaning between the words translated "love" in this conversation—*agapao,* used in Jesus' first two questions (21:15-16); and *phileo,* used in the third (21:17); and again in Peter's three replies (21:15-17). The supposed difference could be demonstrated in the following translation: "Simon son of John, do you love Me with a deep, profound, eternal love?" To which Peter, not able to confess that kind of love, replied, "Yes, Lord, You know that I love You with a natural friendly affection." But why would Peter say "Yes" to Jesus' question if he really meant "No"?

   A careful comparison of John's use of *agapao* and *phileo* throughout his Gospel demonstrates rather conclusively that the two words are used synonymously, in keeping with John's literary style.

11. There is no proper theological distinction to be made between the words "feed" *(boske)* in 21:15 and "take care of" *(poimaive)* in 21:16; nor between the words "lambs" *(arnia)* in 21:15 and "sheep" *(probata)* in 21:16. Once again we have an example of John's fondness for variety in vocabulary. Three times Peter is being commissioned to be the pastor of Christ's flock.

12. Leon Morris, *The Gospel According to John* (Grand Rapids, MI: Eerdmans, 1971), 870, rightly observes that there is nothing in this entire conversation to support the position that Peter was given absolute primacy in the Church, as some assert. Nor does the passage indicate that Peter was in any way superior to John, who is regarded throughout the chapter as specially close to the Lord.

13. There is a well-known tradition that Peter was, in fact, crucified, and that he asked to be nailed to his cross head down because, he said, he was not worthy to die as his Lord had died.

14. Illustrated by that moment at supper when Peter asked John to discover the identity of the betrayer.

15. It would appear that John died a natural death in exile on "the island of Patmos because of the word of God and the testimony of Jesus" (Revelation 1:9).

16. Quoted by Sidlow Baxter in *Awake, My Heart* (Grand Rapids, MI: Zondervan, 1960), 147.

17. Quoted by Sidlow Baxter, ibid., 148.

## Part XII

## *Questions for Reflection or Discussion*

1. Evaluate and discuss this statement: "The resurrection of Jesus Christ sets the Christian faith apart from all other religions." Why is the resurrection of Christ so important to the Christian faith?

2. What is the difference between the gift of the Spirit described in John 20:22 and the gift of the Spirit described in Acts 2? How are they related?

3. What was the nature of Christ's resurrected body? Is there a similarity between it and the body believers will have in their resurrection? (See First Corinthians 15.)

4. How did following Jesus make Peter a "fisher of men"?

5. Compare and contrast the characters of Peter and John.

# A Sinner Rescued

John 7:53-8:11[1]

*53 Then each went to his own home.*[2]

*1 But Jesus went to the Mount of Olives. 2 At dawn he appeared again in the temple courts, where all the people gathered around him, and he sat down to teach them. 3 The teachers of the law and the Pharisees brought in a woman caught in adultery. They made her stand before the group 4 and said to Jesus, "Teacher, this woman was caught in the act of adultery. 5 In the Law Moses commanded us to stone such women. Now what do you say?" 6 They were using this question as a trap, in order to have a basis for accusing him.*

*But Jesus bent down and started to write on the ground with his finger. 7 When they kept on questioning him, he straightened up and said to them, "If any one of you is without sin, let him be the first to throw a stone at her." 8 Again he stooped down and wrote on the ground.*

*9 At this, those who heard began to go away one at a time, the older ones first, until only Jesus was left, with the woman still standing there. 10 Jesus straightened up and asked her, "Woman, where are they? Has no one condemned you?"*

*11 "No one, sir," she said.*

*"Then neither do I condemn you," Jesus declared. "Go now and leave your life of sin."*

A lmost certainly the story of Jesus and the accused adulteress was not part of John's original Gospel. But few doubt that it happened, and most concede that it fits the character of our Lord Jesus. No other recorded episode from His life better illustrates Jesus' respect for women, His compassion for sinners and His abhorrence of hypocrisy. Whatever its origin, this story possesses "the ring of truth."

The incident took place in the temple courts as Jesus taught a group who had gathered around Him (8:2).

## *The Case of the Woman (8:3)*

The wording and the circumstances lead us to suppose the woman in question was married and a habitual adulterer. Witnesses "caught [her] in the act of adultery" (8:4).[3] Likely these witnesses (perhaps friends of her suspicious husband) had purposely followed—and discovered—her. Evidently whoever contracted the witnesses was concerned that *the woman alone* should be put to death.[4]

As the story begins, we see the woman on shameful public display, alone facing the stares and sneers. Conspicuously absent is her male accomplice.

## *The Tactic of the Authorities (8:4-6)*

To ask a rabbi to determine judgment in such a case was not uncommon. But for the scribes and Pharisees to bring the woman to *Jesus* certainly was. It did not evidence any particular concern for the woman. Rather, they wanted to entrap Jesus in a no-win situation (8:6).

"In the Law," they said, "Moses commanded us to stone such women." That was not *exactly* what the Law said, but their version better suited their objectives.[5] "Now what do *you* say?" (8:5).

The trap was obvious! If Jesus said, "This woman should be stoned," they could charge Him with contravening Roman law. And all who favored leniency for the woman would turn against Jesus. If, on the other hand, He said "This woman should be released," they could charge Him with disregarding the law of God. And the strict legalists would turn against Him. If

He refused to make *any* decision, quite possibly the adulteress would have been lynched. The religious authorities were sure they had Jesus in a corner! But they misjudged the Son of God.

## The Rebuttal of Jesus (8:6-9)

Before pronouncing His judgment, Jesus bent down and began to write on the ground with His finger (8:6). Intriguing move! One can only conjecture what He wrote.[6] The astute scholar, T.W. Manson, proposes an interesting possibility. He suggests that Jesus, following Roman criminal law, was writing down the sentence before He delivered it. By this procedure, Manson submits, Jesus was saying, in effect: "You are inviting me to usurp the functions of the Roman Governor. Very well, I will do so in the approved Roman manner." Thus, Manson summarizes, Jesus defeated the plotters by wording a judgment they could not carry out.[7]

What a decision! "If any one of you is without sin, let him be the first to throw a stone at her" (8:7). Go ahead, stone her. But whoever does so must himself be totally innocent of sin and competent to carry out the sentence![8]

Now it is the woman's accusers in a no-win situation! And, stooping down again, Jesus gives them time to let the full import of His words sink in (8:8). Their consciences told them, and everyone there knew, that not one of them was without sin. They could not in good faith put the woman to death. Nor could they carry the discussion further and risk publicly admitting that Jesus was correct. And most certainly they could not divulge their motives for having brought the woman to Jesus. There was only one thing left to do. They must pretend the whole incident had never happened! From eldest to youngest, the delegation silently stole away, leaving the woman and Jesus alone.

## The Redemption of the Sinner (8:10-11)

"Woman, where are they?" Jesus asked as He straightened up. He must have felt some inner enjoyment at the way the incident had turned. "Has no one condemned you?" (8:10).

"No one, sir," the woman replied with genuine relief. Then came the words that must have changed her life forever!

"Neither do I condemn you," said Jesus. "Go now and leave your life of sin" (8:11).

Jesus did not judge her. But neither did He condone her adultery. His word of compassion made it possible for her to seek and receive God's forgiveness for her shameful past. It enabled her to thoroughly repudiate the sin that brought such shame upon her. After her encounter with the Savior, we can hardly imagine her ever retreating to her former immoral lifestyle.

## Conclusion

What lessons this little vignette impresses upon us! It comes as a word of gentle rebuke to the deep-rooted hypocrisy of our hearts. It reminds us, first, of Jesus' piercing word in His Sermon on the Mount: "Do not judge, or you too will be judged" (Matthew 7:1). "Why do you look at the speck of sawdust in your brother's eye and pay no attention to the plank in your own eye?" Jesus asks (7:3). How often do we demand standards in others that we fail—or never try—to meet ourselves! How easy it is to soothe our consciences by condemning in others the sins have comitted! As Paul puts it, "You, then, who teach others, do you not teach yourself? You who preach against stealing, do you steal? You who say that people should not commit adultery, do you commit adultery?" (Romans 2:21-22).

Should not our attitude toward the wretched sinner be, "There, but for the grace of God, go I"? Rather than to harbor a condemning, judgmental spirit, we should, in pity, follow the admonition of Paul: "Brothers, if someone is caught in a sin, you who are spiritual should restore him gently. But watch yourself, or you also may be tempted" (Galatians 6:1). We are well advised to let Fanny Crosby's entreaty guide our attitudes and actions:

> Rescue the perishing,
> Care for the dying,
>     Snatch them in pity from sin and the grave;
> Weep o'er the erring one,
> Lift up the fallen,
>     Tell them of Jesus the mighty to save.[9]

Second, we can show compassion to sinners without treating their sin lightly. Jesus did not say to the woman, "Don't worry; what you have done is not all that bad." Rather, He said, in effect, "I am not passing a final judgment on you now. Go and in deep repentance seek God's forgiveness so that you will be saved from final condemnation."

Third, Jesus gave the adulteress another chance. I recall the words of a young woman whose life before her conversion had been much like the woman's in our text. As she sat with my wife and me in our living room, she exclaimed, "I feel clean inside! It's as if I'm starting life all over again!" The modern adage has it, "Today is the first day of the rest of your life." Jesus says, "Your past can be forgiven, your sins blotted out. You can have a whole new beginning to life!" Someone wistfully wrote,

> How I wish that there was some wonderful place
>  Called the Land of Beginning Again,
> Where all our mistakes and all our heartaches
> And all our poor selfish grief
> Could be dropped like a shabby old coat at the door,
>  And never put on again.[10]

I have news! There *is* such a place! It is at the foot of Jesus' cross. There you can find the mercy that blots out the sinful past. There you can receive the resolve to change!

### Endnotes

1. According to the textual apparatus in *The Greek New Testament,* edited by Aland, Black, Martini, Metzger and Wikgren (Stuttgart, West Germany: United Bible Societies, 1968), this pericope is omitted by the best manuscripts of John's Gospel. These include Sinaiticus and Vaticanus and many other early Greek manuscripts. Some leave a space after 7:52, indicating that the copyist was aware of the passage's existence but thought it right to omit it. It is omitted by the Old and Peshitto Syriac, by the Coptic VSS, by some Old Latin manuscripts and by all early Church Fathers (including Origen, Cyprian, Chrysostom and Nonnus). All the evidence precludes our text from being a part of the original Johannine Gospel.
2. This verse would seem to indicate that the story was originally attached to some other narrative. C.K. Barrett, *The Gospel According to St. John* (London: S.P.C.K., 1955), 491, for example, speculates that it could have been "a piece from the Marcan narrative when Jesus at night went out to Bethany and returned in the morning to the city." But we really have no way of knowing.
3. According to very stringent Jewish law, the witnesses must have seen the couple in the very act of sexual intercourse. Each witness, in each other's presence, must have seen exactly the same act at exactly the same time. Clearly, the fulfilling of such conditions would

be very rare. It may indicate here that someone, perhaps the woman's husband, had the couple under surveillance.

4. If the woman were executed, her husband would succeed to her property.

5. Actually, Old Testament law commanded that *both* guilty parties, the man and the woman, be put to death. The mode of execution was not stipulated. (See Leviticus 20:10; Deuteronomy 22:22.) Stoning was mandated if the woman involved was a betrothed virgin (see Deuteronomy 22:23ff).

6. Some, like William Temple (quoted by Leon Morris, *The Gospel According to John* [Grand Rapids, MI: Eerdmans, 1971], 888), think that Jesus did not wish to look at the sight of professedly godly men hounding a poor woman. It often has been suggested that Jesus was writing down the sins of the accusers. Or that He was showing contempt for the woman's accusers. Or that He was simply trying to gain time and not be rushed into a decision.

7. Quoted by Morris, *The Gospel According to John,* 888.

8. Legally, the witnesses must have first warned the woman, which they probably did not. Otherwise she could not be convicted on their testimony. Had she been stoned under those conditions, the lives of those stoning her would have been at risk.

9. Fanny J. Crosby, "Rescue the Perishing," *Hymns of the Christian Life* (Camp Hill, PA: Christian Publications, Inc. 1978), # 470, stanza 1.

10. The origin of this verse, memorized years ago, is unknown to me.

# The Gospel of John and the Fourfold Gospel

The founder of The Christian and Missionary Alliance, Albert B. Simpson, capsulized the "full gospel" message in four phrases, each of which points to a specific truth concerning our Lord Jesus Christ. He described the Lord as:

- Christ our *Savior*

- Christ our *Sanctifier*

- Christ our *Healer*

- Christ our *Coming King*

To appropriate the Lord Jesus in each of these aspects is to live the deeper life. Let us look one more time into the Gospel of John to see how the writer of this ever-so-spiritual Gospel portrays Christ in each of these aspects.

## *Christ Our Savior*

To say that Christ is our Savior means He has rescued us from the guilt and punishment of our sins. This salvation is grounded in Christ's

sin-atoning death. He gives us eternal life through the regenerating presence of His indwelling Holy Spirit. See how this is clearly set forth in the
Gospel of John.

That we are *sinners* in need of a Savior is very clear. We hear Christ called
"the Lamb of God who takes away the *sin* of the world!" (1:29, emphasis
added). We learn that it was sin that caused the sickness of the invalid at the
pool of Bethesda (see 5:14). The unbelieving Jews are described as "slave[s]
to sin" (8:34). The Pharisees who falsely professed spiritual understanding
are implied to be "guilty of sin" (9:41). The people of the world, to whom Jesus came, have "no excuse for their sin" (15:22). It is the work of the Holy
Spirit to "convict the world in regard to sin" (16:8).

The *punishment due to sinners* is that they *perish* (3:16). But thanks to
Him who lays down his life for the sheep (see 10:17), believers in Jesus
"shall never perish" (10:28). Instead they are *saved* (10:9). They receive the
gift of *eternal life* (3:15-16, 36), as did the woman at the well (4:14). John
tells us that those who hear Christ's words and believe God have eternal life
(5:24). The crowd whom Jesus fed are exhorted to "work [i.e., believe] . . .
for food that endures to eternal life" (6:27). They are to partake of Christ in
order to have eternal life (6:54). (See also 12:25 and 17:2-3.) It is clear that,
for John, eternal life is both a present possession and a future blessing.

John stresses the importance of *believing* on Jesus. At the outset, he portrays Jesus as sole object of belief (1:7). It is to those who believe that "he
gave the right to become children of God" (1:12). The "work" of God is "to
believe in the one he has sent" (6:29). Jesus asked the man whose eyes He
opened, "Do you believe in the Son of Man?" (9:35). When the man discovered Jesus' identity, he exclaimed, "Lord, I believe" (9:38). Martha affirmed
her faith in Christ: "Yes, Lord, . . . I believe that you are the Christ" (11:27).
Jesus exhorted His disciples, "Trust in God; trust [believe] also in me"
(14:1). He prays "for those who will believe in [Him]" (17:20).

Jesus calls us to voluntarily commit to *trust* Him fully and walk in *obedience* to His Word. But while eternal life is a gift to all who believe, we do not
trust in faith itself! The object of our faith is Jesus, whose death atoned for
sin. John makes this clear. Our faith is in "the Lamb of God" who by His
death "takes away" our sin (1:29). He must be "lifted up" if believers are to
have eternal life (3:14). By being "lifted up from the earth" (i.e., by being

crucified), Jesus "will draw all men to [Himself]" (12:32). As "a kernel of wheat falls to the ground and dies" (12:24), it brings forth fruit. From the cross Jesus utters the words, "It is finished" (19:30). The atonement for sin is complete; our debt is paid; we are redeemed by His blood. This is an *objective* work to which we can add nothing!

But there is also a *subjective* aspect to the salvation that Christ provides. It is "through the washing of rebirth and renewal by the Holy Spirit" that we are saved (Titus 3:5). To Nicodemus our Lord said, "No one can enter the kingdom of God unless he is born of water and the Spirit" (John 3:5). "The Spirit gives life," says Jesus in another setting; "the flesh counts for nothing" (6:63). It was this regenerating Spirit that Jesus "breathed" upon His disciples on the evening of His resurrection (20:22). John does, indeed, show us "Christ our Savior."

## Christ Our Sanctifier

To say Christ is our Sanctifier is to say several things. First, He by His Spirit sets us apart from the world, the flesh and the devil for Himself. Second, as God's Spirit fills us, we are made holy (Christlike) and endued with power for witness and service. This service is to God (worship), to the Church (edification) and to the world (evangelism). The Statement of Faith of The Christian and Missionary Alliance describes it this way:

> It is the will of God that each believer should be filled with the Holy Spirit and be sanctified wholly, being separated from sin and the world and fully dedicated to the will of God, thereby receiving power for holy living and effective service. This is both a crisis and a progressive experience wrought in the life of the believer subsequent to conversion.

Such a sanctifying experience is clearly anticipated in the Gospel of John. In His prayer of consecration, our Lord prays for His disciples. "Sanctify them," He asks, "by the truth; your word is truth. . . . For them I sanctify myself, that they too may be truly sanctified" (17:17, 19). The author of the fourth Gospel describes the *ministry of the Holy Spirit* as it relates to holiness and service. He tells us that Jesus, upon whom the Spirit rested, will baptize believers with that same Holy Spirit (1:33). This baptism in the

Spirit will produce "streams of living water [flowing] from within" believers. This will be possible after and because Jesus will be glorified (7:38-39; 16:7). Initially this was fulfilled in the outpouring of the Spirit on the Day of Pentecost (Acts 2).

In those discourses unique to John's Gospel (chapters 14-16), our Lord promises the *Paraclete*[1] and describes His sanctifying ministry to obedient believers.[2] In response to the disciples' loving obedience, He would send "another Counselor to be with [them] forever" (14:16). This Counselor would come to them as the "Spirit of truth" (14:17); the very Spirit of Christ Himself (14:18). He would be their Teacher (14:26), reminding them of all that Jesus had said to them (15:26; 16:13-15). In this way He would bring glory to Jesus (16:14). It is the Spirit who would unite them to Jesus, "the vine" (15:1). As they remained in Him, they would produce the fruit of love (15:9), peace (16:33) and joy (16:17ff). Jesus intends that we today who believe should also appropriate this sanctifying ministry of the Holy Spirit (17:20-21).

Further, John portrays the *empowering ministry* of the Spirit. This power is given that we might continue the works of Christ in the world. Jesus says, "Anyone who has faith in me will do what I have been doing. He will do even greater things than these" (14:12). Jesus commissions us: "As the Father has sent me, I am sending you" (20:21). He assures us that we "did not choose [Him], but [He] chose [us] and appointed [us] to go and bear fruit—fruit that will last" (15:16). He tells God His Father, "As you sent me into the world, I have sent them into the world" (17:18).

Thus Jesus assures us that the Holy Spirit has power both to sanctify us and equip us for ministry. But John also portrays Christ our Sanctifier through the "sign" narratives he recounts. The *water-to-wine* miracle (chapter 2) symbolizes the end of the old, pleasing-God-by-our-works life. In its place we enter a whole new kind of life that is enabled by the "new wine" of the Holy Spirit.[3] The *feeding of the 5,000* illustrates the spiritual nourishment which we may appropriate by faith. We can feast on Jesus, the Bread of life (6:25ff). As Peter puts it, "His divine power has given us everything we need for life and godliness through our knowledge of [Jesus]" (2 Peter 1:3).

## Christ Our Healer

To say Christ is our Healer is to confess that Jesus in His atonement has provided for our physical bodies. This truth is made plain in the Gospel of John. The miracles of Jesus were not only "signs" of deeper spiritual truth,[4] but acts of tender love and compassion. Especially is this true of the *healing miracles* which He performed. John portrays Jesus showing mercy to a "royal official" by healing his son, who was desperately ill (4:43ff). He did for the invalid at the pool of Bethesda what no one else had been able to do (5:1ff). He brought great joy to the heart of the man whose blind eyes he opened (9:1ff). And He showed the mighty power of God in raising Lazarus from the dead (11:1ff). His love and power are still the same today. Let us not be afraid to trust this "Lord for the body."

> Oft on earth He healed the sufferer
>     By His mighty hand;
> Still our sicknesses and sorrows
>     Go at His command.
> He who gave His healing virtue
>     To a woman's touch,
> To the faith that claims His fullness
>     Still will give as much.[5]

## Christ Our Coming King

Finally, to say that Christ is our Coming King is to believe in the imminent, personal, visible, premillennial return of Christ. At that moment believers will rise bodily from the dead to "be with the Lord forever" (1 Thessalonians 4:17). John's Gospel sets before us such a resurrection (John 5:28-29). Jesus warns unbelievers that they will be judged "at the last day" by His words they refused to accept (12:48). Over and over Jesus promises the believer, "I will raise him up at the last day" (6:39-40, 44, 54). He assures Martha, "I am the resurrection and the life. He who believes in me will live, even though he dies; and whoever lives and believes in me will never die" (11:25-26). He prayed, "Father, I want those you have given me to be with me where I am, and to see my glory" (17:24). He promised His disciples, "I am going . . . to prepare a place for you. And . . . I will come back and take you to be with me" (14:2-3). What a comfort to weary pilgrims is our Lord's promised return! And what a motivation to holy living!

Jesus Christ is all-sufficient. He is Christ for body, soul and spirit! He indwells us. This is the Jesus of John's Gospel. This is the Son of God in whom we *believe!*

> Jesus only is our Saviour,
>     All our guilt He bore away,
> All our righteousness He gives us,
>     All our strength from day to day.

> Jesus is our Sanctifier,
>     Cleansing us from self and sin,
> And with all His Spirit's fullness,
>     Filling all our hearts within.

> Jesus only is our Healer,
>     All our sicknesses He bear,
> And His risen life and fullness
>     All His members still may share.

> And for Jesus we are waiting,
>     Listening for the advent call;
> But 'twill still be Jesus only,
>     Jesus ever, all in all.[6]

### Endnotes

1. See chapter 26 of this Deeper Life Pulpit Commentary.
2. The importance of obedience is stressed in 14:23; 15:10, 14, 17.
3. Compare Ephesians 5:18.
4. The healing of the official's son (4:43ff) and the healing at the pool of Bethesda (5:1ff) picture for us our new *life in Christ.* The water turned to wine (2:1ff) signifies new *life in the Spirit.* The feeding of the 5,000 (6:1ff) portrays *Christ as the Bread of Life.* Jesus' walking on the water (6:16ff) encourages us to know that He can calm life's storms. The healing of the blind man (9:1ff) symbolizes Jesus, *the Light of the World.*
5. A.B. Simpson, "Yesterday, Today, Forever," *Hymns of the Christian Life* (Camp Hill, PA: Christian Publications, Inc., 1978), # 119, stanza 3.
6. A.B. Simpson, "Jesus Only," ibid., # 398, stanzas 2-4 and 6.

# Bibliography

Arndt, William F. and Gingrich, F. Wilbur. *A Greek-English Lexicon of the New Testament.* A translation and adaptation of Walter Bauer's German Lexicon. Chicago, IL: The University of Chicago Press, 1957.

Barclay, William. *The Gospel of John,* 2 vols. Philadelphia: The Westminster Press, rev. ed., 1975.

Barrett, C.K. *The Gospel According to St. John.* London: S.P.C.K., 1955.

Beasley-Murray, George R. "John." *Word Biblical Themes.* Dallas, TX: Word Publishing, 1989.

Boice, James Montgomery. *Witness and Revelation in the Gospel of John.* Grand Rapids, MI: Zondervan, 1970.

Bonhoeffer, Dietrich. *The Cost of Discipleship.* London: SCM Press, Ltd., 1959.

Bruce, F.F. *The Gospel of John.* Grand Rapids, MI: Erdmans, 1983.

Bultmann, Rudolph. *The Gospel of John—A Commentary.* Translated from the German by G.R. Beasley-Murray, R.W.N. Hoare and J.K. Riches. Philadelphia: The Westminster Press, 1971.

Cadman, W.H. *The Open Heaven,* edited by G.B. Caird. Oxford: Basil Blackwell, 1969.

Calvin, John. *Commentary on the Gospel According to John,* 2 vols. Edinburgh: The Calvin Translation Society, 1847.

Dodd, C.H. *The Interpretation of the Fourth Gospel.* Cambridge: At the University Press, 1970.

Dods, Marcus. "The Gospel of St. John," *The Expositor's Greek New Testament,* vol I. Grand Rapids, MI: Eerdmans, n.d.

Gesenius, William. *A Hebrew and English Lexicon of the Old Testament.* Oxford: The Clarendon Press, 1955.

Godet, F. *Commentary on the Gospel of St. John,* 3 vols. Edinburgh: T. & T. Clarke, 1881.

401

Gordon, A.J. *How Christ Came to Church.* Philadelphia: American Baptist Publication Society, 1985.

*Hymns of the Christian Life,* Camp Hill, PA: Christian Publications, Inc., 1962, 1978.

Kittel, Gerhard and Friedrich, Gerhard, eds. *Theological Dictionary of the New Testament,* 10 vols. Grand Rapids, MI: Eerdmans, 1964.

Kraeling, Emil G. *Bible Atlas.* New York: Rand McNally, 1956.

Krummacher, F.W. *The Suffering Saviour.* Chicago, IL: Moody Press, 1948.

Ladd, George Eldon. *The Gospel of the Kingdom.* Grand Rapids, MI: Eerdmans, 1959.

Lightfoot, R.H. *St. John's Gospel.* London: Oxford University Press, 1966.

Lloyd-Jones, D. Martyn. *Joy Unspeakable.* Wheaton, IL: Harold Shaw Publishers, 1984.

MacArthur, John E. *The Gospel According to Jesus.* Grand Rapids, MI: Zondervan, 1988.

Maclaren, Alexander. *The Gospel According to St. John.* London: Hodder and Stoughton, 1907.

Morris, Leon. *The Gospel According to John.* Grand Rapids, MI: Eerdmans, 1971.

Murray, Andrew. *Like Christ.* Three Hills, Alberta: Prairie Book Room, n.d.

Piper, John. *Let the Nations Be Glad!* Grand Rapids, MI: Baker Books, 1993.

Sanday, William. *The Authorship and Historical Character of the Fourth Gospel.* London: Macmillan, 1872.

Schnackenburg, Rudolph. *The Gospel According to St. John,* vol. III. Translated from German by David Smith and G.A. Kon. New York: Crossroad, 1982.

Sherwin-White, A.N. *Roman Society and Roman Law in the New Testament.* Oxford: At The Clarendon Press, 1963.

Simpson, A.B. *The Holy Spirit: Power from on High.* Edited for today's reader by Keith M. Bailey. Camp Hill, PA: Christian Publications, 1994.

_____. *Songs of the Spirit.* New York: The Christian Alliance Publishing Co., 1920.

Stevens, George Barker. *The Theology of the New Testament.* Edinburgh: T. & T. Clark, 1899 (reprinted 1956).

Tasker, R.V.G. *The Gospel According to St. John.* London: The Tyndale Press, 1960.

Tenney, Merrill C., ed. *The Zondervan Pictorial Bible Dictionary.* Grand Rapids, MI: Zondervan, 1967.

_____. *New Testament Survey.* Grand Rapids, MI: Eerdmans, 1961.

Tozer, A.W. *Born after Midnight.* Harrisburg, PA: Christian Publications, 1959.

_____. *Man: The Dwelling Place of God.* Harrisburg, PA: Christian Publications, Inc., 1966.

_____. *When He Is Come.* Harrisburg, PA: Christian Publications, Inc., 1968.

Trench, Richard Chenevix. *Synonyms of the New Testament.* Grand Rapids, MI: Eerdmans, 1948.

Westcott, B.F. *Commentary on the Gospel According to St. John.* Grand Rapids, MI: Eerdmans, 1967 (originally 1881).

Willoughby, W. Robert, *First Corinthians: Fostering Spirituality.* Camp Hill, PA: Christian Publications, Inc., 1996.